# A-Level Year 2

# Physics

## Exam Board: AQA

Revising for Physics exams is stressful, that's for sure — even just getting your notes sorted out can leave you needing a lie down. But help is at hand...

This brilliant CGP book explains **everything you'll need to learn** (and nothing you won't), all in a straightforward style that's easy to get your head around. We've also included **exam questions** to test how ready you are for the real thing.

There's even a free Online Edition you can read on your computer or tablet!

**How to get your free Online Edition**

Go to **cgpbooks.co.uk/extras** and enter this code...

0214 1650 3710 5828

This code only works for one person. If somebody else has used this book before you, they might have already claimed the Online Edition.

A-Level revision? It has to be CGP!

# Contents

Option 13: "Electronics" isn't covered in this book.

### Section 7: Option C: — Engineering Physics



### Section 7: Option D — Turning Points in Physics



### Practical and Investigative Skills



### Do Well In Your Exams




Published by CGP

Editors:
Emily Garrett, David Maliphant, Rachael Marshall, Sam Pilgrim, Frances Rooney, Charlotte Whiteley, Sarah Williams and Jonathan Wray.

Contributors:
Mark Edwards, Duncan Kamya, Barbara Mascetti, John Myers, Zoe Nye, Moira Steven and Tony Winzor.

With thanks to Jan Greenway for the copyright research.

ISBN: 978 1 78294 343 3

www.cgpbooks.co.uk

Clipart from Corel®
Printed by Elanders Ltd, Newcastle upon Tyne.

Based on the classic CGP style created by Richard Parsons.






Circular
1) The frequen
The period, T,
seconds). Freq
a complete circ
ne T, so freque
1 — FURTHER M

# Circular Motion

*It's probably worth putting a bookmark in here — this stuff is needed **all over** the place.*

## Angles can be Expressed in Radians

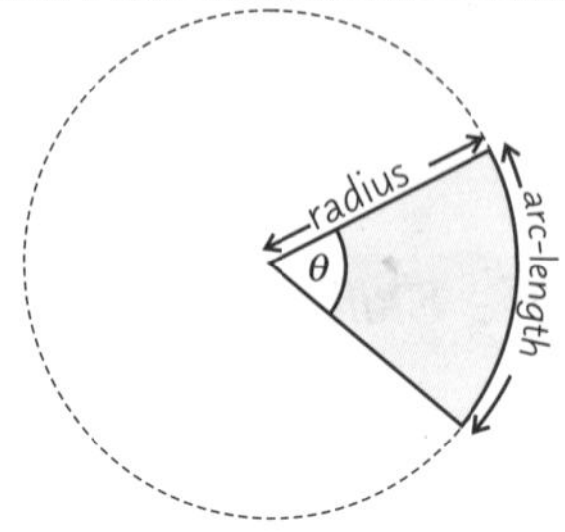


The angle in **radians**, $\theta$, is defined as the **arc-length** divided by the radius of the circle.

For a **complete circle** (360°), the arc-length is just the circumference of the circle ($2\pi r$). Dividing this by the radius ($r$) gives $2\pi$. So there are **$2\pi$ radians** in a complete circle.

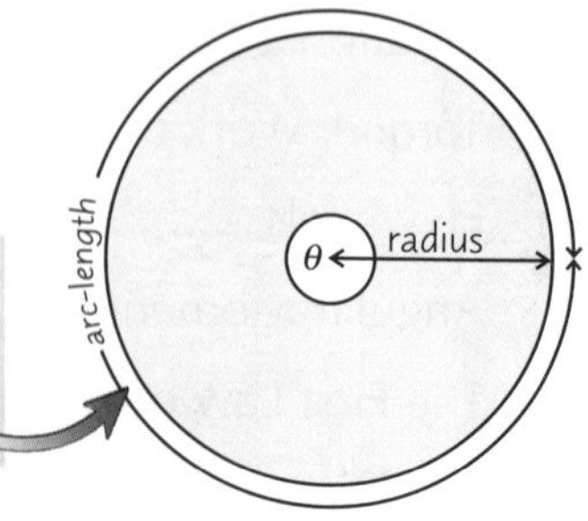


Some common angles:

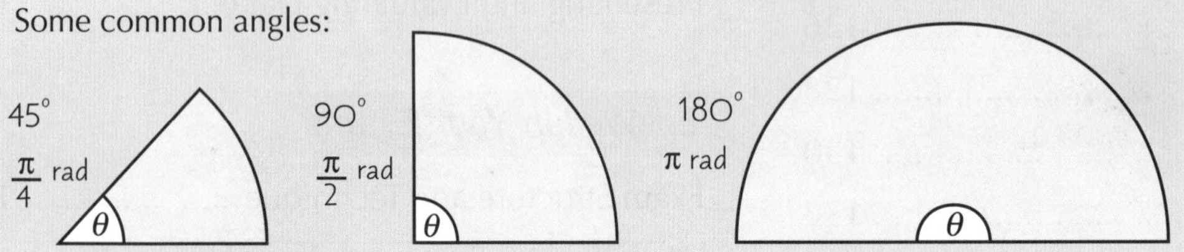


To convert from degrees to radians, multiply by $\frac{\pi}{180}$. To convert from radians to degrees, multiply by $\frac{180}{\pi}$. 1 radian ≈ 57°.

## The Angular Speed is the Angle an Object Rotates Through per Second

1) **Angular speed**, $\omega$, is defined as the **angle turned**, $\theta$, per unit **time** $t$. Its unit is rad s$^{-1}$ — radians per second.

$$\omega = \frac{\theta}{t}$$

2) You can relate **linear speed**, $v$, (sometimes called the **tangential velocity**) and **angular speed**, $\omega$, with:

$$\omega = \frac{v}{r}$$

Where $r$ is the radius of the circle being turned in metres.

**Example:** In a cyclotron, a beam of particles spirals outwards from a central point. The angular speed of the particles remains constant. The beam of particles in the cyclotron rotates through 360° in 35 μs.

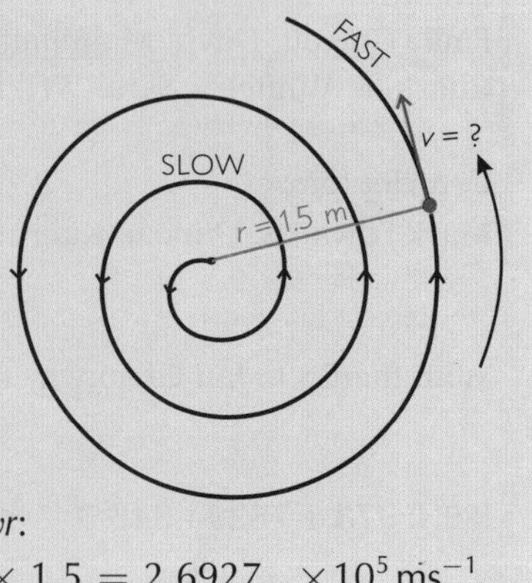


a) Explain why the linear speed of the particles increases as they spiral outwards, even though their angular speed is constant.

Linear speed depends on $r$, the radius of the circle being turned as well as $\omega$. So, as $r$ increases, so does $v$, even though $\omega$ remains constant.

b) Calculate the linear speed of a particle at a point 1.5 m from the centre of rotation.

First, calculate the angular speed:

$$\omega = \frac{\theta}{t} = \frac{2\pi}{35 \times 10^{-6}} = 1.7951... \times 10^5 \text{rad s}^{-1}$$

Then substitute $\omega$ into $v = \omega r$:

$$v = \omega r = 1.7951... \times 10^5 \times 1.5 = 2.6927... \times 10^5 \text{ ms}^{-1}$$

**$v = 2.7 \times 10^5$ ms$^{-1}$ (to 2 s.f.)**

You can find out more about cyclotrons on p. 41.

## ...Motion has a Frequency and Period

...cy, $f$, is the number of complete **revolutions per second** (rev s$^{-1}$ or hertz, Hz).

... is the **time taken** for a complete revolution (in ... ency and period are **linked** by the equation:

$$f = \frac{1}{T}$$

...le, an object turns through **$2\pi$ radians** ... ency and period are related to $\omega$ by:

$$\omega = \frac{2\pi}{T} = 2\pi f$$

$\omega$ = angular speed in rad s$^{-1}$
$f$ = frequency in rev s$^{-1}$ or Hz
$T$ = period in s

# Circular Motion

## Objects Travelling in Circles are **Accelerating** Since Their **Velocity is Changing**

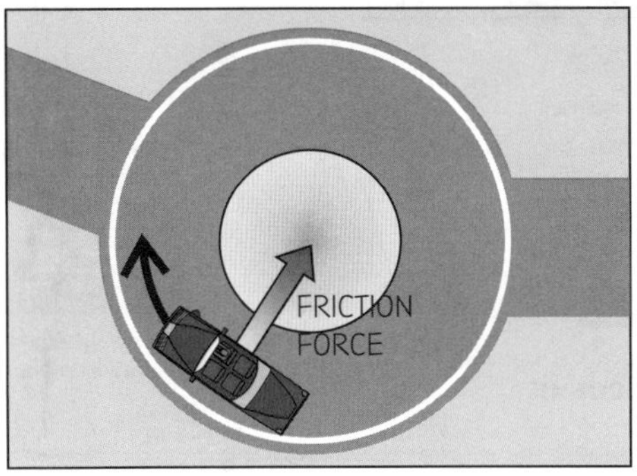


1) Even if the car shown is going at a **constant speed**, its **velocity** is changing since its **direction** is changing.
2) Since acceleration is defined as the **rate of change of velocity**, the car is accelerating even though it isn't going any faster.
3) This acceleration is called the **centripetal acceleration** and is always directed towards the **centre of the circle**.

There are two formulas for centripetal acceleration:

$$a = \frac{v^2}{r}$$

$$a = \omega^2 r$$

$a$ = centripetal acceleration in $ms^{-2}$
$v$ = linear speed in $ms^{-1}$
$\omega$ = angular speed in rad $s^{-1}$
$r$ = radius in m

## The **Centripetal Acceleration** is produced by a **Centripetal Force**

From Newton's laws, if there's a **centripetal acceleration**, there must be a **centripetal force** acting towards the **centre of the circle**.

Since $F = ma$, the centripetal force must be:

$$F = \frac{mv^2}{r} = m\omega^2 r$$

The centripetal force is what keeps the object moving in a circle — remove the force and the object would fly off at a tangent.

Men cowered from the force of the centripede.

## Practice Questions

Q1 How many radians are there in a complete circle?

Q2 How is angular speed defined and what is the relationship between angular speed and linear speed?

Q3 Define the period and frequency of circular motion. What is the relationship between period and angular speed?

Q4 Explain why an object travelling at a constant speed in a circular path is accelerating.

Q5 Write equations for centripetal acceleration, $a$, and centripetal force, $F$, for an object travelling at a linear speed, $v$, in a circular path with a radius $r$.

Q6 In which direction does the centripetal force act, and what happens when this force is removed?

**Exam Questions**

Q1 a) Calculate the angular speed at which the Earth orbits the Sun. (1 year = $3.2 \times 10^7$ s) [2 marks]

b) Calculate the Earth's linear speed. (Assume radius of orbit = $1.5 \times 10^{11}$ m) [1 mark]

c) Calculate the centripetal force needed to keep the Earth in its orbit. (*Mass of Earth = $5.98 \times 10^{24}$ kg*) [2 marks]

d) State what is providing this force. [1 mark]

Q2 A bucket full of water, tied to a rope, is being swung around in a vertical circle (so it is upside down at the top of the swing). The radius of the circle is 1.00 m.

a) By considering the acceleration due to gravity at the top of the swing, calculate the minimum frequency with which the bucket can be swung without any water falling out. [3 marks]

b) The bucket is now swung with a constant angular speed of 5.00 rad $s^{-1}$. Calculate the tension in the rope when the bucket is at the top of the swing if the total mass of the bucket and water is 10.0 kg. [3 marks]

## I'm spinnin' around, move out of my way...

*"Centripetal" just means "centre-seeking". The centripetal force is what actually causes circular motion. What you feel when you're spinning, though, is the reaction (centrifugal) force. Don't get the two mixed up.*

# Simple Harmonic Motion

*Something simple at last — I like the sound of this. And colourful graphs too — you're in for a treat here.*

## SHM is Defined in terms of Acceleration and Displacement

1) An object moving with **simple harmonic motion** (SHM) **oscillates** to and fro, either side of a **midpoint**.
2) The distance of the object from the midpoint is called its **displacement**.
3) There is always a **restoring force** pulling or pushing the object back **towards** the **midpoint**.
4) The **size** of the **restoring force** is directly proportional to the **displacement** — i.e. if the displacement doubles, the restoring force doubles too.
5) As the restoring force causes **acceleration** towards the midpoint, we can also say the **acceleration** is directly **proportional** to **displacement**.

Small displacement, therefore small force.

Large displacement, therefore large force.

There's a negative sign as the acceleration is opposing the displacement.

**Condition for SHM**: an oscillation in which the **acceleration** of an object is **directly proportional** to its **displacement** from the **midpoint**, and is directed **towards the midpoint**.

$a \propto -x$

## The Restoring Force Makes the Object Exchange $E_p$ and $E_k$

1) The **type** of **potential energy** ($E_p$) depends on **what it is** that's providing the **restoring force**. This will be **gravitational $E_p$** for pendulums and **elastic $E_p$** (elastic stored energy) for masses on springs moving horizontally.
2) As the object moves **towards the midpoint**, the restoring force **does work** on the object and so **transfers** some **$E_p$** to **$E_k$**. When the object is moving **away from the midpoint**, all that $E_k$ is transferred **back to $E_p$** again.
3) At the **midpoint**, the object's $E_p$ is **zero** and its $E_k$ is **maximum**.
4) At the **maximum displacement** (the **amplitude**) on both sides of the midpoint, the object's $E_k$ is **zero** and its $E_p$ is at its **maximum**.
5) The **sum** of the **potential** and **kinetic** energy is called the **mechanical energy** and **stays constant** (as long as the motion isn't damped — see p. 8).
6) The **energy transfer** for one complete cycle of oscillation is: $E_p$ to $E_k$ to $E_p$ to $E_k$ to $E_p$ ... and then the process repeats...

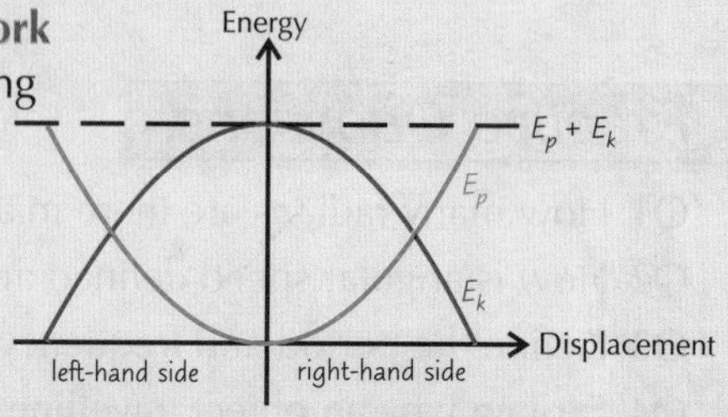


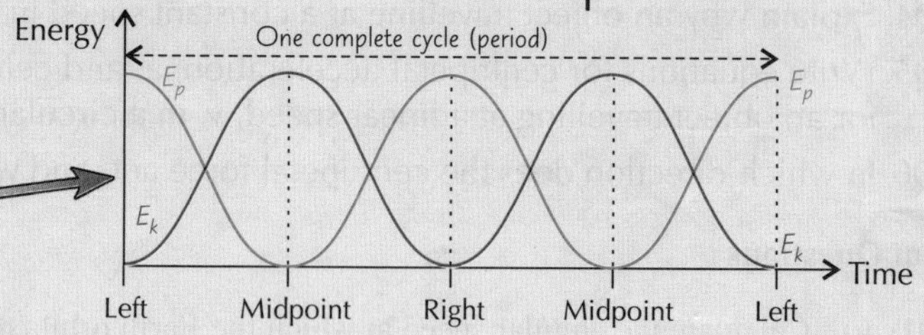


## You can Draw Graphs to Show Displacement, Velocity and Acceleration

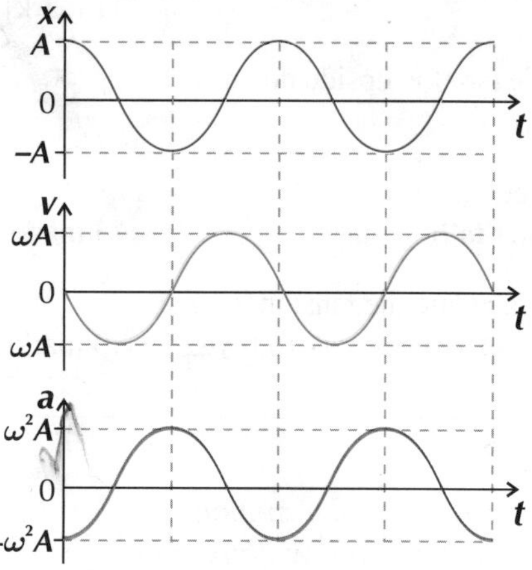


**Displacement**, ***x***, varies as a cosine with a maximum value, ***A*** (the amplitude).

The equations for these graphs are on the next page. You can use a data logger to plot these graphs for a simple oscillator, e.g. a pendulum.

**Velocity**, ***v***, is the gradient of the **displacement**-time graph. It has a maximum value of $\omega A$ (where $\omega$ is the angular frequency of the oscillation — see next page) and is a **quarter of a cycle** in front of the **displacement**.

**Acceleration**, ***a***, is the gradient of the **velocity**-time graph. It has a maximum value of $\omega^2 A$, and is in **antiphase** with the **displacement**.

# Simple Harmonic Motion

## The **Frequency** and **Period** Don't Depend on the **Amplitude**

1) From **maximum positive displacement** (e.g. maximum displacement to the right) to **maximum negative displacement** (e.g. maximum displacement to the left) and **back again** is called a **cycle** of oscillation.
2) The **frequency**, ***f***, of the SHM is the number of cycles per second (measured in Hz).
3) The **period**, ***T***, is the **time** taken for a complete cycle (in seconds).
4) The **angular frequency**, $\omega$, is $2\pi f$. The formulas for $\omega$ are the same as for **angular speed** in circular motion.

In SHM, the **frequency** and **period** are independent of the **amplitude** (i.e. constant for a given oscillation). So a **pendulum clock** will keep ticking in **regular** time **intervals** even if its swing becomes very **small**.

## **Learn** the SHM Equations

You'll be given these formulas in the exam, so just make sure you know what they mean and how to use them.

1) For an object to be moving with SHM, the **acceleration**, *a*, is directly proportional to the **displacement**, *x*.
2) The **constant of proportionality** depends on $\omega$, and the acceleration is always in the **opposite direction** from the displacement (so there's a minus sign in the equation).

   This is the defining equation of SHM: $a = -\omega^2 x$  Maximum acceleration: $a_{max} = \omega^2 A$

Don't forget, *A* is the maximum displacement — it's not acceleration.

3) The **velocity** is **positive** if the object's moving in one direction, and **negative** if it's moving in the **opposite** direction — that's why there's a ± sign.

   $v = \pm\omega\sqrt{A^2 - x^2}$  **Maximum speed = $\omega A$**

4) The **displacement** varies with time according to the equation on the right. To use this equation you need to start timing when the pendulum is at its **maximum displacement** — i.e. when $t = 0$, $x = A$.

   $x = A\cos(\omega t)$

Helene was investigating swinging as a form of simple harmonic motion.

## Practice Questions

Q1 Write down the defining equation of SHM.

Q2 Sketch graphs to show how the displacement, velocity and acceleration for an object in SHM each vary with time. Explain how the velocity and acceleration graphs can be derived from the displacement-time graph.

Q3 Given the amplitude and the frequency, how would you work out the maximum acceleration?

Q4 What is the equation for the velocity of an object moving with SHM? Why does the equation include a ± sign?

**Exam Questions**

Q1 a) Describe the condition necessary for an object to be moving with simple harmonic motion. [2 marks]
b) Explain why the motion of a ball bouncing off the ground is not simple harmonic motion. [1 mark]

Q2 Describe how the total energy, the kinetic energy and the elastic potential energy of a mass-spring system undergoing simple harmonic motion varies as the displacement of the mass varies. [4 marks]

Q3 A pendulum is pulled a distance 0.05 m from its midpoint and released. It oscillates with simple harmonic motion with a frequency of 1.5 Hz. Calculate:
a) its maximum speed [2 marks]
b) its displacement 0.1 s after it is released [2 marks]
c) the time it takes to fall to 0.01 m from the midpoint after it is released [2 marks]

Q4 Two pendulums, C and D are oscillating with simple harmonic motion. Pendulum C has the same maximum displacement, *A*, as pendulum D, but twice the angular speed, $\omega$. Which option correctly describes the maximum acceleration of pendulum C with respect to pendulum D?
A half  B the same  C double  D quadruple [1 mark]

## *"Simple" harmonic motion — hmmm, I'm not convinced...*

*The basic concept of SHM is simple enough (no pun intended). Make sure you can remember the shapes of all the graphs on page 4. You're given the formulas on this page in the exam, but make sure you're comfortable using them.*

# Simple Harmonic Oscillators

*There are a couple more equations to learn on this page I'm afraid. The experiment described at the bottom of the page shows where they come from, though, so that should help you remember them.*

## A **Mass** on a **Spring** is a **Simple Harmonic Oscillator (SHO)**

1) When the mass is **pushed to the left** or **pulled to the right** of the **equilibrium position**, there's a **force** exerted on it. The size of this force (in N) is:

$$F = -kx$$

where $k$ is the **spring constant** (stiffness) of the spring in $\text{Nm}^{-1}$ and $x$ is the **displacement** in m.

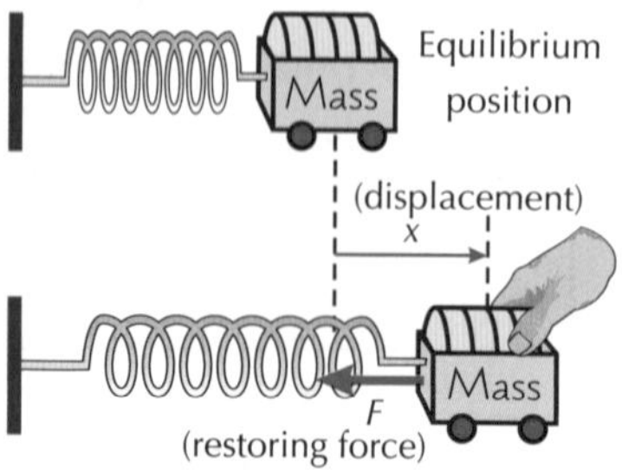


2) After a bit of jiggery-pokery involving Newton's second law and some of the ideas on the previous page, you get the **formula for the period of a mass oscillating on a spring**:

$$T = 2\pi\sqrt{\frac{m}{k}}$$

$T$ = period of oscillation in seconds
$m$ = mass in kg
$k$ = spring constant in $\text{Nm}^{-1}$

A simple theory of how atoms in a lattice (i.e. a solid) behave can be worked out by considering them as masses oscillating on springs. So there you go.

## You Can **Check the Formula Experimentally**

1) Set up the equipment as shown in the diagram.
2) **Pull** the masses down a set amount, this will be your initial **amplitude**. Let the masses go.
3) The masses will now oscillate with **simple harmonic motion**.
4) The **position sensor** measures the **displacement** of the mass over **time**.
5) Connect the position sensor to a computer and create a **displacement-time** graph. Read off the period $T$ from the graph.

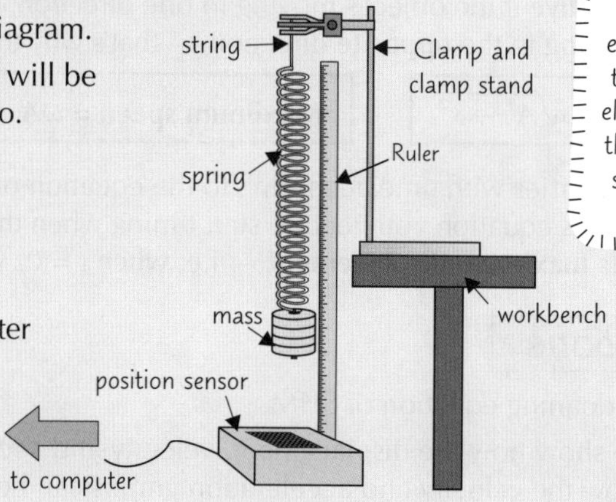


Because the spring in this experiment is hung vertically, the potential energy is both elastic and gravitational. For the horizontal spring system shown above, the potential energy is just elastic.

## You Can Use This Set Up to **Investigate Factors** Which Affect the **Period**

1) Change the **mass**, $m$, by loading more **masses** onto the spring.
2) Change the **spring stiffness constant**, $k$, by using different combinations of springs.
3) Change the **amplitude**, $A$, by pulling the masses down by different distances.

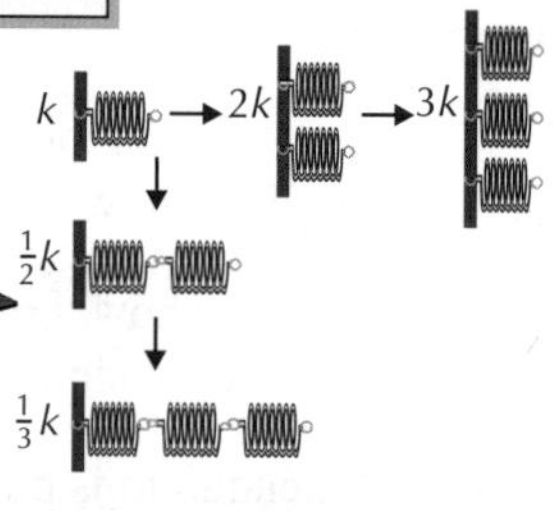


You'll get the following **results**:

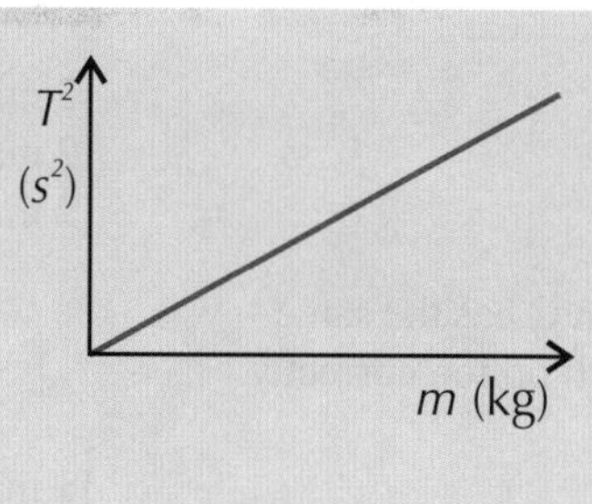


$T \propto \sqrt{m}$ so $T^2 \propto m$

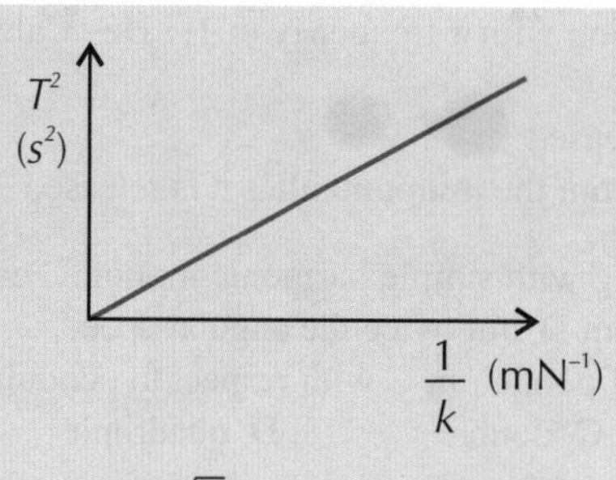


$T \propto \sqrt{\frac{1}{k}}$ so $T^2 \propto \frac{1}{k}$

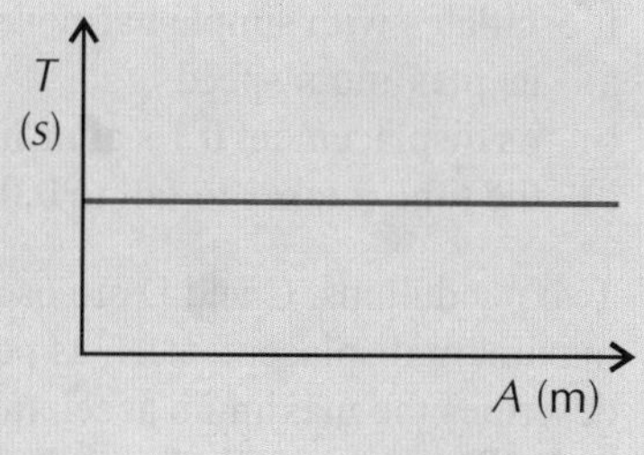


$T$ doesn't depend on amplitude, $A$.

# Simple Harmonic Oscillators

## The Simple Pendulum is the Classic Example of an SHO

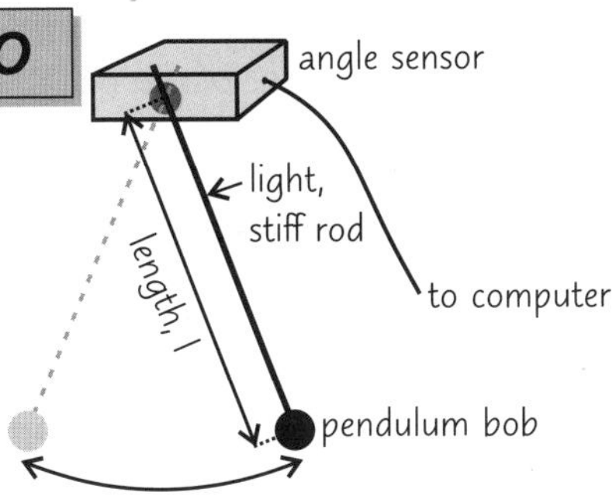


1) Attach a **pendulum** to an **angle sensor** connected to a **computer**.
2) **Displace** the pendulum from its rest position by a small angle (less than 10°) and let it go. The pendulum will oscillate with **simple harmonic motion**.
3) The angle sensor measures how the bob's **displacement** from the **rest** position varies with **time**.
4) Use the computer to plot a **displacement-time** graph and read off the **period**, $T$, from it. Make sure you calculate the average period over **several oscillations** to reduce the **percentage uncertainty** in your measurement (see page 152).
5) Change the **mass** of the pendulum bob, $m$, the **amplitude** of displacement, $A$, and the **length** of the rod, $l$, independently to see how they affect the **period**, $T$.

You can also do this experiment by hanging the pendulum from a clamp and timing the oscillations using a stop watch. Use the clamp stand as a reference point so it's easy to tell when the pendulum has reached the mid-point of its oscillation.

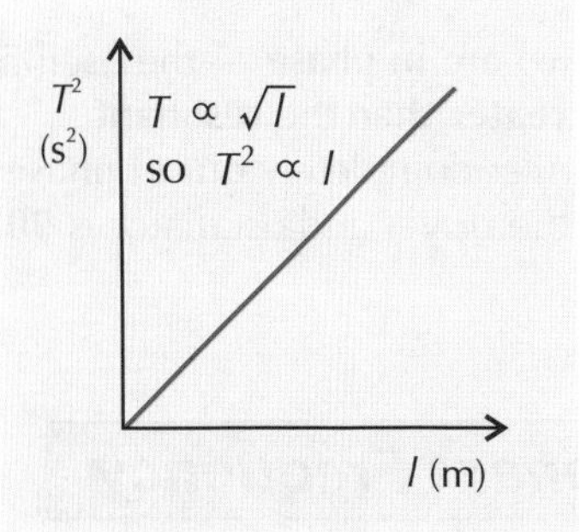


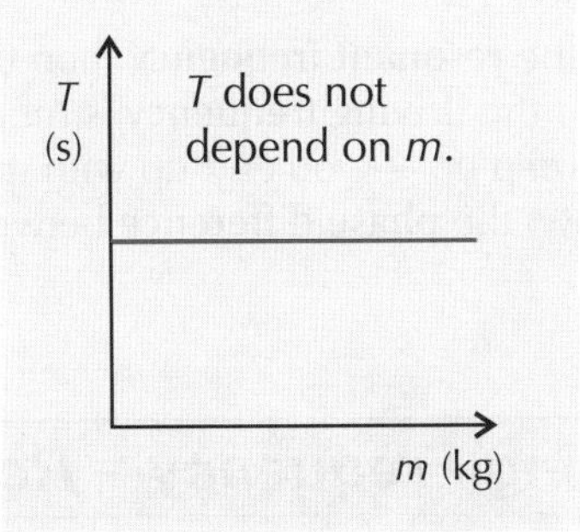


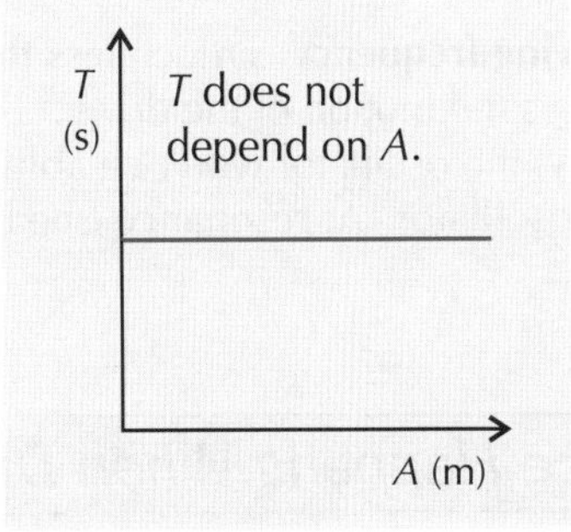

Bob hung around waiting for the experiment to start.

The **formula for the period of a pendulum** is: (The derivation's quite hard, so you don't need to know it.)

This formula only works for small angles of oscillation — up to about 10° from the equilibrium point.

$$T = 2\pi\sqrt{\frac{l}{g}}$$

$T$ = period of oscillation in seconds
$l$ = length of pendulum (between pivot and centre of mass of bob) in m
$g$ = gravitational field strength in $\text{Nkg}^{-1}$

## Practice Questions

Q1 Write down the formula for calculating the period of a mass-spring system.

Q2 Describe an experiment to find how changing the mass in a mass-spring system affects its period of oscillation.

Q3 For a mass-spring system, what graphs could you plot to find out how the period depends on: a) the mass, b) the spring constant, and c) the amplitude? What would they look like?

Q4 Write down the formula for calculating the period of a simple pendulum displaced by a small angle.

**Exam Questions**

Q1 A spring of original length 0.10 m is suspended from a stand and clamp. A mass of 0.10 kg is attached to the bottom and the spring extends to a total length of 0.20 m.

a) Calculate the spring constant of the spring in $\text{Nm}^{-1}$. ($g = 9.81\ \text{Nkg}^{-1}$) [2 marks]

b) The mass is pulled down a further 2.0 cm and then released. Assuming the mass oscillates with simple harmonic motion, calculate the period of the subsequent oscillations. [1 mark]

c) Calculate the mass needed to make the period of oscillation twice as long. [2 marks]

Q2 Two pendulums of different lengths were released from rest at the top of their swing. It took exactly the same time for the shorter pendulum to make five complete oscillations as it took the longer pendulum to make three complete oscillations. The shorter pendulum had a length of 0.20 m. Show that the length of the longer one was 0.56 m. [3 marks]

## Go on — SHO the examiners what you're made of...

*The most important things to remember on these pages are those two period equations. You'll be given them in your exam, but you need to know what they mean and be happy using them. So go and practise using them for a bit.*

# Free and Forced Vibrations

*Resonance... tricky little beast. The Millennium Bridge was supposed to be a feat of British engineering, but it suffered from a severe case of the wobbles caused by resonance. How was it sorted out? By damping, of course — read on...*

## Free Vibrations — No Transfer of Energy To or From the Surroundings

1) If you stretch and release a mass on a spring, it oscillates at its **resonant frequency**.
2) If **no energy's transferred** to or from the surroundings, it will **keep** oscillating with the **same amplitude forever**.
3) In practice this **never happens**, but a spring vibrating in air is called a **free vibration** anyway.

## Forced Vibrations Happen When There's an External Driving Force

1) A system can be **forced** to vibrate by a periodic **external force**.
2) The frequency of this force is called the **driving frequency**.

If the **driving frequency** is much **less than** the **resonant frequency** then the two are **in phase** — the oscillator just follows the motion of the driver. But, if the **driving frequency** is much **greater than** the **resonant frequency**, the oscillator won't be able to keep up — you end up with the driver completely **out of phase** with the oscillator. At **resonance** (see below) the **phase difference** between the driver and oscillator is **90°**.

## Resonance Happens When Driving Frequency = Resonant Frequency

When the **driving frequency** approaches the **resonant frequency**, the system gains more and more energy from the driving force and so vibrates with a **rapidly increasing amplitude**. When this happens the system is **resonating**.

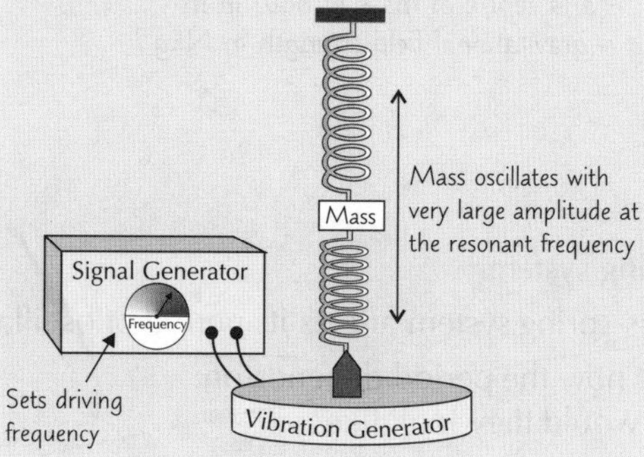


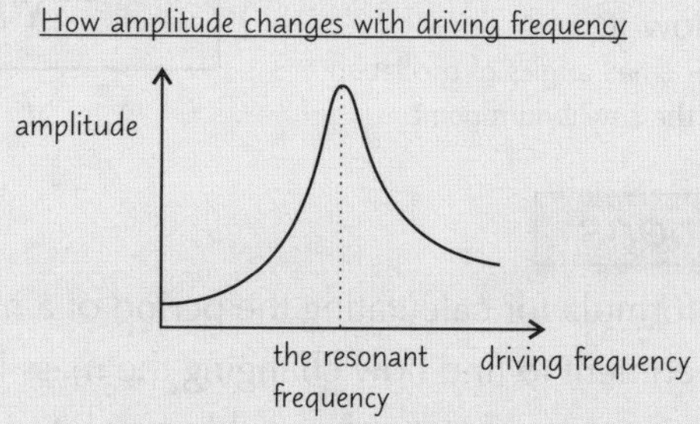


Armies deliberately march 'out of step' when they cross a bridge. This reduces the risk of the bridge resonating and breaking apart.

Examples of resonance:

a) organ pipe

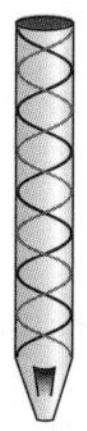

The column of air resonates, setting up a stationary wave in the pipe.

b) swing

A swing resonates if it's driven by someone pushing it at its resonant frequency.

c) glass smashing

A glass resonates when driven by a sound wave at the right frequency.

d) radio

A radio is tuned so the electric circuit resonates at the same frequency as radio broadcasts.

## Damping Happens When Energy is Lost To the Surroundings

1) In practice, **any** oscillating system **loses energy** to its surroundings.
2) This is usually down to **frictional forces** like air resistance.
3) These are called **damping forces**.
4) Systems are often **deliberately damped** to **stop** them oscillating or to **minimise** the effect of **resonance**.

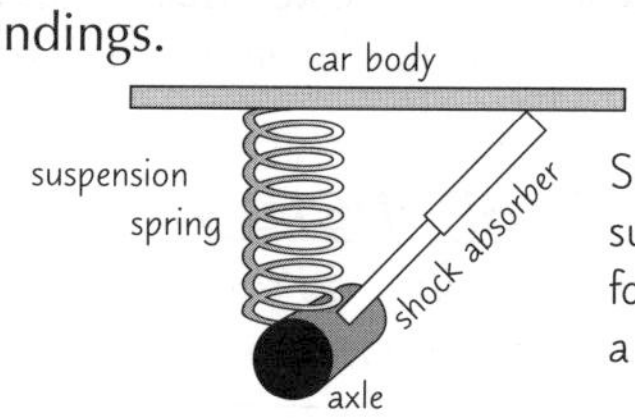


Shock absorbers in a car suspension provide a damping force by squashing oil through a hole when compressed.

# Free and Forced Vibrations

## Different Amounts of Damping have Different Effects

1) The **degree** of damping can vary from **light** damping (where the damping force is small) to **overdamping**.
2) Damping **reduces** the **amplitude** of the oscillation over time. The **heavier** the damping, the **quicker** the amplitude is reduced to zero.
3) **Critical damping** reduces the amplitude (i.e. stops the system oscillating) in the **shortest possible time**.
4) Car **suspension systems** and moving coil **meters** are critically damped so that they **don't oscillate** but return to equilibrium as quickly as possible.
5) Systems with **even heavier damping** are **overdamped**. They take **longer** to return to equilibrium than a critically damped system.

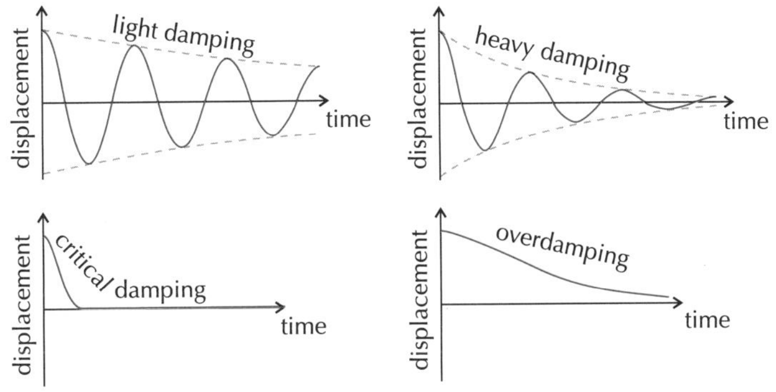


**Plastic deformation** of ductile materials **reduces** the **amplitude** of oscillations in the same way as damping. As the material changes shape, it **absorbs energy**, so the oscillation will be smaller.

## Damping Affects Resonance too

1) **Lightly damped** systems have a **very sharp** resonance peak. Their amplitude only increases dramatically when the **driving frequency** is **very close** to the **resonant frequency**.
2) **Heavily damped** systems have a **flatter response**. Their amplitude doesn't increase very much near the resonant frequency and they aren't as **sensitive** to the driving frequency.
3) Structures are **damped** to avoid being **damaged** by resonance. Taipei 101 is a very tall skyscraper which uses a **giant pendulum** to damp oscillations caused by strong winds.
4) Damping can also be used to **improve performance**. For example, loudspeakers in a room create sound waves in the air. These reflect off of the walls of the room, and at certain frequencies **stationary sound waves** are created between the walls of the room. This causes **resonance** and can affect the quality of the sound — some frequencies are louder than they should be. Places like recording studios use **soundproofing** on their walls which absorb the sound energy and **convert** it into heat energy.

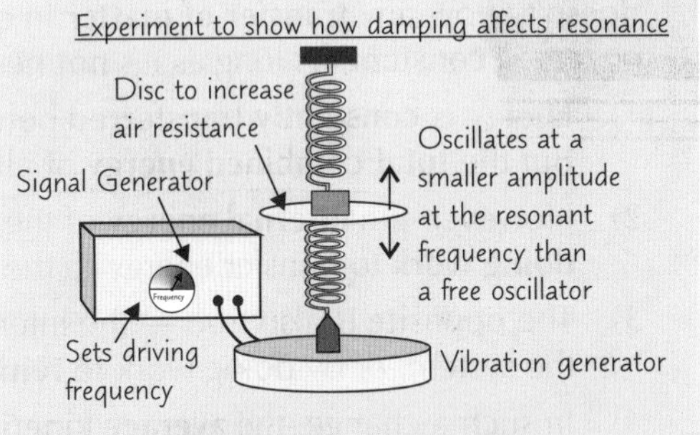


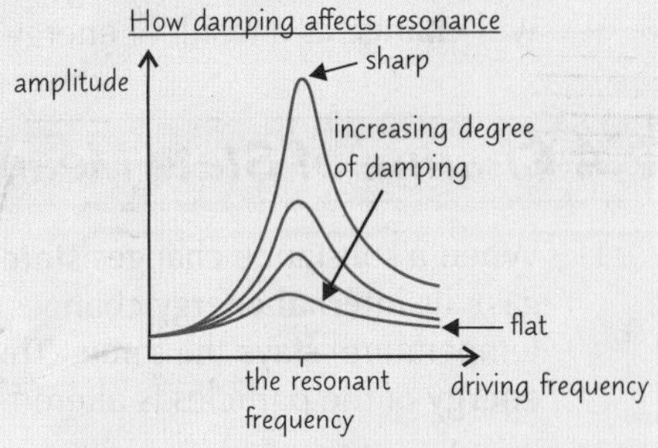


## Practice Questions

Q1 What is a free vibration? What is a forced vibration?

Q2 Draw diagrams to show how a damped system oscillates with time when the system is lightly damped and when the system is critically damped.

Q3 Explain how damping is used to improve sound quality in enclosed spaces.

**Exam Questions**

Q1 a) Describe resonance. [2 marks]
b) Sketch a graph to show how the amplitude of a lightly damped system varies with driving frequency. [2 marks]
c) On the graph, show how the amplitude of the system varies with driving frequency when it is heavily damped. [1 mark]

Q2 a) Describe critical damping. [1 mark]
b) State one situation where critical damping is used. [1 mark]

## A-Level Physics — it can really put a damper on your social life...

*Resonance can be really useful (radios, oboes, swings — yay) or very, very bad...*

# Thermal Energy Transfer

*Thermal physics is really all about energy transfer to and from particles.*

## ***Internal Energy*** *Depends on the* ***Kinetic*** *and* ***Potential Energy*** *of Particles*

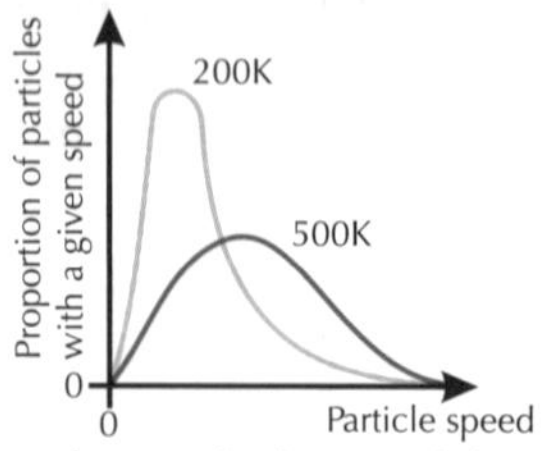


The **particles** in a body **don't** all **travel** at the **same speed**.

1) Some particles will be moving **fast** but others much more **slowly**. The speeds of all the particles are **randomly distributed** (so **kinetic energy** is randomly distributed too). The **largest proportion** will travel at about the **average speed**.
2) The **distribution** of particle speeds depends on the **temperature** of the body. The **higher** the temperature, the **higher** the **average kinetic energy** of the particles.
3) The particles in a body also have **randomly distributed potential energies** that depend on their **relative positions**.

> The **internal energy** of a body is the **sum** of the randomly distributed **kinetic** and **potential energies** of **all** its particles.

## ***Energy Changes*** *Happen Between* ***Particles***

A **system** is just a group of bodies considered as a whole. A **closed system is** one which doesn't allow any **transfer of matter** in or out. For a closed system, the total internal energy is **constant**, as long as it's **not** heated or cooled, and **no work** is done.

1) Energy is **constantly transferred** between particles within a system, through **collisions between particles**. But the **total combined energy** of all the particles **doesn't change** during these collisions.
2) However, the **internal energy** of the system can be **increased** by **heating** it, or by **doing work** to transfer energy to the system (e.g. changing its shape).
3) The **opposite** is also true — the internal energy can be **reduced** by **cooling** the system, or by doing work to **remove energy** from the system.
4) In such a change, the **average kinetic** and/or **potential energy** of the particles will **change** as a result of energy being **transferred to** or **from** the system.

> Changing internal energy through heating or doing work is described by the first law of thermodynamics (p.120).

## *A* ***Change of State*** *Means a* ***Change of Internal Energy***

1) When a substance **changes state** (between solid, liquid or gas), its **internal energy** changes but its **kinetic energy** (and temperature) **stays the same**. This is because the **potential energy** of the particles is altered — not their kinetic energy.
2) As a liquid turns into a gas (for example, boiling water becoming steam) its **potential energy increases** even though the water molecules in both states are at **100 °C**.

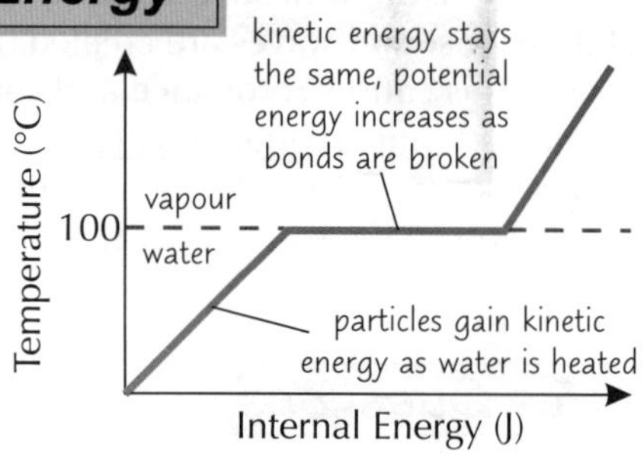


## ***Specific Heat Capacity*** *is how much* ***Energy*** *it Takes to* ***Heat*** *Something*

When you heat something, its particles get more **kinetic energy** and its **temperature** rises.

> The **specific heat capacity** (*c*) of a substance is the amount of **energy** needed to **raise** the **temperature** of **1 kg** of the substance by **1 K** (or 1°C).

or put another way: **energy change = mass × specific heat capacity × change in temperature**

in symbols: $Q = mc\Delta\theta$

$\Delta T$ or $\Delta t$ is sometimes used instead of $\Delta\theta$ for the change in temperature.

$Q$ is the energy change in J, $m$ is the mass in kg and $\Delta\theta$ is the temperature change in K or °C. Units of $c$ are J kg$^{-1}$ K$^{-1}$ or J kg$^{-1}$ °C$^{-1}$.

# Thermal Energy Transfer

## Find Specific Heat Capacity using a Continuous-Flow Calorimeter

**Continuous-flow heating** is when a **fluid** flows continuously over a **heating element**. As it flows, **energy** is **transferred** to the fluid.

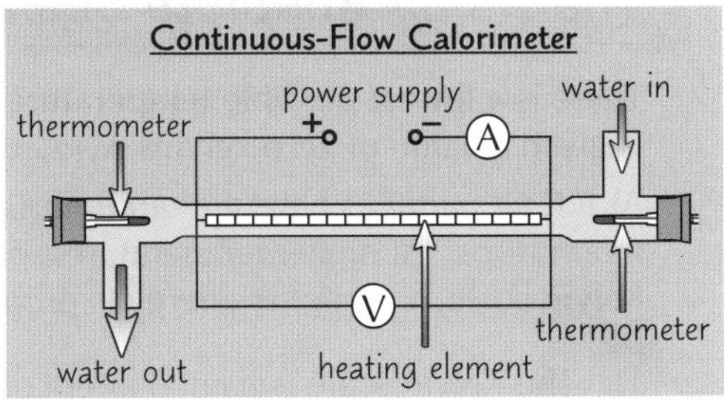


1) Set up the experiment shown and let water flow at a **steady rate** until the water out is at a **constant temperature**.
2) Record the **flow rate** of the water and the duration of the experiment, $t$, (to find the mass of water). You also need to measure the **temperature difference**, $\Delta\theta$, (of the water from the point that it flows in to the point that it flows out) between the thermometers. Also record the **current**, $I$, and **potential difference**, $V$.
3) The **energy supplied** to the water is $Q = mc\Delta\theta + H$, where $H$ is the **heat lost** to the surroundings.
4) **Repeat** the experiment **changing** only the **p.d. of the power supply** and the **flow rate** (mass) so $\Delta\theta$ remains **constant**. You should now have an equation for each experiment: $Q_1 = m_1c\Delta\theta + H$ and $Q_2 = m_2c\Delta\theta + H$.
5) The values of $c$, $\Delta\theta$ and $H$ are the same, so $Q_2 - Q_1 = (m_2 - m_1)c\Delta\theta$. Rearranging gives: $c = \frac{Q_2 - Q_1}{(m_2 - m_1)\Delta\theta}$.
6) $Q$ is just the **electrical energy** supplied over time $t$ in each case, so you can use $Q = VIt$ to find $Q_1$ and $Q_2$, and therefore **c**, the **specific heat capacity** of water.

## Specific Latent Heat is the Energy Needed to Change State

To **melt** a **solid** or **boil or evaporate a liquid**, you need **energy** to **break the bonds** that hold the particles in place. The **energy** needed for this is called **latent heat**. The **larger** the **mass** of the substance, the **more energy** it takes to **change** its **state**. That's why the **specific latent heat** is defined per kg:

The **specific latent heat** ($l$) of **fusion** or **vaporisation** is the quantity of **thermal energy** required to **change the state** of **1 kg** of a substance.

So: **energy change = mass of substance changed × specific latent heat** or: $Q = ml$

Where $Q$ is the energy change in J and $m$ is the mass in kg. The units of $l$ are J kg$^{-1}$.

You'll usually see the latent heat of vaporisation (melting or freezing) written $l_v$ and the latent heat of fusion (boiling or condensing) written $l_f$.

## Practice Questions

Q1 Give the definition of internal energy.

Q2 Define specific heat capacity and specific latent heat.

Q3 Show that the thermal energy needed to heat 2 kg of water from 20 °C to 50 °C is ~250 kJ ($c_{water}$ = 4180 J kg$^{-1}$ K$^{-1}$).

**Exam Questions**

Q1 A 2.0 kg metal cylinder is heated uniformly from 4.5 °C to 12.7 °C in 3 minutes. The electric heater supplies electrical energy at a rate of 90 Js$^{-1}$. Assuming that heat losses are negligible, calculate the specific heat capacity of the metal. State a correct unit for your answer. [4 marks]

Q2 A kettle transfers energy at a rate of $3.00 \times 10^3$ Js$^{-1}$.

a) If the kettle contains 0.500 kg of water at 20.0 °C, calculate how long it will take the water to reach 100.0 °C and then boil dry, assuming the kettle remains switched on throughout and no energy is lost to the surroundings. ($l_v$(water) = 2260 kJkg$^{-1}$, $c_{water}$ = 4180 J kg$^{-1}$ K$^{-1}$) [5 marks]

b) Which of the following statements is true about the energy of the particles in the water during this process?

A The temperature of the water increases steadily throughout the time found in part a).

B At the point of boiling, only the potential energy of the water particles is changing.

C Once the water starts boiling, the kinetic energy of the water particles starts increasing.

D Both the kinetic and potential energy of the water particles are continually increasing throughout the time found in part a). [1 mark]

## My specific eat capacity — 24 pies...

*This stuff's a bit dull, but hey... make sure you're comfortable using those equations. Interesting(ish) fact for the day — the huge difference in specific heat capacity between the land and the sea is one of the causes of monsoons in Asia.*

# Gas Laws

*Laws for gases? What ever next... I give it about 5 minutes before the no-win no-fee lawyers start calling you.*

## There's an **Absolute Scale** of **Temperature**

There is a **lowest possible temperature** called **absolute zero***. Absolute zero is given a value of **zero kelvins**, written **0 K**, on the absolute temperature scale.

At **0 K** all particles have the **minimum** possible **kinetic energy** — everything pretty much stops. At higher temperatures, particles have more energy. In fact, with the **Kelvin scale**, a particle's **energy** is **proportional** to its **temperature** (see page 18).

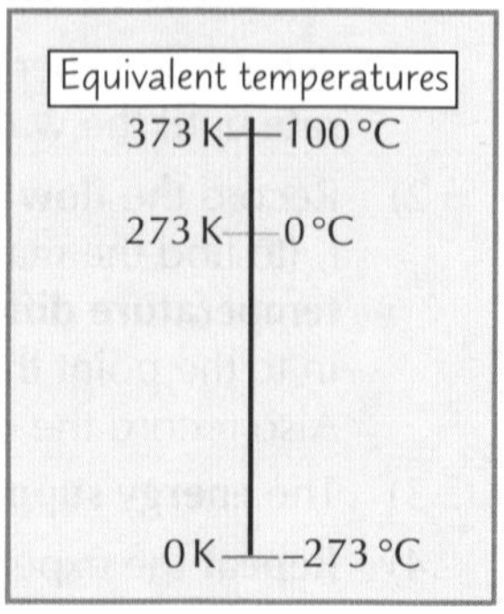


1) The Kelvin scale is named after Lord Kelvin who first suggested it.
2) A change of **1 K** equals a change of **1 °C**.
3) To change from degrees Celsius into kelvins you **add 273** (or 273.15 if you need to be really precise).

$$K = C + 273$$

**All equations** in **thermal physics** use temperatures measured in kelvins.

**It's true. −273.15 °C is the lowest temperature theoretically possible. Weird, huh. You'd kinda think there wouldn't be a minimum, but there is.*

## There are **Three Gas Laws**

The three gas laws were each worked out **independently** by **careful experiment**. Each of the gas laws applies to a **fixed mass** of gas.

### Boyle's Law: $pV$ = constant

At a **constant temperature** the **pressure** $p$ and **volume** $V$ of a gas are **inversely proportional**.

E.g. if you **reduce** the volume of a gas, its particles will be **closer together** and will **collide** with each other and the container more often, so the pressure **increases**.

A (theoretical) gas that obeys Boyle's law at all temperatures is called an **ideal gas**.

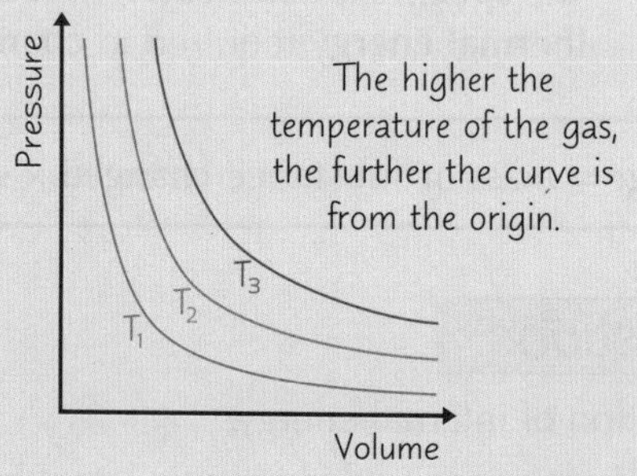


### Charles's Law: $V/T$ = constant

'Ello, 'ello...

At constant **pressure**, the **volume** $V$ of a gas is **directly proportional** to its **absolute temperature** $T$.

When you **heat** a gas the particles **gain** kinetic energy (page 10). At a constant pressure, this means they move **more quickly** and **further apart**, and so the **volume** of the gas **increases**.

**Ideal gases** obey this law and the pressure law as well.

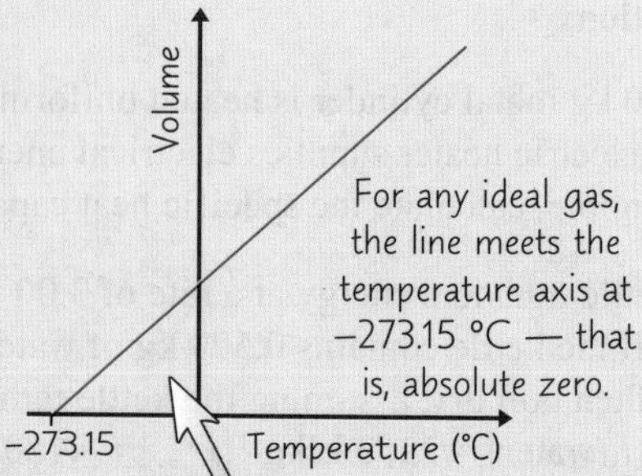


If you'd plotted these graphs in kelvins, they'd both have gone through the origin.

### The Pressure Law: $p/T$ = constant

At constant **volume**, the **pressure** $p$ of a gas is **directly proportional** to its **absolute temperature** $T$.

If you **heat** a gas, the particles **gain** kinetic energy. This means they move **faster**. If the volume doesn't change, the particles will **collide** with each other and their container more often and at higher speed, **increasing** the pressure inside the container.

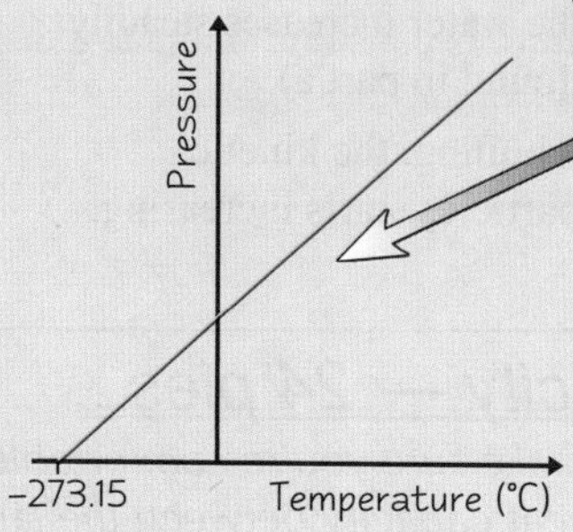

# Gas Laws

## ***Investigate*** *the Gas Laws with these* ***Experiments***

**Experiment to investigate Boyle's Law**

You can investigate the effect of **pressure** on **volume** by setting up the experiment shown. The **oil** traps a pocket of air in a sealed **tube** with **fixed dimensions**. A **tyre pump** is used to **increase** the pressure on the oil and the **Bourdon gauge** records the **pressure**. As the pressure increases, more oil will be pushed into the tube, the **oil level** will **rise**, and the air will **compress**. The volume occupied by air in the tube will **reduce**.

Measure the volume of air when the system is at **atmospheric pressure**, then gradually increase the pressure, keeping the **temperature constant**. Note down both the pressure and the volume of air as it changes. Multiplying these together at any point should give the **same value**.

If you plot a **graph** of $p$ against $\frac{1}{V}$ you should get a **straight line**.

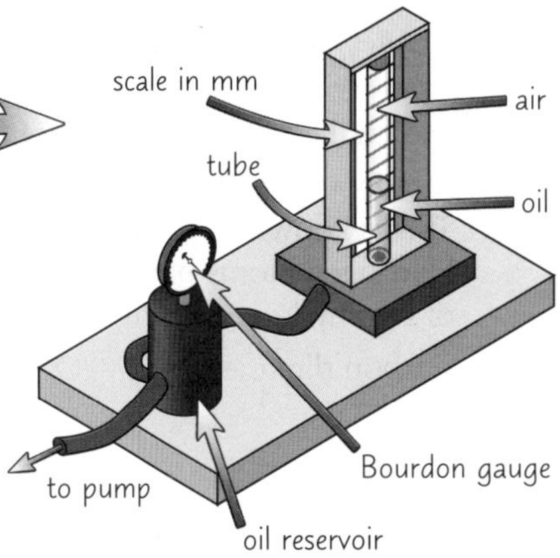


**Experiment to investigate Charles's Law**

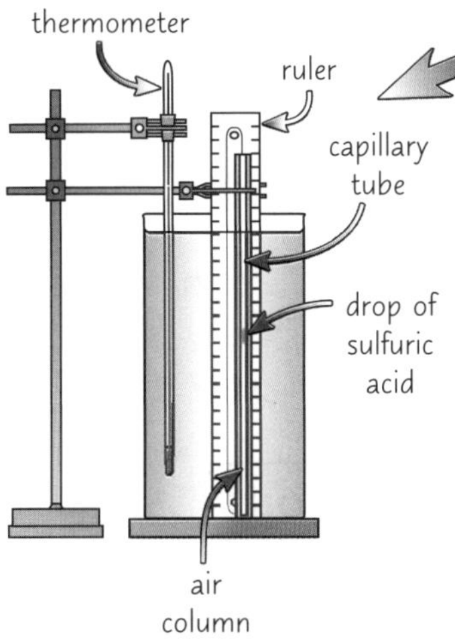


You can investigate the effect of **temperature** on **volume** by setting up the experiment shown. A **capillary tube** is **sealed** at the bottom and contains a drop of **concentrated sulfuric acid** halfway up the tube — this traps a **column of air** between the bottom of the tube and the acid drop. The beaker is filled with **near-boiling water**, and the **length** of the trapped column of air increases. As the water cools, the length of the air column **decreases**.

Regularly record the **temperature** of the water and the air column **length** as the water cools. **Repeat** with fresh near-boiling water twice more, letting the tube adjust to the new temperature between each repeat. Record the length at the **same temperatures** each time and take an **average** of the three results.

If you plot your **average results** on a graph of **length** against **temperature** and draw a line of best fit, you will get a **straight line**. This shows that the length of the air column is **proportional** to the temperature. The volume of the column of air is equal to the volume of a cylinder, which is proportional to its length ($V = \pi r^2 l$), so the **volume** is also proportional to the temperature. This agrees with **Charles's law**.

## *Practice Questions*

Q1 Give the value of absolute zero in kelvins and degrees Celsius.

Q2 State Boyle's law, Charles's law and the pressure law.

Q3 The pressure of a gas is 100 000 Pa and its temperature is 27 °C. The gas is heated — its volume stays fixed but the pressure rises to 150 000 Pa. Show that its new temperature is 177 °C.

Q4 Describe an experiment to demonstrate the effect of temperature on the volume of a gas when pressure is constant.

**Exam Questions**

Q1 An unknown solution boils at 107.89 °C. Calculate its boiling temperature in kelvins. [1 mark]

Q2 A gas expands from 2.42 m$^3$ to 6.43 m$^3$. The final temperature of the gas is 293 K. Calculate the initial temperature of the gas, assuming the pressure remains constant. [2 marks]

Q3 a) Describe an experiment to investigate the effect of pressure on the volume of a gas when temperature is constant. Include a description of your method and the relationship you would expect to see. [4 marks]

b) A parcel of air has a volume of 0.460 m$^3$ at $1.03 \times 10^5$ Pa. Calculate its volume at $3.41 \times 10^5$ Pa. Assume that the temperature does not change. [2 marks]

## *Don't feel under pressure — take some time to chill out...*

*Three laws, two practicals, one thing to do — learn it all. Learning laws probably isn't your favourite way to spend your time (unless you want to be a lawyer) but it'll stop a nasty question from slowing you down in the exams.*

# Ideal Gas Equation

*Aaahh... great... another one of those 'our equation doesn't work properly with real gases, so we'll invent an ideal gas that it does work for and they'll think we're dead clever' situations. Hmm. Physicists, eh...*

## *The **Molecular Mass** of a **Gas** is the Mass of **One Molecule** of that Gas*

1) Molecular mass is the **sum** of the **masses** of **all the atoms** that make up a **molecule**.
2) Molecular mass is usually given relative to the mass of a **carbon-12** atom. This is known as **relative molecular mass**. Carbon-12 has a relative mass of **12**. Hydrogen atoms have a relative mass of 1, but hydrogen molecules are made up of **two** hydrogen atoms, so the relative **molecular mass** of hydrogen is **2**.
3) Carbon dioxide ($^{12}_{6}C + ^{16}_{8}O + ^{16}_{8}O$) has a relative molecular mass of 12 + 16 + 16 = 44.

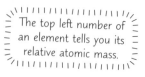

The top left number of an element tells you its relative atomic mass.

## *The **Molar Mass** is the Mass of **One Mole** of a **Gas***

1) At a fixed **pressure** and **temperature**, a fixed volume of gas will contain the **same amount** of gas molecules, **no matter** what the gas is. This leads to a unit called a **mole**.
2) **One mole** of any **gas** contains the same number of particles. This number is called **Avogadro's constant** — it has the symbol $N_A$ and is equal to **6.02 × 10^23 particles per mole**.
3) The **molar mass** of a substance is the mass that **1 mole** of that substance would have (usually in **grams**). It is **equal** to the **relative molecular mass** of that substance. So the molar mass of helium ($^{4}_{2}He$) is 4 g and the molar mass of an oxygen molecule, which consists of 2 oxygen atoms, is 16 g + 16 g = 32 g.
4) The **number of moles** in a substance is usually given by ***n***, and its units are '**mol**'. The number of molecules in a mass of gas is given by the number of moles, *n*, **multiplied by** Avogadro's constant. So the number of molecules, $N = nN_A$.

## *If you **Combine** All Three Gas Laws you get the **Ideal Gas Equation***

1) Remember the gas laws from page 12? **Combining all three** of them gives the equation: $$\frac{pV}{T} = \text{constant}$$
2) The constant in the equation depends on the amount of gas used. The amount of **gas** can be **measured** in **moles**, ***n***.

(Pretty obvious... if you have more gas it takes up more space.)

3) The constant then becomes ***nR***, where ***R*** is called the **molar gas constant**. Its value is **8.31 J mol⁻¹ K⁻¹**. Plugging this into the equation gives:

$$\frac{pV}{T} = nR \quad \text{or rearranging,} \quad pV = nRT \text{ — the ideal gas equation}$$

This equation works well (i.e., a real gas approximates to an ideal gas) for gases at **low pressures** and fairly **high temperatures**.

Ideal gases obey Boyle's, Charles's and the pressure laws.

## *__Boltzmann's Constant__ k is like a **Gas Constant** for **One Particle** of **Gas***

1) **Boltzmann's constant, *k***, is equivalent to $R/N_A$ (molar gas constant / Avogadro's constant) — you can think of Boltzmann's constant as the **gas constant** for **one particle of gas**, while ***R*** is the gas constant for **one mole of gas**.
2) The value of Boltzmann's constant is **1.38 × 10⁻²³ JK⁻¹**.
3) If you combine $N = nN_A$ and $k = R/N_A$ you'll see that $Nk = nR$ — which can be substituted into the ideal gas equation:

$$pV = NkT \text{ — the equation of state}$$

The equation $pV = NkT$ is called the equation of state of an ideal gas.

# Ideal Gas Equation

## Work is Done to Change the Volume of a Gas at Constant Pressure

1) For a gas to **expand** or **contract** at **constant pressure**, **work** must be **done** — i.e. there must be a transfer of energy.
2) This normally involves the **transfer** of **heat energy** — e.g. if you **heat** a gas-filled balloon, it will **expand**. **Remove** the heat source and it will **contract** back to its **original size** as the heat is transferred back to its surroundings.
3) The **work done** in **changing** the **volume** of a gas at a constant pressure is given by: where $p$ is **pressure** and $\Delta V$ is change in **volume**.

**work done = $p\Delta V$**

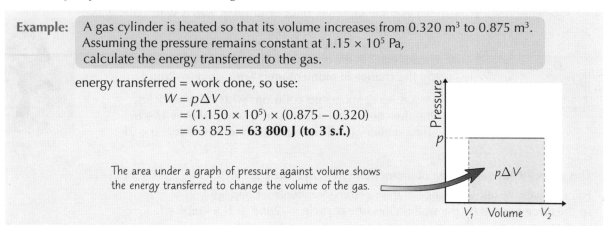

**Example:** A gas cylinder is heated so that its volume increases from 0.320 m³ to 0.875 m³. Assuming the pressure remains constant at $1.15 \times 10^5$ Pa, calculate the energy transferred to the gas.

energy transferred = work done, so use:

$$W = p\Delta V$$
$$= (1.150 \times 10^5) \times (0.875 - 0.320)$$
$$= 63\,825 = \mathbf{63\,800\ J\ (to\ 3\ s.f.)}$$

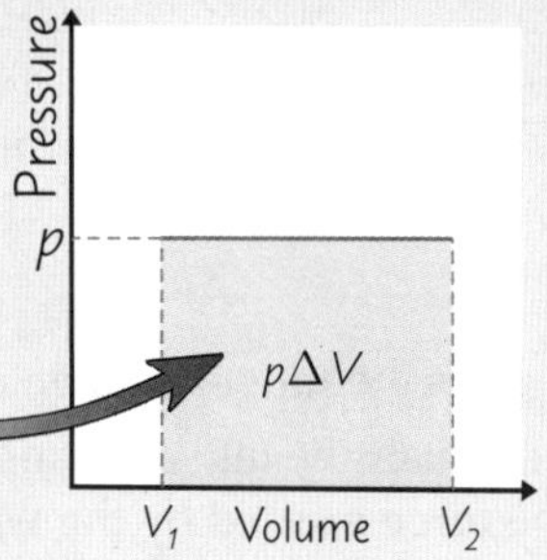


The area under a graph of pressure against volume shows the energy transferred to change the volume of the gas.

## Practice Questions

Q1 What is meant by molecular mass and relative molecular mass?

Q2 What is the molar mass of carbon-12 ($^{12}_{6}C$)?

Q3 How many atoms are there in one mole of krypton?

Q4 What is the ideal gas equation?

Q5 What is the equation of state of an ideal gas?

Q6 Show that the work done when a gas expands from 3.4 m³ to 9.3 m³ at $1.0 \times 10^{15}$ Pa is $5.9 \times 10^{15}$ J.

**Exam Questions**

Q1 The mass of one mole of nitrogen gas is 0.028 kg.

a) A flask contains 0.014 kg of nitrogen gas. Calculate the number of:
   i) moles of nitrogen gas in the flask. [1 mark]
   ii) nitrogen molecules in the flask. [1 mark]

b) The flask has a volume of 0.0130 m³ and its temperature is 27.2 °C. Calculate the pressure of the gas inside it. ($R = 8.31$ J mol⁻¹ K⁻¹) [2 marks]

c) Explain what would happen to the pressure inside the flask if the number of molecules of nitrogen in the flask were halved. [2 marks]

Q2 A large helium balloon has a volume of 10.0 m³ at ground level. The temperature of the gas in the balloon is 293 K and the pressure is $1.00 \times 10^5$ Pa. The balloon is released and rises to a height where its volume becomes 25.0 m³ and its temperature is 261 K. Calculate the pressure inside the balloon at its new height. [3 marks]

Q3 470 kJ of work (to 3 significant figures) is done to increase the volume of a gas to 10.3 m³. Calculate the original volume of the gas assuming a constant pressure of $1.12 \times 10^5$ Pa. [2 marks]

## Ideal revision equation: marks = (pages read × questions answered)²...

*All this might sound a bit theoretical, but most gases you'll meet in the everyday world come fairly close to being 'ideal'. They only stop obeying these laws well when the pressure's too high or they're getting close to their condensation point.*

# The Pressure of an Ideal Gas

*Kinetic theory tries to explain the gas laws. It basically models a gas as a series of hard balls that obey Newton's laws.*

## You Need to be Able to **Derive** the **Pressure** of an **Ideal Gas**

### Start by **Deriving** the **Pressure** on **One Wall** of a Box — in the x direction

Imagine a cubic box with sides of length $l$ containing $N$ particles each of mass $m$.

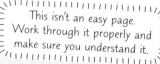

This isn't an easy page. Work through it properly and make sure you understand it.

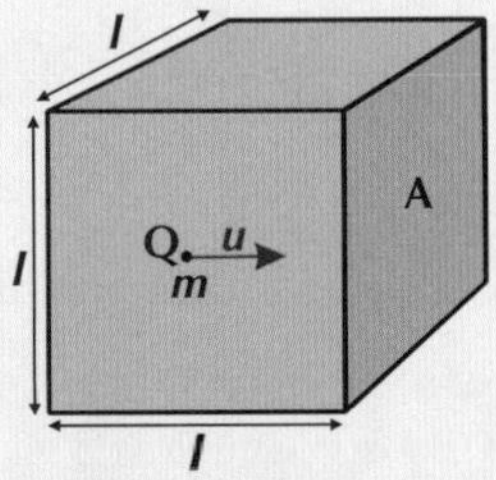


1) Say particle **Q** moves directly towards **wall A** with velocity $u$. Its **momentum** approaching the wall is $mu$. It strikes wall **A**. Assuming the **collisions** are perfectly **elastic**, it rebounds and heads back in the opposite direction with momentum $-mu$. So the **change in momentum** is $-mu - mu = -2mu$.
2) Assuming **Q** suffers no collisions with other particles, the **time between collisions** of **Q** and wall **A** is $2l \div u$. The number of **collisions per second** is therefore $u \div 2l$.

Gases under pressure can be udderly delightful.

3) This gives the **rate of change of momentum** as $-2mu \times u \div 2l$.
4) Force equals the rate of change of momentum (Newton's second law), so the **force exerted by the wall** on this one particle $= -2mu^2 \div 2l = -mu^2 \div l$.
5) Particle **Q** is only one of many in the cube. Each particle will have a different velocity $u_1$, $u_2$ etc. towards **A**.

   The total force, $F$, of all these particles on wall **A** is: $$F = \frac{m(u_1^2 + u_2^2 + ...)}{l}$$

   This force is now positive as we're talking about the force **on** the wall.

6) You can define a quantity called the **mean square speed**, $\overline{u^2}$ as: $$\overline{u^2} = \frac{u_1^2 + u_2^2 + ...}{N}$$
7) If you put that into the equation above, you get: $$F = \frac{Nm\overline{u^2}}{l}$$
8) So, the pressure of the gas on end **A** is given by: $$\text{pressure, } p = \frac{\text{force}}{\text{area}} = \frac{Nm\overline{u^2} \div l}{l^2} = \frac{Nm\overline{u^2}}{l^3} = \frac{Nm\overline{u^2}}{V}$$
   where $V$ = volume of the cube

### ...Then for the **General Equation** you need to think about **All 3 Directions** — **x, y** and **z**

A gas particle can move in **three dimensions** (i.e. the $x$, $y$ and $z$ directions).

1) You can calculate its **speed**, $c$, from Pythagoras' theorem in three dimensions:
   $c^2 = u^2 + v^2 + w^2$ where $u$, $v$ and $w$ are the components of the particle's velocity in the $x$, $y$ and $z$ directions.
2) If you treat all $N$ particles in the same way, this gives an **overall** mean square speed of: $\overline{c^2} = \overline{u^2} + \overline{v^2} + \overline{w^2}$
3) Since the particles move **randomly**: $\overline{u^2} = \overline{v^2} = \overline{w^2}$ so $\overline{c^2} = 3\overline{u^2}$ and so $\overline{u^2} = \frac{\overline{c^2}}{3}$.
4) You can substitute this into the equation for pressure that you derived above to give:

$$pV = \frac{1}{3}Nm\overline{c^2}$$

# The Pressure of an Ideal Gas

## A Useful Quantity is the **Root Mean Square Speed** or $c_{rms}$

As you saw on the previous page, it often helps to think about the motion of a **typical particle** in kinetic theory.

1) $\overline{c^2}$ is the **mean square speed** and has **units $m^2s^{-2}$**.
2) $\overline{c^2}$ is the average of the **square speeds** of **all** the particles, so the square root of it gives you the typical speed.
3) This is called the **root mean square speed** or, usually, the **r.m.s. speed**. It's often written as $c_{rms}$.
   The **unit** is the same as any speed — **$ms^{-1}$**.

$$\text{r.m.s. speed} = \sqrt{\text{mean square speed}} = \sqrt{\overline{c^2}} = c_{rms}$$

4) So you can write the equation on the previous page as:

$$pV = \frac{1}{3}Nm(c_{rms})^2$$

## Lots of **Simplifying Assumptions** are Used in **Kinetic Theory**

In **kinetic theory**, physicists picture gas particles moving at **high speed** in **random directions**.
To get **equations** like the one you just derived though, some **simplifying assumptions** are needed:

1) The molecules continually **move about randomly**.
2) The motion of the molecules follows **Newton's laws**.
3) **Collisions** between molecules themselves or at the walls of a container are **perfectly elastic**.
4) Except for during collisions, the molecules always move in **straight lines**.
5) Any **forces** that act during collisions last for **much less time** than the time between collisions.

A **gas obeying** these **assumptions** is called an **ideal** gas. Ideal gases also follow the three **gas laws**, and have an **internal energy** (p.10) that is dependent only on the kinetic energy of their particles.
(The **potential energy** = **0 J** as there are no forces between them except when they are **colliding**.)
Real gases behave like ideal gases as long as the **pressure isn't too big** and the **temperature** is **reasonably high** (compared with their boiling point), so they're useful assumptions.

## Practice Questions

Q1 What is the change in momentum when a gas particle hits a wall of its container head-on?

Q2 What is the force exerted on the wall by this one particle? What is the total force exerted on the wall?

Q3 What is the pressure exerted on this wall? What is the total pressure on the container?

Q4 What is 'root mean square speed'? How would you find it?

Q5 Give three of the assumptions made about ideal gas behaviour.

**Exam Question**

Q1 Some helium gas is contained in a flask of volume $7.00 \times 10^{-5}$ m$^3$. Each helium atom has a mass of $6.65 \times 10^{-27}$ kg, and there are $2.17 \times 10^{22}$ atoms present. The pressure of the gas is $1.03 \times 10^5$ Pa.

a) Calculate the mean square speed of the atoms. [2 marks]

b) Calculate the r.m.s. speed of a typical helium atom in the flask. [1 mark]

c) If the absolute temperature of the gas is doubled, calculate the new r.m.s. speed of its atoms. [2 marks]

## Help — these pages are de-riving me crazy...

*Make sure you know the derivation inside out and back to front — it's not easy, so you might want to go through it a few times, but it is worth it. Remember — mean square speed is the average of the squared speeds — i.e. square all the speeds, then find the average. Don't make the mistake of finding the average speed first and then squaring. No, no no...*

# Kinetic Energy and the Development of Theories

*If, like me, you've spent this whole section wondering just how such spiffing physics came to be, you're in luck.*

## *Average Kinetic Energy* is *Proportional* to *Absolute Temperature*

There are **two equations** for the **product *pV*** of a gas — the ideal gas equation (page 14), and the equation involving the mean square speed of the particles (page 17). You can **equate these** to get three expressions for the **average kinetic energy**.

*N* is the number of molecules in the gas, $(c_{rms})^2$ is their mean square speed, and *m* is the mass of one molecule.

1) The **ideal gas equation**: $pV = nRT$
2) The **pressure** of an **ideal gas** given by kinetic theory: $pV = \frac{1}{3}Nm(c_{rms})^2$
3) **Equating** these two gives: $\frac{1}{3}Nm(c_{rms})^2 = nRT$
4) **Multiplying** by **3/2** gives: $\frac{3}{2} \times \frac{1}{3}Nm(c_{rms})^2 = \frac{3nRT}{2}$, so: $\frac{1}{2}m(c_{rms})^2 = \frac{3}{2}\frac{nRT}{N}$
5) $\frac{1}{2}m(c_{rms})^2$ is the **average kinetic energy** of a **particle**.
6) You can substitute ***Nk*** for ***nR***, where ***k*** is the **Boltzmann constant** (see page 14) to show that the **average kinetic energy** of a particle is **directly proportional** to ***T*** (**absolute temperature**). $\frac{1}{2}m(c_{rms})^2 = \frac{3}{2}kT$
   You can use $\frac{3}{2}kT$ as an **approximation** for the **average kinetic energy** of the molecules in **any substance**.
7) Finally, the Boltzmann constant is equivalent to $R/N_A$ (see p.14), so you can substitute this for ***k*** in the equation above, to get: $\frac{1}{2}m(c_{rms})^2 = \frac{3}{2}\frac{RT}{N_A}$

## *The **Gas Laws** are **Empirical, Kinetic Theory** is **Theoretical***

1) **Empirical laws** are based on **observations** and **evidence**. This means that they can **predict what will happen** but they **don't explain why**.
2) For example, the **gas laws** (page 12) and the **ideal gas** equation (page 14) are all based on **observations** of how a gas responds to changes in its environment. They were discovered by scientists making **direct observations** of the gases' **properties** and can be **proven** with **simple experiments**.
3) **Kinetic theory** (pages 16-17) is based on **theory** — the clue is in the name. This means it's based on **assumptions** and **derivations** from **knowledge** and **theories** we already had.

## Our ***Understanding*** of Gases has ***Developed*** over ***Thousands*** of ***Years***

Our knowledge and understanding of gases has **changed significantly** over time. The gas laws in this section (see p.12) were developed by lots of different scientists over **thousands of years**.

1) **Ancient Greek** and **Roman philosophers** including **Democritus** had ideas about gases **2000 years ago**, some of which were quite close to what we now know to be true.
2) **Robert Boyle** discovered the relationship between **pressure** and **volume** at a constant temperature in **1662** — this is Boyle's law.
3) This was followed by **Charles's law** in **1787** when **Jacques Charles** discovered that the **volume** of a gas is proportional to **temperature** at a constant pressure.
4) The **pressure law** was discovered by **Guillaume Amontons** in **1699**, who noticed that at a constant volume, **temperature** is proportional to **pressure**. It was then **re-discovered** much later by **Joseph Louis Gay-Lussac** in **1809**.
5) In the **18th century** a physicist called **Daniel Bernoulli** explained Boyle's Law by assuming that gases were made up of tiny particles — the beginnings of **kinetic theory**. But it took another couple of hundred years before kinetic theory became widely accepted.
6) **Robert Brown** discovered **Brownian motion** in **1827**, which helped support kinetic theory — see next page.

*Thanks for calling the scientific community, please hold while we validate your ideas for 2000 years.*

# Kinetic Energy and the Development of Theories

## Scientific Ideas Aren't Accepted Immediately

You might have thought that when Bernoulli published his work on kinetic theory (see previous page) everyone would **immediately agree** with it. Not so. The scientific community **only** accepts new ideas when they can be **independently validated** — that is, other people can reach the **same conclusions**. Otherwise anyone could make up **any old nonsense**.

I hereby postulate that the Moon is made of cheese.

In the case of kinetic theory, most physicists thought it was just a **useful hypothetical model** and atoms **didn't really exist**. It wasn't until the **1900s**, when Einstein was able to use kinetic theory to make predictions for Brownian motion, that **atomic** and **kinetic theory** became **widely accepted**.

## Brownian Motion Supports Kinetic Theory

1) In 1827, botanist Robert Brown noticed that pollen grains in water moved with a **zigzag**, **random motion**.
2) This type of movement of any particles suspended in a fluid is known as **Brownian motion**. It **supports** the **kinetic particle theory** of the different states of matter. It says that the random motion is a result of **collisions** with **fast**, **randomly-moving** particles in the fluid.
3) You can see this when **large**, **heavy** particles (e.g. smoke) are moved with Brownian motion by **smaller**, **lighter** particles (e.g. air) travelling at **high speeds** — it is why smoke particles in air appear to **move around randomly** when you observe them in the lab.
4) This is **evidence** that the air is made up of **tiny atoms** or **molecules** moving **really quickly**.
5) So Brownian motion really helped the idea that everything is made from atoms **gain acceptance** from the **scientific community**.

A strong Brownian motion generator (with biscuits)

## Practice Questions

Q1 Give an equation linking absolute temperature and average kinetic energy.

Q2 What happens to the average kinetic energy of a particle if the temperature of a gas doubles?

Q3 Discuss the differences between theories and empirical laws.

Q4 Describe how our knowledge and understanding of the behaviour of gases has evolved over time.

**Exam Questions**

Q1 The mass of one mole of nitrogen molecules is $2.80 \times 10^{-2}$ kg. There are $6.02 \times 10^{23}$ molecules in one mole. Calculate the typical speed of a nitrogen molecule at 308 K. $k = 1.38 \times 10^{-23}$ $JK^{-1}$. [4 marks]

Q2 Some air freshener is sprayed at one end of a room. The room is 8.19 m long and the temperature is 21.2 °C.

a) Assuming the average air freshener molecule moves at 395 $ms^{-1}$, calculate how long it would take for a particle to travel directly to the other end of the room. [1 mark]

b) The perfume from the air freshener only slowly diffuses from one end of the room to the other. Explain why this takes much longer than suggested by your answer to part a). Include reference to Brownian motion in your answer. [3 marks]

## Make your own Brownian motion — mix some greenian and redian motion...

*This topic has it all. Lovely little equations, a couple of handy definitions, a brief historical interlude and even a cuppa. Ooh, don't mind if I do. Mine's white with two sugars please. And have you got any of those little jammy biscuits? Ta. Right, you'd best get learning this now. Make sure you can handle the equations — don't get caught out in the exam.*

# Gravitational Fields

*Gravity's all about masses **attracting** each other. If the Earth didn't have a **gravitational field**, apples wouldn't fall to the ground and you'd probably be floating off into space instead of sitting here reading this page...*

## A **Gravitational Field** is a **Force Field**

Tides are caused by gravitational fields.

1) A **force field** is a **region** where an object will experience a **non-contact force**.
2) Force fields cause **interactions** between objects or particles — e.g. between **static** or **moving charges** (p. 26), or in the case of gravity, between **masses**.
3) Any object with mass will **experience an attractive force** if you put it in the **gravitational field** of another object.
4) Only objects with a **large** mass, such as stars and planets, have a significant effect. E.g. the effects of the gravitational fields of the **Moon** and the **Sun** are noticeable here on Earth — they're the main cause of our **tides**.

## You can Draw **Lines of Force** to Show the **Field** Around an Object

**Force fields** can be represented as **vectors**, showing the **direction** of the force they would exert on an object placed in that field. **Gravitational field lines** (or "**lines of force**") are arrows showing the **direction of the force** that masses would feel in a gravitational field. Simply look at the direction the arrows are pointing to find the direction of the force — easy.

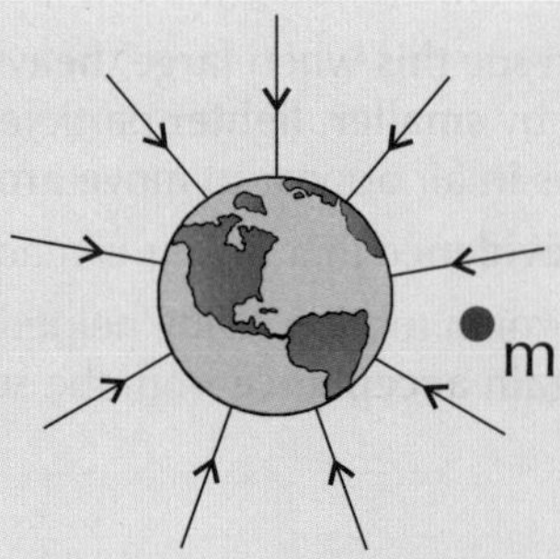


1) If you put a small mass, ***m***, anywhere in the Earth's gravitational field, it will always be attracted **towards** the Earth.
2) The Earth's gravitational field is **radial** — the lines of force meet at the centre of the Earth.
3) If you move mass *m* further away from the Earth — where the **lines** of force are **further apart** — the **force** it experiences **decreases**.
4) The small mass, *m*, has a gravitational field of its own. This doesn't have a noticeable effect on the Earth though, because the Earth is so much **more massive**.
5) Close to the Earth's surface, the field is (almost) uniform — the **field lines** are (almost) **parallel** and **equally spaced**.

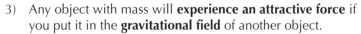

## You can **Calculate Forces** Using **Newton's Law of Gravitation**

The **force** experienced by an object in a gravitational field is always **attractive**. It's a **vector** which depends on the **masses** involved and the **distances** between them. It's easy to work this out for **point masses** — or objects which behave as if all their mass is concentrated at the centre, e.g. uniform spheres. You just put the numbers into this equation...

Newton's Law of Gravitation:

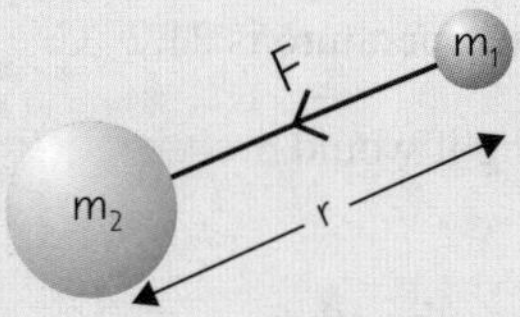

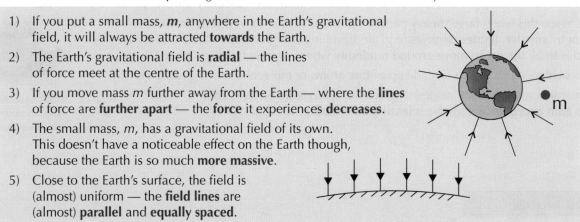

$$F = \frac{Gm_1m_2}{r^2}$$

*F* is the magnitude of the gravitational force between masses $m_1$ and $m_2$.
*G* is the gravitational constant — $6.67 \times 10^{-11}$ Nm$^2$kg$^{-2}$.
*r* is the distance (in metres) between the centres of the two masses.

The diagram shows the force acting on $\boldsymbol{m_1}$ due to $\boldsymbol{m_2}$. (The force on $m_2$ due to $m_1$ is equal but in the opposite direction.)

The law of gravitation is an **inverse square law** so:

1) If the distance *r* between the masses **increases** then the force *F* will **decrease**.
2) If the **distance doubles** then the **force** will be one **quarter** the strength of the original force.

$$F \propto \frac{1}{r^2}$$

If you're trying to estimate the gravitational force between objects, remember their distance has a bigger impact than their mass.

# Gravitational Fields

## The *Field Strength* is the *Force per Unit Mass*

Gravitational field strength, **g**, is the **force per unit mass**. Its value depends on **where you are** in the field. There's a really simple equation for working it out:

$$g = \frac{F}{m}$$

*g* has units of newtons per kilogram ($Nkg^{-1}$)

The **value** of **g** at the **Earth's surface** is approximately **9.81** $\mathbf{Nkg^{-1}}$ (or 9.81 $ms^{-2}$).

1) *F* is the force experienced by a mass *m* when it's placed in the gravitational field. Divide *F* by *m* and you get the **force per unit mass**.
2) *g* is a **vector** quantity, always pointing towards the centre of the mass whose field you're describing.
3) Since the gravitational field is almost uniform at the Earth's surface, you can assume *g* is a constant (as long as you don't go too high above the Earth's surface).
4) *g* is just the **acceleration** of a mass in a gravitational field. It's often called the **acceleration due to gravity**.

## In a *Radial Field, g* is *Inversely Proportional* to *r²*

Point masses have **radial** gravitational fields (see previous page).
The **magnitude** of *g* depends on the distance *r* from the point mass *M*.

$$g = \frac{GM}{r^2}$$

where *g* is the gravitational field strength ($Nkg^{-1}$),
*G* is the gravitational constant ($6.67 \times 10^{-11}\ Nm^2kg^{-2}$),
*M* is a point mass (kg)
and *r* is the distance from the centre (m).

And it's an **inverse square law** again — as ***r* increases, *g* decreases**.
If you plot a graph of *g* against *r* for the **Earth**, you get a curve like this.
It shows that *g* is greatest at the surface of the Earth, but decreases rapidly as *r* increases and you move further away from the centre of the Earth.

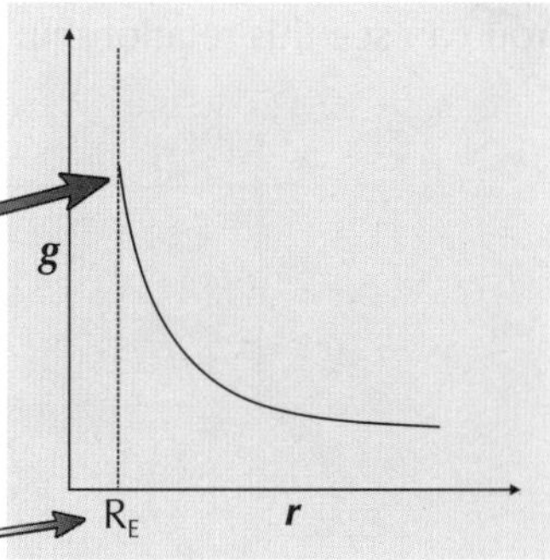


$R_E$ is the **radius** of the Earth.

## Practice Questions

Q1 What is a force field?

Q2 Draw the gravitational field lines for a uniform spherical mass.

Q3 Draw the direction of the force acting on the Moon caused by the Earth. Assume they're both uniform spheres.

Q4 Write down Newton's law of gravitation.

Q5 Sketch a graph of distance from mass (*r*) against gravitational field strength (*g*) for a point mass.

**Exam Questions**

Q1 The Earth's radius is approximately 6400 km. The mass of the Sun is $1.99 \times 10^{30}$ kg.
The average distance from the Earth to the Sun is $1.5 \times 10^{11}$ m.

a) Estimate the mass of the Earth (*use g = 9.81* $Nkg^{-1}$ *at the Earth's surface*). [2 marks]

b) Estimate the force of gravitational attraction between the Sun and the Earth. [2 marks]

Q2 The Moon has a mass of $7.35 \times 10^{22}$ kg and a radius of 1740 km.
Calculate the force acting on a 25 kg mass on the Moon's surface. [2 marks]

Q3 Two planets, A and B, have gravitational fields such that an object placed three quarters of the way along from A to B will experience no net force due to gravity. Which option correctly describes the mass, $M_B$ of planet B, in terms of the mass of planet A, $M_A$? Assume no other gravitational fields are present.

A $\frac{1}{9} M_A$ B $\frac{9}{16} M_A$ C $\frac{1}{3} M_A$ D $\frac{3}{4} M_A$ [1 mark]

## *If you're really stuck, put 'Inverse Square Law'...*

*Clever chap, Newton, but famously tetchy. He got into fights with other physicists, mainly over planetary motion and calculus... the usual playground squabbles. Then he spent the rest of his life trying to turn scrap metal into gold. Weird.*

# Gravitational Potential

*Gravitational potential is all to do with the energy something has based on where it is in a gravitational field.*

## Gravitational Potential is Potential Energy per Unit Mass

The **gravitational potential**, $V$, at a point is the **gravitational potential energy** that a **unit mass** at that point would have. For example, if a **1 kg** mass has **–62.5 MJ of potential energy** at a point **Z**, then the **gravitational potential at Z is –62.5 MJkg⁻¹**. The reason the potential energy is **negative** is covered below.

In a **radial field** (like the Earth's), the equation for gravitational potential is:

$$V = -\frac{GM}{r}$$

$V$ is gravitational potential ($Jkg^{-1}$), $G$ is the gravitational constant, $M$ is the mass of the object causing the gravitational field (kg), and $r$ is the distance from the centre of the object (m).

**Gravitational potential** is **negative** on the **surface** of the mass and **increases with distance** from the mass. You can think of this **negative energy** as being caused by you having to **do work against** the **gravitational field** to move an object out of it. This means that the gravitational potential at an **infinite distance** from the mass will be **zero.** **Gravitational potential energy** is also negative — you might have worked out positive values in the past (from $mgh$) but this is just the **gain** in potential energy. Potential energy becomes **less negative** as the object moves upwards.

**Gravitational field strength**, $g$, can be calculated from the amount the **gravitational potential**, $V$, varies with **distance**, $r$.

$$g = \frac{-\Delta V}{\Delta r}$$

You can see this relationship by plotting graphs of $V$ against $r$ and $g$ against $r$:

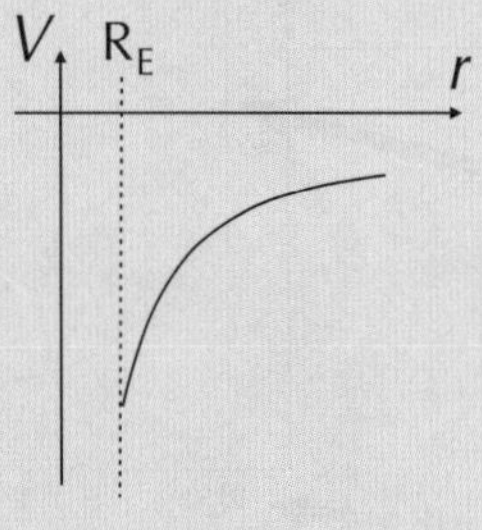


If you find the **gradient** of this graph at a particular **point**, you get the value of $g$ at that point.

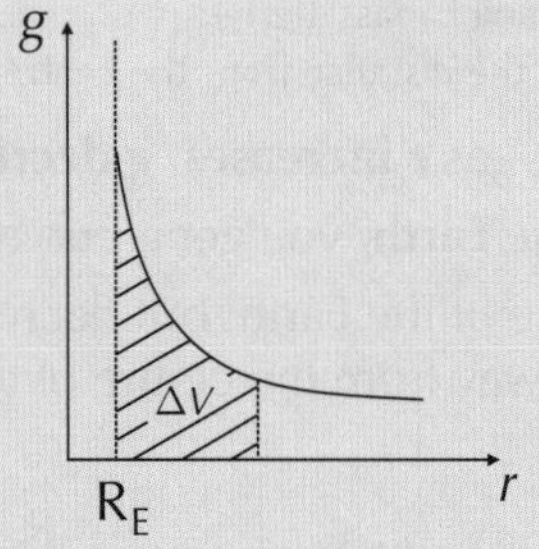


If you find the **area** under this graph it gives you the change in gravitational potential, $\Delta V$.

Remember you can estimate the area below this curve by counting squares (if it's plotted on squared paper) or by splitting it into trapeziums and adding together the areas of each trapezium.

## To Escape a *Gravitational Field*, a Mass Must Travel at the *Escape Velocity*

The **escape velocity** is defined as the velocity at which an object's **kinetic energy** is **equal** to minus its **gravitational potential energy**. This means the **total energy** is **zero**. The formula for it is:

$$v = \sqrt{\frac{2GM}{r}}$$

$v$ is escape velocity ($ms^{-1}$)

### Deriving Escape Velocity

1) First, **multiply** $V$ (the gravitational potential energy per unit mass) by a mass $m$ to get the **gravitational potential energy**.
2) Then, as you know total energy is zero: $\frac{1}{2}mv^2 - \frac{GMm}{r} = 0$ so $\frac{1}{2}mv^2 = \frac{GMm}{r}$
3) **Cancel** out $m$: $\frac{1}{2}v^2 = \frac{GM}{r}$
4) **Rearrange** for velocity, $v$: $v^2 = \frac{2GM}{r} \longrightarrow v = \sqrt{\frac{2GM}{r}}$

The escape velocity is the same for all masses in the same gravitational field.

**Example:** Find the escape velocity from the Earth's surface. Mass of Earth = $5.98 \times 10^{24}$ kg, radius of Earth = $6.37 \times 10^6$ m and $G = 6.67 \times 10^{-11}$ $Nm^2kg^{-2}$.

Simply substitute in the given values:

$$v = \sqrt{\frac{2GM}{r}} = \sqrt{\frac{2 \times 6.67 \times 10^{-11} \times 5.98 \times 10^{24}}{6.37 \times 10^6}} = 11\,190.7... = \mathbf{11\,200\ ms^{-1}\ (to\ 3\ s.f.)}$$

This means you'd have to throw a ball upwards at 11.2 km/s for it to fully escape Earth's pull. That's probably faster than you can manage.

# Gravitational Potential

## Gravitational Potential Difference is the Energy Needed to Move a Unit Mass

**Two points** at different distances from a mass will have **different** gravitational potentials (because gravitational potential increases with distance) — this means that there is a **gravitational potential difference** between these two points.

When you **move** an object you do **work** against the force of **gravity** — the **amount of energy** you need depends on the **mass** of the object and the **gravitational potential difference** you move it through:

$$\Delta W = m\Delta V$$

where $\Delta W$ is the work done (J), $m$ is the mass of the object (kg) and $\Delta V$ is the gravitational potential difference ($\text{Jkg}^{-1}$).

A short derivation of this is on p. 29.

## Equipotentials Show All Points of Equal Potential in a Field

1) **Equipotentials** are **lines** (in 2D) and **surfaces** (in 3D) that join all of the points with the **same potential**, $V$.
2) This means as you travel along an equipotential, your potential doesn't change — you **don't lose or gain energy**.
3) This means that for the journey the **gravitational potential difference**, $\Delta V = 0$.
4) As $\Delta W = m\Delta V$, this means that the amount of **work done** is also **zero**.
5) For a uniform spherical mass (you can usually assume the Earth's one) the equipotentials are **spherical surfaces**.
6) **Equipotentials** and **field lines** are **perpendicular**.

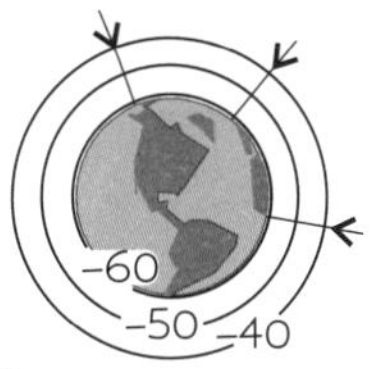


Equipotentials of −60, −50 and −40 $\text{MJkg}^{-1}$ around Earth.

## Practice Questions

Q1 What is gravitational potential? Write an equation for it.

Q2 Write down the equation linking gravitational field strength and gravitational potential.

Q3 What quantity does the gradient of a tangent to the curve of a $V$-$r$ graph represent?

Q4 Describe how you would find the change in gravitational potential between two points in a gravitational field from a graph of $g$ against $r$ for the field.

Q5 Write down the equation for escape velocity.

Q6 What is an equipotential surface?

**Exam Question**

$G = 6.67 \times 10^{-11}\ \text{Nm}^2\text{kg}^{-2}$

Q1 A 300 kg probe is sent to the asteroid Juno to collect rock samples before returning to Earth. Juno has a mass of $2.67 \times 10^{19}$ kg.

a) The gravitational potential, $V$, at the surface of the asteroid is $-1.52 \times 10^4\ \text{Jkg}^{-1}$. At a point 1.54 km above the surface, $V$ is $-1.50 \times 10^4\ \text{Jkg}^{-1}$. Calculate the value of $g$ at the surface of the asteroid, assuming it is constant across this range. [2 marks]

b) Calculate the radius of the asteroid Juno. [2 marks]

c) Calculate the speed at which an object would need to be launched from the surface of Juno for it to fully escape Juno's gravitational field. [1 mark]

d) Calculate the work done by the probe as it travels from the surface to a point 2020 m above the surface. [3 marks]

## With enough work you have the potential for brilliance...

*So quite a lot of new stuff here, but hopefully you can see how everything links together. It's all to do with energy — you do work to change your gravitational potential energy or you do none and merrily travel along an equipotential. Just remember the few simple formulas and once you've got the basic info like radius and mass, you're set.*

# Orbits and Gravity

*Any object travelling with a circular or elliptical path around something is said to be in orbit.*

## The Period and Radius of an Orbit are Related

Any object undergoing **circular motion** (e.g. a satellite) is kept in its path by a **centripetal force**. What causes this force depends on the object — in the case of satellites it's the **gravitational attraction** of the mass they're orbiting. This means that, in this case the centripetal force is the gravitational force.

The **force** acting on an object in **circular motion** (p. 3) is given by:

$$F = \frac{mv^2}{r}$$

The force of **attraction** due to **gravity** between two objects with masses $m$ and $M$ (p. 20) is given by:

$$F = \frac{GMm}{r^2}$$

Make the two equations **equal** each other and rearrange to find the **speed**, $v$, of a satellite in a gravitational field:

$$\frac{mv^2}{r} = \frac{GMm}{r^2} \Rightarrow v^2 = \frac{GMmr}{r^2 m} \Rightarrow v = \sqrt{\frac{GM}{r}}$$

So the **speed** of a satellite is **inversely proportional** to the **square root** of its orbital **radius**, or $v \propto \frac{1}{\sqrt{r}}$.

The **time** taken for a satellite to make **one orbit** is called the **orbital period**, $T$.
Remember, speed = $\frac{\text{distance}}{\text{time}}$, and the **distance** for a circular orbit is $2\pi r$, so $v = \frac{2\pi r}{T}$. Rearrange for $T$:

$$v = \frac{2\pi r}{T} \Rightarrow T = \frac{2\pi r}{v}$$

Then substitute the expression for $v$ found above and rearrange:

$$T = \frac{2\pi r}{v} = \frac{2\pi r}{\left(\sqrt{\frac{GM}{r}}\right)} = \frac{2\pi r\sqrt{r}}{\sqrt{GM}}$$

To make it a bit easier to deal with, **square** both sides:

$$T^2 = \frac{2^2\pi^2 r^2 r}{GM} = \frac{4\pi^2 r^3}{GM}$$

This leads to the relationship: $T^2 \propto r^3$ (Period squared is proportional to the radius cubed)

## You Can Solve Problems About Orbital Radius and Period

**Example:** Planets A and B are orbiting the same star. Planet A has an orbital radius of $8.0 \times 10^{10}$ m and a period of 18 hours. Planet B has an orbital radius of $1.0 \times 10^{12}$ m. Calculate the orbital period of planet B in hours.

As $T^2 \propto r^3$, this means $\frac{T^2}{r^3}$ = constant. So $\frac{T_A^2}{r_A^3} = \frac{T_B^2}{r_B^3}$ so $T_B^2 = \frac{T_A^2 r_B^3}{r_A^3}$

$$T_B = \sqrt{\frac{T_A^2 r_B^3}{r_A^3}} = \sqrt{\frac{(18 \times 60 \times 60)^2 \times (1.0 \times 10^{12})^3}{(8.0 \times 10^{10})^3}}$$

$$= \sqrt{8.20125 \times 10^{12}} = 2\,863\,782.46480... \text{ s}$$

2 863 782.46480... ÷ 3600 = 795.4851... hours = **800 hours (to 2 s.f.)**

# Orbits and Gravity

## The Energy of an Orbiting Satellite is Constant

An orbiting **satellite** has **kinetic** and **potential energy** — its **total energy** (i.e. kinetic + potential) is always **constant**.

1) In a **circular orbit**, a satellite's **speed** and **distance** above the mass it's orbiting are **constant**. This means that its **kinetic energy** and **potential energy** are also both **constant**.
2) In an **elliptical orbit**, a satellite will **speed up** as its **height decreases** (and slow down as its height increases). This means that its **kinetic energy increases** as its **potential energy decreases** (and vice versa), so the **total energy** remains **constant**.

When calculating gravitational potential, remember that $r$ is from the centre of the orbit, not the height above the surface.

## Geostationary Satellites Orbit the Earth once in 24 hours

1) A **synchronous** orbit is one where the **orbital period** of the orbiting object is the **same** as the **rotational period** of the orbited object.
2) **Geostationary** satellites are a type of synchronous orbit — they're always above the **same point on Earth**.
3) To do this they must always be **directly above** the **equator** — i.e. their **plane** of orbit follows the Earth's equator.
4) A geostationary satellite travels at the **same angular speed as the Earth** turns below it.
5) Their orbit takes exactly **one day**.
6) Their **orbital radius** is about **42 000 km** — about 36 000 km above the **surface** of Earth.
7) These satellites are really useful for sending TV and telephone signals — the satellite is **stationary** relative to a certain point on the **Earth**, so you don't have to alter the angle of your receiver (or transmitter) to keep up.

## Low Orbit Satellites Orbit Below 2000 km Above the Earth's Surface

1) **Low orbiting satellites** are defined as any satellites which orbit between **180-2000 km** above Earth.
2) Satellites designed for low earth orbits are **cheaper** to launch and require less powerful **transmitters** as they're closer to Earth.
3) This makes them useful for **communications**. However, their proximity to Earth and relatively **high orbital speed** means you need multiple satellites **working together** to maintain constant coverage.
4) Low orbit satellites are close enough to see the Earth's surface in a **high level** of detail. **Imaging** satellites are usually placed in this type of orbit and are used for things like **spying** and monitoring the **weather**.
5) Their orbits usually lie in a **plane** that includes the **north** and **south pole**.
6) Each orbit is over a **new** part of the Earth's surface as the Earth rotates underneath — so the **whole** of the Earth can be scanned.

## Practice Questions

Q1 Derive the relationship between the period and radius of an orbit.

Q2 The International Space Station orbits the Earth with velocity $v$. If another vehicle docks with it, increasing its mass, what difference, if any, does this make to the speed or radius of the orbit?

Q3 Compare the advantages and disadvantages of geostationary and low orbit satellites.

**Exam Questions**

Q1 Which of the following correctly describes a satellite's new velocity compared to its original velocity, $v_o$, if its orbital radius is doubled?

A $0.25\ v_o$ B $0.64\ v_o$ C $0.71\ v_o$ D $2.0\ v_o$ [1 mark]

Q2 A satellite has an orbital period of 3 hours around a planet. The velocity of the satellite is then halved. Calculate the new orbital period. [4 marks]

## All this talk of orbits is putting my head in a spin...

*When I hear the word 'satellite' I just think of man-made ones, e.g. for phones or TV, and tend to forget that moons are satellites too — don't make the same mistake. You're probably best off learning all the stuff about satellites and their orbits too, including the advantages of different types — just knowing what they are won't get you too far in the exam.*

# Electric Fields

*Electric fields can be attractive or repulsive, so they're different from gravitational ones. It's all to do with charge.*

## There is an **Electric Field** around a **Charged Object**

Any object with **charge** has an **electric field** around it — the region where it can attract or repel other charges.

1) Electric charge, **Q**, is measured in **coulombs** (C) and can be either positive or negative.
2) **Oppositely** charged particles **attract** each other. **Like** charges **repel**.
3) If a **charged object** is placed in an electric field, then it will experience a **force**.
4) If the charged object is a **sphere**, you can assume all of its **charge** is at its **centre**.
5) Just like with gravitational fields, **electric fields** can be represented by **field lines**.

Electric fields are force fields (p. 20) where charged objects will experience a non-contact force.

## You can **Calculate Forces** using **Coulomb's Law**

**Coulomb's law** gives the force of attraction or repulsion between two **point charges** in a **vacuum**:

$$F = \frac{1}{4\pi\varepsilon_0}\frac{Q_1 Q_2}{r^2}$$

$\varepsilon_0$ ("epsilon-nought") is the **permittivity of free space** and is equal to $8.85 \times 10^{-12}$ $Fm^{-1}$,
$Q_1$ and $Q_2$ are the **charges**,
$r$ is the **distance** between $Q_1$ and $Q_2$.

This unit is a 'farad per metre' — see p.32.

1) The force on $Q_1$ is always **equal** and **opposite** to the force on $Q_2$ — the **direction** depends on the charges.

If the charges are **opposite** then the force is **attractive**. *F* will be **negative**.

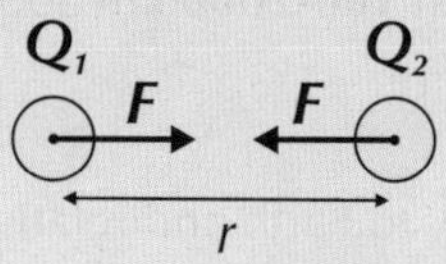


If $Q_1$ and $Q_2$ are **alike** then the force is **repulsive**. *F* will be **positive**.

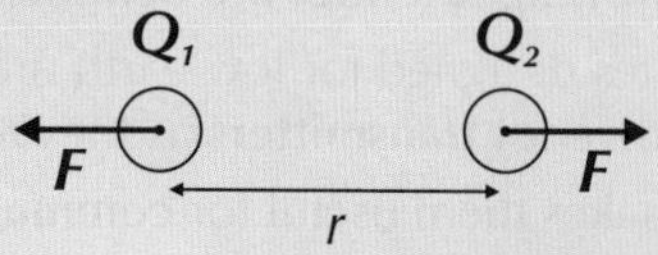


2) Coulomb's law is an **inverse square law**. The **further apart** the charges, the **weaker** the force between them.
3) If the point charges aren't in a vacuum, then the size of the force *F* also depends on the **permittivity**, ε, of the material between them. **Air** can be treated as a **vacuum** when using Coulomb's law.

Mr Allan liked to explain Coulomb's law using prairie dogs.

## **Electric Field Strength** is **Force per Unit Charge**

**Electric field strength**, ***E***, is defined as the **force per unit positive charge**.
It's the force that a charge of +1 C would experience if it was placed in the electric field.

*F* is the force on a 'test' charge *Q*.

$$E = \frac{F}{Q}$$

where *E* is **electric field strength** ($NC^{-1}$), *F* is the **force** (N) and *Q* is the **charge** (C).

1) ***E*** is a **vector** pointing in the **direction** that a **positive charge** would **move**.
2) The units of ***E*** are **newtons per coulomb** ($NC^{-1}$).
3) Field strength depends on **where you are** in the field.
4) A **point charge** — or any body that behaves as if all its charge is concentrated at the centre — has a **radial** field.

The electric field lines around a charged sphere would look the same as for a point charge.

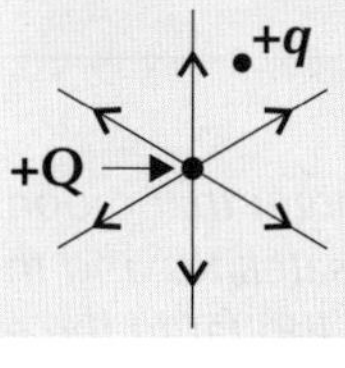


For a **positive *Q***, the small positive 'test' charge *q* would be **repelled**, so the field lines point **away** from *Q*.

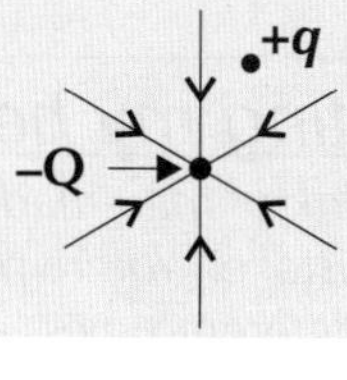


For a **negative *Q***, the small positive charge *q* would be **attracted**, so the field lines point **towards *Q***.

# Electric Fields

## In a Radial Field, E is Inversely Proportional to r²

1) In a **radial field**, the electric field strength, ***E***, depends on the distance ***r*** from the point charge ***Q***:

$$E = \frac{1}{4\pi\varepsilon_0}\frac{Q}{r^2}$$

where ***E*** is the **electric field strength** ($NC^{-1}$),
$\varepsilon_0$ is the **permittivity of free space** ($8.85 \times 10^{-12}$ $Fm^{-1}$), ***Q*** is the **point charge** (C)
and ***r*** is the **distance** from the point charge (m).

2) It's another **inverse square law.**
3) Field strength **decreases** as you go **further away** from ***Q*** — on a diagram, the **field lines** get **further apart.**

$$E \propto \frac{1}{r^2}$$

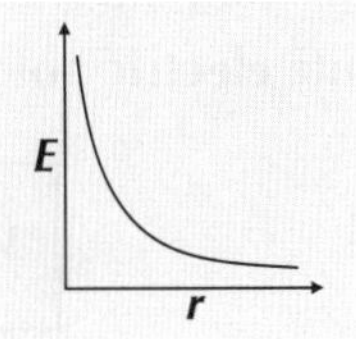


## In a Uniform Field, E is Inversely Proportional to d

A **uniform field** can be produced by connecting two **parallel plates** to the opposite poles of a battery. The field strength, ***E***, is the **same** at **all points** between the two plates.

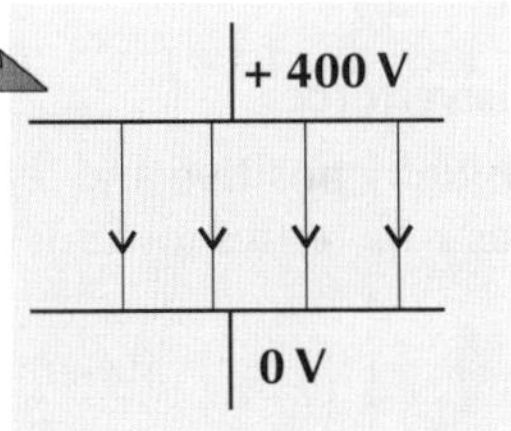


$$E = \frac{V}{d}$$

where ***E*** is the **electric field strength** ($Vm^{-1}$ or $NC^{-1}$),
***V*** is the **potential difference** between the plates (V)
and ***d*** is the distance between them (m)

Uniform electric fields can be used to determine whether a particle is **charged** or not. The **path** of a charged particle moving through an electric field will **bend** — the **direction** depends on whether it's a positive or negative charge.

1) A charged particle that enters an electric field at **right angles** to the field feels a **constant force parallel** to the electric **field lines.**
2) If the particle is **positively** charged then the force acts on it in the **same direction** as the field lines. If it's **negatively** charged, the force is in the **opposite** direction to the field lines.
3) This causes the particle to **accelerate** at right angles to the particle's original **motion** — and so it follows a **curved** path (a **parabola**).
4) In a **3D** situation, the **motion** is the **same** (a parabola) as there are no other significant forces acting on the charged particle.

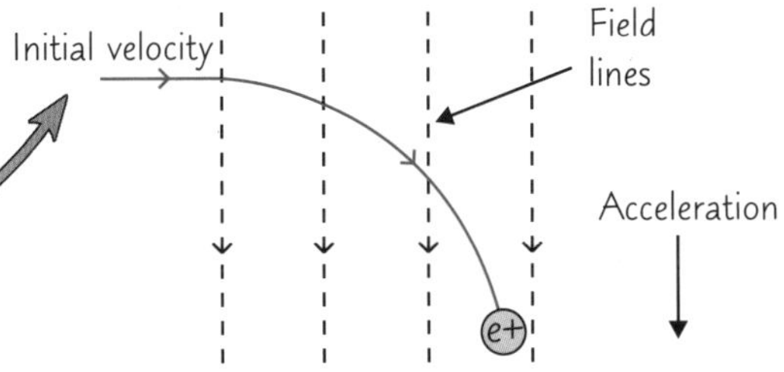


## Practice Questions

Q1 Write down Coulomb's law.

Q2 Sketch a radial electric field and a uniform electric field. How would you find *E* for each?

Q3 Sketch the path of an electron entering a uniform electric field at right angles to the field lines.

**Exam Questions**

Q1 An alpha particle (charge $+2e$) was deflected while passing through thin gold foil. The alpha particle passed within $5.0 \times 10^{-12}$ m of a gold nucleus (charge $+79e$). What was the magnitude and direction of the electrostatic force experienced by the alpha particle? ($e = 1.60 \times 10^{-19}$ C) [4 marks]

Q2 a) Two parallel plates are connected to a 1500 V dc supply, and separated by an air gap of 4.5 mm. What is the electric field strength between the plates? State the direction of the field. [2 marks]

b) The plates are now pulled further apart so that the distance between them is doubled. The electric field strength remains the same. What is the new voltage between the plates? [1 mark]

## Electric fields — one way to roast beef...

*At least you get a choice here — uniform or radial, positive or negative, attractive or repulsive, chocolate or strawberry...*

# Electric Potential and Work Done

*Some more about potential energy and doing work — but this time it's charges instead of masses.*

## Absolute Electric Potential is Potential Energy per Unit Charge

All points in an **electric field** have an **absolute electric potential**, ***V***. This is the electric **potential energy** that a **unit positive charge** (+ 1 C) would have at that point. The **absolute electric potential** of a point depends on **how far** it is from the **charge** creating the **electric field** and the **size** of that charge.

In a **radial field, absolute electric potential** is given by:

$$V = \frac{1}{4\pi\varepsilon_0}\frac{Q}{r}$$

where $V$ is absolute electric potential (V), $Q$ is the size of the charge (C) and $r$ is the distance from the charge (m).

1) The **sign** of ***V*** depends on the charge ***Q*** — i.e. ***V*** is **positive** when ***Q*** is positive and the force is **repulsive**, and **negative** when ***Q*** is negative and the force is **attractive**.
2) The **absolute magnitude** of ***V*** is **greatest** on the **surface of the charge**, and **decreases** as the **distance** from the charge **increases** — ***V*** will be **zero** at an **infinite distance** from the charge.

**Repulsive force**

***V*** is initially **positive** and tends to **zero** as ***r*** increases towards **infinity**.

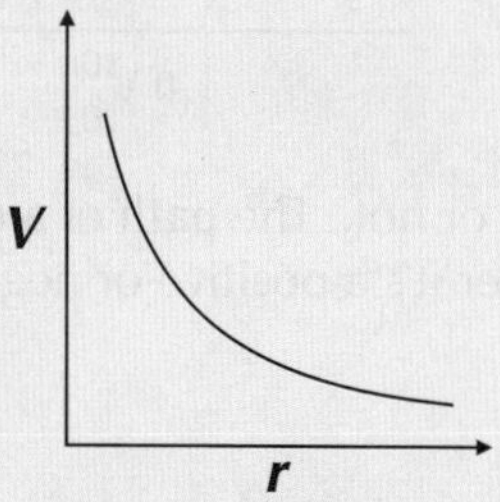


**Attractive force**

***V*** is initially **negative** and tends to **zero** as ***r*** increases towards **infinity**.

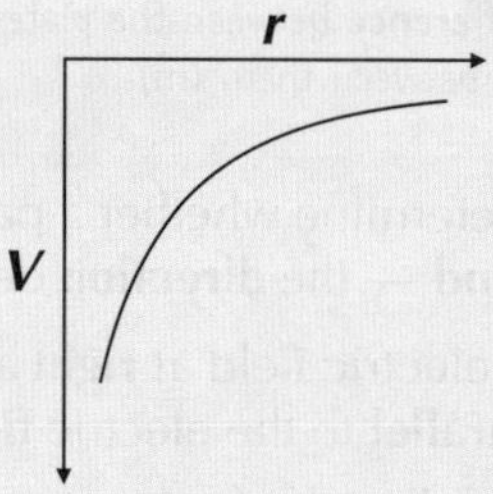


The **gradient** of a **tangent** to either graph gives the **field strength** at that point:

$$E = \frac{\Delta V}{\Delta r}$$

You can also find $\Delta V$ between two points from the **area** under a graph of ***E*** (see p.27) against ***r***.

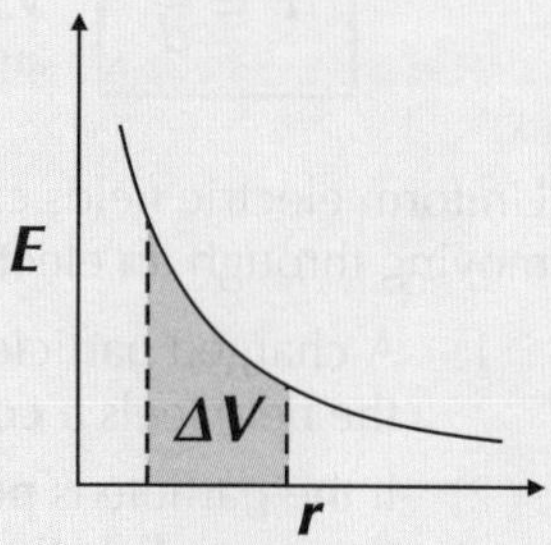


## Electric Potential Difference is the Energy Needed to Move a Unit Charge

If **two points** in an **electric field** have different potential, then there is an **electric potential difference** between them. To **move a charge** across a **potential difference** (i.e. from one electric potential to another) you need to use **energy**.

The **amount of energy** you need (or the **work done**) depends on the **size** of the **charge** you're moving and the size of the **potential difference** you want to move it across:

$$\Delta W = Q\Delta V$$

where $\Delta W$ is the work done (J), $Q$ is the charge being moved (C) and $\Delta V$ is the electric potential difference (V).

### Deriving the Formula for Uniform Field Strength

There are two parallel plates with a potential difference of $\Delta V$ across them, creating a **uniform electric field**.

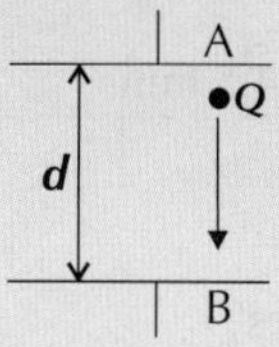


The field strength is force per unit charge, $E = \frac{F}{Q}$.

1) To move a charge ***Q*** from A to B, the **work done = force × distance moved** = ***Fd***. So $\Delta W = Fd$.
2) Since $\Delta W = Q\Delta V$ and $F = \Delta W \div d$, then $F = \frac{Q\Delta V}{d}$.
3) So $E = \frac{F}{Q} = \frac{\Delta V}{d}$ where $\Delta V$ is the p.d. across the plates (page 27).

# Electric Potential and Work Done

## You Can Also Derive **Work Done** for a **Gravitational Field**

At the **Earth's surface** the **gravitational field** is **uniform**.

The field strength is $g = \frac{-\Delta V}{\Delta r} = \frac{F}{m}$

g in a uniform field — g as force per unit mass

F is negative because you're working against gravity

which rearranges to give $m\Delta V = -F\Delta r$

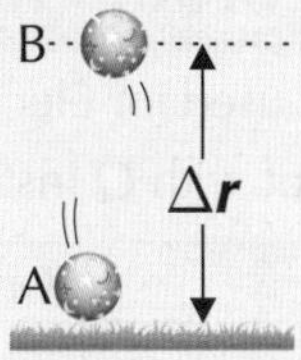

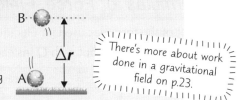

There's more about work done in a gravitational field on p.23.

1) To throw a ball $m$ from A to B, the **work done** = **force** × **distance moved** = $m\Delta V$
2) So the energy needed to move a mass $m$ against a gravitational potential difference is given by $m\Delta V$.

## **Equipotentials** Show All Points of **Equal Potential** in a **Field**

1) Just like in **gravitational fields**, you find **equipotentials** (p.23) in electric fields too.
2) For a **point charge**, the equipotentials are **spherical surfaces**. Between **parallel plates**, the equipotentials are **flat planes**.
3) Remember, **no work** is done when you travel **along** an equipotential — an electric charge can travel along an equipotential without any **energy** being transferred.

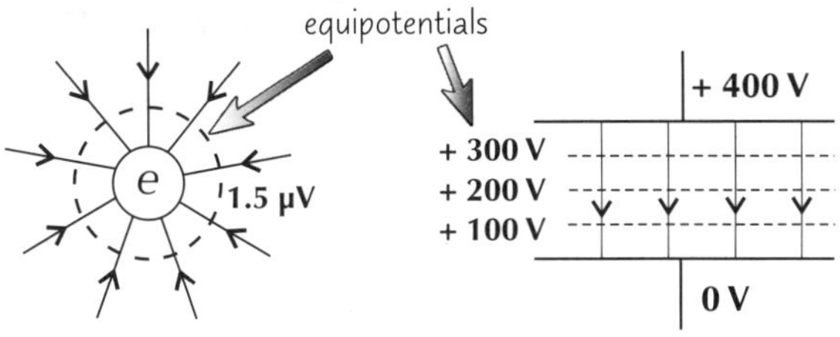


## Practice Questions

Q1 What is meant by 'absolute electric potential'? What value would it have at infinity?
Q2 How would you find the absolute electric potential in a radial field?
Q3 Sketch a graph of absolute electric potential against distance for an attractive and a repulsive charge.
Q4 What quantity does the area under the curve of a graph of $E$ against $r$ represent?
Q5 What is 'potential difference'?
Q6 Define the term 'equipotential'.
Q7 What shapes are the equipotentials in the electric field of a point charge?

**Exam Questions**

Q1 Calculate the absolute electric potential at a point $6.0 \times 10^{-10}$ m from an electron.
($e = 1.60 \times 10^{-19}$ C, $\varepsilon_0 = 8.85 \times 10^{-12}$ Fm$^{-1}$) [2 marks]

Q2 Show how the formula for uniform electric field strength can be derived from $W = Q\Delta V$. [2 marks]

Q3 Two parallel charged plates form a uniform electric field, as shown in the diagram.

a) Calculate the work done in moving the electron from A to C. [1 mark]

b) Explain why no work is done if the electron moves from A to B. [1 mark]

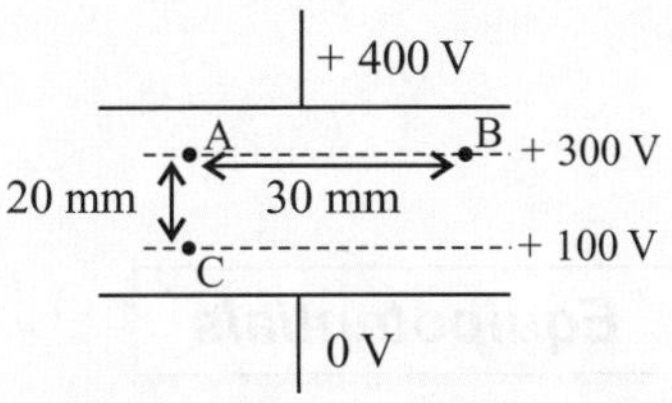


## I prefer gravitational fields — electric fields are repulsive...

*Revising fields is a bit like a buy-one-get-one-free sale — you learn all about gravitational fields and they throw electric fields in for free. You just have to remember to change your ms for Qs and your Gs for $1/4\pi\varepsilon_0$s... okay, so it's not quite a BOGOF sale. Maybe more like a buy-one-get-one-half-price sale... anyway, you get the point — go learn some stuff.*

# Comparing Electric and Gravitational Fields

*You might have thought a lot of the formulas from the last topic looked familiar — electric and gravitational fields are more similar than you might think...*

## Formulas for **Force**, **Field Strength** and **Potential** All Have the Same Layout

A lot of the formulas used for electric fields are the same as those used for gravitational fields but with $Q$ instead of $m$ (or $M$) and $\frac{1}{4\pi\varepsilon_0}$ instead of $G$.

| | Gravitational Fields | Electric Fields |
|---|---|---|
| Force due to | $F = \frac{Gm_1m_2}{r^2}$ | $F = \frac{1}{4\pi\varepsilon_0}\frac{Q_1Q_2}{r^2}$ |
| Field strength | $g = \frac{GM}{r^2}$ | $E = \frac{1}{4\pi\varepsilon_0}\frac{Q}{r^2}$ |
| Potential | $V = -\frac{GM}{r}$ | $V = \frac{1}{4\pi\varepsilon_0}\frac{Q}{r}$ |

Both the have **inverse-square** relationships with $r$.

## There Are Lots of **Similarities**...

### Field Strengths

Gravitational field strength, $\boldsymbol{g}$, is force per unit mass. $g = \frac{F}{m}$

Electric field strength, $\boldsymbol{E}$, is force per unit positive charge. $E = \frac{F}{Q}$

### Field Lines

The gravitational field lines for a point mass point towards the centre of mass.

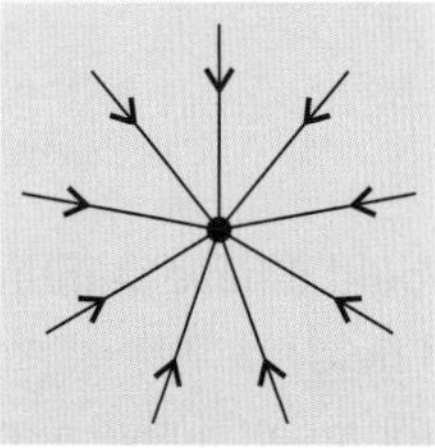

The electric field lines for a negative point charge point towards the centre of charge.

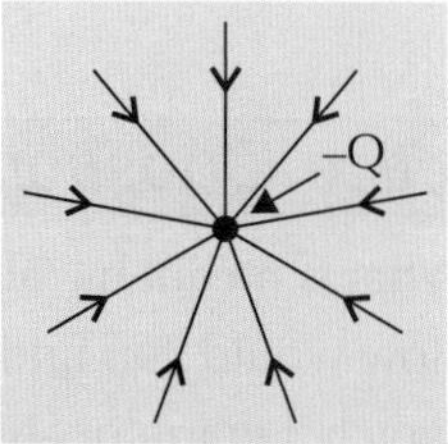


The gravitational field lines near the surface of a large object are parallel lines.

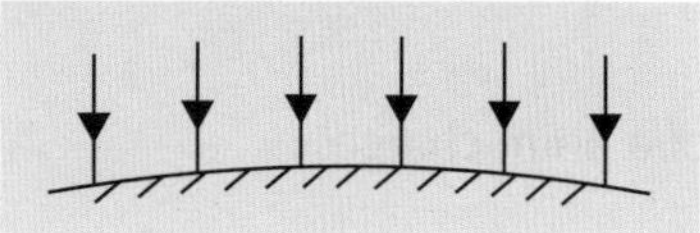

The electric field lines for a uniform field between two parallel plates are parallel lines.

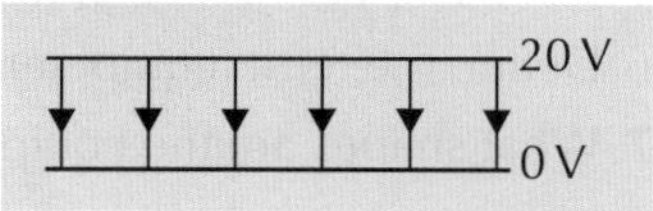


### Potential

Gravitational potential, $V$, is potential energy per unit mass and is zero at infinity.

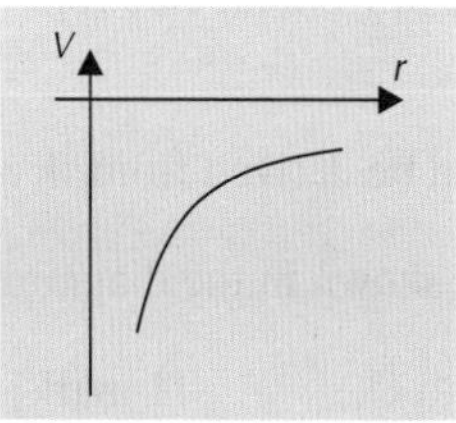


Absolute electric potential, $V$, is potential energy per unit positive charge and is zero at infinity.

This is the graph for a negative charge.

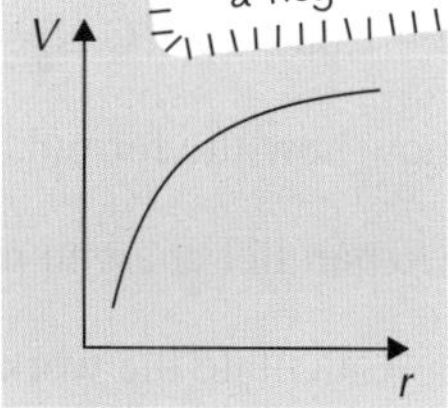


### Equipotentials

The equipotentials for a **uniform spherical mass** and a **point charge** both form a **spherical surface**.

### Work Done

Work done to move a unit mass through a gravitational potential. $\Delta W = m\Delta V$

Work done to move a unit charge through an electric potential. $\Delta W = Q\Delta V$

# Comparing Electric and Gravitational Fields

## ... And One Important **Difference**

Although gravitational and electric fields are similar, they're not the same. The main thing to keep in mind is that gravitational forces are **always attractive**, whereas electric forces can be **attractive** or **repulsive**.

## Comparing **Forces** at **Subatomic Levels**

When you get down to the subatomic level of electrons, protons and neutrons, the distances between particles becomes **tiny**. As both the gravitational and electrostatic forces have an **inverse square** relationship with **distance**, you'd expect these forces to be huge.

1) However, **gravity** at this level can pretty much be ignored. This is because although they're close together, all of the particles have incredibly **small masses** — the gravitational force at these distances is much **weaker** than the electrostatic force.
2) Thankfully, the nucleus doesn't break apart from all of this electrostatic **repulsion** — there are **other forces** at work (you met these forces in year 1 of A level).

Despite being small, Lola wouldn't be ignored.

**Example:** Two protons in a nucleus are 3.00 fm apart. Calculate the gravitational and electrostatic forces between them. $m_p = 1.67 \times 10^{-27}$ kg, $Q_{proton} = 1.6 \times 10^{-19}$ C, $\varepsilon_0 = 8.85 \times 10^{-12}$ Fm$^{-1}$ and $G = 6.67 \times 10^{-11}$ m$^3$kg$^{-1}$s$^{-2}$.

**Gravitational:**

$$F = \frac{Gm_1m_2}{r^2} = \frac{6.67 \times 10^{-11} \times (1.67 \times 10^{-27})^2}{(3.00 \times 10^{-15})^2}$$

$F = 2.066... = \mathbf{2.07 \times 10^{-35}}$ **N**

**Electrostatic:**

$$F = \frac{1}{4\pi\varepsilon_0}\frac{Q_1Q_2}{r^2} = \frac{(1.60 \times 10^{-19})^2}{4\pi \times 8.85 \times 10^{-12} \times (3.00 \times 10^{-15})^2}$$

$F = 25.57... = \mathbf{25.6}$ **N**

So here, the force on the protons due to electrostatic repulsion is $10^{36}$ **times bigger** than the force on the protons due to gravity.

## Practice Questions

Q1 Write down the equations for the forces due to electric and gravitational fields. Comment on their relationship with distance.

Q2 Draw field lines to show the gravitational field for a point mass and the electric field for a negative point charge.

Q3 Draw the graphs of gravitational potential against distance and absolute electric potential against distance for a negative charge.

Q4 What are the values of gravitational and electric potential at infinity?

Q5 What do the equipotentials for a uniform spherical mass look like? How do they compare to the equipotentials of a point charge?

Q6 State one difference between gravitational and electric fields.

**Exam Question**

$e = 1.60 \times 10^{-19}$ C, $m_e = 9.11 \times 10^{-31}$ kg, $\varepsilon_0 = 8.85 \times 10^{-12}$ Fm$^{-1}$ and $G = 6.67 \times 10^{-11}$ Nm$^2$kg$^{-2}$

Q1 Two electrons are $8.00 \times 10^{-10}$ m apart.

a) Compare the magnitude and direction of the gravitational and electric forces between them, supporting your comments with calculations. [4 marks]

b) Use your answer to a) to explain why gravitational forces can be ignored at a subatomic level. [1 mark]

## Double the physics, double the fun — right?

*Or maybe not, but it makes it a bit easier to remember all of this stuff. Get cracking and start learning all of this information, especially the stuff on subatomic particles, then reward yourself with a break before doing any more work.*

# Capacitors

*Capacitors are things that store electrical charge — like a charge bucket. The capacitance of one of these things tells you how much charge the bucket can hold. Sounds simple enough... ha... ha, ha, ha...*

## Capacitors Build Up Charge on Plates

1) A capacitor is an electrical component made up of two **conducting plates** separated by a **gap** or a **dielectric** (an insulating material, see below).
2) When a capacitor is connected to a **power source**, **positive** and **negative** charge build up on **opposite** plates, creating a uniform **electric field** between them (p.27).
3) The amount of **charge per unit potential difference** (voltage) stored by a capacitor is called its **capacitance**.

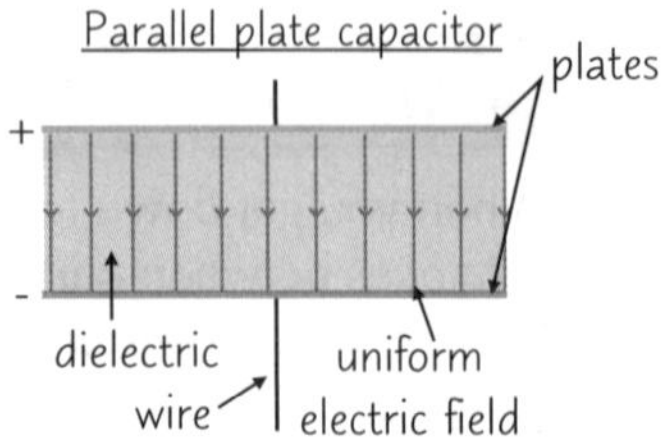


$$C = \frac{Q}{V}$$

where $Q$ is the **charge** in coulombs, $V$ is the **potential difference** in volts and $C$ is the **capacitance** in **farads (F)** — **1 farad = 1 $CV^{-1}$**.

4) A farad is a **huge** unit so you'll usually see capacitances expressed in terms of:

**μF** — microfarads ($\times 10^{-6}$) **nF** — nanofarads ($\times 10^{-9}$) **pF** — picofarads ($\times 10^{-12}$)

## You Can Increase Capacitance Using Dielectrics

1) **Permittivity** is a measure of how difficult it is to generate an **electric field** in a certain material.
2) The **relative permittivity** is the ratio of the permittivity of a material to the permittivity of free space:

$$\varepsilon_r = \frac{\varepsilon_1}{\varepsilon_0}$$

Where $\varepsilon_r$ is the relative permittivity of material 1, $\varepsilon_1$ is the permittivity of material 1 in $Fm^{-1}$, $\varepsilon_0$ is the permittivity of free space.

3) Relative permittivity is sometimes also called the **dielectric constant**.

**No charge is applied**

1) Imagine a dielectric is made up of lots of **polar molecules** — they have a positive end and a negative end.
2) When no charge is stored by the capacitor, there is **no electric field** — so these molecules point in a bunch of **random directions**.

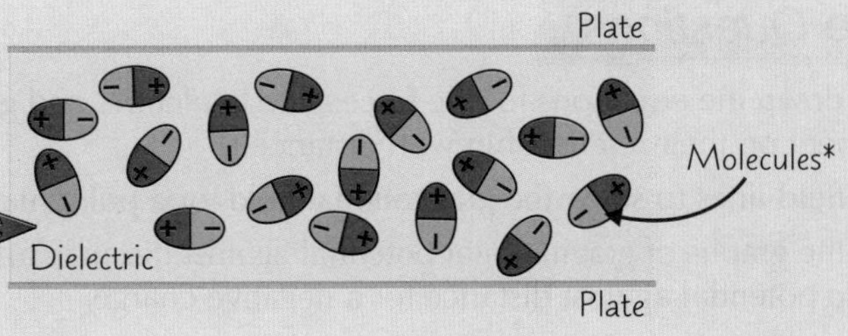


*Not to scale.

**Charge is applied**

1) When a charge is applied to a capacitor, an **electric field** is generated.
2) The **negative ends** of the molecules are attracted to the **positively charged plate** and vice versa.
3) This causes all of the molecules to **rotate** and **align** themselves with the electric field.
4) The molecules each have their own **electric field**, which in this alignment now **opposes** the **applied** electric field of the capacitor. The larger the **permittivity**, the larger this opposing field is.
5) This **reduces** the overall electric field, which reduces the **potential difference** needed to charge the capacitor — so the capacitance **increases**.

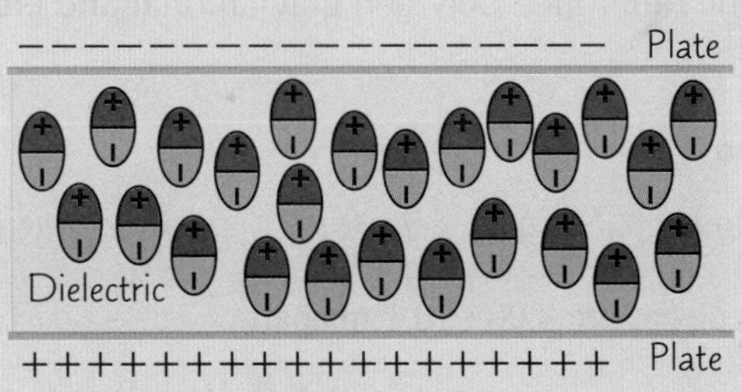


You can calculate the capacitance of a capacitor using the **dimensions** of the capacitor and the **permittivity** of the **dielectric**:

$$C = \frac{A\varepsilon_0\varepsilon_r}{d}$$

Where $A$ is the **area** of the plates ($m^2$), $\varepsilon_0$ is the permittivity of **free space** ($Fm^{-1}$), $\varepsilon_r$ is the **relative permittivity** of the **dielectric** and $d$ is the **separation** of the plates (m).

# Capacitors

## Capacitors Store Energy

1) When **charge** builds up on the plates of a **capacitor**, **electrical energy** is **stored** by the capacitor.
2) You can find the **energy stored** in a capacitor from the **area** under a **graph** of **charge stored** against **potential difference** across the capacitor.

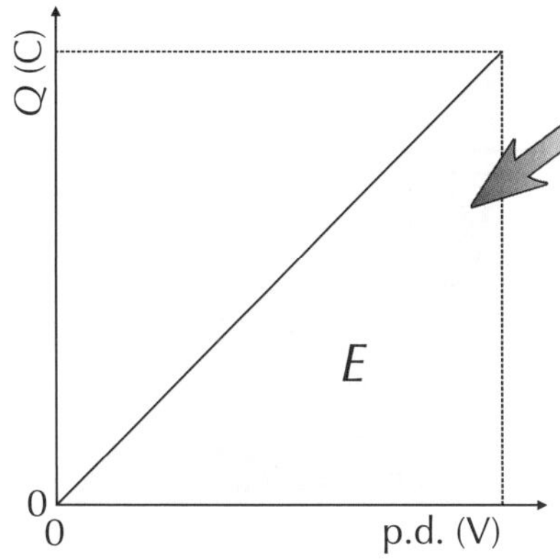


3) The potential difference across the capacitor is directly **proportional** to the charge stored on it, so the graph will be a **straight line** through the origin.
4) On this graph, the **energy stored** is given by the **yellow triangle**.
5) The greater the **capacitance**, the more **energy** is stored by the capacitor for a given potential difference.
6) **Area of a triangle = ½ × base × height** so the energy stored by the capacitor is:

$$E = \frac{1}{2}QV$$

Where ***E*** is the **energy stored** (J), ***Q*** is the **charge** on the capacitor (C) and ***V*** is the **potential difference** (V).

Samantha had heard there was energy stored on plates.

The gradient of a *Q-V* graph effectively gives the capacitance.

## Practice Questions

Q1 Define capacitance.

Q2 What is the relationship between charge, potential difference and capacitance?

Q3 What is the dielectric constant of a material also known as?

Q4 Describe and explain what happens to the molecules in a dielectric when they're exposed to an electric field.

Q5 Write down the formula for capacitance involving plate area, plate separation and permittivity.

Q6 How would you find the energy stored by a capacitor for a given potential difference from a graph of charge against potential difference?

Q7 Write down an equation that relates the energy stored in a capacitor to the charge it stores and the potential difference between its plates.

**Exam Questions**

Q1 The potential difference of a test circuit was measured as a capacitor was charged. The graph below was plotted from the recorded data.

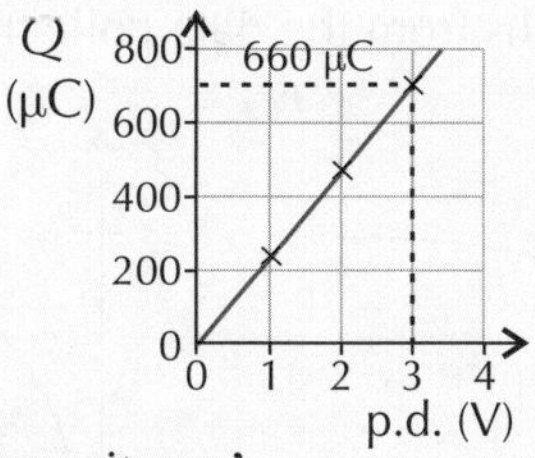


a) Explain what is meant by the term 'capacitance'. [1 mark]

b) Calculate the capacitance of the capacitor. [2 marks]

Q2 A capacitor with capacitance 137 pF is charged until it stores a charge of 2.47 nC and is then disconnected. It has a dielectric with a relative permittivity of 3.1. The dielectric is removed, so there is now a vacuum between the plates, but nothing else is changed. Calculate the change in potential difference across the capacitor. [4 marks]

Q3 A 8.0 μF capacitor is fully charged from a 12 V supply. Calculate the energy stored by the capacitor. [3 marks]

## *Capacitance — fun, it's not...*

*Capacitors are really useful in the real world. Pick an appliance, any appliance, and it'll probably have a capacitor or several. If I'm being honest, though, the only saving grace of these pages for me is that girl eating a plate...*

# Charging and Discharging

*Charging and discharging — pushing electrons onto a capacitor, then letting them scamper off again.*

## There are **Three** Expressions for the **Energy Stored** by a Capacitor

When you charge a capacitor, you store energy on it. Starting from the energy equation on page 33, you can find two more.

$$E = \frac{1}{2}QV$$

$C = \frac{Q}{V}$, so $Q = CV$. Substitute this into the equation above and you get:

$$E = \frac{1}{2}CV^2$$

$C = \frac{Q}{V}$, so $V = \frac{Q}{C}$. Substitute this into the first equation and you get:

$$E = \frac{1}{2}\frac{Q^2}{C}$$

**Example:** A 900 μF capacitor is charged up to a potential difference of 240 V. Calculate the energy stored by the capacitor.

First, choose the best equation to use — you've been given $V$ and $C$, so you need $E = \frac{1}{2}CV^2$.

Substitute the values in: $E = \frac{1}{2} \times (9 \times 10^{-4}) \times 240^2 = 25.92 =$ **30 J (to 1 s.f.)**

## You can **Investigate** What Happens When you **Charge** a **Capacitor**

1) Set up the test circuit shown in the circuit diagram.
2) Close the switch to connect the **uncharged** capacitor to the dc power supply.
3) Let the capacitor **charge** whilst the **data logger** records both the **potential difference** (from the voltmeter) and the **current** (from the ammeter) over time.
4) When the current through the ammeter is **zero**, the capacitor is fully charged.

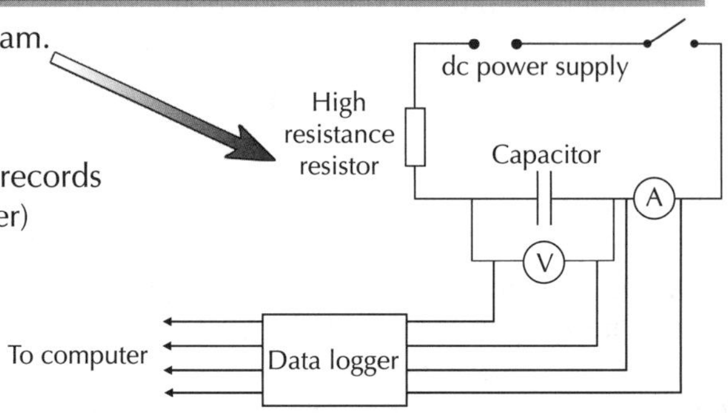


## You Can Plot Graphs of **Current**, **Potential Difference** and **Charge** Against **Time**

You should be able to plot the following graphs from the data collected from this experiment:

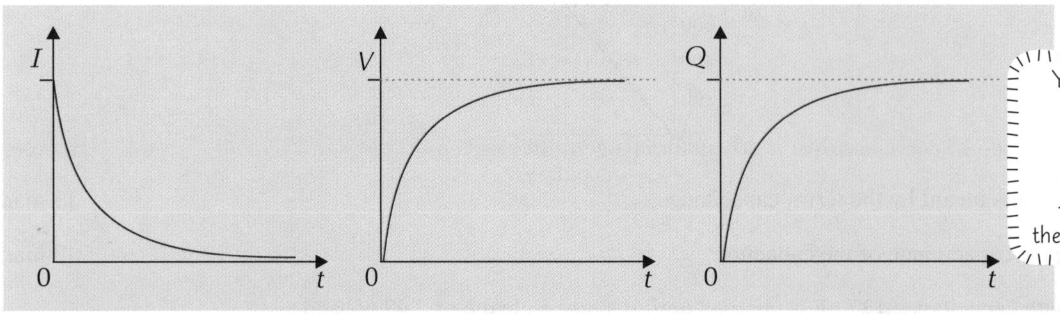

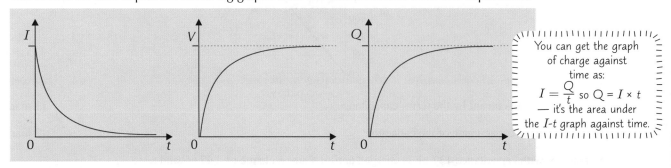

You can get the graph of charge against time as: $I = \frac{Q}{t}$ so $Q = I \times t$ — it's the area under the $I$-$t$ graph against time.

Once a capacitor begins charging:

1) As soon as the switch closes, current starts to flow. The electrons flow onto the plate connected to the **negative terminal** of the dc power supply, so a **negative charge** builds up.
2) This build-up of negative charge **repels** electrons off the plate connected to the **positive terminal** of the power supply, making that plate positive. These electrons are attracted to the positive terminal of the power supply.
3) An **equal** but **opposite** charge builds up on each plate, causing a **potential difference** between the plates. Remember that **no charge** can flow **between** the plates because they're **separated** by an **insulator** (a vacuum, gap or dielectric).
4) As **charge** builds up on the plates, **electrostatic repulsion** makes it **harder** and **harder** for more electrons to be deposited. When the p.d. across the **capacitor** is equal to the p.d. across the **power supply**, the **current** falls to **zero**.

# Charging and Discharging

## To Discharge a Capacitor, Remove the Power Supply and Close the Switch

1) **Remove the power supply** from the test circuit on page 34 and close the **switch** to complete the circuit.
2) Let the capacitor **discharge** whilst the data logger records **potential difference** and **current** over time.
3) When the **current** through the ammeter and the **potential difference** across the plates are **zero**, the capacitor is fully discharged.

You can then plot graphs of current, potential difference and charge against time once more.

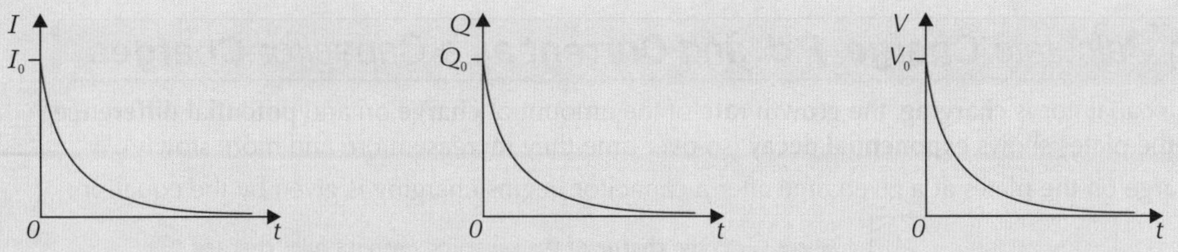


1) The current flows in the **opposite direction** from the **charging current**.
2) As the **potential difference** decreases, the **current** decreases as well.
3) When a capacitor is **discharging**, the amount of **charge** on and **potential difference** between the plates falls **exponentially** with time. That means it always takes the **same length** of time for the charge or potential difference to **halve**, no matter what value it starts at — like radioactive decay (see p.58).
4) The same is true for the amount of **current flowing** around the circuit.

## Practice Questions

Q1 Write down the three formulas for calculating the energy stored by a capacitor.

Q2 Describe how you could investigate how the potential difference across a charging capacitor varies with time.

Q3 Sketch graphs to show the variation of the current round the circuit and potential difference across the plates of a capacitor with time for: a) charging a capacitor, b) discharging a capacitor.

Q4 Explain the shape of the *Q-t* graph for a charging capacitor.

**Exam Questions**

Q1 A 250 μF capacitor is fully charged to 1.5 μC and then discharged through a fixed resistor.

a) Calculate the energy stored by the capacitor when it is fully charged. [1 mark]

b) Calculate the voltage of the battery used to charge the capacitor. [2 marks]

c) Sketch the graph of charge against time as the capacitor discharges. [1 mark]

Q2 The graph of current against time for a charging capacitor is shown on the right. Explain the shape of the graph. [1 mark]

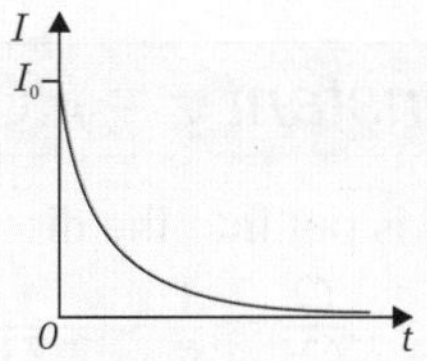


Q3 The charge stored on a capacitor is kept constant while the potential difference across the plates is increased by a factor of two. Which of the following statements is true? [1 mark]

A The capacitance of the capacitor will increase.
B The energy stored by the capacitor will half.
C The energy stored by the capacitor will quadruple.
D The energy stored by the capacitor will remain the same.

## An analogy — consider the lowly bike pump...

*A good way to think of the charging process is like pumping air into a bike tyre. To start with, the air goes in easily, but as the pressure in the tyre increases, it gets harder and harder to squeeze any more air in. The tyre's 'full' when the pressure of the air in the tyre equals the pressure of the pump. The analogy works just as well for discharging...*

# More Charging and Discharging

*Even more charging and discharging — now it's time for some fun exponential relationships.*

## The **Time Taken** to **Charge** or **Discharge** Depends on **Two Factors**

The **time** it takes to charge or discharge a capacitor depends on:

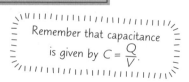

1) The **capacitance** of the capacitor (**C**). This affects the amount of **charge** that can be transferred at a given **potential difference**.
2) The **resistance** of the circuit (**R**). This affects the **current** in the circuit.

Remember that capacitance is given by $C = \frac{Q}{V}$.

## You can Calculate **Charge, P.d.** and **Current** as a Capacitor **Charges**

1) When a capacitor is **charging**, the **growth rate** of the amount of **charge** on and **potential difference** across the plates shows **exponential decay** (so over time they increase more and more slowly).
2) The charge on the plates at a given time after a capacitor begins charging is given by the equation:

$$Q = Q_0(1 - e^{\frac{-t}{RC}})$$

where $Q_0$ is the **charge** of the capacitor when it's **fully charged** (C), $t$ is **time since** charging began (s), $R$ is the resistance (Ω) and $C$ is the capacitance (F).

3) The potential difference between the plates at a given time is given by:

$$V = V_0(1 - e^{\frac{-t}{RC}})$$

4) The **charging current** is different however, as it decreases exponentially — the formula to calculate the charging current at a given time is:

$$I = I_0 e^{\frac{-t}{RC}}$$

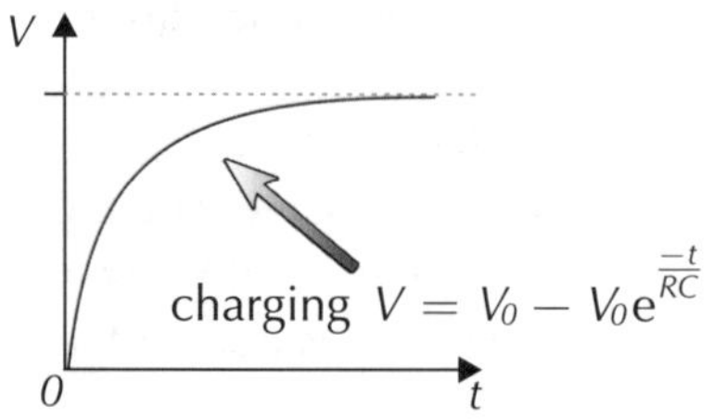


## You can do the Same for a **Discharging Capacitor**

1) Because the amount of **charge** left on the plates falls **exponentially with time** as a capacitor discharges, it always takes the **same length of time** for the charge to **halve**, no matter **how much charge** you start with.
2) The charge left on the plates at a given time after a capacitor begins discharging from being fully charged is given by the equation:

$$Q = Q_0 e^{\frac{-t}{RC}}$$

3) As the **potential difference** and **current** also decrease **exponentially** as a capacitor discharges, the formulas for calculating the current or potential difference at a certain time are similar:

$$I = I_0 e^{\frac{-t}{RC}} \qquad V = V_0 e^{\frac{-t}{RC}}$$

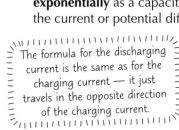

The formula for the discharging current is the same as for the charging current — it just travels in the opposite direction of the charging current.

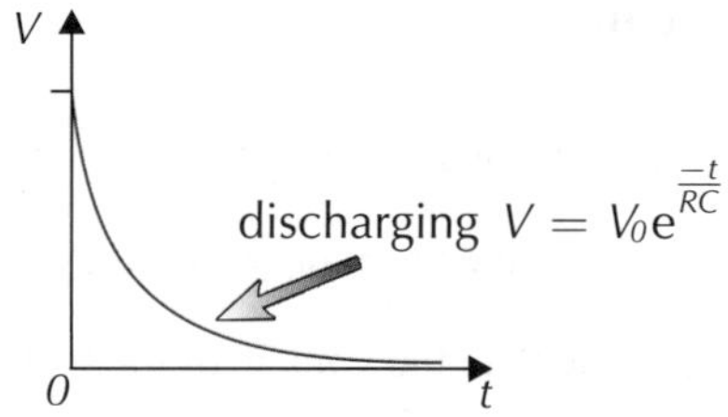


## Time Constant $\tau$ = RC

$\tau$ is the Greek letter 'tau'

If $t = \tau = RC$ is put into the **discharging** equations above, then $Q = Q_0 e^{-1}$, $V = V_0 e^{-1}$ and $I = I_0 e^{-1}$.

So when $t = \tau$: $\frac{Q}{Q_0} = \frac{1}{e} \approx \frac{1}{2.718} \approx 0.37$

1) $\tau$, the time constant, is the time taken for the charge, potential difference or current of a discharging capacitor to fall to 37% of its value when fully charged.
2) It's also the time taken for the charge or potential difference of a charging capacitor to **rise** to **63%** of its value when fully charged.
3) So the **larger** the **resistance** in series with the capacitor, the **longer it takes** to charge or discharge.
4) In practice, the time taken for a capacitor to charge or discharge **fully** is taken to be about $5RC$.

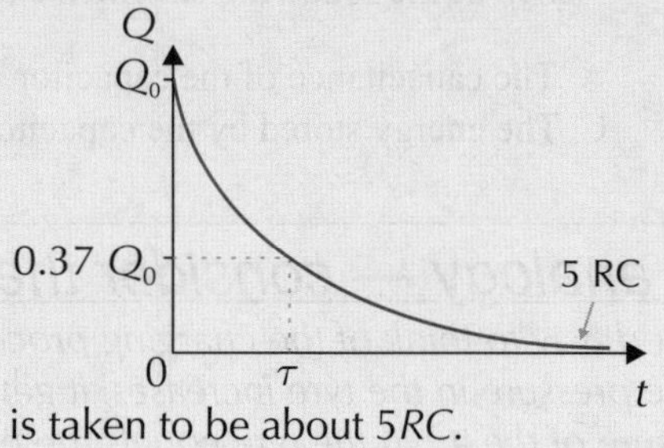

# More Charging and Discharging

## You Can Find the Time Constant from Log-Linear Graphs

Instead of using $\tau = RC$, you can create **log-linear graphs** from data (p. 158) to find the time constant. Here **charge** is used, but this works for potential difference and current as well.

1) Starting from the equation for $Q$ on a discharging capacitor, take the **natural log** of both sides and rearrange:

   $Q = Q_0 e^{\frac{-t}{RC}}$ becomes $\boldsymbol{\ln(Q) = \left(\frac{-1}{RC}\right)t + \ln(Q_0)}$

2) The equation is now in the form of $y = mx + c$. This means if you plotted a graph of **ln(Q)** against time, ***t***, you would get a **straight line**.

3) The **gradient** of this line would be $\frac{-1}{RC}$ or $\frac{-1}{\tau}$ and the $y$-intercept would be $\ln(Q_0)$.

4) To get the time constant from the graph, you **divide –1 by the gradient** of the line.

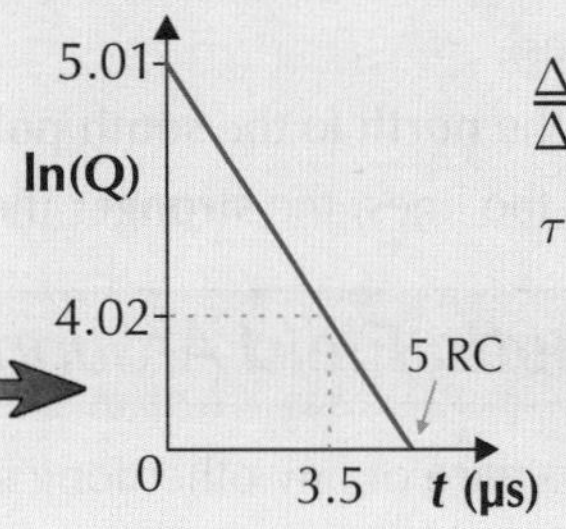

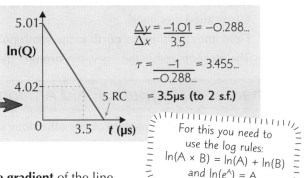

$\frac{\Delta y}{\Delta x} = \frac{-1.01}{3.5} = -0.288...$

$\tau = \frac{-1}{-0.288...} = 3.455...$

$= \mathbf{3.5 μs}$ **(to 2 s.f.)**

For this you need to use the log rules: $\ln(A \times B) = \ln(A) + \ln(B)$ and $\ln(e^A) = A$

## Time to Halve, $T_{½}$ = 0.69RC

The 'time to halve' is the time taken for the **charge**, **current** or **potential difference** of a **discharging** capacitor to reach **half** of the value it was when it was **fully charged**.

$$T_{½} = 0.69RC$$

Where $T_{½}$ is the time to halve (s), $R$ is the resistance in the circuit (Ω) and $C$ is the capacitance of the capacitor (F).

**Example:** Find the time taken for the charge of a capacitor to drop to half of its initial value.

We're looking for the time when $Q = \frac{1}{2}Q_0$ so $Q = \frac{1}{2}Q_0 = Q_0 e^{\frac{-t}{RC}} \Longrightarrow \frac{1}{2} = e^{\frac{-t}{RC}}$

Take the natural log of both sides: $\ln\left(\frac{1}{2}\right) = \ln\left(e^{\frac{-t}{RC}}\right) \Longrightarrow \ln(1) - \ln(2) = \frac{-t}{RC}$

Rearrange to get $t = \ln(2)RC$. $\ln(2) = 0.693...$ so $t = \mathbf{0.69}\boldsymbol{RC}$ **(to 2 s.f.)**

For this you need to use another log rule: $\ln(A \div B) = \ln(A) - \ln(B)$.

## Practice Questions

Q1 What two factors affect how quickly a capacitor charges?

Q2 Write down the formula for calculating potential difference at a given time for a charging capacitor.

Q3 Write down the formula for calculating charge at a given time for a discharging capacitor.

Q4 Describe how you would calculate the time constant from a plot of $\ln(V)$ against $t$.

Q5 Write down the formula for the 'time to halve'.

**Exam Questions**

Q1 A 250 μF capacitor is fully charged from a 6.0 V battery and then discharged through a 1.0 kΩ resistor.

a) Calculate the time taken for the charge on the capacitor to fall to 37% of its original value. [2 marks]

b) Calculate the percentage of the total charge remaining on the capacitor after 0.7s. [2 marks]

c) The charging voltage is increased to 12 V. Explain the effect this has on the total charge stored on the capacitor, the capacitance of the capacitor and the time taken to fully charge the capacitor. [3 marks]

Q2 A fully charged 320 μF capacitor is discharged through a 1.6 kΩ resistor.
Calculate the time taken for its voltage to drop to half of its value when it was fully charged. [2 marks]

### I'll spare you a log cabin joke...

*That's a lot of maths. You're given the formulas for charge in the exam though, so remember how these compare to potential difference and current and life will become much simpler. Best swat up on your log skills too — they're pretty tricky and you need them to create those nice straight line plots to get the time constant from.*

# Magnetic Fields

*Magnetic fields — making pretty patterns with iron filings before spending an age trying to pick them off the magnet.*

## A **Magnetic Field** is a **Region** Where a **Force** is Exerted on **Magnetic Materials**

1) Magnetic fields can be represented by **field lines** (also called flux lines).
2) Field lines go from the **north** to the **south pole** of a magnet.
3) The **closer** together the lines, the **stronger** the field.

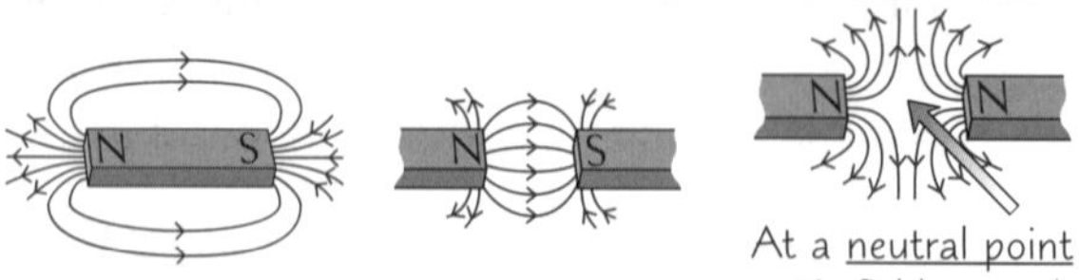

At a neutral point magnetic fields cancel out.

## There is a **Magnetic Field** Around a **Wire** Carrying **Electric Current**

When **current** flows in a **wire** or any other long straight conductor, a **magnetic field** is induced around the wire.

1) The **field lines** are **concentric circles** centred on the wire.
2) The **direction** of a magnetic **field** around a current-carrying wire can be worked out with the **right-hand rule**.
3) If you loop the wire into a **coil**, the field is **doughnut-shaped**, while a coil with length (a **solenoid**) forms a **field** like a **bar magnet**.

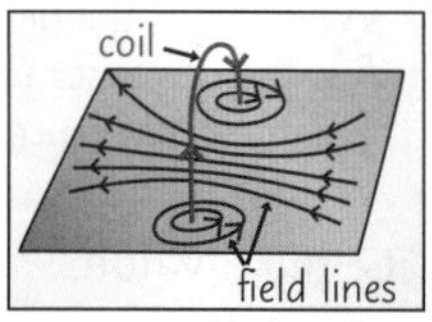


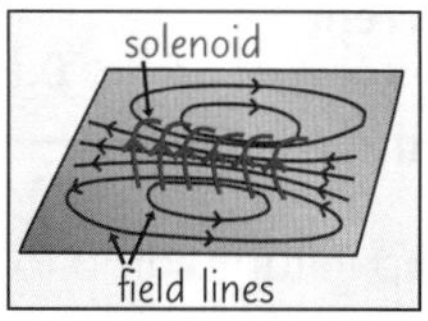


RIGHT-HAND RULE

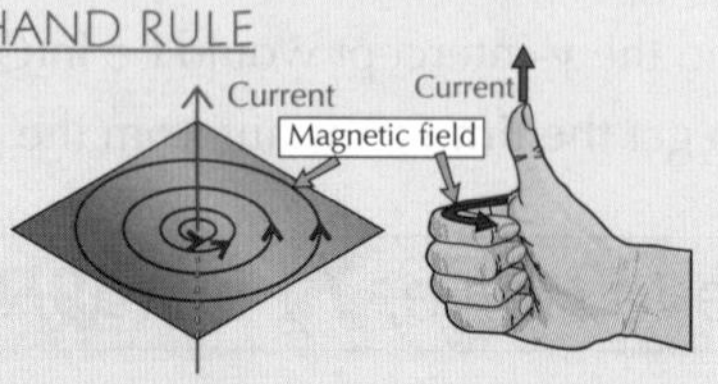

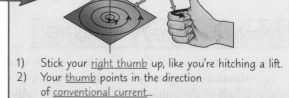

1) Stick your right thumb up, like you're hitching a lift.
2) Your thumb points in the direction of conventional current...
3) ...your curled fingers point in the direction of the field.

## A **Wire** Carrying a **Current** in a **Magnetic Field** will **Experience** a **Force**

1) If you put a **current-carrying wire** into an **external** magnetic field (e.g. between two magnets), the field around the wire and the field from the magnets are **added together**. This causes a **resultant field** — lines **closer together** show where the magnetic field is **stronger**. These bunched lines cause a 'pushing' **force** on the wire.
2) The direction of the force is always **perpendicular** to both the current direction and the magnetic field — it's given by **Fleming's left-hand rule**.
3) If the current is **parallel** to the field lines the size of the force is **0 N** — there is **no component** of the magnetic field perpendicular to the current.

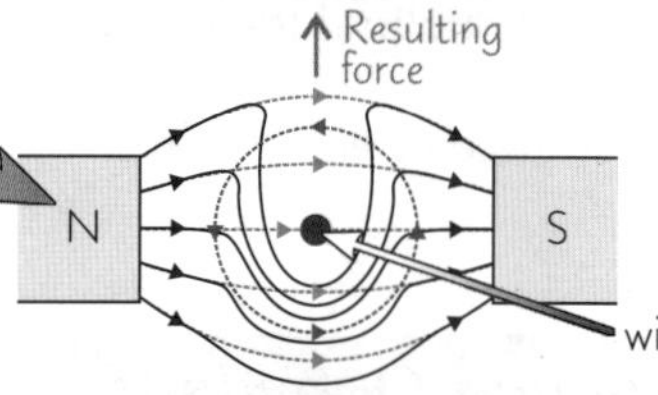


**Fleming's Left-Hand Rule**

The First finger points in the direction of the external uniform magnetic Field, the seCond finger points in the direction of the conventional Current. Then your thuMb points in the direction of the force (in which Motion takes place).

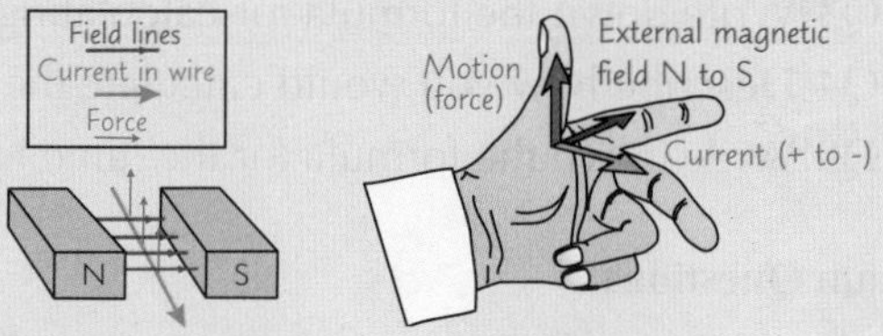


## The **Force** on a Wire is **Proportional** to the **Flux Density**

1) The **force** on a **current-carrying** wire at a **right angle** to an external magnetic field is proportional to the **magnetic flux density**, ***B***. Magnetic flux density is sometimes called the **strength** of the magnetic field.
2) **Magnetic flux density**, ***B***, is **defined** as:

> The **force** on **one metre** of wire carrying a **current** of **one amp** at **right angles** to the **magnetic field**.

3) When current is at 90° to the magnetic field, the size of the **force**, ***F*** is proportional to the **current**, ***I***, the **length of wire** in the field, ***l***, as well as the **flux density**, ***B***. This gives the equation:

$$F = BIl$$

4) **Flux density** is a **vector** quantity with both a **direction** and **magnitude**. It's measured in **teslas**, **T**:

$$1 \text{ tesla} = \frac{\text{Wb}}{\text{m}^2}$$

It helps to think of flux density as the number of flux lines (measured in webers (Wb), see p.42) per unit area.

# Magnetic Fields

## Use a Top Pan Balance to Investigate Flux Density

You need to be able to use this diagram to set up a circuit.

You can use the set-up shown to investigate the relationship between the **force on a wire**, the **length of wire perpendicular** to a magnetic field, the **current** through it and **flux density** ($F = BIl$).

1) A **square hoop** of metal wire is positioned so that the **top** of the hoop, **length *l***, passes through the magnetic field, **perpendicular** to it. When a current flows, the **length of wire** in the magnetic field will experience a downwards **force** (Fleming's left-hand rule).
2) The power supply should be connected to a **variable resistor** so that you can **alter** the **current**. Zero the digital balance when there is **no** current through the wire so that the mass reading is due to the electromagnetic force only. Turn on the power supply.
3) Note the **mass** and the **current**. Use the variable resistor to **change** the current and record the new mass — do this for a **large range** of currents. Repeat this until you have 3 mass readings for each current. Calculate the **mean** for each mass reading.
4) Convert your mass readings into **force** using $F = mg$. **Plot** the data on a graph of **force *F*** against **current *I***. Draw a line of best fit.
5) Because $\boldsymbol{F = BIl}$, the **gradient** of your graph is equal to $B \times l$. Measure the gradient, then divide by length $l$ to **get a value for *B***.
6) Alternatively, you could vary the **length of wire** perpendicular to the magnetic field by using **different sized hoops**. You could also keep current and wire length the same and instead vary the **magnetic field** by changing the **strength** of the magnets.

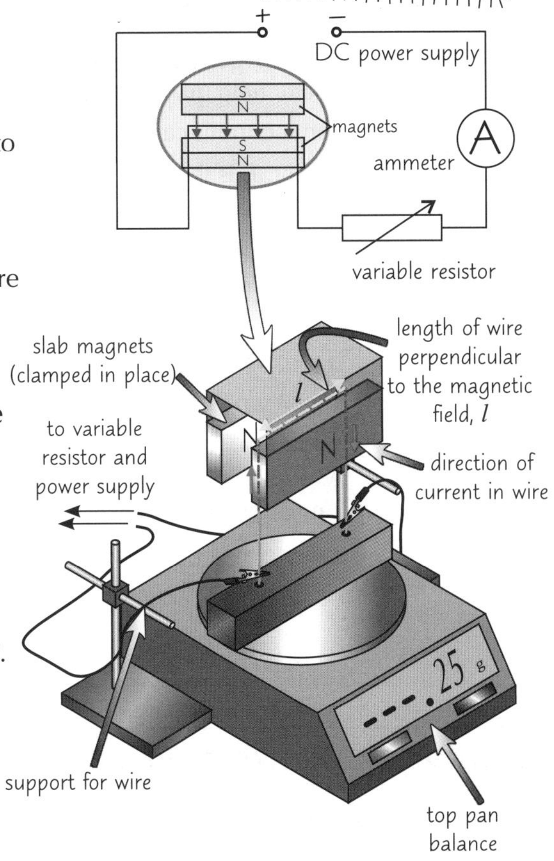


## Practice Questions

Q1 Sketch the magnetic field lines around a long, straight, current-carrying wire. Show the directions of the current and the magnetic field.

Q2 Write the rule that relates the directions of force, current and $B$ field. What is this rule called?

Q3 A copper bar can roll freely on two copper supports, as shown in the diagram. When current is applied in the direction shown, which way will the bar roll?

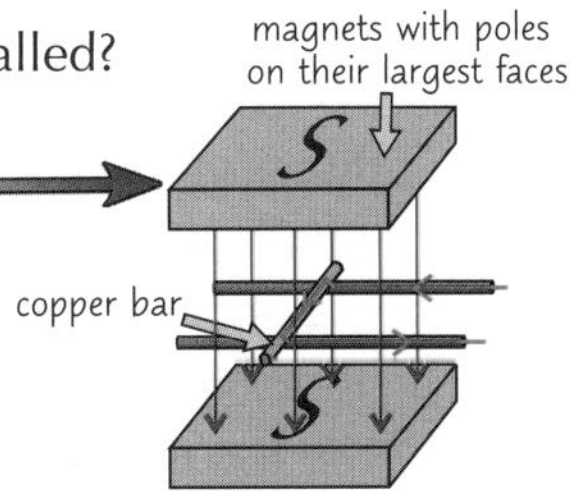


Q4 What is magnetic flux density? What are its units?

Q5 Describe an experiment using a top pan balance to investigate the force on a wire carrying current that is flowing perpendicular to a magnetic field.

### Exam Questions

Q1 A wire carrying a current of 3.00 A runs perpendicular to a magnetic field of strength $2.00 \times 10^{-5}$ T. 4.00 cm of the wire is within the field.

a) Calculate the magnitude of the force on the wire. [2 marks]

b) The wire is rotated so that it runs parallel to the magnetic field. Give the new force on the wire. Explain your answer. [2 marks]

Q2 A student plots a graph of force against wire length for a current carrying wire in a magnetic field. The current-carrying wire is perpendicular to the field. Which of the following statements is true?

A The flux density is the gradient of the best fit line.

B The force is inversely proportional to the wire length.

C The force is proportional to the wire length.

D The flux density is the $y$-intercept of the best fit line.

[1 mark]

## Left-hand rule. Left-hand rule. LEFT-HAND RULE. LEFT-HAND RULE.

*Fleming's left hand rule is the key to this section — so make sure you know how to use it and understand what it all means. Remember that the direction of the magnetic field is from N to S, and that the current is from +ve to –ve — this is as important as using the correct hand. You need to get those right or it'll all go to pot...*

# Charged Particles in a Magnetic Field

*Magnetic fields don't just exert a force on current-carrying wires — they have the same effect on all charged particles.*

## Forces Act on Charged Particles in Magnetic Fields

A **force** acts on a charged particle **moving** in a **magnetic field**. This is why a **current-carrying wire** experiences a force in a magnetic field (page 38) — electric current in a wire is the **flow** of **negatively charged electrons**.

- The force on a current-carrying wire in a magnetic field that is **perpendicular** to the current is given by $\boldsymbol{F = BIl}$.
- Electric current, $I$, is the flow of charge, $Q$, per unit time, $t$. So $I = \frac{Q}{t}$.
- A **charged** particle which moves a distance $l$ in time $t$ has a velocity, $v = \frac{l}{t}$. So $\boldsymbol{l = vt}$.

Putting all these equations together gives the force acting on a single charged particle moving through a magnetic field, where its velocity is perpendicular to the magnetic field:

$$F = BIl = B\frac{Q}{\cancel{t}}v\cancel{t} \longrightarrow \boldsymbol{F = BQv}$$

where $\boldsymbol{F}$ = force in N,
$\boldsymbol{B}$ = magnetic flux density in T,
$\boldsymbol{Q}$ = charge on the particle in C,
$\boldsymbol{v}$ = velocity of the particle in $ms^{-1}$

In many exam questions, Q is the magnitude of the charge on the electron, which is $1.60 \times 10^{-19}$ C.

**Example:** An electron travels at a velocity of $2.00 \times 10^4\ ms^{-1}$ perpendicular to a uniform magnetic field with a magnetic flux density of 2.00 T. What is the magnitude of the force acting on the electron?

Just use the equation $F = BQv$ and put the correct numbers in:

$F = BQV = 2.00 \times (1.60 \times 10^{-19}) \times (2.00 \times 10^4) = \boldsymbol{6.40 \times 10^{-15}}$ **N**

## Charged Particles in a Magnetic Field are Deflected in a Circular Path

1) **Fleming's left-hand rule** says that the force on a **moving charge** in a magnetic field is always **perpendicular** to its **direction of travel**.
2) Mathematically, that is the condition for **circular** motion.
3) To use Fleming's left-hand rule for charged particles, use your **second finger** (normally current) as the **direction of motion** for a **positive** charge.
4) If the particle carries a **negative** charge (e.g. an **electron**) point your **second finger** in the **opposite direction** to its motion.

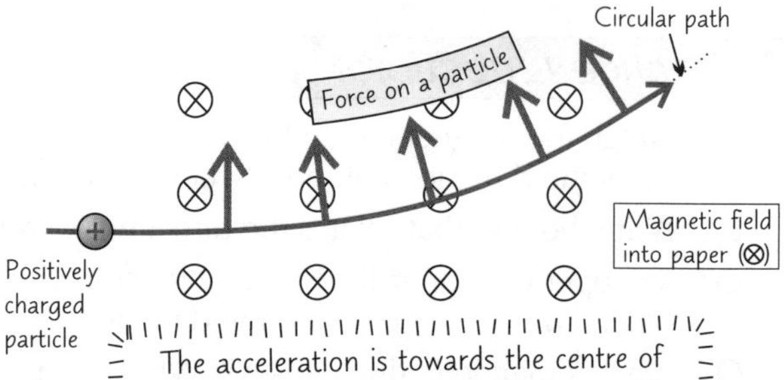


The acceleration is towards the centre of the circle — it is centripetal (see page 3).

5) The **force** due to the magnetic field ($F = BQv$) experienced by a particle travelling through a magnetic field is **independent** of the particle's **mass**, but the **centripetal acceleration** it experiences **will depend** on the **mass** — from Newton's 2nd law of motion.
   - The particle's acceleration will be $a = \frac{v^2}{r}$.
   - Combining this with **Newton's 2nd law**, $F = ma$, gives the force on a particle in a circular orbit $\boldsymbol{F = \frac{mv^2}{r}}$ (see page 3).

The **radius** of the circular path followed by a charged particle in a magnetic field can be found by **combining** the equations for the force on a charged particle in a **magnetic field** and for the force on a particle in a **circular orbit**:

$$F = \frac{mv^2}{r} \text{ and } F = BQv \text{ so } \frac{mv^2}{r} = BQv$$

$$\text{which gives you } \boldsymbol{r = \frac{mv}{BQ}}$$

This means:

- The radius **increases** (i.e. the particle is **deflected less**) if the **mass** or **velocity** of the particle **increases**.
- The radius **decreases** (i.e. the particle is **deflected more**) if the **strength** of the **magnetic field** or the **charge** on the particle **increases**.

# Charged Particles in a Magnetic Field

## **Cyclotrons** Make Use of **Circular Deflection**

This is not a cyclotron.

1) Circular deflection is used in particle accelerators such as **cyclotrons**.
2) Cyclotrons have many uses, for example in **medicine**. Cyclotrons are used to produce **radioactive tracers** or high-energy beams of radiation for use in **radiotherapy**.
3) A **cyclotron** is made up of two hollow **semicircular electrodes** with a uniform magnetic field applied perpendicular to the plane of the electrodes, and an **alternating** potential difference applied between the electrodes:

- Charged particles are **fired** into one of the electrodes. The magnetic field makes them follow a (semi)circular path and then **leave** the electrode.
- An applied potential difference between the electrodes **accelerates** the particles across the gap until they enter the next electrode.
- Because the particle's speed is **slightly higher**, it will follow a circular path with a **larger** radius (see page 2) before leaving the electrode again.
- The potential difference is **reversed** so the particle is **accelerated again** before entering the next electrode. This process repeats as the particle **spirals outwards**, increasing in speed, before eventually **exiting** the cyclotron.

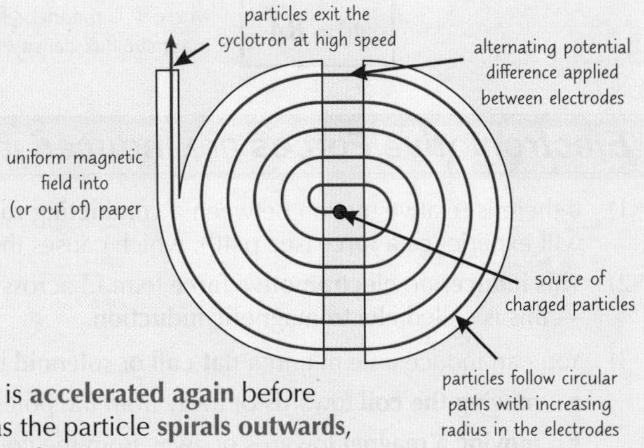


## Practice Questions

Q1 What is the equation for the force acting on a single charged particle that is moving through a magnetic field perpendicular to the field lines? Why is the particle deflected in a circular path?

Q2 Give the hand rule for working out the direction of motion of a positively charged particle in a magnetic field.

Q3 What happens to the radius of the circular path of a charged particle in a magnetic field if the velocity of the particle increases?

Q4 Describe how a cyclotron works.

**Exam Questions**

Q1 An electron is travelling through a uniform magnetic field of flux density 1.10 T. A force of $4.91 \times 10^{-15}$ N is acting on the electron. Calculate the velocity of the electron perpendicular to the field. [2 marks]

Q2 State the direction of force acting on a negative particle in a power transmission line moving from east to west in a uniform magnetic field that acts vertically downwards. [1 mark]

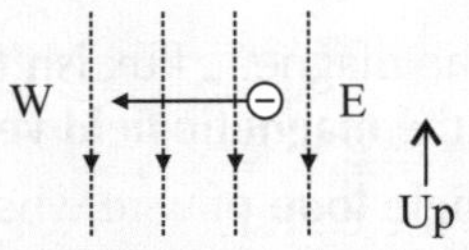


Q3 a) Show that the radius of the circular path followed by charged a particle in a magnetic field is equal to the product of the mass and the velocity of the particle divided by the product of magnetic flux density and the charge of the particle. [2 marks]

b) An electron is travelling in a circular path of radius $3.52 \times 10^{-2}$ m in a magnetic field of flux density 0.00510 T Calculate the velocity of the electron. *Mass of an electron* = $9.11 \times 10^{-31}$ *kg* [1 mark]

## A Cyclotrons' Legacy — a load of very dizzy and rather queasy electrons...

*So how do all those poor particles know which way they should be turning without getting dizzy, I hear you cry. We can only assume that they make excellent use of Fleming's left hand rule. But if the particle is negative, remember to point your second finger in the opposite direction to its motion. Got all that? Good.*

# Electromagnetic Induction

*So it turns out that if you waggle a bit of metal around near a magnet you can make your own electricity — don't ever let anybody tell you that physics isn't seriously cool. Chemistry's got nothing on this.*

## Think of the Magnetic Flux as the Total Number of Field Lines

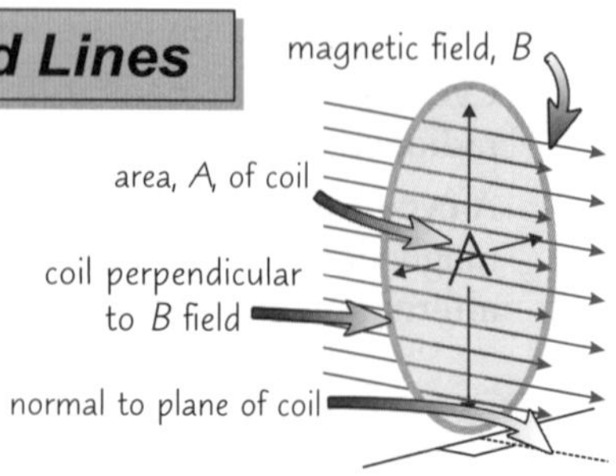


1) **Magnetic flux density**, ***B***, is a measure of the **strength** of a magnetic field. It helps to think of it as the **number** of field lines **per unit area**.
2) The total **magnetic flux**, ***Φ***, passing through an **area**, ***A***, perpendicular to a **magnetic field**, ***B***, is defined as:

$$\Phi = BA$$

where $\Phi$ is magnetic flux (Wb), $B$ is magnetic flux density (T) and $A$ is area ($m^2$).

## Electromotive Forces are Induced in Conductors when they Cut Magnetic Flux

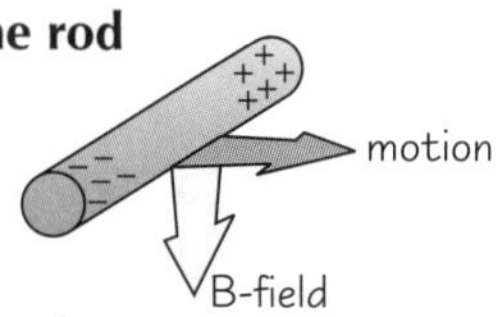


1) If there is relative motion between a **conducting rod** and a magnetic field, the **electrons in the rod** will experience a **force** (see p.40), which causes them to **accumulate** at one end of the rod.
2) This **induces** an **electromotive force** (**e.m.f.**) across the ends of the rod — this is called **electromagnetic induction**.
3) You can induce an e.m.f. in a **flat coil** or **solenoid** by:
   - **moving the coil** towards or away from the poles of a magnet.
   - **moving a magnet** towards or away from the coil.
4) In either case, the e.m.f. is a caused by the **magnetic field** (or '**magnetic flux**') that passes through the coil **changing**.
5) If the coil is part of a **complete circuit**, an **induced current** will flow through it.

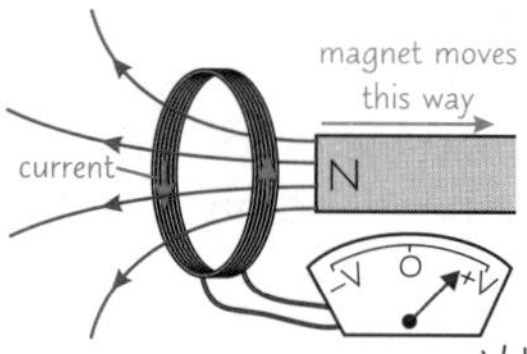


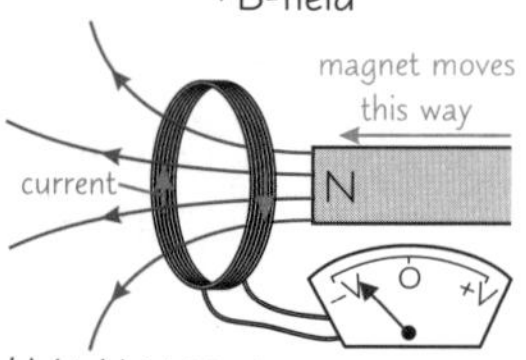


Remember e.m.f. is a voltage — check your Year 1 notes.

## More Turns in a Coil of Wire Mean a Bigger e.m.f. will be Induced

1) When you move a **coil** in a magnetic field, the size of the e.m.f. induced depends on the **magnetic flux** passing through the coil, ***Φ***, and the **number of turns** in the coil that **cut the flux**, ***N***. The product of these is called the **flux linkage**. For a coil with $N$ turns, perpendicular to a field with flux density $B$, the flux linkage is given by:

$$N\Phi = BAN$$

The unit of both flux linkage and $\Phi$ is the **weber, Wb**.

2) The rate of change in flux linkage tells you how **strong** the **electromotive force** will be in **volts**:

A **change** in **flux linkage** of **one weber per second** will induce an **electromotive force** of **1 volt** in a loop of wire.

Flux linkage is sometimes given in "weber-turns" or "Wb turns"

## Use Trig if the Magnetic Flux Isn't Perpendicular to the Area

When the magnetic flux **isn't perpendicular** to the area you're interested in, you need to use **trig** to resolve the **magnetic field vector** into components that are **parallel** and **perpendicular** to the area.

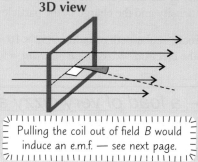

For a **single loop** of wire when ***B*** is **not perpendicular** to **area**, you can find the **magnetic flux** using this equation:

$$\Phi = BA\cos\theta$$

where $\theta$ is the angle between the field and the normal to the plane of the loop.

**Top-down view**

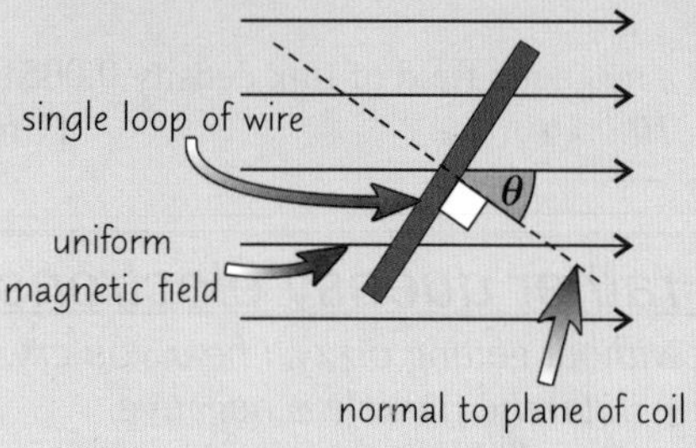


**3D view**

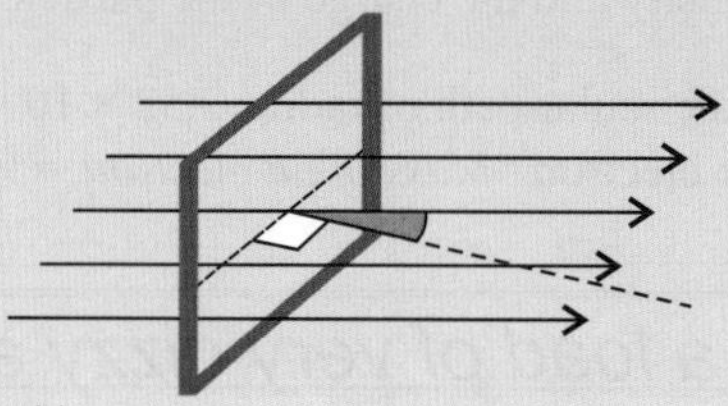

Pulling the coil out of field $B$ would induce an e.m.f. — see next page.

For a **coil** with ***N*** turns the **flux linkage** is:

$$N\Phi = BAN\cos\theta$$

Remember SOH CAH TOA: $\cos\theta$ = adjacent ÷ hypotenuse

# Electromagnetic Induction

## The **Angle** of a Coil in a B Field Affects the **Induced E.M.F.**

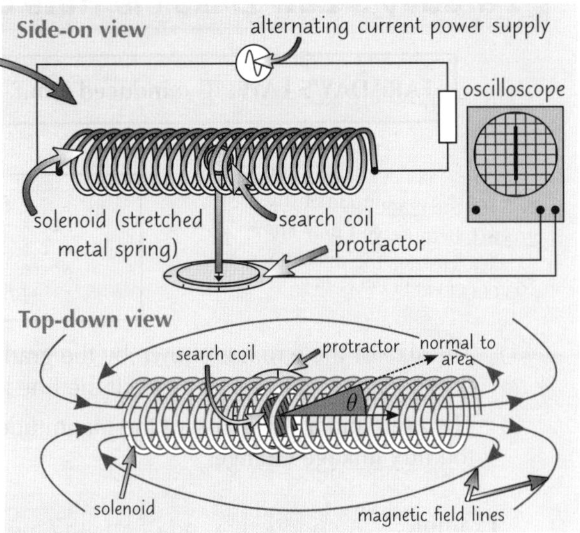


1) You can investigate the effect of **angle** to the **flux lines** on **effective magnetic flux linkage** using this apparatus.
2) The stretched metal spring acts as a solenoid and is connected to an **alternating** power supply (so the **flux** through the search coil is **constantly changing**). The search coil should have a **known area** and a **set number of loops** of fine wire. It is connected to an **oscilloscope** (see p.46) to record the induced e.m.f. in the coil.
3) Set up the oscilloscope so that it only shows the **amplitude** of the e.m.f. as a **vertical line** (i.e. turn off the time base).
4) Position the search coil so that it is about **halfway** along the solenoid. Orientate the search coil so that it is **parallel** to the **solenoid** (and its area is **perpendicular** to the **field**), then **record** the induced e.m.f. in the search coil from the amplitude of the oscilloscope trace.
5) **Rotate** the search coil so its **angle** to the solenoid changes by **10°**. Record the induced e.m.f. and **repeat** until you have rotated the search coil by 90°.
6) You'll find that as you turn the search coil, the induced e.m.f. **decreases**. This is because the search coil is cutting **fewer** flux lines as the **component** of the magnetic field **perpendicular** to the area of the coil **gets lower**, so the t**otal magnetic flux passing** through the search coil is **lower**. This means that the magnetic flux linkage experienced by the coil is lower.
7) Plot a **graph** of **induced e.m.f.** against $\theta$. The induced e.m.f. should be **maximum** at **0°**, and a **zero** at **90°**.

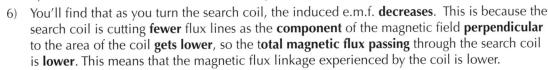

## Practice Questions

Q1 Describe the three ways an e.m.f. can be induced in a conductor in a magnetic field.

Q2 What is the difference between magnetic flux density, magnetic flux and magnetic flux linkage?

Q3 A coil consists of $N$ turns, each of area $A$ in magnetic field $B$. State the equation to calculate its flux linkage if:
  a) the normal to the plane of the coil is perpendicular to a uniform magnetic field.
  b) the normal to the plane of the coil is at an angle to a uniform magnetic field.

Q4 Describe an experiment you could carry out to investigate how the magnetic flux density experienced by a search coil in a magnetic field changes when you vary the angle of it relative to the field.

**Exam Questions**

Q1 The magnetic flux density of a uniform magnetic field is $2.00 \times 10^{-3}$ T.
  a) Calculate the magnetic flux passing through an area of 0.230 m$^2$ at right angles to the field lines. [1 mark]
  b) A coil of area 0.230 m$^2$ with 151 turns is placed in the field at right angles to the field lines. Calculate the magnetic flux linkage in the coil. [1 mark]
  c) Over a period of 2.50 seconds the magnetic field is reduced uniformly to $1.50 \times 10^{-3}$ T. Calculate the e.m.f induced across the ends of the coil. [3 marks]

Q2 A 0.010 m$^2$ coil of 550 turns is perpendicular to a magnetic field of strength 0.92 T generated.
  a) Calculate the magnetic flux linkage in the coil. [1 mark]
  b) The coil is rotated until the normal to the plane of the coil is at 90° to the magnetic field. The movement is uniform and takes 0.5 s. Calculate the e.m.f. induced by this movement. [2 marks]

Q3 The graph shows how the flux through a coil varies over time. Sketch a graph to show how the induced e.m.f. in the coil varies over this same time period. [3 marks]

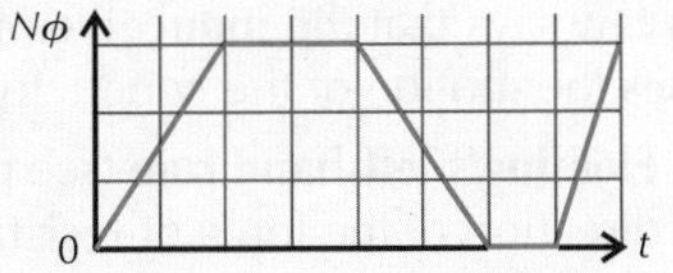


### Beware — physics can induce extreme confusion...

*Make sure you know the difference between flux and flux linkage, and that you can calculate both. Although I'd love to NΦ all tricky stuff, there's simply nothing else to do but learn it. And if you didn't get the flux-tastic pun in that last sentence, you haven't learnt the equations well enough — back to the start with you, don't stop until you're laughing.*

# Induction Laws and Alternators

*Congratulations, your application has been accepted. Now you must be inducted into our laws. And our alternators.*

## **Faraday's Law** Links the **Rate of Change** of **Flux Linkage** with **E.M.F.**

**FARADAY'S LAW:** The **induced e.m.f.** is **directly proportional** to the **rate of change of flux linkage**.

It can be written as:

$$\varepsilon = \frac{\textbf{flux linkage change}}{\textbf{time taken}} = N\frac{\Delta\Phi}{\Delta t}$$

where $\varepsilon$ is the **magnitude** of induced e.m.f.
($N$ = 1 if it's just a loop, not a coil)

It's the magnitude of the e.m.f. because you only know its size, not the direction.

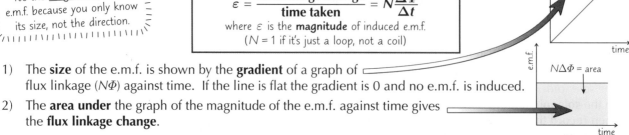

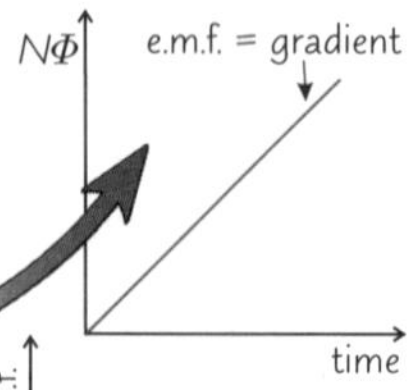


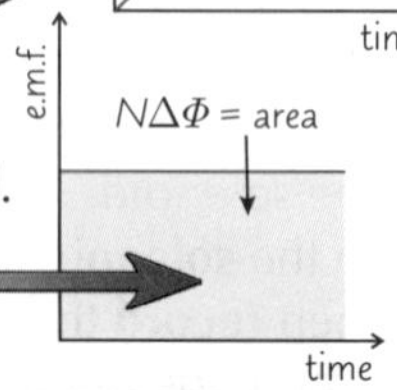


1) The **size** of the e.m.f. is shown by the **gradient** of a graph of flux linkage ($N\Phi$) against time. If the line is flat the gradient is 0 and no e.m.f. is induced.
2) The **area under** the graph of the magnitude of the e.m.f. against time gives the **flux linkage change**.

**Example:** A conducting rod of length $l$ moves through a perpendicular uniform magnetic field, $B$, at a constant velocity, $v$. Show that the magnitude of the e.m.f. induced in the rod is equal to $Blv$.

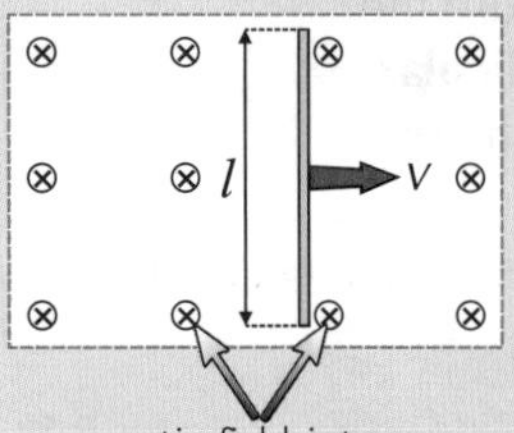


magnetic field into page

Distance travelled, $s = v\Delta t$ (distance = speed × time)

Area of flux it cuts, $A = lv\Delta t$

Total magnetic flux cut through, $\Delta\phi = BA = Blv\Delta t$

Faraday's law gives $\varepsilon = \frac{\Delta(N\phi)}{\Delta t} = \frac{\Delta\phi}{\Delta t}$ (since $N = 1$)

So induced e.m.f., $\varepsilon = \frac{\Delta\phi}{\Delta t} = \frac{Blv\Delta t}{\Delta t} = \boldsymbol{Blv}$

You might be asked to find the e.m.f. induced on something more interesting than a rod, e.g. the Earth's magnetic field across the wingspan of a plane. Just think of it as a moving rod and use the equation as usual.

## The **Direction** of the **Induced E.M.F.** and **Current** are given by **Lenz's Law...**

**LENZ'S LAW:** The **induced e.m.f.** is always in such a **direction** as to **oppose** the **change** that caused it.

1) **Lenz's law** and **Faraday's law** can be **combined** to give one formula that works for both:

$$\varepsilon = \frac{\textbf{– flux linkage change}}{\textbf{time taken}} = -N\frac{\Delta\Phi}{\Delta t}$$

where $\varepsilon$ is the induced e.m.f.

Kevin's lenses always acted in the opposite direction.

2) The **minus sign** shows the direction of the **induced e.m.f.**
3) The idea that an induced e.m.f. will **oppose** the change that caused it agrees with the principle of the **conservation of energy** — the **energy used** to pull a conductor through a magnetic field, against the **resistance** caused by magnetic **attraction**, is what **produces** the **induced current**.
4) **Lenz's law** can be used to find the **direction** of an **induced e.m.f.** and **current** in a conductor travelling at right angles to a magnetic field.

- **Lenz's law** says that the **induced e.m.f.** will produce a force that **opposes** the motion of the conductor — in other words a **resistance**.
- Using **Fleming's left-hand rule** (see p.38), point your thumb in the direction of the force of **resistance** — which is in the **opposite direction** to the motion of the conductor.
- Point your **first finger** in the direction of the **field**. Your **second finger** will now give you the direction of the **induced e.m.f.**.
- If the conductor is **connected** as part of a **circuit**, a current will be induced in the **same direction** as the induced e.m.f..

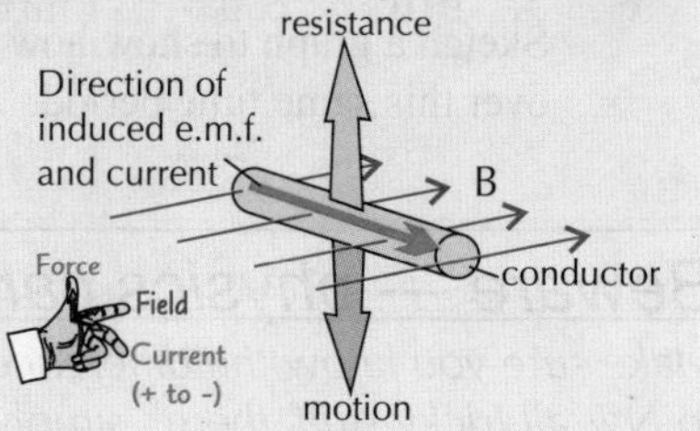

# Induction Laws and Alternators

## An *Alternator* is a *Generator* of *Alternating Current*

1) **Generators**, or dynamos, **convert** kinetic energy into **electrical energy** — they **induce** an electric **current** by **rotating** a **coil** in a magnetic field.
2) The diagram shows a simple **alternator** — a generator of **ac**. It has **slip rings** and **brushes** to connect the coil to an external circuit.
3) The output **voltage** and **current** change direction with every **half rotation** of the coil, producing **alternating current** (**ac**).

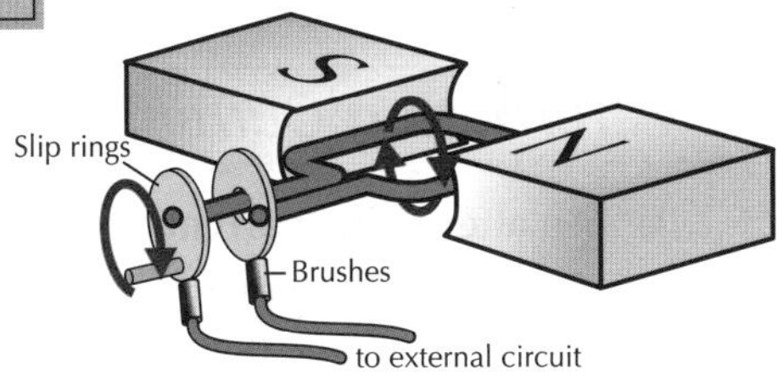


## *Flux Linkage* and *Induced Voltage* are *90° Out of Phase*

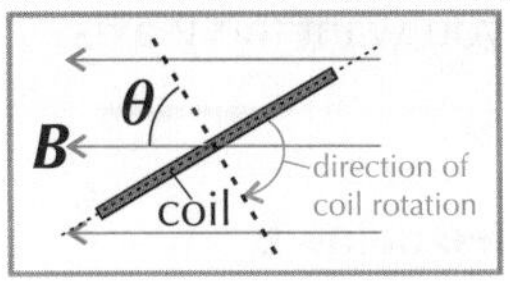


1) The amount of flux cut by the coil (**flux linkage**) is: $N\Phi = BAN\cos\theta$ See page 42.
   ($\theta$ is the angle between the normal to the coil and the flux lines)
2) As the coil rotates $\theta$ changes, so the **flux linkage** varies **sinusoidally** between $+BAN$ and $-BAN$.
3) How fast $\theta$ changes depends on the angular speed, $\omega$, of the coil (see page 2), $\theta = \omega t$. So you can write:

   **flux linkage** $= N\Phi = BAN\cos\omega t$

4) The **induced e.m.f.**, $\varepsilon$, depends on the **rate of change** of **flux linkage** (Faraday's law), so it also varies **sinusoidally**. The equation for the e.m.f. at time $t$ is:

   $\varepsilon = BAN\omega\sin\omega t$

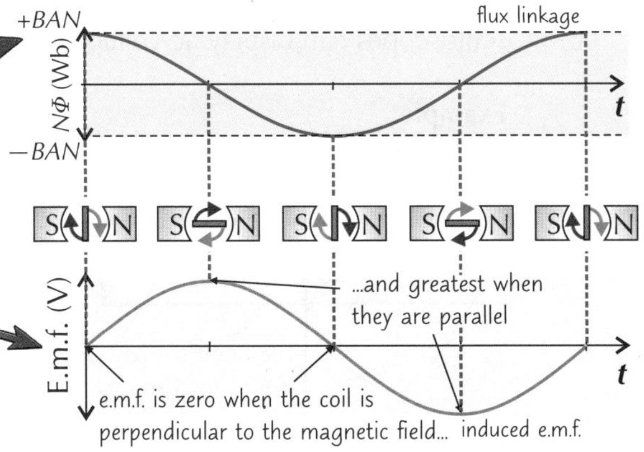


**Example:** A rectangular coil with 30.0 turns, each with an area of 0.200 m$^2$, is rotated as shown at 20.0 rad s$^{-1}$ in a uniform 1.50 mT magnetic field. Calculate the maximum e.m.f. induced in the coil.

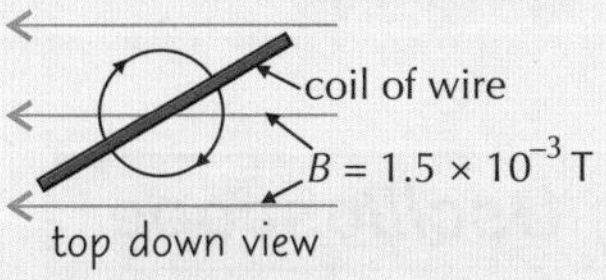


$\varepsilon = BAN\omega\sin\omega t$. So, $\varepsilon$ will be greatest when $\sin\omega t = \pm 1$, which gives $\varepsilon = 1.50 \times 10^{-3} \times 0.200 \times 30.0 \times 20.0 \times \pm 1$
$= \mathbf{\pm 0.180\ V}$

rad stands for radians — see page 2.

## Practice Questions

Q1 State Faraday's law and Lenz's law.

Q2 Describe how to find the direction of an induced e.m.f. in a copper bar moving at right angles to a magnetic field.

Q3 Show that flux linkage and induced e.m.f. are 90° out of phase in an alternator.

**Exam Questions**

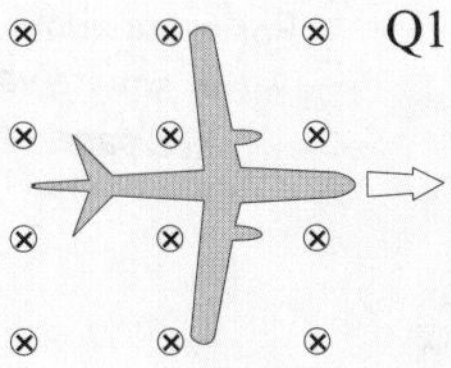

Q1 An aeroplane with a wingspan of 33.9 m flies at a speed of 148 ms$^{-1}$ perpendicular to the Earth's magnetic field, as shown. The Earth's magnetic field at the aeroplane's location is $6.00 \times 10^{-5}$ T.

a) Calculate the induced e.m.f. between the wing tips. [3 marks]

b) Copy and complete the diagram to show the direction of the induced e.m.f. between the wing-tips. [1 mark]

Q2 A 0.0105 m$^2$ coil of 521 turns is rotated on an axis that is perpendicular to a magnetic field of 0.900 T.

a) Find the flux linkage when the angle between its normal and the magnetic field is 60.0°. [1 mark]

b) Calculate the peak e.m.f. induced when the coil is rotated at an angular speed of $40\pi$ rad s$^{-1}$. [3 marks]

## *Alternators and laws of induction? They generatorly don't phase me...*

*Bless my soul — there are so many Greek letters on this page it looks like Hercules had a few too many and spewed the alphabet all over everywhere. Go from zero to (physics) hero and learn what they all mean, then find your way through all the equations too. Then when you get into the exam you'll easily be able to go the distance — just like that.*

# Alternating Currents

*Oh alternating current, you're just no good for me. You're up then you're down, you're in then you're out, you're positive at peak voltage then negative in a trough. I should know that you're always going to cha-a-aange...*

## **Alternating** Current is **Constantly Changing**

alternating currants

1) An **alternating current** or voltage is one that changes direction with time.
2) This means the voltage across a resistance goes up and down in a **regular pattern** — some of the time it's positive and some of the time it's negative.
3) You can use an **oscilloscope** to **display** the **voltage** of an alternating current (and **direct current** too). Oscilloscopes are just like really **fancy voltmeters** — the **vertical height** of the trace at any point shows the **input voltage** at that point.
4) The oscilloscope screen has a **grid** on it — you can select how many **volts per division** you want the *y*-axis scale to represent using the *Y*-gain control dial, e.g. 5 V per division.
5) An alternating current (ac) source gives a regularly repeating **sinusoidal waveform.** A direct current (dc) source is always at the same voltage, so you get a **horizontal line** (see below).
6) Oscilloscopes can display ac voltage as a **vertical line** and dc voltage as a **dot** if you **turn off** the time base.

**Example:**
A **sinusoidal alternating voltage** signal.

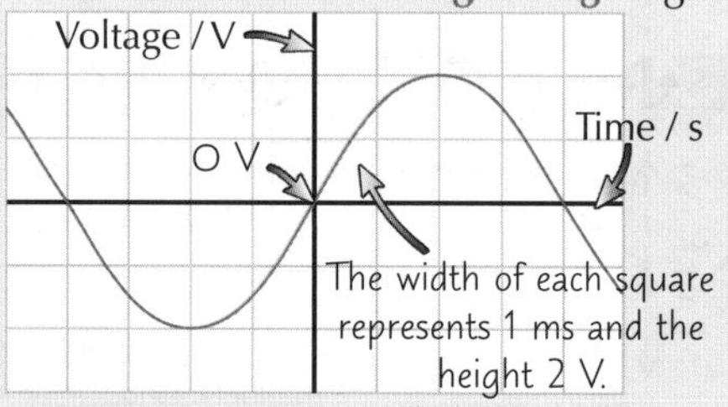


Oscilloscope settings:
*Y*-gain = 2 V per division,
time base = 1 ms per division.

A sinusoidal alternating voltage with the **time base** turned **off**.

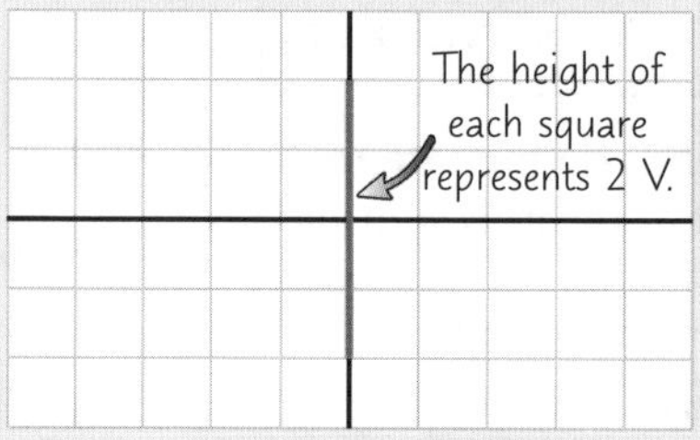


Oscilloscope settings:
*Y*-gain = 2 V per division,
time base turned off.

A **direct current** supply.

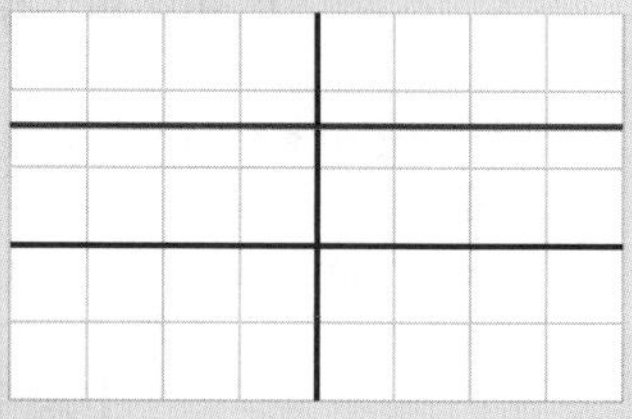

Oscilloscope settings:
*Y*-gain = 2 V per division,
time base = 1 ms per division.

## Find the **rms**, **Peak** and **Peak-to-Peak Voltages** using an **Oscilloscope**

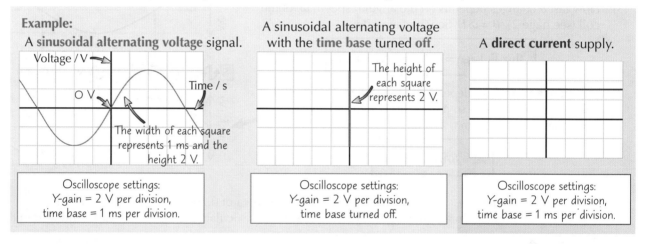

1) There are three basic pieces of information you can get from an ac oscilloscope trace — the **time period**, ***T***, the **peak voltage**, $V_0$, and the **peak-to-peak voltage**.

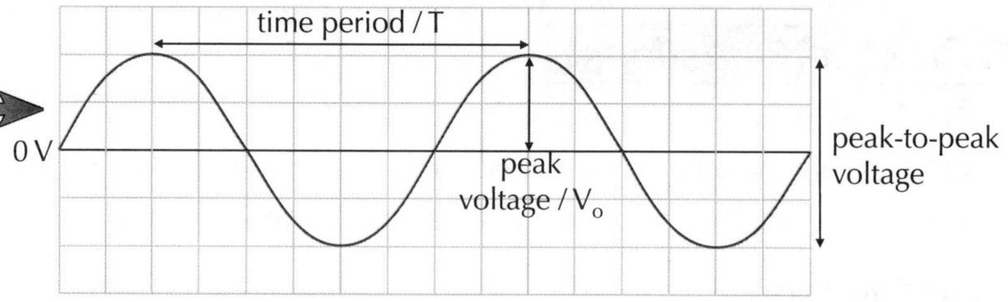


2) An ac supply with a peak voltage of 2 V will be **below** 2 V **most of the time**. That means it **won't** have as high a **power output** as a 2 V **dc** supply. To compare them properly, you need to calculate the **root mean square** (rms) **voltage**.
3) For a sine wave, you can calculate the rms voltage ($V_{rms}$)by **dividing** the **peak voltage**, $V_0$, by $\sqrt{2}$. You do the same to calculate the rms current $I_{rms}$:

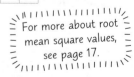

For more about root mean square values, see page 17.

$$V_{rms} = \frac{V_0}{\sqrt{2}}$$

$V_0$ = peak voltage in volts (V)

$$I_{rms} = \frac{I_0}{\sqrt{2}}$$

$I_0$ = peak current in amperes (A)

To work out **rms power** for an ac supply, just use the **rms values** of voltage and current: $\textbf{power}_{rms} = I_{rms} \times V_{rms}$

4) Measuring the distance **between** successive **peaks** along the **time axis** (the horizontal axis) gives you the **time period** (as long as you know the time base setting). You can use this to calculate the **frequency**:

$$\textbf{frequency} = \frac{1}{\textbf{time period}}, \text{ or } f = \frac{1}{T}$$

# Alternating Currents

## You'll Need to Use those **Equations** to **Answer Questions**

**Example:** A light is powered by a sinusoidal ac power supply with a peak voltage of 2.12 V and a root mean square current of 0.40 A.

a) Calculate the root mean square voltage of the power supply.

$$V_{rms} = \frac{V_0}{\sqrt{2}} = \frac{2.12}{\sqrt{2}} = 1.499... = \mathbf{1.50\ V\ (to\ 3\ s.f.)}$$

b) Calculate the power of the power supply.

$$\text{Power} = I_{rms} \times V_{rms} = 1.499... \times 0.40 = 0.5996... = \mathbf{0.60\ W\ (to\ 2\ s.f.)}$$

## **Mains Electricity** is an **Alternating Current**

The UK's mains electricity supply is **around 230 V**, although this does vary a little.
This is an **alternating** supply, so the value of 230 V stated is actually the **rms value**.

**Example:** Calculate the peak-to-peak voltage of the UK mains electricity supply.

Just rearrange $V_{rms} = \frac{V_0}{\sqrt{2}}$ into $V_0 = \sqrt{2}\,V_{rms}$:

$V_0 = \sqrt{2} \times V_{rms} = \sqrt{2} \times 230 = 325.26...\text{ V}$
$= 330$ (to s.f.)

$V_{peak\text{-}to\text{-}peak} = 2 \times V_0 = 650.53...$
$= \mathbf{650\ V\ (to\ 2\ s.f.)}$

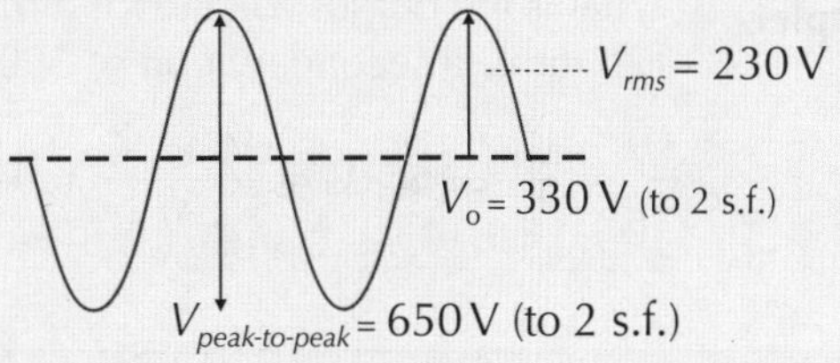


## Practice Questions

Q1 What is an alternating current?

Q2 Describe the waveform of the voltage in an alternating current.

Q3 Write down the equations for calculating root mean square voltage and root mean square current from peak voltage and peak current.

Q4 The frequency of UK mains alternating current is 50 Hz. Show that its time period is 0.02 s.

**Exam Questions**

Q1 Two students are trying to use an oscilloscope to display an alternating current.

a) One student sets up her power supply and connects it to the oscilloscope. She sees a vertical line in the middle of the screen. What setting must she adjust to display a sinusoidal wave form? [1 mark]

b) Another student sets up his power supply and connects it to the oscilloscope. He sees a flat horizontal line at 7 V. Explain what he has done wrong. [1 mark]

Q2 a) The peak current in an ac circuit is 9.13 A. Calculate the root mean square current. [1 mark]

b) The root mean square voltage of the same alternating supply is 119 V. Calculate the peak-to-peak voltage. [2 marks]

## Careful on your surfboard — these currents keep changing direction...

*If it helps, have a quick daydream about a summer beach holiday. Ah, the sand, waves, ice cream, torrential rain, wind, woolly hats, waterproof trousers, hypothermia and then the roaring fire... I love Cornwall in August. But you can't enjoy any of that until you've done your exams, so you might as well do a good job and learn all this alternating current stuff.*

# Transformers

*Turns out electromagnetic induction is quite useful in the real world — remember that place?*

## *Transformers* Work by Electromagnetic *Induction*

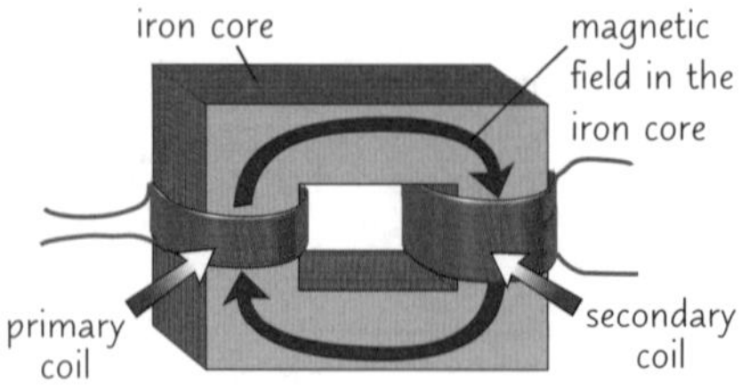

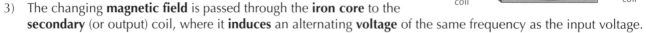

1) **Transformers** are devices that make use of electromagnetic induction to **change** the size of the **voltage** for an **alternating current**.
2) An alternating current flowing in the **primary** (or input) **coil** produces **magnetic flux**.
3) The changing **magnetic field** is passed through the **iron core** to the **secondary** (or output) coil, where it **induces** an alternating **voltage** of the same frequency as the input voltage.
4) From Faraday's law, the **induced** e.m.f.s in both the **primary** and **secondary** coils can be calculated:

Primary coil $V_p = N_p \frac{\Delta \Phi}{\Delta t}$ Secondary coil $V_s = N_s \frac{\Delta \Phi}{\Delta t}$
(where $N$ is the number of turns in a coil)

⟹ These can be combined to give the **transformer equation** for an **ideal** transformer: ⟹

$$\frac{N_s}{N_p} = \frac{V_s}{V_p}$$

(where $N$ is the number of turns in a coil)

5) **Step-up** transformers **increase** the **voltage** by having **more turns** on the **secondary** coil than the primary. **Step-down** transformers **reduce** the voltage by having **fewer** turns on the secondary coil.

**Example:** What is the output voltage for a transformer with a primary coil of 120 turns, a secondary coil of 350 turns and an input voltage of 230 V?

$$\frac{N_s}{N_p} = \frac{V_s}{V_p} \Rightarrow V_s = \frac{V_p \times N_s}{N_p} = V_s = \frac{230 \times 350}{120} = 670.83... = \mathbf{670\ V\ (to\ 2\ s.f.)}$$

## Transformers are *Not 100% Efficient*

You can put the two ideal transformer equations together to give: $\frac{V_p}{V_s} = \frac{N_p}{N_s} = \frac{I_s}{I_p}$

1) If a transformer was **100% efficient**, the **power in** would **equal** the **power out**.
2) Power is current × voltage. This means that for an **ideal transformer**: $I_p V_p = I_s V_s$ or $\frac{I_s}{I_p} = \frac{V_p}{V_s}$
3) However, in practice there will be **small losses** of **power** from the transformer, mostly due to **eddy currents** in the transformer's iron **core**.
4) Eddy currents are looping currents induced by the changing magnetic flux in the core. They create a **magnetic field** that **acts against** the field that induced them, reducing the field strength. They also dissipate energy by **generating heat**.
5) The effect of eddy currents can be reduced by **laminating** the core with layers of **insulation**.
6) Heat is also generated by **resistance** in the coils — to minimise this, **thick copper wire** is used, which has a **low resistance**.
7) The **efficiency** of a transformer is simply the **ratio** of **power out** to **power in**, so: (this gives the efficiency as a **decimal** — multiply by 100 to get a **percentage**).

$$\text{efficiency} = \frac{I_s V_s}{I_p V_p}$$

**Example:** a) A transformer has an input current of 173 A and doubles the input voltage to give an output voltage of 35 600 V. Calculate the maximum possible current output by the transformer.

$V_p = 35\,600 \div 2 = 17\,800$ V

$I_p V_p = I_s V_s$ so $I_s = \frac{I_p \times V_p}{V_s} = \frac{173 \times 17\,800}{35\,600} = \mathbf{86.5\ A}$

You could also work this out by realising that if the voltage doubles, the current must halve, as they are inversely proportional.

b) The efficiency of another transformer is 0.871. It decreases an initial voltage of 11 560 V to 7851 V and $I_p$ is 195 A. Calculate the current output by the transformer.

$\text{efficiency} = \frac{I_s V_s}{I_p V_p}$ so $I_s = \frac{\text{efficiency} \times I_p \times V_p}{V_s} = \frac{0.871 \times 195 \times 11560}{7851}$

$= 250.083... = \mathbf{250\ A\ (to\ 3\ s.f.)}$

# Transformers

## *Transformers* are an *Important* Part of the *National Grid...*

1) **Electricity** from power stations is sent round the country in the **national grid** at the **lowest** possible current, because the **power losses** due to the **resistance** of the cables is equal to $P = I^2R$ — so if you double the transmitted current, you **quadruple** the power lost.
2) Since **power** = **current** × **voltage**, a **low current** means a **high voltage**.
3) **Transformers** allow us to **step up** the voltage to around **400 000 V** for **transmission** through the national grid, and then **reduce** it again to **230 V** for domestic use.

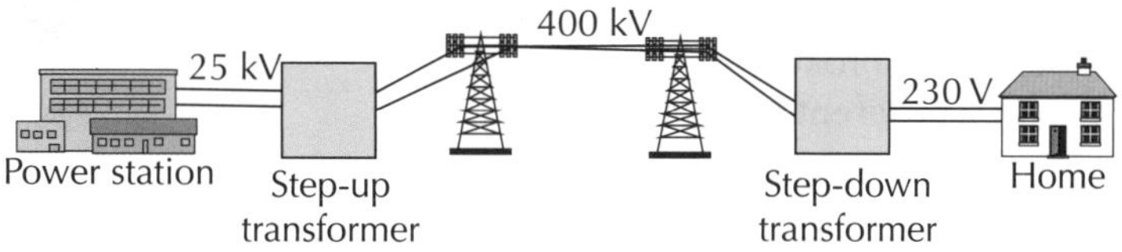

... robots in disguise

## ...and You Need to be Able to *Work Out* the Power *Wasted* in *Transmission*

**Example:** A current of 1330 A is used to transmit 1340 MW of power through 147 km of cables. The resistance of the transmission wire is 0.130 Ω per kilometre. Calculate the power wasted.

Total resistance = 0.130 × 147 = 19.11 Ω

Power lost = $I^2R = 1330^2 \times 19.11 = 3.3803... \times 10^7 = \mathbf{3.38 \times 10^7}$ **W (to 3 s.f.)**

## Practice Questions

Q1 Draw a diagram of a simple transformer.

Q2 State the transformer equation.

Q3 What is meant by a step-down transformer?

Q4 Describe how eddy currents are formed in a transformer and explain why they reduce a transformer's efficiency.

Q5 Why is electricity transmitted across the national grid at as low a current as possible?

**Exam Questions**

Q1 A simple transformer with 158 turns in the primary coil has an input voltage of 9.30 V.

a) Calculate the number of turns needed in the secondary coil to step up the voltage to 45.0 V. [1 mark]

b) The input current for the transformer is 1.50 A.
Assuming the transformer is ideal, calculate the output current. [2 marks]

c) Calculate the actual efficiency of the transformer given that the power output is measured as 10.8 W. [1 mark]

d) Describe a change that could be made to the transformer to improve its efficiency by reducing the effect of eddy currents. [1 mark]

Q2 A substation receives 943 kW of electricity from a power station through wires with a total resistance 132 Ω. The input current was 15.6 A
Calculate the electrical power originally transmitted from the power station. [2 marks]

## Arrrrrrrrrgggggghhhhhhh...

*Breathe a sigh of relief, pat yourself on the back and make a brew — well done, you've reached the end of the section. That was pretty nasty stuff (the section, not your tea), but don't let all of those equations get you down — once you've learnt the main ones and can use them blindfolded, even the trickiest looking exam question will be a walk in the park...*

# Rutherford Scattering and Atomic Structure

*You'll be learning about the 'nuclear model' of the atom shortly. But first it's time for a trip back in time to see how scientists came up with it. And it's got a bit to do with plum puddings.*

## Scientists Thought **Atoms** Were Like a **Plum Pudding**

1) The idea of **atoms** has been around since the time of the Ancient Greeks in the 5th Century BC. A man called Democritus proposed that all matter was made up of little, **identical lumps** called 'atomos'.
2) Much later, in 1804, a scientist called John Dalton put forward a hypothesis that agreed with Democritus — that matter was made up of tiny spheres ('atoms') that couldn't be broken up. He reckoned that each **element** was made up of a **different** type of 'atom'.
3) Nearly 100 years later, J. J. Thomson discovered that **electrons** could be removed from atoms. So Dalton's theory wasn't quite right (atoms could be broken up).
4) Thomson suggested that atoms were **spheres** of **positive charge** with tiny negative electrons stuck in them like fruit in a **plum pudding**.
5) Until this point though, nobody had proposed the idea of the **nucleus**. Rutherford was the first to suggest atoms did not have **uniformly** distributed **charge** and **density**.

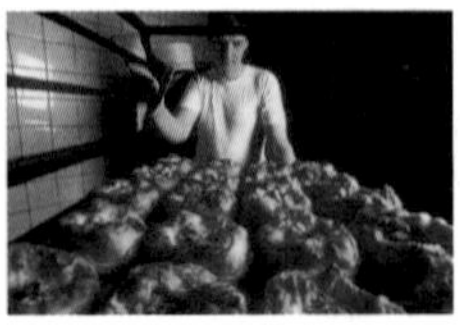

James fancied doing a bit of nuclear physics

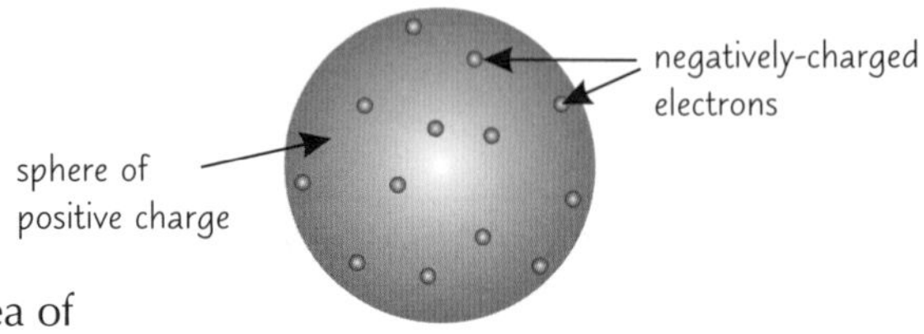


## **Rutherford Scattering** Showed the Existence of a **Nucleus**

1) In 1909, Rutherford and Marsden tried firing a beam of **alpha particles** (see p.54) at thin gold foil.
2) A circular detector screen surrounding the gold foil and the alpha source was used to detect alpha particles deflected by any angle.
3) They expected that the positively-charged alpha particles would be **deflected** by the electrons by a very **small amount** if the plum pudding model was true.
4) Instead, most of the alpha particles just went **straight through** the foil, while a small number were deflected by a **large angle**.
5) Some were even deflected by more than **90°**, sending them back the way they came — this was confusing at the time and called for a change to the **model** of the atom.

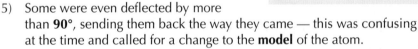

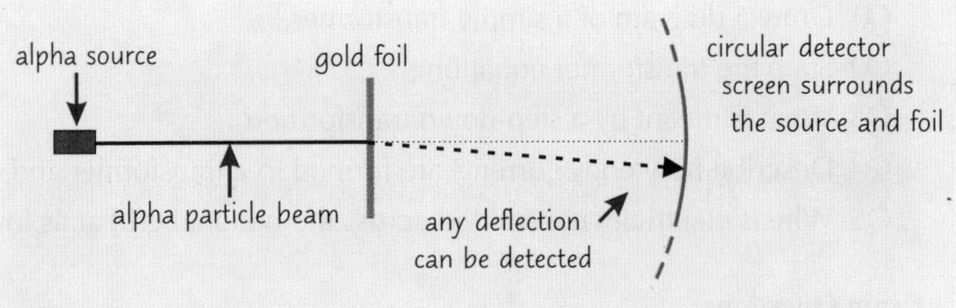


The results of Rutherford scattering suggested that atoms must have a small, positively-charged **nucleus** at the centre:

1) Most of the atom must be **empty space** because most of the alpha particles passed straight **through** the foil.
2) The nucleus must have a large **positive** charge, as some positively-charged alpha particles were **repelled** and deflected by a **large angle**.
3) The nucleus must be **small** as very **few** alpha particles were deflected back.
4) Most of the mass must be in the **nucleus**, since the fast alpha particles (with high momentum) are **deflected** by the nucleus.

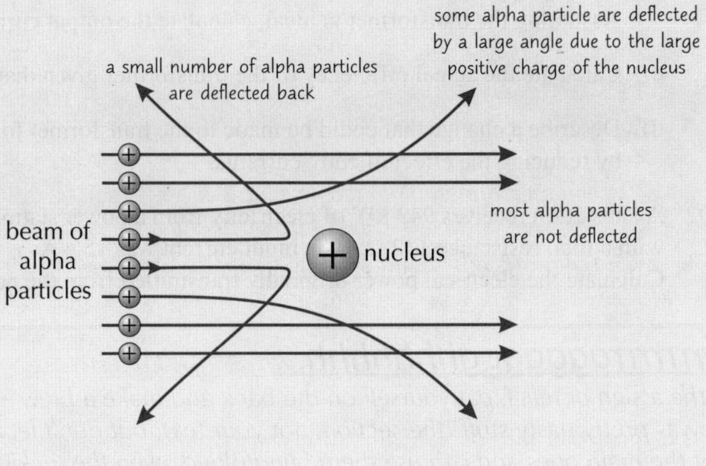

# Rutherford Scattering and Atomic Structure

## You can **Estimate** the **Closest Approach** of a **Scattered Particle**

1) When you fire an alpha particle at a gold nucleus, you know its **initial kinetic energy**.
2) An alpha particle that 'bounces back' and is deflected through 180° will have reversed direction a short distance from the nucleus. It does this at the point where its **electric potential energy** (see p.28) **equals** its **initial kinetic energy**.
3) It's just conservation of energy — and you can use it to find how close the particle can get to the nucleus.
4) Using a form of Coulomb's law (p.26) to find the electric potential energy:

$$E_k = E_{elec} = \frac{Q_{gold}Q_{alpha}}{4\pi\varepsilon_0 r}$$

where $\varepsilon_0 = 8.85 \times 10^{-12}$ Fm$^{-1}$ is the permittivity of free space (p.26) and $r$ is the distance from the centre of the nucleus (m)

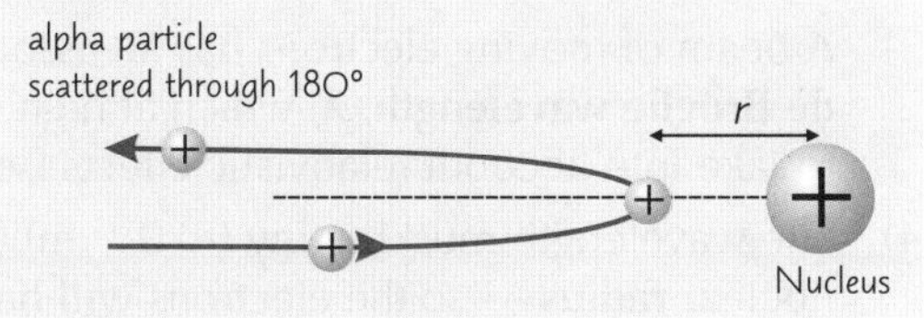


5) To find the charge of a nucleus you need to know the atom's **proton number, *Z*** — that tells you how many protons are in the nucleus (surprisingly). A proton has a charge of **+e** (where e is the size of the charge on an electron), so the charge of a nucleus must be ***+Ze***.
6) The **distance of closest approach** is an **estimate** of **nuclear radius** — it gives a **maximum** value for it. However, electron diffraction (next page) gives much more accurate values for nuclear radii.

**Example:** An alpha particle with an initial kinetic energy of 6.0 MeV is fired at a gold nucleus. Estimate the radius of the nucleus by finding the closest approach of the alpha particle to the nucleus.

Initial particle energy = 6.0 MeV = $6.0 \times 10^6$ eV

Convert this energy into joules: $(6.0 \times 10^6) \times (1.60 \times 10^{-19}) = 9.6 \times 10^{-13}$ J

You know that this equals the electric potential energy at the distance of closest approach:

$$\frac{Q_{gold}Q_{alpha}}{4\pi\varepsilon_0 r} = 9.6 \times 10^{-13}$$

$$r = \frac{Q_{gold}Q_{alpha}}{(9.6 \times 10^{-13}) \times 4\pi\varepsilon_0} = \frac{(79 \times 1.60 \times 10^{-19}) \times (2 \times 1.60 \times 10^{-19})}{4\pi \times (9.6 \times 10^{-13}) \times 8.85 \times 10^{-12}}$$

A gold nucleus has 79 protons and an alpha particle is made up of two protons and two neutrons.

$r = 3.788... \times 10^{-14} = \mathbf{3.8 \times 10^{-14}}$ **m (to 2 s.f.)**

## Practice Questions

Q1 Describe the plum pudding model of the atom.

Q2 Describe Rutherford scattering and explain how the results from the experiment showed that a nucleus is both small and positively charged.

Q3 Describe how you could estimate the nuclear radius of an atom.

**Exam Question**

$\varepsilon_0 = 8.85 \times 10^{-12}\ Fm^{-1}$, $e = 1.60 \times 10^{-19}\ C$, $Z_{gold} = 79$

Q1 A beam of alpha particles is directed onto a very thin gold film. Each alpha particle has a kinetic energy of 4.8 MeV.

a) Explain why the majority of alpha particles are not scattered. [2 marks]

b) Explain how alpha particles are scattered by atomic nuclei. [3 marks]

c) Calculate the distance of closest approach for an alpha particle that has been deflected by 180°. [2 marks]

d) What is the kinetic energy of the alpha particle at the distance of closest approach? [1 mark]

## Alpha scattering — It's positively repulsive...

*Scattering is a key idea you need to understand for questions about atomic size and structure. Just one experiment managed to change how we view the atom, proving the old-fashioned 'plum pudding' model to be wrong. We now know the atom is mostly made of empty space, and it contains a small nucleus with a large positive charge.*

# Nuclear Radius and Density

*The tiny nucleus — such a weird place, but one that you need to become ultra familiar with. Lucky you...*

## You Can Use *Electron Diffraction* to *Estimate Nuclear Radius*

1) **Electrons** are a type of particle called a **lepton**. Leptons **don't interact** with the **strong nuclear force** (whereas neutrons and alpha particles do). Because of this, electron diffraction is an **accurate** method for estimating the **nuclear radius**.
2) Like other particles, electrons show **wave-particle duality** (you met this in year 1 of A-level)— so **electron beams** can be diffracted.
3) A beam of moving electrons has an associated **de Broglie wavelength**, $\lambda$, which at high speeds (where you have to take into account relativistic effects (see p.148)) is approximately:

$$\lambda \simeq \frac{hc}{E}$$

*E* is electron energy (J), *h* is the Planck constant and *c* is the speed of light in a vacuum

4) The wavelength must be **tiny** (~$10^{-15}$ m) to investigate the nuclear **radius** — so the electrons will have a very **high** energy.
5) If a beam of **high-energy electrons** is directed onto a thin film of material in front of a screen, a **diffraction pattern** will be seen on the screen.
6) The first minimum appears where:

$$\sin\theta \approx \frac{1.22\lambda}{2R}$$

*R* is the radius of the nucleus it has been scattered by.

7) Using measurements from this diffraction pattern, you can rearrange the above equation to find the **radius** of the nucleus.

**Example:** A beam of 300 MeV electrons is fired at a piece of thin foil, and produces a diffraction pattern on a fluorescent screen. The first minimum of the diffraction pattern is at an angle of 30° from the straight-through position. Estimate the radius of the nuclei the electrons were diffracted by.

$E = 300 \text{ MeV} = (3.00 \times 10^8) \times (1.60 \times 10^{-19}) = 4.8 \times 10^{-11} \text{ J}$

$$\lambda = \frac{hc}{E} = \frac{6.63 \times 10^{-34} \times 3.00 \times 10^8}{4.8 \times 10^{-11}} = 4.143... \times 10^{-15} \text{m}$$

$$R \approx \frac{1.22\lambda}{2\sin\theta} = \frac{1.22 \times 4.143... \times 10^{-15}}{2\sin(30)} = 5.055... \times 10^{-15} \text{m} = \mathbf{5 \text{ fm (to 1 s.f.)}}$$

## *Intensity* Varies With *Diffraction Angle*

1) The diffraction pattern is very similar to that of a light source shining through a **circular aperture** — a **central bright** maximum (circle) containing the majority of the incident electrons, surrounded by other **dimmer** rings (maxima).
2) The **intensity** of the maxima **decreases** as the **angle of diffraction** increases. The graph shows the **relative intensity** of electrons in each maximum.
(You might also see a **logarithmic plot** of this graph, where the **difference** in the **peak heights** is less pronounced).

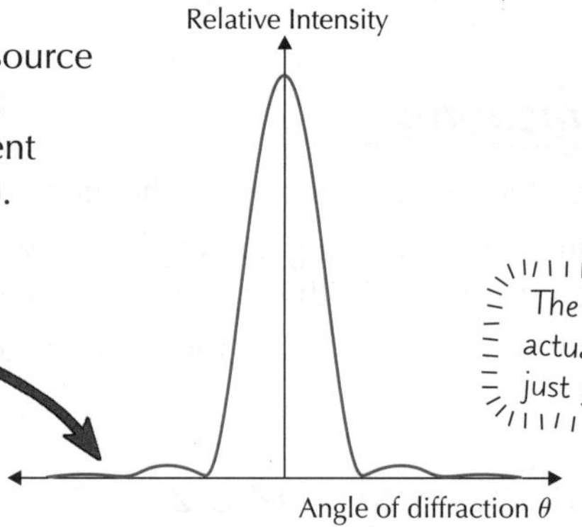


The intensity never actually hits zero, it just gets very close.

## The *Nuclear Radius* is Very *Small* in Comparison to the *Atomic Radius*

By **probing atoms** using scattering and diffraction methods, we know that:
1) The **radius of an atom** is about 0.05 nm ($5 \times 10^{-11}$ m)
2) The radius of the smallest **nucleus** is about 1 fm ($1 \times 10^{-15}$ m — pronounced 'femtometres').

So **nuclei** are really **tiny** compared with the size of the **whole atom**.

Imagine a Ferris wheel is the size of an atom. If you put a **grain of rice** in the centre, this would be the size of the atom's **nucleus**.

Make sure you know that the typical radius of a nucleus is ≈ $1 \times 10^{-15}$ m.

# Nuclear Radius and Density

## The Nucleus is Made Up of Nucleons

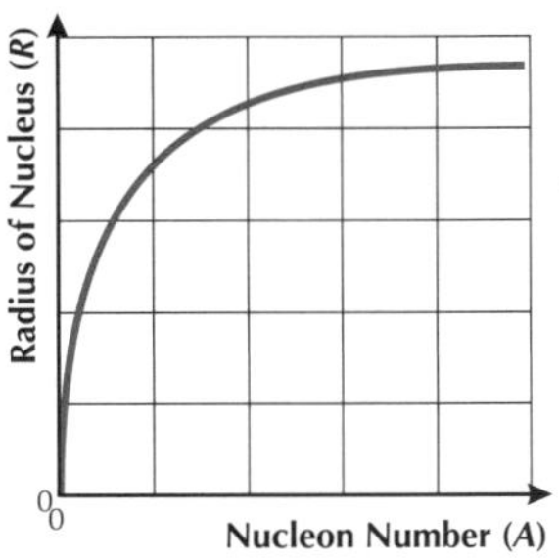


1) The **particles** that make up the nucleus (i.e. **protons** and **neutrons**) are called **nucleons**.
2) The **number of nucleons** in an atom is called the **nucleon** (or mass) **number, *A***.
3) As **more nucleons** are added to the nucleus, it gets **bigger**.
4) And as we all know by now, you can measure the size of a nucleus by firing particles at it (see previous page).

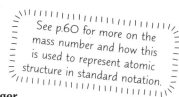

See p.60 for more on the mass number and how this is used to represent atomic structure in standard notation.

## Nuclear Radius is Proportional to the Cube Root of the Nucleon Number

1) When data from nuclear radii experiments is plotted on a **graph** of **nuclear radius *R*** against the **cube root** of the **nucleon number $A^{1/3}$**, the line of best fit gives a **straight line**.
2) This shows a **linear relationship** between $R$ and $A^{1/3}$. As the nucleon number increases, the radius of the nucleus increases proportionally to the cube root of $A$.
3) This relationship can be written as: $R \propto A^{1/3}$.
4) You can make this into an equation by introducing a constant, $R_0$, giving:

$$R = R_0A^{1/3}$$

Where $R_0$ is roughly 1.4 fm.

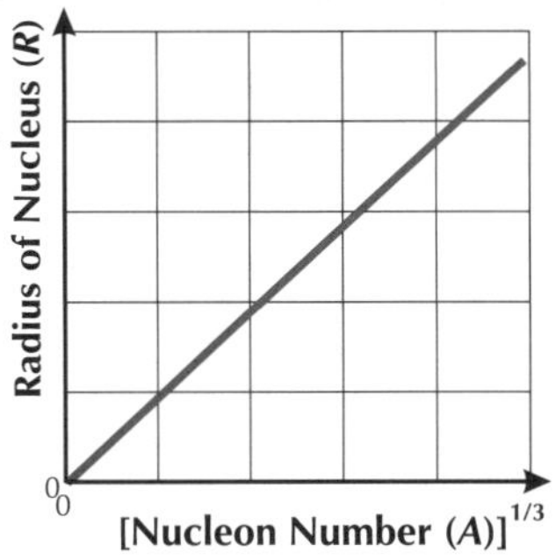


## The Density of Nuclear Matter is Enormous

1) The **volume** that each nucleon (i.e. a **proton** or a **neutron**) takes up in a nucleus is about the **same**.
2) Because protons and neutrons have nearly the **same mass** (we'll call it $m_{nucleon}$), it means that all nuclei have a **similar density** ($\rho$), which you can quickly prove:

$$\rho = \frac{\text{mass}}{\text{volume}} = \frac{A \times m_{nucleon}}{\frac{4}{3}\pi R^3} = \frac{A \times m_{nucleon}}{\frac{4}{3}\pi (R_0 A^{\frac{1}{3}})^3} = \frac{3m_{nucleon}}{4\pi R_0^3} = \text{constant}$$

3) If you substitute the constants into this formula, you'll get that nuclear density is around $1.45 \times 10^{17}$ kgm$^{-3}$.
4) Nuclear matter is **no ordinary** stuff. Its density is **enormous** — much larger than **atomic density**. This suggests that an atom contains lots of **empty space**, with **most** of its **mass** being in a **small nucleus**.

## Practice Questions

Q1 What order of magnitude is the radius of a typical nucleus?

Q2 Write down the formula relating nuclear radius and nucleon number.

**Exam Questions**

Q1 High-energy electrons with a de Broglie wavelength of 3.00 fm are diffracted by a carbon-12 nucleus (radius = $2.7 \times 10^{-15}$ m).

a) Estimate the angle at which the first minimum appears on the electron beam's diffraction pattern. [2 marks]

b) Sketch a graph of relative intensity against angle of diffraction for the electrons. [2 marks]

Q2 Show that the density of a carbon-12 nucleus and the density of a gold nucleus are roughly the same. [4 marks]
($R_0$ = 1.4 fm, carbon-12 nucleus mass = $2.00 \times 10^{-26}$ kg and $A$ = 12, gold nucleus mass = $3.27 \times 10^{-25}$ kg and $A$ = 197)

## Time to fill all that empty space in your head...

*Thankfully this isn't too tricky — just a couple of formulas and a graph to learn. Cover these pages, scribble down what you can remember and see how you've done. Then read again any bits you missed — not too fun, but it works.*

# Radioactive Emissions

*Now it's time to see the big consequences of when a tiny nucleus starts to break down.*

## Unstable Nuclei are Radioactive

1) If a nucleus is **unstable**, it will **break down** to **become** more stable. Its **instability** could be caused by having **too many neutrons**, **not enough neutrons**, or just **too much energy** in the nucleus.
2) The nucleus **decays** by **releasing energy** and/or **particles**, until it reaches a **stable form** — this is called **radioactive decay**.
3) When a radioactive particle **hits** an **atom** it can **knock off electrons**, creating an **ion** — so, **radioactive emissions** are also known as **ionising radiation**.
4) An individual radioactive decay is **random** — it can't be predicted.

## There are Four Types of Nuclear Radiation

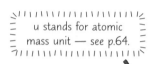

u stands for atomic mass unit — see p.64.

| Radiation | Symbol | Constituent | Relative Charge | Mass (u) |
|---|---|---|---|---|
| Alpha | $\alpha$ | A helium nucleus — 2 protons & 2 neutrons | +2 | 4 |
| Beta-minus (Beta) | $\beta$ or $\beta^-$ | Electron | -1 | (negligible) |
| Beta-plus | $\beta^+$ | Positron | +1 | (negligible) |
| Gamma | $\gamma$ | Short-wavelength, high-frequency electromagnetic wave | 0 | 0 |

## You Can Use Penetrating Power to Investigate Radiation Types

Different types of radiation have different **penetrating powers**, and so can be stopped by different types of **material**:

1) Record the **background radiation** count rate when no source is present (p.56).
2) Place an **unknown** source near to a **Geiger counter** and record the count rate.
3) Place a sheet of **paper** between the source and the Geiger counter. Record the count rate.
4) Repeat step two, replacing the paper with a **3 mm** thick sheet of **aluminium.**

Depending on when the count rate **significantly decreased**, you can calculate what **kind of radiation** the source was emitting. For example, if **paper** has **no effect** and **aluminium** causes a significant (but not complete) **reduction** in count rate, the source must be emitting **beta** and **gamma** radiation.

| Radiation | Symbol | Ionising | Speed | Penetrating power | Affected by magnetic field? |
|---|---|---|---|---|---|
| Alpha | $\alpha$ | Strongly | Slow | Absorbed by paper or a few cm of air | Yes |
| Beta-minus (Beta) | $\beta$ or $\beta^-$ | Weakly | Fast | Absorbed by ~3 mm of aluminium | Yes |
| Beta-plus | $\beta^+$ | Annihilated by electron — so virtually zero range | | | |
| Gamma | $\gamma$ | Very weakly | Speed of light | Absorbed by many cm of lead, or several m of concrete. | No |

## You Can Control How Thick Material Is Using Radiation

1) When creating **sheets of material** like paper, foil or steel, ionising radiation can be used to control its **thickness**.
2) The material is flattened as it is fed through **rollers**.
3) A radioactive **source** is placed on one side of the material, and a radioactive **detector** on the other. The **thicker** the material, the **more** radiation it **absorbs** and **prevents** from reaching the detector.
4) If **too much** radiation is being absorbed, the rollers move **closer** together to make the material **thinner**. If too **little** radiation is being absorbed, they move further **apart**.

# Radioactive Emissions

## **Alpha** and **Beta** Particles have **Different Ionising Properties**

What a radioactive source can be used for often depends on its **ionising properties**.

1) **Alpha** particles are **strongly positive** — so they can **easily pull electrons** off atoms.
2) Ionising an atom **transfers** some of the **energy** from the **alpha particle** to the **atom**. The alpha particle **quickly ionises** many atoms (about 10 000 ionisations per mm in air for each alpha particle) and **loses** all its **energy**. This makes alpha-sources suitable for use in **smoke alarms** because they allow **current** to flow, but won't **travel very far**.
3) Although alpha particles can't penetrate your skin, sources of alpha particles are **dangerous** if they are **ingested**. They quickly **ionise body tissue** in a small area, causing lots of **damage**.
4) The **beta**-minus particle has **lower mass** and **charge** than the alpha particle, but a **higher speed**. This means it can still **knock electrons** off atoms. Each **beta** particle will ionise about 100 atoms per mm in air, **losing energy** at each interaction.
5) This **lower number of interactions** means that beta radiation causes much **less damage** to body tissue.
6) **Beta radiation** is commonly used for controlling the **thickness** of a **material** (see previous page).

## **Gamma** Rays Are Used In **Medicine**

Gamma radiation is even more **weakly ionising** than beta radiation, so will do even **less damage** to body tissue. This means it can be used in medicine:

1) **Radioactive tracers** are used to help **diagnose** patients without the need for **surgery**. A radioactive source with a **short half-life** to prevent prolonged radiation exposure is either eaten or injected into the patient. A **detector**, e.g. a PET scanner, is then used to detect the emitted gamma rays.
2) Gamma rays can be used in the **treatment** of **cancerous tumours** — damaging cells and sometimes curing patients of cancer. Radiation **damages all cells** though — cancerous or not, and so sometimes a **rotating beam** of gamma rays is used. This **lessens** the damage done to surrounding tissue, whilst giving a high dose of radiation to the tumour at the centre of rotation.
3) Damage to other, healthy cells is not completely prevented however and treatment can cause patients to suffer **side effects** — such as tiredness and reddening or soreness of the skin.
4) Exposure to gamma radiation can also cause **long term** side effects like **infertility** for certain treatments.
5) As well as patients, the risks towards **medical staff** giving these treatments must be kept as low as possible. **Exposure time** to radioactive sources is kept to a minimum, and generally staff leave the room (which is itself **shielded**) during treatment.

Eric and his mates knew the importance of a shield.

Simply put, radiation use in medicine has **benefits** and **risks**. The key is trying to use methods which **reduce** the risks (shielding, rotating beams etc.) while still giving you the results you want. It's all one big balancing act.

## Practice Questions

Q1 What makes a nucleus radioactive?

Q2 Name three types of nuclear radiation and give three properties of each.

Q3 Describe how radiation can be used to control the thickness of steel sheets during manufacture.

Q4 Suggest why alpha sources are not used in medical treatments.

**Exam Questions**

Q1 Briefly describe an absorption experiment to distinguish between alpha, beta and gamma radiation. You may wish to include a sketch in your answer. [4 marks]

Q2 Gamma rays are often used in medicine. State one example of where they are used and describe one benefit and one risk of using gamma rays in this way. [3 marks]

## Radioactive emissions — as easy as $\alpha$, $\beta$, $\gamma$...

*You need to learn the different types of radiation and their properties. Remember that alpha particles are by far the most ionising and so cause more damage if they get inside your body than the same dose of any other radiation — which is one reason we don't use alpha sources as medical tracers. Learn this all really well, then go and have a brew.*

# Investigations of Radioactive Emissions

*Radiation is all around us... Not quite as catchy as the original, but it is true at least...*

## *We're **Surrounded** by **Background Radiation***

Put a Geiger counter anywhere and the counter will click — it's detecting **background radiation**.

When you take a reading from a **radioactive source**, you need to measure the **background radiation** separately and **subtract** it from your measurement.

There are many **sources** of background radiation:

1) **The air**: Radioactive **radon gas** is released from **rocks**. It emits alpha radiation. The concentration of this gas in the atmosphere varies a lot from place to place, but it's usually the largest contributor to the background radiation.
2) **The ground and buildings**: **All rock** contains radioactive isotopes.
3) **Cosmic radiation**: Cosmic rays are particles (mostly high-energy protons) from **space**. When they collide with particles in the upper atmosphere, they produce nuclear radiation.
4) **Living things**: All plants and animals contain **carbon**, and some of this will be radioactive **carbon-14**. They also contain other radioactive materials such as potassium-40.
5) **Man-made radiation**: In most areas, radiation from **medical** or **industrial** sources makes up a tiny, tiny fraction of the background radiation.

## *The **Intensity** of **Gamma Radiation** Obeys the **Inverse Square Law***

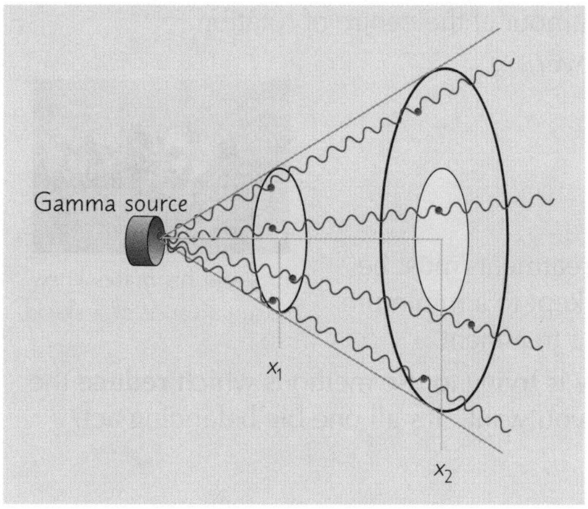


1) A **gamma source** will **emit** gamma **radiation** in **all directions**.
2) This radiation **spreads out** as you get **further away** from the source.
3) This means the amount of **radiation per unit area** (the **intensity**) will **decrease** the further you get from the source.
4) If you took a reading of **intensity**, $I$, at a **distance**, $x$, from the source you would find that it **decreases** by the **square of the distance** from the source.
5) This can be written as the equation:

$$I = \frac{k}{x^2}$$

where k is a constant

6) This **relationship** can be **proved** by taking **measurements of intensity** at different distances from a gamma source, using a **Geiger counter** (see next page).
7) If the **distance** from the source is **doubled**, the **intensity** is found to **fall to a quarter** — which **verifies** the inverse square law.

## *Consider the **Inverse Square Law** When Working With **Radioactive Sources***

1) Using a radioactive source becomes **significantly** more dangerous the closer you get to the source. This is why you should always hold a source **away from your body** when transporting it through the lab.
2) Long handling **tongs** should also be used to minimise the radiation absorbed by the body.
3) For those not working directly with radioactive sources, it's best to just keep as **far away** as possible.

Will thought the roof would be far enough away to be safe.

# Investigations of Radioactive Emissions

## You Can **Investigate** the **Inverse Square Law**

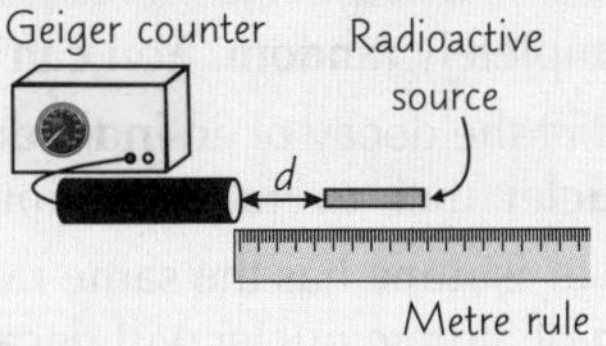


The collection area of the tube stays constant in this experiment, so the intensity of the radiation is proportional to the count rate it records.

1) Set up the equipment as shown in the **diagram**, leaving out the **source** at first.
2) Turn on the Geiger counter and take a reading of the **background radiation count rate** (in counts per sec). Do this **3** times and take an **average**.
3) Place the **tube** of the Geiger counter so it is lined up with the **start** of the rule.
4) Carefully place the radioactive source at a **distance** *d* from the tube.
5) **Record** the count rate at that distance. Do this **3** times and take an **average**.
6) Move the source so the **distance** between it and the Geiger counter doubles (2*d*).
7) Repeat steps 5 and 6 for distances of 3*d*, 4*d* etc.
8) Once the experiment is finished, put away your source **immediately** — you don't want to be exposed to more radiation than you need to be.
9) Correct your data for **background radiation** (previous page). Then plot a graph of **corrected count rate** against **distance** of the counter from the source. You should see that as the distance doubles, the corrected count rate drops to a quarter of its starting value, supporting the **inverse square law**.

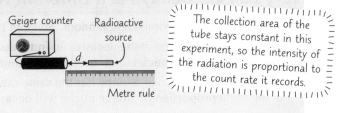

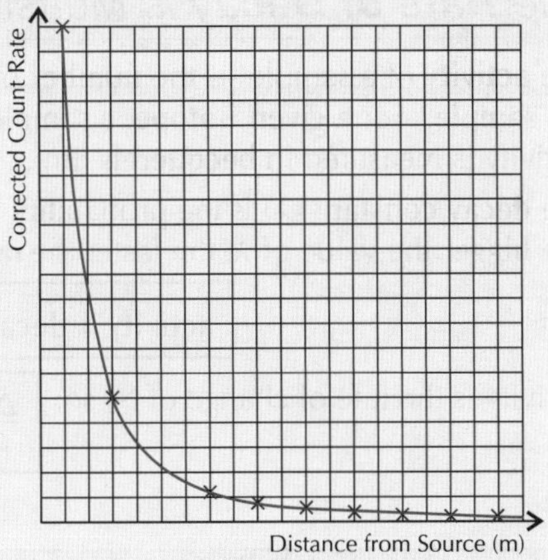


You could also plot a graph of the relative intensity for each distance — both graphs will give you the **same curve**.

## Practice Questions

Q1 Give three sources of background radiation.

Q2 What is usually the largest contributor to background radiation?

Q3 Write down the equation that links intensity and distance from the source for gamma radiation.

Q4 Explain why handling tongs are used to handle radioactive sources, with reference to the inverse square law.

Q5 Briefly describe an experiment you could do to demonstrate the inverse square law for the intensity of gamma radiation.

Q6 Sketch a graph of the relative intensity against distance for a radioactive gamma source.

**Exam Question**

Q1 The count rate detected by a Geiger counter, 10.0 cm from a gamma source, is 240 counts per second (cps) (to 3 s.f.). If the source is removed, there is a count rate of 60 counts per minute (to 2 s.f.).

a) Estimate the counts per second at a distance of 20.0 cm from the source, to the nearest cps. [2 marks]

b) Estimate the counts per second at a distance of 35.0 cm from the source, to the nearest cps. [1 mark]

Q2 A Geiger counter is moved gradually away from a gamma source, and the graph of the corrected count rate per second against distance shown to the right is plotted. Calculate the distance from the source to the Geiger counter at point A. [2 marks]

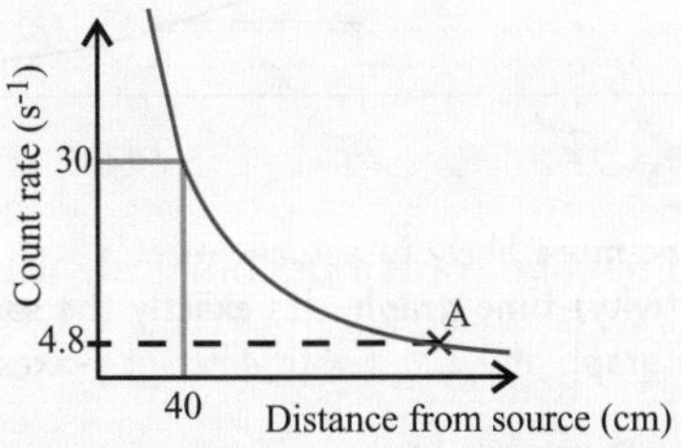


## *Inverse square laws aren't very funny...*

*True, there's nothing particularly fascinating on these pages, but they're also not too difficult — mostly just banging on about this inverse square law and how you can show it. But we don't go on about anything unless it's important, so even though the equation is given in the exam, make sure you are happy sticking numbers in and using it.*

# Exponential Law of Decay

*Oooh look — some more maths. Good.*

## Every Isotope Decays at a Different Rate

1) **Radioactive decay** is completely **random**. You **can't predict which** atom's nucleus will decay **when**.
2) Although you can't predict the decay of an **individual nucleus**, if you take a **very large number of nuclei**, their **overall behaviour** shows a **pattern**.
3) Any sample of a particular **isotope** has the **same rate of decay**, i.e. the same **proportion** of atomic nuclei will **decay** in a **given time**.

> Isotopes of an element have the same number of protons, but different numbers of neutrons in their nuclei.

## The Rate of Decay is Measured by the Decay Constant

The **activity** of a sample — the **number** of nuclei ($N$) that **decay each second** — is **proportional** to the **size of the sample**. For a **given isotope**, a sample **twice** as big would give **twice** the **number of decays** per second. Activity is measured in **becquerels** (Bq). 1 Bq = 1 decay per second.

The **decay constant** ($\lambda$) is the probability of a given nucleus decaying per second. The **bigger** the value of $\lambda$, the faster the rate of decay. Its unit is $s^{-1}$.

**activity = decay constant × number of nuclei or $A = \lambda N$**

> If you get given a molar mass you'll need to calculate the number of moles (p.14). Then, no. atoms = no. moles × Avogadro's constant, $N_A = 6.02 \times 10^{23}$ mol$^{-1}$.

Activity is the rate of change of N, so: $\frac{\Delta N}{\Delta t} = -\lambda N$

There's a negative because the number of atoms left is always decreasing.

> You could model this equation with a spreadsheet — see p.158.

## You Need to Learn the Definition of Half-Life

The **half-life** ($T_{1/2}$) of an **isotope** is the **average time** it takes for the **number of unstable nuclei** to **halve**.

Measuring the **number of unstable nuclei** isn't the easiest job in the world. **In practice**, half-life isn't measured by counting nuclei, but by measuring the **time it takes** the **activity** to **halve**.

The **longer** the **half-life** of an isotope, the **longer** it stays **radioactive**.

## The Number of Undecayed Particles Decreases Exponentially

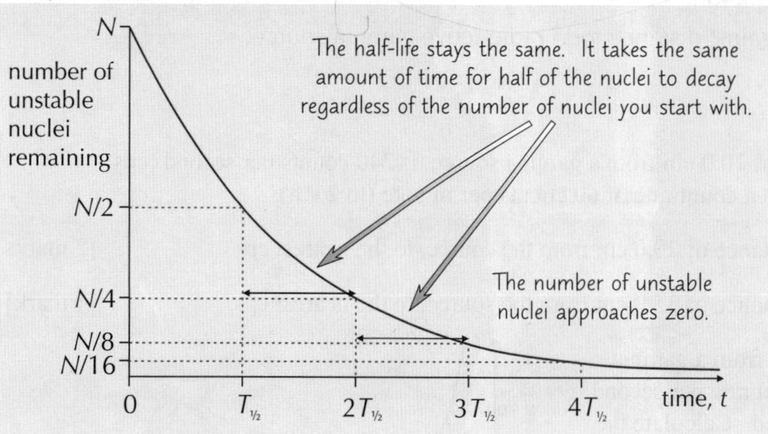


You'd be **more likely** to actually meet a **count rate (activity)-time graph**. It's **exactly the same shape** as the graph above, but with different **y-axes**.

Plotting the natural log ('ln' button on your calculator) of the **number** of radioactive **atoms** (or the activity) against **time** gives a **straight-line** graph (see p.158). The gradient is the negative decay constant. You can use this to **calculate half-life** (next page).

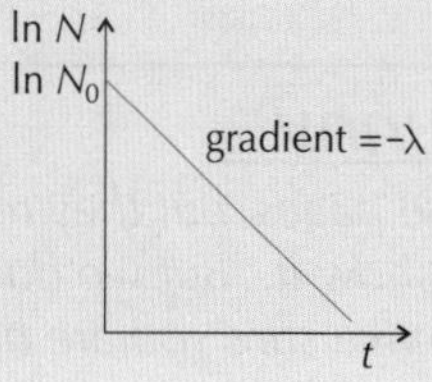


> When you're **measuring** the **activity** and **half-life** of a **source**, you've got to **remember background radiation**. The **background radiation** needs to be **subtracted** from the **activity readings** to give the **source activity**.

**How to find the half-life of an isotope:**

1) Read off the value of count rate (activity) or the particles when $t = 0$.
2) Go to **half** the original value.
3) Draw a horizontal line to the curve, then a vertical line down to the x-axis.
4) Read off the half-life where the line crosses the **x-axis**.
5) Check the units carefully.
6) It's always a good idea to **check** your answer. Repeat steps 1–4 for a quarter the original value. Divide your answer by two. This will also give you the half-life. Check that you get the same answer both ways.

# Exponential Law of Decay

## You Need to Know the Equations for Half-Life and Decay...

1) The number of radioactive nuclei decaying per second (**activity**) is proportional to the number of nuclei remaining.
2) The **half-life** can be **calculated** using the equation:

$$T_{½} = \frac{\ln 2}{\lambda} \approx \frac{0.693}{\lambda}$$

(where ln is the natural log)

3) The **number of unstable nuclei** remaining, $N$, depends on the **number originally** present, $N_0$. The **number remaining** can be calculated using the equation:

$$N = N_0 e^{-\lambda t}$$

4) As a sample decays, its activity goes down — there's an equation for that too:

$$A = A_0 e^{-\lambda t}$$

Here $t$ = time, measured in seconds.

## Different Half-Lives have Different Uses

Radioactive substances are extremely useful. You can use them for all sorts — to **date** organic material, diagnose **medical problems**, **sterilise** food, and in **smoke alarms**. Knowledge about half-lives can be used for:

1) **Radioactive dating of objects** — the radioactive isotope **carbon-14** is used in **radioactive dating**. Living plants take in carbon dioxide from the atmosphere as part of **photosynthesis**, including the **radioactive isotope carbon-14**. When they die, the **activity** of carbon-14 in the plant starts to **fall**, with a **half-life** of around **5730 years**. Archaeological finds made from once living material (like wood) can be tested to find the **current amount** of carbon-14 in them, and date them.
2) **Medical diagnosis** — radioactive tracers (p.55) are used to help diagnose patients. Technetium-99m is suitable for this use because it emits **γ-radiation**, has a **half-life of 6 hours** (long enough for data to be recorded, but short enough to limit the radiation to an acceptable level) and **decays** to a **much more stable isotope**.

## Long Half-Lives can be Dangerous

As well as being useful, radioactive substances can be **dangerous** too (p.55). This is an even bigger problem if the substances stay radioactive for a **long time**. Some isotopes found in waste products of nuclear power generation have incredibly **long half-lives**. This means that we must **plan ahead** about how nuclear waste **will be stored** — e.g. in water tanks or **sealed underground** — to prevent **damage** to the **environment** or **people** not only now but years into the **future** too (p.63).

## Practice Questions

Q1 Define radioactive activity and state the two formulas for calculating it. What unit is it measured in?

Q2 Define what is meant by the decay constant.

Q3 What is meant by the term 'half-life'?

Q4 Sketch a general radioactive decay graph showing the activity of a sample against time and describe how it could be used to find the half-life.

Q5 Describe how radioactive dating works.

**Exam Questions**

Q1 Explain what is meant by the random nature of radioactive decay. [1 mark]

Q2 A reading of 750 Bq is taken from a pure radioactive source. The radioactive source initially contains $8.3 \times 10^{-20}$ moles (to 2 s.f.), and background activity in the lab is measured as 50 Bq (to 2 s.f.).

a) Determine the half-life of this sample. ($N_A = 6.02 \times 10^{23}\ mol^{-1}$) [5 marks]

b) Approximately how many atoms of the radioactive source will there be after 300 seconds? [1 mark]

Q3 Explain the implications of the half-life of highly radioactive nuclear waste on its safe disposal and storage. [2 marks]

## Radioactivity is a random process — just like revision shouldn't be...

*Remember the shape of that graph — whether it's count rate, activity or number of atoms plotted against time, the shape's always the same. Then it's just lots of mathsy stuff — make sure you really practise using all of those equations.*

# Nuclear Decay

*The stuff on these pages covers the most important facts about nuclear decay that you're just going to have to make sure you know inside out. I'd be very surprised if you didn't get a question about it in your exam...*

## Atomic Structure can be Represented Using Standard Notation

**STANDARD NOTATION:**

$$^{12}_{6}\mathrm{C}$$

The **nucleon number** or **mass number** (*A*) — there are a total of 12 protons and neutrons in a carbon-12 atom.

The **proton number** or **atomic number** (*Z*) — there are six protons in a carbon atom.

The symbol for the element carbon.

Atoms with the **same number of protons** but **different numbers of neutrons** are called **isotopes**. The following examples are all isotopes of carbon: $^{12}_{6}\mathrm{C}$, $^{13}_{6}\mathrm{C}$, $^{14}_{6}\mathrm{C}$.

## Some Nuclei are More Stable than Others

The nucleus is under the **influence** of the **strong nuclear force holding** it **together** and the **electromagnetic force pushing** the **protons apart** (you met the electromagnetic force in year 1 of A-level). It's a very **delicate balance**, and it's easy for a nucleus to become **unstable**. You can get a stability graph by plotting ***Z*** (atomic number) against ***N*** (number of neutrons).

A nucleus will be **unstable** if it has:

1) **too many neutrons**
2) **too few neutrons**
3) **too many nucleons** altogether, i.e. it's **too heavy**
4) too much energy

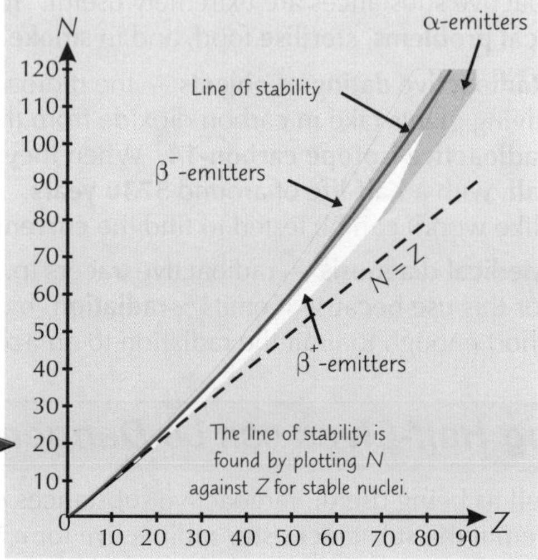


## α Emission Happens in Heavy Nuclei

When an alpha particle is **emitted**:
The **proton number decreases** by **two**, and the **nucleon number decreases** by **four**.

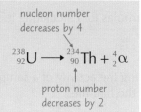

$$^{238}_{92}\mathrm{U} \longrightarrow {}^{234}_{90}\mathrm{Th} + {}^{4}_{2}\alpha$$

nucleon number decreases by 4

proton number decreases by 2

1) **Alpha emission** only happens in **very heavy** atoms, like **uranium** and **radium**.
2) The **nuclei** of these atoms are **too massive** to be stable.

## β⁻ Emission Happens in Neutron Rich Nuclei

1) **Beta-minus** (usually just called beta) decay is the emission of an **electron** from the **nucleus** along with an **antineutrino**.
2) Beta decay happens in isotopes that are **"neutron rich"** (i.e. have many more **neutrons** than **protons** in their nucleus).
3) When a nucleus ejects a beta particle, one of the **neutrons** in the nucleus is **changed** into a **proton**.

In **beta-plus emission**, a **proton** gets **changed** into a **neutron**. The **proton number decreases** by **one**, and the **nucleon number stays the same.**

When a **beta-minus** particle is **emitted**:
The **proton number increases** by **one**, and the **nucleon number stays the same.**

$$^{188}_{75}\mathrm{Re} \longrightarrow {}^{188}_{76}\mathrm{Os} + {}^{0}_{-1}\beta + {}^{0}_{0}\bar{\nu}_e$$

nucleon number stays the same

proton number increases by 1

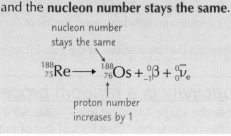

# Nuclear Decay

## γ Radiation is Emitted from Nuclei with Too Much Energy

1) **After alpha** or **beta** decay, the **nucleus** often has **excess energy** — it's **excited**. This energy is **lost** by emitting a **gamma ray**.
2) During **gamma emission**, there is **no change** to the nuclear **constituents** — the nucleus just **loses excess energy**.
3) **Another way** that gamma radiation is produced is when a nucleus **captures** one of its own orbiting **electrons**.
4) **Electron capture** causes a **proton** to **change** into a **neutron**. This makes the **nucleus unstable** and it **emits** gamma radiation.

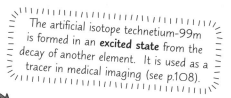

The artificial isotope technetium-99m is formed in an **excited state** from the decay of another element. It is used as a tracer in medical imaging (see p.108).

$$p + e \rightarrow n + \nu_e + \gamma$$

## You Can Draw Energy Level Diagrams for Nuclear Reactions

**Energy level diagrams** are used to represent these radioactive processes.

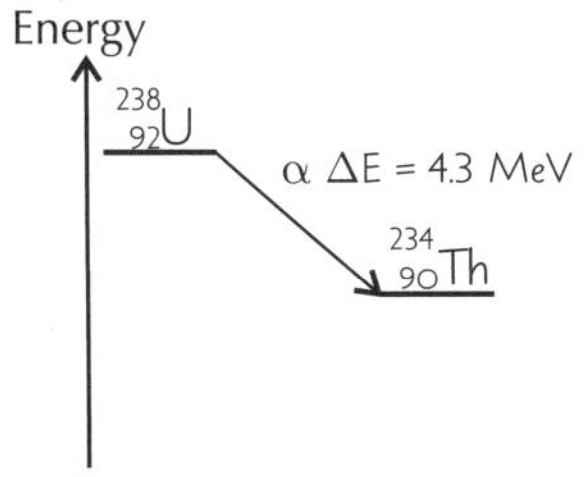


An alpha decay

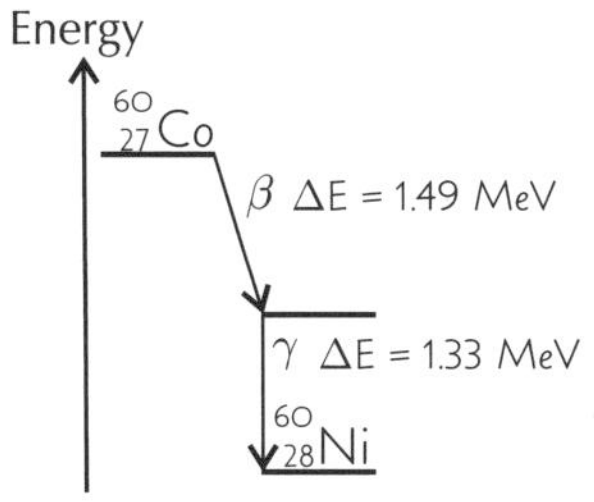


A beta decay followed by gamma emission

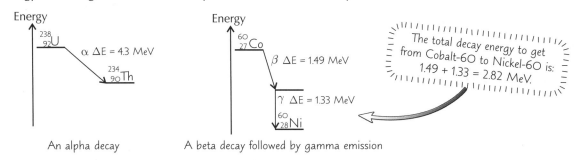

The total decay energy to get from Cobalt-60 to Nickel-60 is: 1.49 + 1.33 = 2.82 MeV.

## There are Conservation Rules in Nuclear Reactions

In every nuclear reaction **energy, momentum, charge** and **nucleon number** must be conserved.

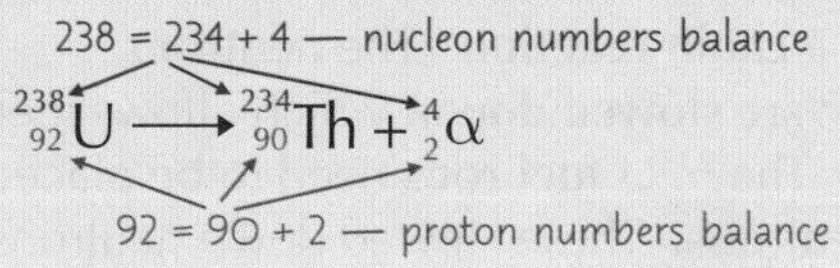

238 = 234 + 4 — nucleon numbers balance
$^{238}_{92}U \longrightarrow ^{234}_{90}Th + ^{4}_{2}\alpha$
92 = 90 + 2 — proton numbers balance

Eugene was all about balance.

## Practice Questions

Q1 Sketch a graph of *N* against *Z*, marking on the line of stability and the regions where beta-minus and alpha decays occur.

Q2 What can make a nucleus unstable?

Q3 Describe the changes that happen in the nucleus during alpha, beta-minus, beta-plus and gamma decay.

Q4 What is the isotope technetium-99m used for?

Q5 List the circumstances in which gamma radiation may be emitted.

Q6 Draw an energy level diagram for a nucleus $^{14}_{6}C$ that undergoes beta decay and releases 0.16 MeV of energy.

**Exam Questions**

Q1 Radium-226 undergoes alpha decay to radon, releasing 4.78 MeV of energy.

a) Complete the balanced nuclear equation for this reaction. $^{226}_{88}Ra \rightarrow Rn$ [2 marks]

b) Draw an energy level diagram showing this transition. [1 mark]

Q2 Potassium-40 ($Z = 19$, $A = 40$) undergoes beta decay to calcium. Write a balanced nuclear equation for this reaction. [3 marks]

## Nuclear decay — it can be enough to make you unstable...

*Unstable nuclei will decay, and energy, momentum, proton number and nucleon number are conserved when they do. Make sure you learn how to draw and read those level diagrams — you could be asked about them in your exam.*

# Nuclear Fission and Fusion

*Nuclear power provides shed-loads of energy whilst not creating as many greenhouse gases as traditional fossil fuels.*

## Fission Means Splitting Up into Smaller Parts

1) **Large nuclei**, with at least 83 protons (e.g. uranium), are **unstable** and some can randomly **split** into two **smaller** nuclei — this is called **nuclear fission**.
2) This process is called **spontaneous** if it just happens **by itself**, or **induced** if we **encourage** it to happen.
3) Fission can be **induced** by making a neutron enter a $^{235}U$ nucleus, causing it to become very unstable. Only **low energy** neutrons (called **thermal neutrons**) can be captured in this way.
4) **Energy is released** during nuclear fission because the new, smaller nuclei have a **higher binding energy per nucleon** (see p. 64).
5) The **larger** the nucleus, the more **unstable** it will be — so large nuclei are **more likely** to **spontaneously fission**.
6) This means that spontaneous fission **limits** the **number of nucleons** that a nucleus can contain — in other words, it **limits** the number of **possible elements**.

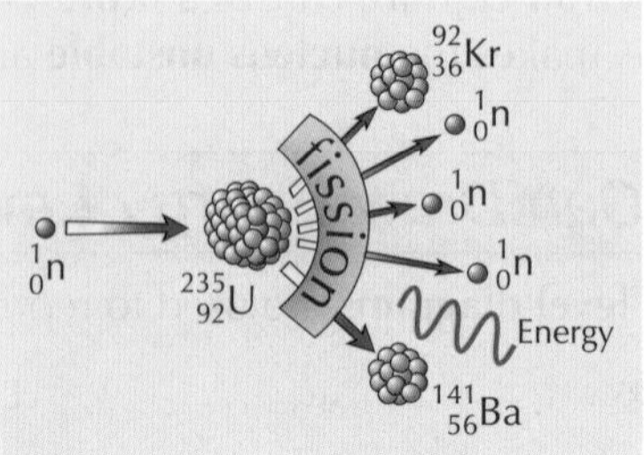


## Controlled Nuclear Reactors Produce Useful Power

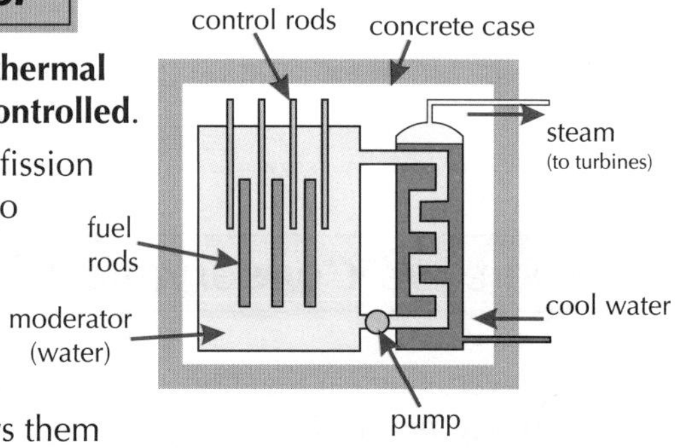


We can **harness** the **energy** released during nuclear **fission reactions** in a **thermal nuclear reactor**, but it's important that these reactions are very **carefully controlled**.

1) Nuclear reactors use **rods of uranium** that are rich in $^{235}$**U** as '**fuel**' for fission reactions. (The rods also contain a lot of $^{238}$**U**, but that doesn't undergo fission.) These are placed into the reactor **remotely** which keeps workers as far away from the radiation as possible (p.56).
2) These **fission** reactions produce more **neutrons** which then **induce** other nuclei to fission — this is called a **chain reaction**. The **neutrons** will only cause a chain reaction if they are **slowed down**, which allows them to be **captured** by the uranium nuclei. The $^{235}U$ **fuel rods** need to be placed in a **moderator** (for example, **water**) to further **slow down** and/or absorb **neutrons.** These slowed down neutrons are called **thermal neutrons.**
3) This happens through **elastic collisions** (kinetic energy is conserved) with **nuclei** of the moderator material. Choosing a moderator with a **similar mass** to the neutrons (e.g. **water**) is more efficient at **slowing** neutrons down.
4) You want the chain reaction to continue on its own at a **steady rate**, where **one** fission follows another. The amount of 'fuel' you need to do this is called the **critical mass** — any less than the critical mass (**sub-critical mass**) and the reaction will just peter out. Nuclear reactors use a **supercritical** mass of fuel (where several new fissions normally follow each fission) and **control the rate of fission** using **control rods**.
5) Control rods control the **chain reaction** by **limiting** the number of **neutrons** in the reactor. These **absorb neutrons** so that the **rate of fission** is controlled. **Control rods** are made up of a material that **absorbs neutrons** (e.g. boron), and they can be inserted by varying amounts to control the reaction rate. In an **emergency**, the reactor will be **shut down** automatically by the **release of the control rods** into the reactor, which will stop the reaction as quickly as possible.
6) **Coolant** is sent around the reactor to **remove heat** produced in the fission — often the coolant is the **same water** that is being used in the reactor as a **moderator**. The **heat** from the reactor can then be used to make **steam** for powering **electricity-generating turbines**.
7) The nuclear reactor is surrounded by a thick **concrete case**, which acts as **shielding**. This prevents **radiation escaping** and reaching the people working in the power station.

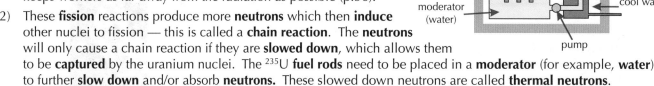

The neutrons are first slowed from very high speeds by inelastic collisions with U-238 but you don't need to know about those.

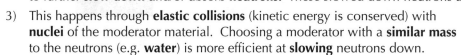

If the chain reaction in a nuclear reactor is **left to continue unchecked**, large amounts of **energy** are **released** in a very **short time**. **Many new fissions** will follow each fission, causing a **runaway reaction** which could lead to an **explosion**. This is what happens in a **fission (atomic) bomb**.

Before a new power plant is built, it has to be decided whether the benefits of nuclear power outweigh the risks (e.g. power plant meltdowns). Shielding and control rods help to reduce the risks involved with using nuclear power. It will never be risk-free but there are lots of measures in place to make it as safe as possible. A good understanding of nuclear physics can help society to make informed decisions about how electricity should be generated.

# Nuclear Fission and Fusion

## *Waste Products of Fission Must be Stored Carefully*

1) Although nuclear fission produces **lots** of **energy** and creates less **greenhouse gases** than burning fossil fuels, there are still lots of dangerous waste products.
2) The **waste products** of **nuclear fission** usually have a **larger proportion of neutrons** than nuclei of a similar atomic number — this makes them **unstable** and **radioactive**.
3) The products can be used for **practical applications** such as **tracers** in medical diagnosis (see p.108).
4) However, they may be **highly radioactive** and so their **handling** and **storage** needs **great care**.
5) When material is removed from the reactor, it is initially **very hot**, so is placed in **cooling ponds** until the **temperature falls** to a safe level.
6) This is done **remotely** — just like the handling of **fuel** — to limit the radiation workers are exposed to.
7) The radioactive waste is then **stored** in **sealed containers** until its **activity has fallen** sufficiently. Areas for storage are chosen where there will be **minimal impact** on animals and the environment — and any **people** that live nearby are **consulted** about the decision to store nuclear waste near them.

## *Fusion Means Joining Nuclei Together*

1) **Two light nuclei** can **combine** to create a larger nucleus — this is called **nuclear fusion**.
2) A lot of **energy** is released during nuclear fusion because the new, heavier nuclei have a **much higher binding energy per nucleon** (see p.64).

In the Sun, **hydrogen nuclei** fuse in a series of reactions to form **helium**.

e.g. $^{2}_{1}H + ^{1}_{1}H \rightarrow ^{3}_{2}He + \text{energy}$

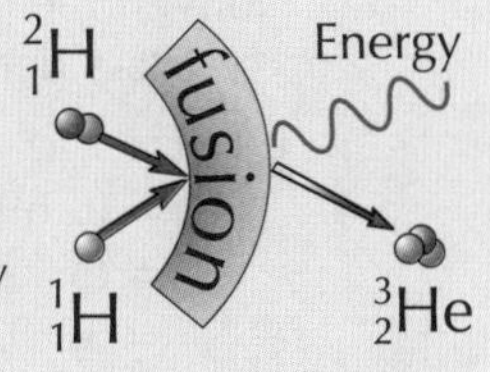


### *Nuclei Need Lots of Energy to Fuse*

1) All nuclei are **positively charged** — so there will be an **electrostatic** (or Coulomb) **force** of **repulsion** between them.
2) Nuclei can only **fuse** if they **overcome** this electrostatic force and get **close** enough for the attractive force of the **strong interaction** to hold them both together.
3) About **1 MeV** of kinetic energy is **needed** to make nuclei fuse together — and that's **a lot of energy**.

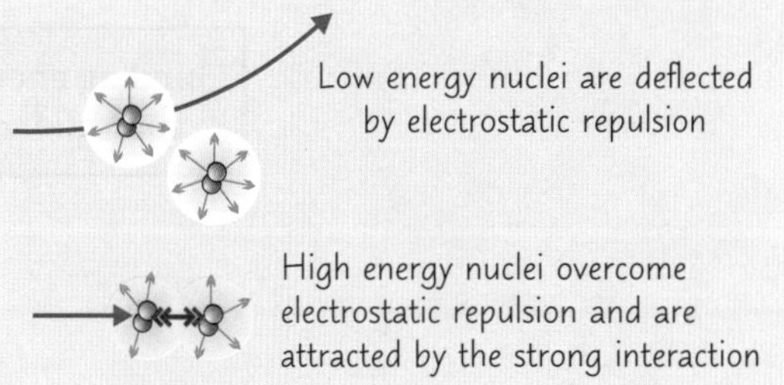

Low energy nuclei are deflected by electrostatic repulsion
High energy nuclei overcome electrostatic repulsion and are attracted by the strong interaction


## *Practice Questions*

Q1 What is the difference between spontaneous and induced fission and how can fission be induced in $^{235}U$?

Q2 Describe and explain the roles of the moderator, coolant and shielding in a nuclear reactor, giving examples of the materials commonly used for them and the reasons for choosing these materials.

Q3 Why must the waste products of nuclear fission be handled remotely and disposed of very carefully?

Q4 Why is a lot of energy required for nuclear fusion to occur?

**Exam Questions**

Q1 Nuclear reactors use carefully controlled chain reactions to produce energy.

a) Explain what is meant by the expressions 'chain reaction' and 'critical mass' in terms of nuclear fission. [3 marks]

b) State one feature of a nuclear reactor whose role is to control the rate of fission and describe how it works. Include an example of a suitable material for the feature you have chosen. [3 marks]

c) Explain what happens in a nuclear reactor during an emergency shut-down. [2 marks]

Q2 State two advantages and two disadvantages of using nuclear fission to produce electricity. [4 marks]

## *If anyone asks, I've gone fission... that joke never gets old...*

*So many words... But all of them pretty important. You already knew fission created loads of energy, but now you have to learn all the grizzly details about how reactors actually work and what to do with all the waste they produce.*

# Binding Energy

*Turn off the radio and close the door, 'cos you're going to need to concentrate hard on this stuff about binding energy...*

## *The **Mass Defect** is **Equivalent** to the **Binding Energy***

1) The **mass** of a **nucleus** is **less than** the mass of its **constituent parts** — the difference is called the **mass defect**.
2) Einstein's equation, $\boldsymbol{E = mc^2}$, says that mass and energy are **equivalent**. It applies to **all** energy changes.
3) So, as nucleons join together, the total mass **decreases** — this '**lost**' mass is **converted** into energy and **released**.
4) The amount of **energy released** is **equivalent** to the **mass defect**.
5) If you **pulled** the nucleus completely **apart**, the **energy** you'd have to use to do it would be the **same** as the energy **released** when the nucleus formed.

The energy needed to **separate** all of the nucleons in a nucleus is called the **binding energy** (measured in **MeV**), and it is **equivalent** to the **mass defect**.

**Example:** Estimate the binding energy in eV of the nucleus of a lithium atom, $^6_3\text{Li}$, given that its mass defect is 0.0343 u.

1) Convert the mass defect into kg.
   Mass defect = $0.0343 \times (1.661 \times 10^{-27}) = 5.697... \times 10^{-29}$
2) Use $E = mc^2$ to calculate the binding energy.
   $E = (5.697... \times 10^{-29}) \times (3.00 \times 10^8)^2 = 5.127... \times 10^{-12}$ J
   $= (5.127... \times 10^{-12}) \div (1.60 \times 10^{-13})$
   $= 32.0...$ MeV = **32.0 MeV (to 3 s.f.)**

Atomic mass is usually given in atomic mass units (u) where 1 u = $1.661 \times 10^{-27}$ kg

1 MeV = $1.60 \times 10^{-13}$ J

Captain Skip didn't believe in ghosts, marmalade and that things could be bound without rope.

6) A mass defect of **1 u** is equivalent to about **931.5 MeV** of binding energy.

$$\frac{\textbf{binding energy}}{\textbf{mass defect}} \approx \textbf{931.5 MeVu}^{-1}$$

You could get 1 u equivalent to 931.75 MeV using the numbers on this page. The value of 931.5 MeV is found from using more precise values of u, c and e.

## *The **Average Binding Energy Per Nucleon** is at a **Maximum** around **N = 50***

A useful way of **comparing** the binding energies of different nuclei is to look at the average **binding energy per nucleon**.

$$\textbf{Average binding energy per nucleon (in MeV)} = \frac{\textbf{Binding energy } (B)}{\textbf{Nucleon number } (A)}$$

So, the binding energy per nucleon for $^6_3\text{Li}$ (in the example above) is 32 ÷ 6 = 5.3 MeV.

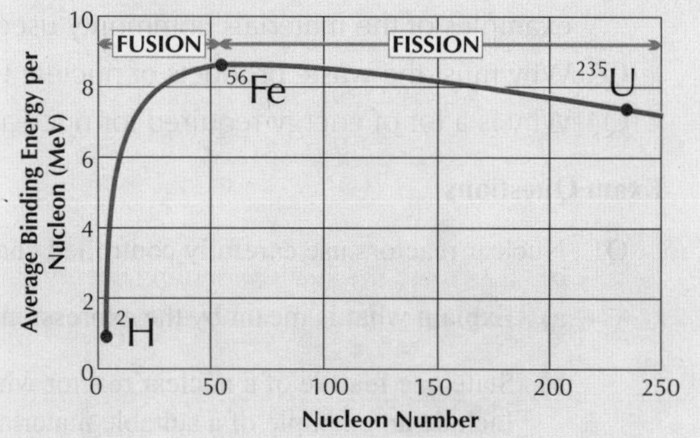


1) A **graph** of **average binding energy per nucleon** against **nucleon number**, for all elements, shows a **curve**. **High** average binding energy per nucleon means that **more energy** is needed to **remove** nucleons from the nucleus.
2) In other words, the **most stable** nuclei occur around the **maximum point** on the graph — which is at **nucleon number 56** (i.e. **iron**, Fe).
3) **Combining small nuclei** is called nuclear **fusion** (see p.63) — this **increases** the **average binding energy per nucleon** dramatically, which means a lot of **energy is released** during nuclear fusion.
4) **Fission** is when **large nuclei** are **split in two** (see p.62) — the **nucleon numbers** of the two **new nuclei** are **smaller** than the original nucleus, which means there is an **increase** in the average binding energy per nucleon. So, energy is also **released** during nuclear fission (but not as much energy per nucleon as in nuclear fusion).

# Binding Energy

## The Change in Average Binding Energy Gives the Energy Released

The average **binding energy per nucleon graph** can be used to **estimate** the **energy released** from nuclear reactions.

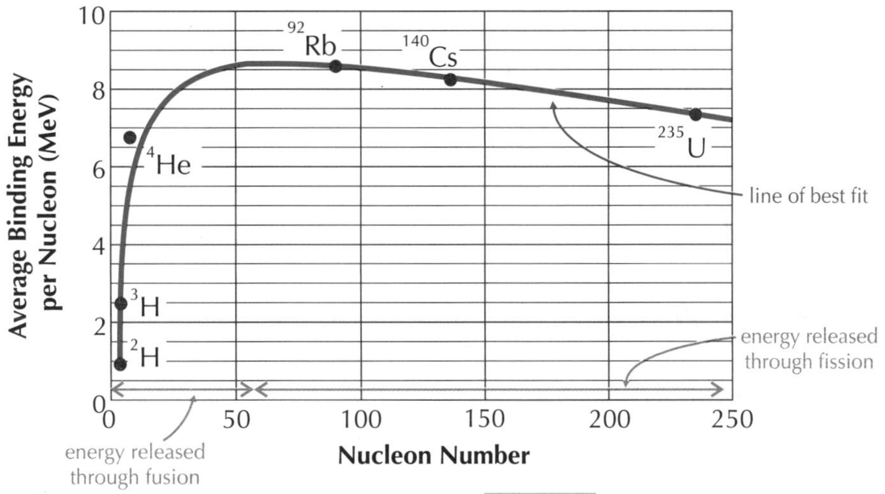


**Fusion**

1) $^4$**He** nuclei have **4 nucleons**, so the **binding energy** of $^4$He = 4 × 6.8 = **27.2 MeV**.
2) The binding energy of $^2$**H** and $^3$**H** = (2 × 1.0) + (3 × 2.6) = **9.8 MeV**.
3) So if $^2$H and $^3$H nuclei were **fused** together to form $^4$He (and a neutron), the **energy released** would be **27.2 – 9.8 = 17 MeV**.

**Fission**

1. The **binding energy** of $^{235}$U = 235 × 7.4 = **1739 MeV**.
2. The binding energy of $^{92}$**Rb** and $^{140}$**Cs** = (92 × 8.8) + (140 × 8.2) = **1957.6 MeV**.
3. So if a $^{235}$U nucleus **splits** into $^{92}$**Rb** and $^{140}$**Cs** (plus a few neutrons) during nuclear **fission**, the **energy released** would be = 1957.6 – 1739 = 218.6 = **220 MeV** (to 2 s.f.)

## Practice Questions

Q1 State the formula relating energy to mass and the speed of a light in a vacuum.

Q2 What is the binding energy of a nucleus?

Q3 What is the binding energy in MeV equivalent to a mass defect of 1 u?

Q4 What is meant by the binding energy per nucleon?

Q5 Sketch a graph of average binding energy per nucleon against nucleon number, labelling the regions where fusion and fission occur and the element with the highest average binding energy per nucleon.

Q6 How would you calculate the energy released by a fission reaction, given the masses of the products and reactants?

**Exam Questions**

Q1 The mass defect of a uranium-235 nucleus is 1.864557 u.

a) Calculate the binding energy, in joules, of a uranium-235 nucleus. *(1 MeV = 1.60 × 10$^{-13}$ J)* [2 marks]

b) Calculate the average binding energy (in MeV) per nucleon for uranium-235. [1 mark]

Q2 The following equation represents a nuclear reaction that takes place in the Sun:

$$^1_1p + ^1_1p \rightarrow ^2_1H + ^0_{+1}\beta^+$$ where p is a proton and $\beta^+$ is a positron

a) State the type of nuclear reaction shown. [1 mark]

b) Given that the binding energy per nucleon for a proton is 0 MeV and for a $^2_1$H nucleus it is approximately 0.86 MeV, estimate the energy released by this reaction. [2 marks]

## *A mass defect of 1 u is equivalent to a binding energy of 931.5 MeV...*

*Remember this useful little fact, and it'll save loads of time in the exam — because you won't have to fiddle around with converting atomic mass from u to kg and binding energy from J to MeV. What more could you possibly want...*

# Optical Telescopes

*Some optical telescopes use lenses (no, really), so first, here's a bit of lens theory...*

## **Converging** Lenses Bring Light Rays **Together**

1) **Lenses** change the **direction** of light rays by **refraction**.
2) Rays **parallel** to the **principal axis** of the lens converge onto a point called the **principal focus**. Parallel rays that **aren't** parallel to the principal axis converge somewhere else on the **focal plane** (see diagram).
3) The **focal length**, ***f***, is the distance between the **lens axis** and the **focal plane**.

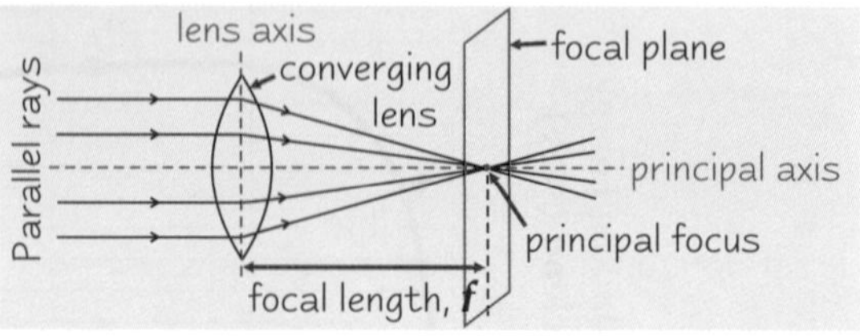


## ***Images*** *can be* ***Real*** *or* ***Virtual***

1) A **real image** is formed when light rays from an object are made to **pass through** another point in space. The light rays are **actually there**, and the image can be **captured** on a **screen**.
2) A **virtual image** is formed when light rays from an object **appear** to have come from another point in space. The light rays **aren't really where the image appears to be**, so the image **can't** be captured on a screen.
3) Converging lenses can form both **real** and **virtual** images, depending on where the object is. If the object is **further** than the **focal length** away from the lens, the image is **real**. If the object's **closer**, the image is **virtual**.
4) To work out where an image will appear, you can draw a **ray diagram**. Draw **two rays** from the same point on the object (the top is best) one **parallel** to the principal axis that passes through the **principal focus**, and one passing through the **centre** of the lens that **doesn't get refracted** (bent). The image will form where the **two rays meet** if the image is real, or where the two rays appear to have **come from** if the image is virtual:

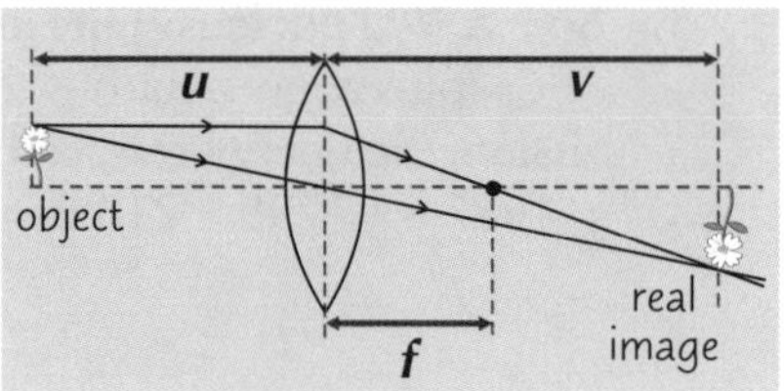


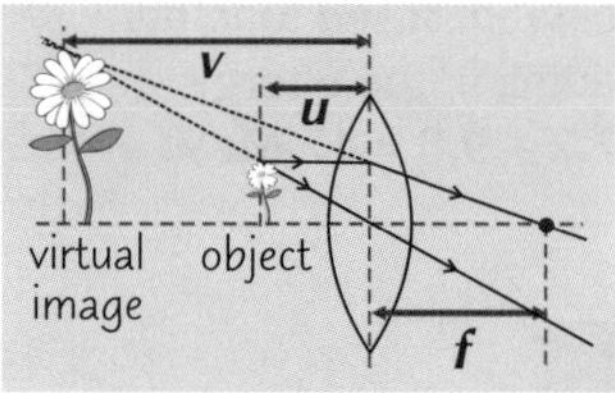


If an object sits on the principal axis, so will the image.

In the diagram, ***u*** = distance between object and lens axis, ***v*** = distance between image and lens axis (**positive** if image is **real**, **negative** if image is **virtual**), ***f*** = focal length.

4) The values ***u***, ***v*** and ***f*** are related by the **lens equation**:

$$\frac{1}{f} = \frac{1}{u} + \frac{1}{v}$$

## *A* ***Refracting Telescope*** *uses* ***Two*** *Converging Lenses*

1) The **objective lens** converges the rays from the object to form a **real image**.
2) The **eye lens** acts as a **magnifying glass** on this real image to form a **magnified virtual image**.

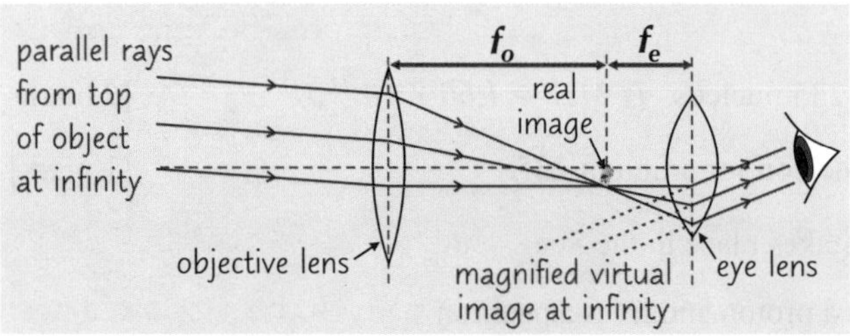


3) If you assume the object is at infinity, then the rays from it are **parallel**, and the real image is formed on the **focal plane**.
4) A **telescope** (in normal adjustment) is set up so that the **principal focus** of the **objective** lens is in the **same position** as the principal focus of the **eye** lens, so the **final magnified image** appears to be at **infinity**.
5) The **magnification**, ***M***, of the telescope can be calculated in terms of angles, or the focal length. The **angular magnification** is the **angle** subtended by the **image** $\theta_i$ over the **angle** subtended by the **object** $\theta_o$ at the eye:

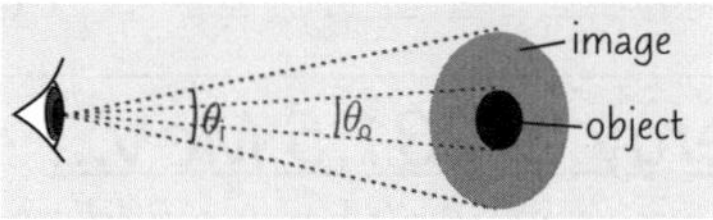


$$M = \frac{\theta_i}{\theta_o}$$

or in terms of **focal length** (with the telescope in normal adjustment as shown above):

$$M = \frac{f_o}{f_e}$$

A large magnification is needed — so $f_o > f_e$

# Optical Telescopes

## A Reflecting Telescope use Two Mirrors and a Converging Lens

1) A **parabolic concave mirror** (the **primary mirror**) converges parallel rays from an object, forming a **real image**.
2) An **eye lens magnifies** the image as before.
3) The principle focus of the mirror (where the image is formed) is **in front** of the mirror, so an arrangement needs to be devised where the observer doesn't **block out** the light.
4) A set-up called the **Cassegrain arrangement**, which uses a **convex secondary mirror**, is a common solution to this problem.

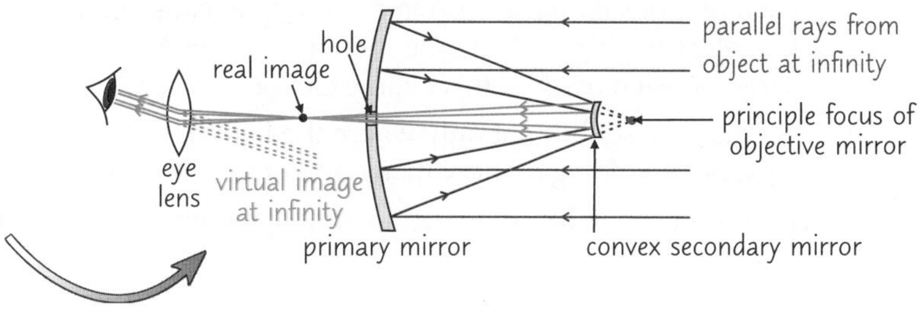


## The Resolving Power of a Telescope — How Much Detail You Can See

1) The **resolving power** of a telescope is just a **measure** of how much **detail** you can see. It's dependent on the **minimum angular resolution** — the **smallest** angular **separation** at which the instrument can **distinguish two points**. The **smaller** the minimum angular resolution, the **better** the resolving power.

About half of the stars that we see in the night sky are actually collections of two or more stars. Our eyes see them as a single star since the angle between them is too small to resolve.

2) Resolution is limited by diffraction. If a beam of light passes through a circular **aperture**, then a **diffraction pattern** is formed. The central circle is called the **Airy disc** (see p. 144 for an example of the pattern).
3) **Two** light sources can **just** be distinguished if the **centre** of the **Airy disc** from one source is **at least as far away** as the **first minimum** of the other source. This led to the **Rayleigh criterion**:

$$\theta \approx \frac{\lambda}{D}$$

where $\theta$ is the **minimum angular resolution**, $\lambda$ is the **wavelength** of the light in **metres** and $D$ is the **diameter** of the **aperture** in **metres**.

4) For **telescopes**, $D$ is the diameter of the **objective lens** or the **objective mirror**. So **very large** lenses or mirrors are needed to see **fine detail**.

## There are Big Problems with Refracting Telescopes

1) Glass refracts **different colours** of light by **different amounts** and so the image for each colour is in a slightly **different position**. This **blurs** the image and is called **chromatic aberration**.
2) Any **bubbles** and **impurities** in the glass **absorb** some of the light, which means that **very faint** objects **aren't seen**. Building large lenses that are of a **sufficiently good quality** is **difficult** and **expensive**.

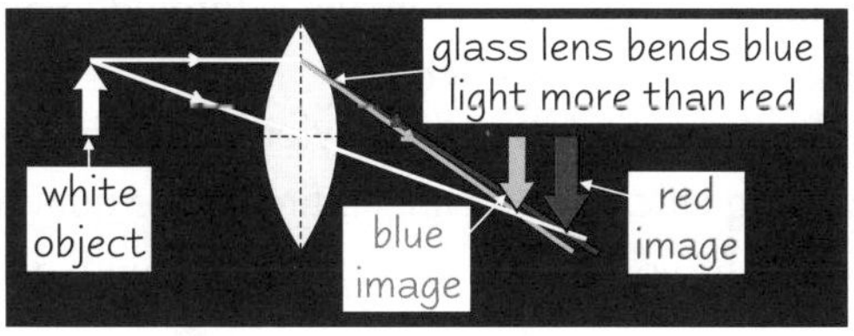


3) **Large lenses** are very **heavy** and can only be **supported** from their **edges**, so their **shape** can become **distorted**.
4) For a **large magnification**, the **objective lens** needs to have a **very long focal length**. This means that refracting telescopes have to be **very long**, leading to very **large** and **expensive buildings** needed to house them.

## Reflecting Telescopes are Better than Refractors but Still Have Problems

1) **Large mirrors** of **good quality** are much **cheaper** to build than large lenses. They can also be **supported** from **underneath** so they don't **distort** as much as lenses.
2) Mirrors don't suffer from **chromatic aberration** (see above) but can have **spherical aberration**:

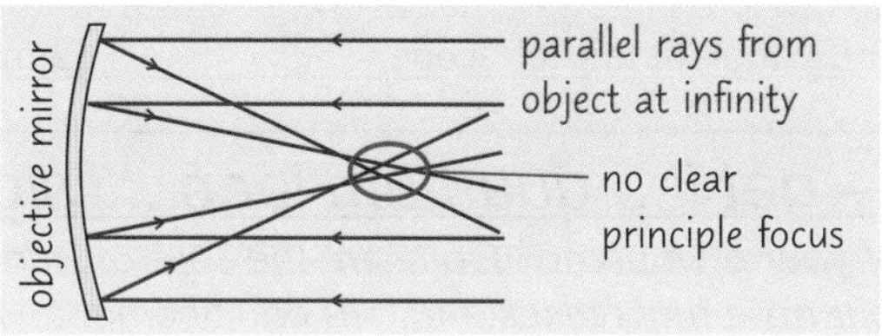


If the **shape** of the mirror isn't quite **parabolic**, parallel rays reflecting off different parts of the mirror do not all **converge** onto the same point.

When the **Hubble Space Telescope** was first launched it suffered from **spherical aberration**. They had to find a way round the problem before it could be used.

# Optical Telescopes

## Charge-Coupled Devices (CCDs) are Very Sensitive Image Detectors

1) CCDs are **silicon chips** about the size of a postage stamp, divided up into a grid of millions of **identical pixels**.
2) When photons hit the silicon in a pixel, they cause **electrons** to be released (via the photoelectric effect, which you met in year 1 of A-level). These electrons alter the charge on each pixel — this charge can be measured and used to create a **digital signal**.
3) This signal describes not only **where** the light hits, but its **brightness/intensity** too, as the charge on each pixel will vary depending on how many photons hit it. This allows a **digital image** of an object to be created.
4) CCDs are used in **lots** of places — **digital cameras**, barcode scanners and giant astronomical **telescopes**.

## CCDs and the Human Eye can be Compared as Image Detectors

1) **Quantum Efficiency** — Quantum efficiency is the **proportion** of the incident photons that are **detected**. For a CCD it's typically **80%** or more. The quantum efficiency of the eye is of the order of **1%**, so **CCDs detect far more** of the light that falls on them than the eye does.
2) **Detectable Light Spectrum** — The eye can only detect **visible light**, whereas CCDs can detect **infrared**, **visible** and **UV** light.
3) **Resolution** — If you were to project the **whole visual field** of an eye onto a screen, you'd need over **500 megapixels** for the eye not to see any **pixelation**. CCDs on the other hand have of the order of **50 megapixels**, so it seems like the eye **captures more** detail than a CCD. However, what's also important is how **far apart** different parts of the object being viewed need to be in order for them to be **distinguishable** — this is called **spatial resolution**. The minimum resolvable distance of the human eye is around **100 μm**, whereas CCDs can have a spatial resolution of around **10 μm**. So CCDs are **better** for capturing **fine detail**.
4) **Convenience** — The human eye doesn't need any **extra equipment**, and looking down a telescope is **simpler** than setting up a CCD, but CCDs produce **digital images** which can be **stored**, **copied**, and **shared** globally.

The numbers here are a bit rough and ready — it's hard to measure things like quantum efficiency for the eye, and CCDs come with a range of different specifications. You may be asked about these figures in the exam, so make sure you learn them, but remember they're only a rough guide.

## Practice Questions

Q1 Define the focal length and principal focus of a converging lens.

Q2 Draw ray diagrams to show how an image is formed in a refracting telescope in normal adjustment and a reflecting (Cassegrain) telescope.

Q3 Explain resolving power and state the Rayleigh criterion.

Q4 What does quantum efficiency mean? Estimate the quantum efficiency of a CCD.

Q5 Give two reasons why you would use a telescope with a CCD to collect data instead of one without a CCD.

**Exam Questions**

Q1 a) A telescope has a dish diameter of 1.6 m. It is being used to detect light with wavelength 620 nm from two stars. Calculate the minimum angular separation of the two stars in order for them to be distinguishable by the telescope. [1 mark]

b) If the dish of the telescope is made smaller, explain what happens to its resolving power. [1 mark]

Q2 An objective lens with a focal length of 5.0 m and an eye lens with a focal length of 0.10 m are used in a refracting telescope.

a) Calculate how far apart the lenses should be placed for the telescope to be in normal adjustment. [1 mark]

b) Define angular magnification and calculate the angular magnification of this telescope. [2 marks]

## CCDs were a quantum leap for astronomy — get it... quantum leap... *sigh*

*With CCDs, you can get all the images you want from the comfort of your own home. Gone are the days of standing on a hill with a telescope and a flask hoping the sky clears before your nose turns black and falls off. Shame.*

# Non-Optical Telescopes

*Some telescopes don't use visible light — they use radio waves, IR, UV or X-rays instead — read on to learn more...*

## ***Radio*** *Telescopes are* ***Similar*** *to* ***Optical*** *Telescopes in Some Ways*

1) The most obvious feature of a radio telescope is its **parabolic dish**. This works in exactly the same way as the **objective mirror** of an **optical reflecting** telescope.
2) An **antenna** is used as a detector at the **focal point** instead of an eye or camera in an optical telescope, but there is **no equivalent** to the **eye lens**.

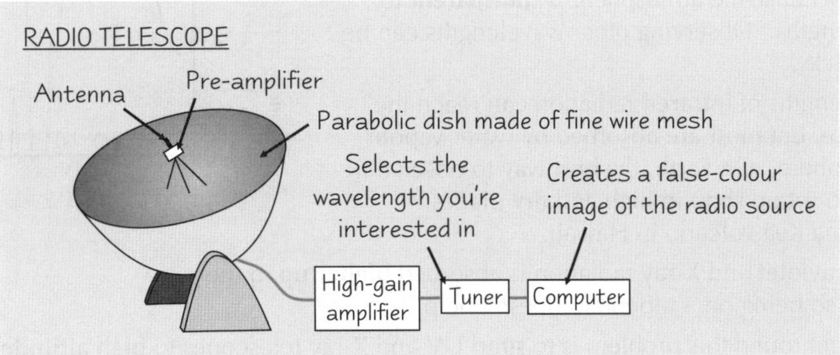


3) Most radio telescopes are **manoeuvrable**, allowing the source of the waves to be **tracked** (in the same way as optical telescopes). The telescope moves with the source, stopping it 'slipping out of view' as the Earth rotates.

## ***Radio Waves*** *have a Much* ***Longer Wavelength*** *than Light...*

1) The **wavelengths** of **radio waves** are about a **million times longer** than the wavelengths of **light**.
2) The **resolving power** of a telescope is dependent on the **Rayleigh criterion** (see p.67), which is $\theta \approx \lambda/D$.
3) So for a radio telescope to have the **same resolving power** as an optical telescope, its dish would need to be a **million times bigger** (about the size of the UK for a decent one). The **resolving power** of a radio telescope is **worse** than the **unaided eye**.

Radio astronomers get around this by **linking** lots of telescopes together.
Using some nifty computer programming, their data can be combined to form a **single image**. This is equivalent to one **huge dish** the size of the **separation** of the telescopes.
Resolutions **thousands** of times better than optical telescopes can be achieved this way.

## *...so* ***Radio*** *Telescopes aren't as* ***Fiddly*** *to Make as Optical Reflectors*

1) Instead of a **polished mirror**, a **wire mesh** can be used since the long wavelength radio waves don't notice the gaps. This makes their **construction** much **easier** and **cheaper** than optical reflectors.
2) The **shape** of the dish has to have a **precision** of about $\lambda/20$ to avoid **spherical aberration** (see page 67). So the dish does not have to be **anywhere near as perfect** as a mirror.
3) However, unlike an optical telescope, a radio telescope has to **scan across** the radio source to **build up** the **image**.

# Non-Optical Telescopes

## The Atmosphere Blocks Certain EM Wavelengths

1) One of the big problems with doing astronomy on Earth is trying to look through the atmosphere.
2) Our atmosphere only lets **certain wavelengths** of **electromagnetic radiation** through and is **opaque** to all the others. The graph shows how the **transparency** of the atmosphere varies with **wavelength**.

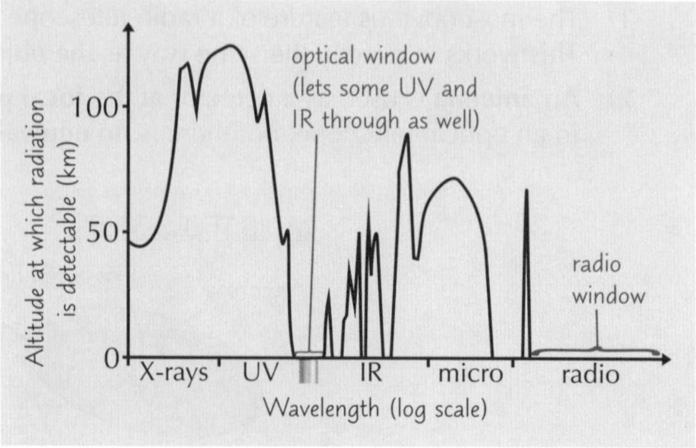


3) We can use **optical** and **radio** telescopes on the surface of the Earth because the atmosphere is **transparent** to these wavelengths. Observing other wavelengths can be a bit more tricky.
4) A few wavelengths of **infrared** radiation can reach the Earth's surface, but most are absorbed by water vapour in the atmosphere. On Earth, the best way to observe IR radiation is to set up shop in **high** and **dry** places, like the Mauna Kea volcano in Hawaii.
5) But most **ultraviolet** and **X-ray** radiation is absorbed **higher up** in the atmosphere, so being on a mountain doesn't help.
6) One way to get round this problem is to strap UV and X-ray telescopes to **high altitude weather balloons** or **aeroplanes**. They can take the telescope high enough into the atmosphere to detect the radiation.
7) The ideal situation is to get your telescope **above the atmosphere** altogether, by launching it into **space** and setting it in orbit around the Earth.

## IR and UV Telescopes have a Very Similar Structure to Optical Telescopes

1) Infrared and ultraviolet telescopes are very similar to optical reflecting telescopes. They use the same **parabolic mirror** set-up to focus the radiation onto a detector.
2) In both cases, **CCDs** (see p. 68) or **special photographic paper** are used as the radiation detectors, just as in optical telescopes.
3) The **longer** the **wavelength** of the radiation, the **less** it's affected by imperfections in the mirror (see previous page). So the mirrors in **infrared** telescopes **don't** need to be as perfectly shaped as in optical telescopes. But the mirrors in **UV** telescopes have to be even **more** precisely made.

**IR telescopes** have the added problem that they produce their **own** infrared radiation due to their **temperature**. They need to be **cooled** to very low temperatures using liquid helium, or refrigeration units.

## X-ray Telescopes have a Different Structure from Other Telescopes

1) X-rays don't reflect off surfaces in the same way as most other EM radiation. Usually X-ray radiation is either **absorbed** by a material or it **passes straight through** it.

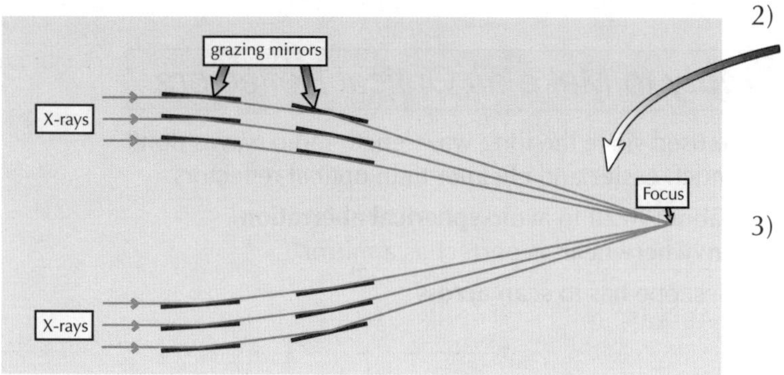


2) X-rays **do** reflect if they just **graze** a mirror's surface though. By having a series of **nested mirrors**, you can gradually alter the direction of X-rays enough to bring them to a **focus** on a detector. This type of telescope is called a **grazing telescope**.
3) The X-rays can be detected using a modified **Geiger counter** or a **fine wire mesh**. Newer X-ray telescopes such as the XMM-Newton telescope use highly sensitive X-ray **CCD** cameras.

# Non-Optical Telescopes

## Different Telescopes have Different **Resolving** and **Collecting Powers**

The **RESOLVING POWER** of a telescope is limited by two main factors:

1) The **Rayleigh criterion** (see page 67):
This depends on the **wavelength** of the radiation and the **diameter** of the objective mirror or dish.
So, for the **same size** of dish, a UV telescope has a much better resolving power than a radio telescope.
2) The quality of the **detector**:
Just like in digital cameras, the resolving power of a telescope is limited by the resolution of the detector. That can be how many **pixels** there are on a CCD, or for a wire mesh X-ray detector, how **fine** the wire mesh is.

The **COLLECTING POWER** of a telescope is proportional to its **collecting area**.

1) A **bigger dish** or **mirror** collects **more energy** from an object in a given time.
This gives a **more intense image**, so the telescope can observe **fainter** objects.
2) The **collecting power** (energy collected per second) is proportional to the area:

$$\textbf{Power} \propto \textbf{Diameter}^2$$

The bigger the dish, the greater the collecting power. Mmm....

3) For a **radio**, **optical**, **UV** or **IR** telescope, this is the area of the objective mirror or dish.
4) For **X-ray** telescopes, it's the area of the **opening** through which X-rays can enter the telescope.
In general, X-ray telescopes have a much **smaller collecting power** than other types of telescope.

## Practice Questions

Q1 Why do radio telescopes tend to have poor resolving powers?

Q2 Why is it easier to make a parabolic dish for a radio telescope than it is to make a parabolic mirror for an optical telescope?

Q3 Why don't astronomers install UV and X-ray telescopes on the top of mountains?

**Exam Questions**

Q1 Describe and explain the differences in resolving and collecting powers of a radio telescope and a UV telescope with the same surface area, given that their detectors have the same resolution. [4 marks]

Q2 In 1983, the IRAS satellite observed the entire sky in infrared wavelengths. The satellite was kept at a temperature of 2 K by a reservoir of liquid helium which cooled the satellite by evaporation.

a) Explain why the satellite needed to be kept at such a low temperature. [2 marks]

b) Some infrared telescopes are on the surface of the Earth.
State the typical location of this type of telescope [1 mark]

Q3 a) Many X-ray and UV telescopes are housed on satellites that orbit high above the Earth's atmosphere.
Where else are X-ray and UV telescopes positioned? Explain why this is necessary. [2 marks]

b) Describe and explain the major differences between the mirrors in X-ray and UV telescopes. [3 marks]

Q4 a) State how the collecting power of a telescope is related to its objective diameter. [1 mark]

b) The Arecibo radio telescope has a dish diameter of 300 m (to 2 s.f.). The Lovell radio telescope has a dish diameter of 76 m. Calculate the ratio of their collecting powers. [2 marks]

## Power is proportional to diameter$^2$? Bring on the cakes...

*If you can't observe the radiation you want to from Earth, just strap your telescope to a rocket and blast it into space. Sounds easy enough till you remember it's going to be reeeally hard to repair if anything goes wrong.*

# Distances and Magnitude

*There are a couple of ways to classify stars — the first is by luminosity, using the magnitude scale.*

## The **Luminosity** of a Star is the **Total Energy** Emitted **per Second**

1) Stars can be **classified** according to their luminosity — that is, the **total** amount of energy emitted in the form of electromagnetic radiation **each second** (see p.74).
2) The **Sun's** luminosity is about $4 \times 10^{26}$ W (luminosity is measured in watts, since it's a sort of power). The **most luminous** stars have a luminosity about a **million** times that of the Sun.
3) The **intensity**, $I$, of an object that we observe is the power **received** from it per unit area **at Earth**. This is the effective **brightness** of an object.

## **Apparent Magnitude, m,** is Based on how **Bright** things **Appear** from **Earth**

1) The **brightness** of a star in the night sky depends on **two** things — its **luminosity** and its **distance from us** (if you ignore weather and light pollution, etc.). So the **brightest** stars will either be **close** to us or have a **high luminosity**.
2) An Ancient Greek called **Hipparchus** invented a system where the very **brightest** stars were given an **apparent magnitude** of **1** and the **dimmest** visible stars an apparent magnitude of **6**, with other levels catering for the stars in between.
3) In the 19th century, the scale was redefined using a strict **logarithmic** scale:

   A **magnitude 1** star has an **intensity 100 times** greater than a **magnitude 6** star.

   This means a difference of **one magnitude** corresponds to a difference in **intensity** of $\mathbf{100^{1/5}}$ **times**. So a magnitude 1 star is about **2.51 times brighter** than a magnitude 2 star.
4) At the same time, the range was **extended** in **both directions** with the very brightest objects in the sky having **negative apparent magnitude**.

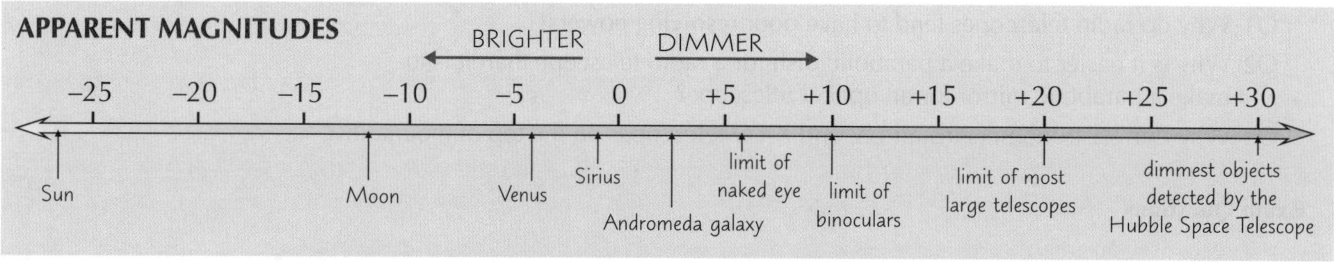


5) You can calculate the **brightness** (or intensity) **ratio** between **two stars** using:

$$\frac{I_2}{I_1} \approx 2.51^{m_1 - m_2}$$

where $I_1$ is the **intensity** of **star 1**,
$I_2$ is the **intensity** of **star 2**,
$m_1$ is the **apparent magnitude** of **star 1** and
$m_2$ is the **apparent magnitude** of **star 2**.

## The **Distance** to **Nearby Stars** can be Measured in **Parsecs**

1) Imagine you're in a **moving car**. You see that (stationary) objects in the **foreground** seem to be **moving faster** than objects in the **distance**. This **apparent change in position** is called **parallax**.
2) Parallax is measured in terms of the **angle of parallax**. The **greater** the **angle**, the **nearer** the object is to you.
3) The distance to **nearby stars** can be calculated by observing how they **move relative** to **very distant stars** when the Earth is in **different parts** of its **orbit**. This gives a **unit** of distance called a **parsec** (**pc**).

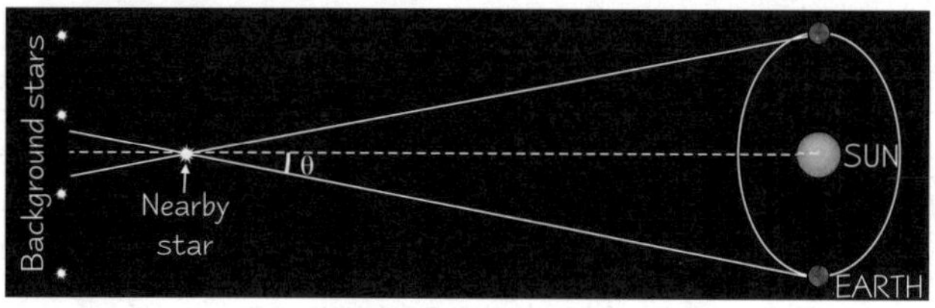


A star is exactly **one parsec** (**pc**) away from Earth if the **angle of parallax**, $\theta$, is:

$$\theta = 1\,\text{arcsecond} = \left(\frac{1}{3600}\right)^\circ$$

1 parsec = $3.08 \times 10^{16}$ m.

# Distances and Magnitude

## Absolute Magnitude, M, is based only on the Luminosity of the Star

1) The **absolute magnitude** of a star or galaxy, ***M***, does not depend on its distance from Earth. It is defined as what its apparent magnitude **would be** if it were **10 parsecs** away from Earth.
2) The relationship between ***M*** and ***m*** is given by the formula:

$$m - M = 5\log\left(\frac{d}{10}\right)$$

where *d* is the distance in parsecs

If you know the absolute magnitude of a star, you can use this equation to calculate its **distance** from Earth. This is really handy, since the distance to most stars is **too big** to measure using parallax (see previous page).

This method uses objects like **type 1a supernovae** that are known as **standard candles**. Standard candles are objects that you can calculate the luminosity of **directly**. So, if you find a type 1a supernova within a galaxy, you can work out how far that galaxy is from us. This is how the **Hubble constant** was worked out (see p.86).

## Distances in the Solar System can be Measured in Astronomical Units (AU)

The **parsec** is only one measurement used in **astrophysics** — luckily the others you need to know are much **simpler**.

1) From the time of **Copernicus** (in the 1500s) onwards, astronomers could work out the **distances** between the **planets** and the Sun **relative** to the Earth, using **astronomical units** (AU). But they couldn't work out the **actual distances**.

   One **astronomical unit** (AU) is defined as the **mean distance** between the **Earth** and the **Sun**.

2) The **size** of the AU ($1.50 \times 10^{11}$ m) wasn't known until 1769 — when it was carefully **measured** during a **transit of Venus** (when Venus passed between the Earth and the Sun).

## Another Measure of Distance is the Light-Year (ly)

1) All **electromagnetic waves** travel at the **speed of light**, *c*, in a vacuum ($c = 3.00 \times 10^8$ ms$^{-1}$).

   The **distance** that electromagnetic waves travel through a vacuum in **one year** is called a **light-year** (**ly**).

2) If we see the light from a star that is, say, **10 light-years away** then we are actually seeing it as it was **10 years ago**. The further away the object is, the further **back in time** we are actually seeing it.
3) **1 ly** is equivalent to about **$9.46 \times 10^{15}$ m**, and 1 pc is equal to about **3.26 ly**.

## Practice Questions

Q1 What is the relationship between apparent magnitude and intensity?

Q2 What is the equation that links apparent magnitude, absolute magnitude and distance?

Q3 Give three units of distance used in astrophysics. Explain the meaning of each one.

**Exam Questions**

Q1 Define the absolute magnitude of a star. [2 marks]

Q2 Calculate the absolute magnitude of the Sun given that the Sun's apparent magnitude is –27.
(1 pc = $2.1 \times 10^5$ AU) [3 marks]

Q3 The star Sirius has an apparent magnitude of –1.46 and an absolute magnitude of +1.4.
The star Canopus has an apparent magnitude of –0.72 and an absolute magnitude of –5.5.

a) State which of the two stars appears brighter from Earth. [1 mark]

b) Calculate the distance from Earth to the furthest star. [3 marks]

## Learn all this and you'll look like the brightest in class...

*The magnitude scale is a pretty weird system, but like with a lot of astronomy, the old ways have stuck. Remember — the lower the number, the brighter the object. The definition of absolute magnitude is a bit random as well — I mean, why ten parsecs? Ours not to reason why, ours but to... erm... learn it. (Doesn't have quite the same ring does it.)*

# Stars as Black Bodies

*Now they're telling us the Sun's black. Who writes this stuff?*

## A Black Body is a Perfect Absorber and Emitter

1) Objects emit **electromagnetic radiation** due to their **temperature**. At everyday temperatures this radiation lies mostly in the **infrared** part of the spectrum (which we can't see) — but heat something up enough and it will start to **glow**.
2) **Pure black** surfaces emit radiation **strongly** and in a **well-defined way**. We call it **black body radiation**.
3) A black body is defined as:

> A body that **absorbs all wavelengths** of electromagnetic radiation (that's why it's called a **black** body) and can **emit all wavelengths** of electromagnetic radiation.

4) The graph of **intensity** against **wavelength** for black body radiation varies with **temperature**, as shown in the graph:
5) To a reasonably good approximation **stars** behave as **black bodies** and their black body radiation produces their **continuous spectrum**.

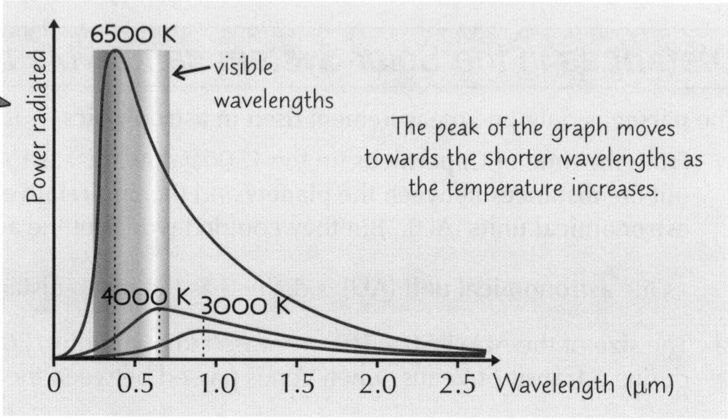


## The Peak Wavelength gives the Temperature

1) For each temperature, there is a **peak** in the black body curve at a wavelength called the **peak wavelength**, $\lambda_{max}$.
2) $\lambda_{max}$ is related to the **temperature** by **Wien's displacement law**:

$$\lambda_{max}T = \text{constant} = 2.9 \times 10^{-3}\ \text{mK}$$

where T is the temperature in kelvin and mK is a metre-kelvin.

## The Power Output of a Star Depends on its Temperature and Surface Area

1) The **power output** of a star (its **luminosity**) is the **total energy** it emits **per second** and is related to the **temperature** of the star and its **surface area**. You might see it shown as ***P*** or ***L***.
2) The power output is proportional to the **fourth power** of the star's **temperature** and is **directly proportional** to the **surface area**. This is **Stefan's law**:

$$P = \sigma A T^4$$

where $P$ is the power output of the star (in W), $A$ is its surface area (in $m^2$), $T$ is its surface temperature (in K) and $\sigma$ (a little Greek "sigma") is Stefan's constant.

3) Measurements give Stefan's constant as $\sigma = 5.67 \times 10^{-8}\ \text{Wm}^{-2}\text{K}^{-4}$.
4) From **Earth**, we can measure the **intensity** of the radiation received from the star. The intensity is the **power** of radiation **per square metre**, so as the radiation spreads out and becomes **diluted**, the intensity **decreases**. If the energy has been emitted from a **point** or a **sphere** (like a star, for example) then it obeys the **inverse square law**:

$$I = \frac{P}{4\pi d^2}$$

where $P$ is the power output of the star (in W), and $d$ is the distance from the star (in m).

# Stars as Black Bodies

## You Can Put the **Equations Together** to **Solve Problems**

**Example:** The star Sirius B has a surface area of $4.1 \times 10^{13}$ m$^2$ and produces a black body spectrum with a peak wavelength of 115 nm. The intensity of the light from Sirius B when it reaches Earth is $1.12 \times 10^{-11}$ Wm$^{-2}$. How many years does the light from Sirius B take to reach Earth? *($\sigma = 5.67 \times 10^{-8}$ Wm$^{-2}$K$^{-4}$)*

First, find the **temperature of Sirius B**:

$\lambda_{max}T = 2.9 \times 10^{-3}$ mK, so $T = 2.9 \times 10^{-3} \div \lambda_{max} = 2.9 \times 10^{-3} \div 115 \times 10^{-9} = 25\,217.39...$ K

Now, you can use **Stefan's law** to find the **luminosity**:

$P = \sigma AT^4 = (5.67 \times 10^{-8}) \times (4.1 \times 10^{13}) \times 25\,217.39...^4 = 9.400... \times 10^{23}$ W

Then use $I = \frac{P}{4\pi d^2}$ to find the **distance** of **Sirius B from Earth**:

$$d = \sqrt{\frac{P}{4\pi I}} = \sqrt{\frac{9.400... \times 10^{23}}{4\pi \times 1.12 \times 10^{-11}}} = 8.17... \times 10^{16}$$

Remember, $c = 3.00 \times 10^8$ ms$^{-1}$.

Use $c = d \div t$ to find the **time taken** $t = d \div c = 8.17... \times 10^{16} \div 3.00 \times 10^8 = 272\,426\,013.226...$ s

Finally, convert this to years: $272\,426\,013.226... \div (60 \times 60 \times 24 \times 365) = 8.638... =$ **8.6 years (to 2 s.f.)**

## It's Hard to get **Accurate** Measurements

1) **Wien's displacement law**, **Stefan's law** and the **inverse square law** can all be used to work out various **properties** of stars. This needs very **careful measurements**, but our **atmosphere** mucks up the results.
2) It only lets through **certain wavelengths** of **electromagnetic radiation** — **visible** light, most **radio** waves, **very near infrared** and a bit of **UV**. It's **opaque** to the rest.
3) And then there are things like **dust** and **man-made light pollution** to contend with. Observatories are placed at **high altitudes**, well away from **cities**, and in **low-humidity** climates to minimise the problem. The best solution, though, is to send up **satellites** that can take measurements **above** the atmosphere.
4) Our **detectors** don't do us any favours either. The **measuring devices** that astronomers use aren't perfect since their **sensitivity** depends on the **wavelength**.
5) For example, **glass absorbs UV** light but is **transparent** to **visible light**, so any instruments that use glass affect UV readings straight off.
6) All you can do about this is choose the best materials for what you want to measure, and then **calibrate** your instruments really carefully.

## Practice Questions

Q1 What is Wien's displacement law and what is it used for?

Q2 What is the relationship between luminosity, surface area and temperature?

Q3 Why are accurate measurements of black body radiation difficult on the Earth's surface?

**Exam Questions**

Q1 A star, X, has a surface temperature of 4000 K and the same power output as the Sun ($3.9 \times 10^{26}$ W). The Sun has a surface temperature of 6000 K.

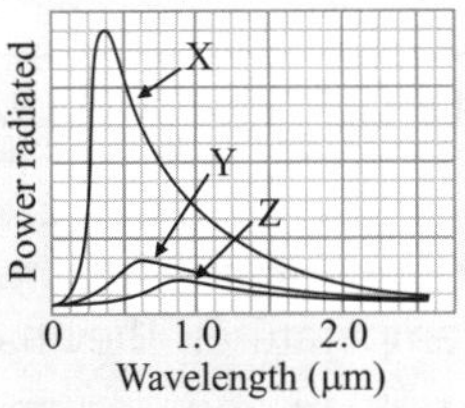


a) State which radiation curve represents this star — X, Y or Z. Explain your answer. [2 marks]

b) State whether star X or the Sun is larger. Explain your answer. [2 marks]

Q2 The star Procyon A, which has a luminosity of $2.3 \times 10^{27}$ W, produces a black body spectrum with a peak wavelength of 436 nm.

Calculate the surface area of Procyon A. [3 marks]

### Astronomy — theories, a bit of guesswork and a whole load of calibration...

*Astronomy isn't the most exact of sciences, I'm afraid. The Hubble Space Telescope's improved things a lot, but try to get a look at some actual observational data. Then look at the error bars — they'll generally be about the size of a house.*

# Spectral Classes and the H-R Diagram

*As well as classifying stars by luminosity (the magnitude scale, p.72), they can be classified by colour.*

## The **Balmer Series** is a Set of Lines in the **Spectrum** of **Hydrogen**

1) The lines in **emission** and **absorption spectra** occur because electrons in an atom can only exist at certain well-defined **energy levels**.
2) In **atomic hydrogen**, the electron is usually in the **ground state** (*n* = 1), but there are lots of energy levels (*n* = 2 to *n* = ∞ — called excitation levels) that the electron **could** exist in if it was given more energy.

The wavelengths corresponding to the **visible bit** of hydrogen's spectrum are caused by electrons moving from **higher energy levels** to the **first excitation level** (*n* = 2). This leads to a series of **lines** called the **Balmer series.**

## The **Strengths** of the **Spectral Lines** Show the **Temperature** of a Star

1) For a **hydrogen absorption line** to occur in the **visible** part of a star's spectrum, electrons in the hydrogen atoms already need to be in the ***n* = 2** state.
2) This happens at **high temperatures**, where **collisions** between the atoms give the electrons extra energy.
3) If the temperature is **too high**, though, the majority of the electrons will reach the ***n* = 3** level (or above) instead, which means there won't be so many Balmer transitions.
4) So the **intensity** of the Balmer lines depends on the **temperature** of the star.
5) For a particular intensity of the Balmer lines, **two temperatures** are possible. Astronomers get around this by looking at the **absorption lines** of **other atoms** and **molecules** as well.

## The **Relative Strength** of Absorption Lines gives the **Spectral Class**

Well... quite.

1) For historical reasons the stars are classified into **spectral classes:**

**O** (hottest), **B**, **A**, **F**, **G**, **K** and **M**

Use a **mnemonic** to remember the order. The standard one is the rather non-PC **'Oh Be A Fine Girl, Kiss Me'**.

2) The graph shows how the **intensity** of the visible spectral lines changes with **temperature**:

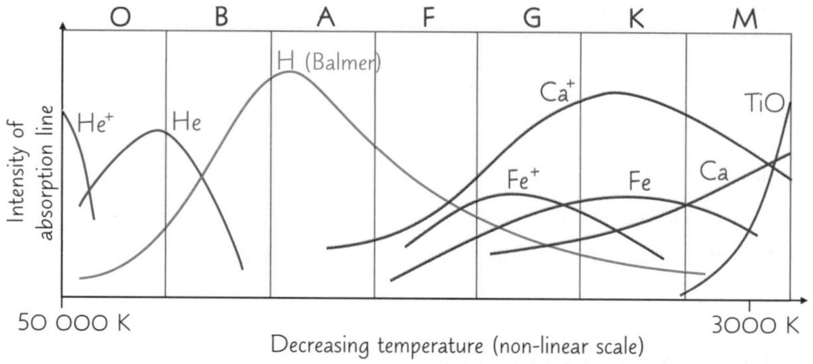


A quick note on the temperature axis: These diagrams, and the H-R diagram (next page), tend to be drawn with spectral class along the horizontal axis. The relationship between spectral class and temperature isn't linear or logarithmic.

**THE VISIBLE SPECTRAL CHARACTERISTICS OF SPECTRAL CLASSES**

**O** **Blue** stars: temperature **25 000 – 50 000 K**. The strongest spectral lines are **helium ion** and **helium atom** absorptions, since these need a really high temperature. They have weak **hydrogen Balmer** lines too.

**B** **Blue** stars: **11 000 – 25 000 K**. These spectra show strong **helium atom** and **hydrogen** absorptions.

**A** **Blue-white** stars: **7500 – 11 000 K**. Visible spectra are governed by the strongest Balmer **hydrogen** lines, but there are also some **metal ion** absorptions.

**F** **White** stars: **6000 – 7500 K**. These spectra have strong **metal ion** absorptions.

**G** **Yellow-white** stars: **5000 – 6000 K**. These have both **metal ion** and **metal atom** absorptions.

**K** **Orange** stars: **3500 – 5000 K**. At this temperature, most spectral lines are from neutral **metal atoms.**

**M** **Red** stars: **< 3500 K. Molecular band** absorptions from compounds like **titanium oxide** are present in the spectra of these stars, since they're cool enough for molecules to form.

# Spectral Classes and the H-R Diagram

## *Absolute Magnitude* vs *Temperature/Spectral Class — the H-R diagram*

1) Independently, Hertzsprung and Russell noticed that a plot of **absolute magnitude** (see p.73) against **temperature** (or **spectral class**) didn't just throw up a random collection of stars but showed **distinct areas**.

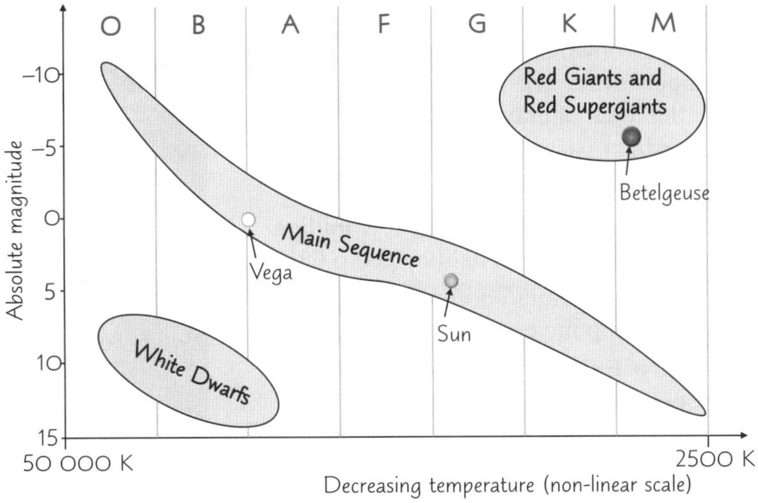

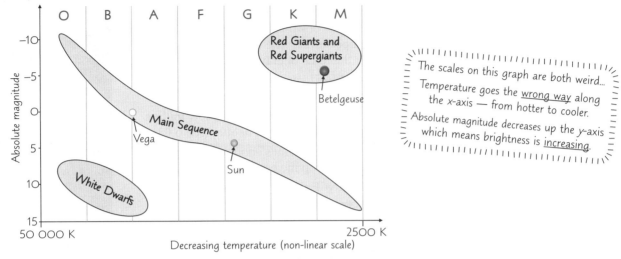

*The scales on this graph are both weird... Temperature goes the wrong way along the x-axis — from hotter to cooler. Absolute magnitude decreases up the y-axis which means brightness is increasing.*

2) The **long, diagonal band** is called the **main sequence**. Main sequence stars are in their long-lived **stable phase** where they are fusing **hydrogen** into **helium**. The Sun is a main sequence star.
3) Stars that have a **high luminosity** and a relatively **low surface temperature** must have a **huge** surface area because of Stefan's law (page 74). These stars are called **red giants** and **red supergiants** and are found in the **top-right** corner of the H-R diagram. These are stars that have **moved off** the main sequence and fusion reactions other than hydrogen to helium are also happening in them.
4) Stars that have a **low luminosity** but a **high temperature** must be very **small**, again because of Stefan's law. These stars are called **white dwarfs** and are about the size of the Earth. They lie in the **bottom-left** corner of the H-R diagram. White dwarfs are stars at the **end** of their lives, where all of their fusion reactions have stopped and they are just **slowly cooling down**.

## *Practice Questions*

Q1 Why does hydrogen have to be at a particular temperature before Balmer absorption lines are seen?

Q2 List the spectral classes in order of decreasing temperature and outline their spectral characteristics.

Q3 What is an H-R diagram and what are the three main groups of stars that emerge when the diagram is plotted?

**Exam Questions**

Q1 The spectral classes of stars can be identified by examining the lines in their absorption spectra.

a) Explain how temperature affects the strength of the Balmer lines in stellar absorption spectra. [3 marks]

b) State the two spectral classes of star in which strong Balmer lines are observed. [2 marks]

c) Describe the visible spectral characteristics and temperature of a star in class F. [3 marks]

Q2 The spectra of M stars have absorption bands corresponding to energy levels of molecules. Explain why this only occurs in the lowest temperature stars. [1 mark]

Q3 Draw the basic features of an H-R diagram, indicating where you would find main sequence stars, red giants and white dwarfs. Plot where you would find our Sun. [5 marks]

## *'Ospital Bound — A Furious Girl Kicked Me...*

*Spectral classes are another example of astronomers sticking with tradition. The classes used to be ordered alphabetically by the strength of the Balmer lines. When astronomers realised this didn't quite work, they just fiddled around with the old classes rather than coming up with a sensible new system. Just to make life difficult for people like you and me.*

# Stellar Evolution

*Stars go through several different stages in their lives and move around the H-R diagram as they go (see p.77). What happens to them depends on their mass — who said size doesn't matter?...*

## **Stars** Begin as Clouds of **Dust** and **Gas**

1) Stars are born in a **cloud** of **dust** and **gas**, most of which was left when previous stars blew themselves apart in **supernovae**. The denser clumps of the cloud **contract** (very slowly) under the force of **gravity**.
2) When these clumps get dense enough, the cloud fragments into regions called **protostars**, that continue to contract and **heat up**.
3) Eventually the **temperature** at the centre of the protostar reaches a **few million degrees**, and **hydrogen nuclei** start to **fuse** together to form helium (see p.63).
4) This releases an **enormous** amount of **energy** and creates enough radiation **pressure** (along with the star's gas pressure) to stop the **gravitational collapse**.
5) The star has now reached the **MAIN SEQUENCE** and will stay there, relatively **unchanged**, while it fuses hydrogen into helium.

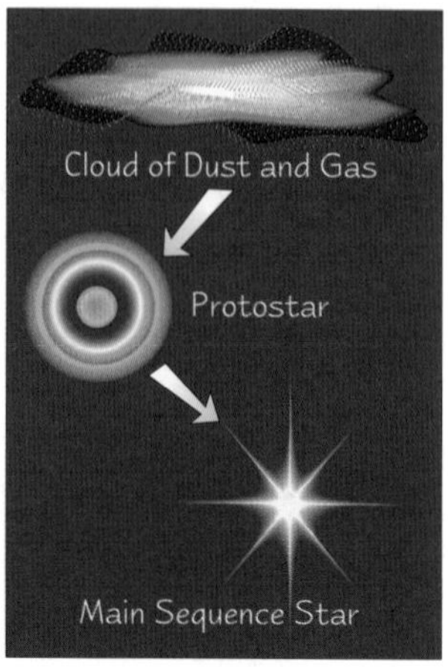


## **Main Sequence** Stars become **Red Giants** when they **Run Out** of **Fuel**

1) Stars spend most of their lives as **MAIN SEQUENCE** stars. The **pressure** produced from **hydrogen fusion** in their **core balances** the **gravitational force** trying to compress them. This stage is called **core hydrogen burning**.
2) When all the **hydrogen** in the **core** has fused into helium, nuclear fusion **stops**, and with it the **outward pressure stops**. The helium core **contracts** and **heats up** under the **weight** of the star. The outer layers **expand** and **cool**, and the star becomes a **RED GIANT**.

   The material **surrounding** the core still has **plenty of hydrogen**. **Heat** from the contracting helium **core** raises the **temperature** of this material enough for the hydrogen to **fuse**. This is called **shell hydrogen burning**. (Very low-mass stars stop at this point. They use up their fuel and slowly fade away...)
3) The helium core continues to contract until, eventually, it gets **hot** enough and **dense** enough for **helium** to **fuse** into **carbon** and **oxygen**. This is called **core helium burning**. This releases a **huge** amount of energy, which **pushes** the **outer layers** of the star further outwards.
4) When the **helium** runs out, the carbon-oxygen core **contracts again** and heats a **shell** around it so that helium can fuse in this region — **shell helium burning**.

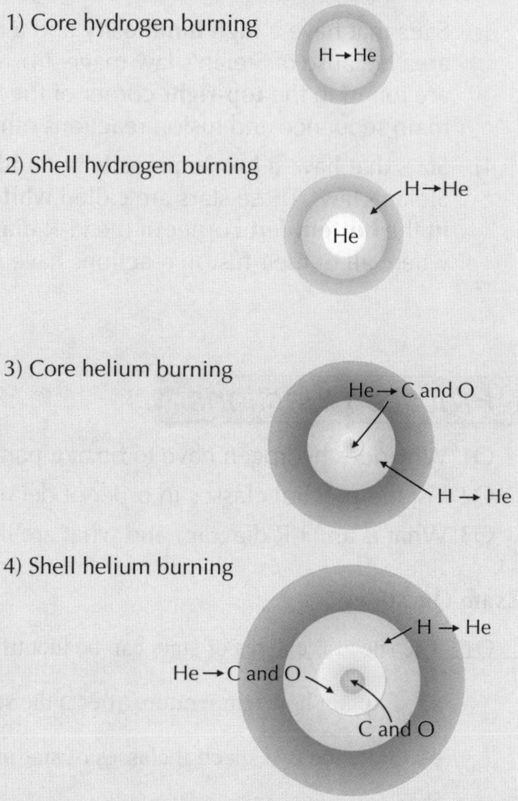


## **Low Mass** Stars (like the Sun) **Eject** their Shells, leaving behind a **White Dwarf**

1) In low-mass stars, the **carbon-oxygen core isn't hot enough** for any further **fusion** and so it continues to **contract** under its own **weight**. Once the core has shrunk to about **Earth-size**, **electrons** exert enough pressure (**electron degeneracy pressure**) to stop it collapsing any more (fret not — you don't have to know how).
2) The **helium shell** becomes more and more **unstable** as the core contracts. The star **pulsates** and **ejects** its outer layers into space as a **planetary nebula**, leaving behind the dense core.
3) The star is now a very **hot**, **dense solid** called a **WHITE DWARF**, which will simply **cool down** and **fade away**.

# Stellar Evolution

## As Stars Age Their **Position** On The H-R Diagram **Changes**

1) **Where** a star is on a Hertzsprung-Russell diagram changes as it **evolves**.
2) Our Sun won't stay in the **main sequence** forever — its position on the diagram will drift to the **top-right** as it becomes a red giant. It will be **colder** and appear **brighter** than it was on the main sequence.
3) Once it has run out of helium to burn in its core, it will then become a **white dwarf** and its position will move to the **bottom-left** of the diagram. It will be **hotter** but will also be **dimmer** than it was on the main sequence.

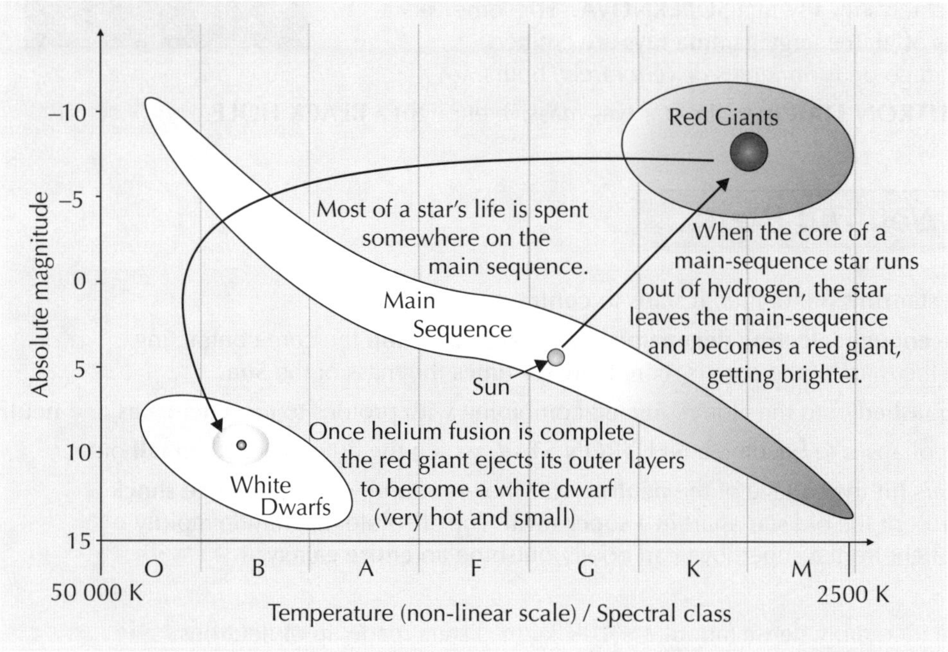


Star formation, from a cloud of gas to the main sequence, happens off this side of the H-R diagram.

## Practice Questions

Q1 What is a protostar?

Q2 Describe fully the four stages of fuel burning in a low mass star.

Q3 Describe what is meant by a white dwarf and explain how it is formed.

Q4 Describe the transitions the Sun will undertake in the rest of its lifetime.

Q5 Draw these transitions on a Hertzsprung-Russell diagram.

**Exam Questions**

Q1 Describe briefly how main sequence stars are formed. [3 marks]

Q2 A low mass star is on the main sequence.

a) Describe what happens to the star just after it runs out of hydrogen fuel to fuse within its core. [2 marks]

b) State the name of the type of star it has now become. [1 mark]

c) State the name of the type of star it will become when it runs out of fuel completely. [1 mark]

## Our Sun will one day fade away...

*But don't worry, that's not for a few billion years. Make sure you can describe the lifetime of a star like our Sun — all the way from a cloud of dust to a cooling white dwarf. Then make sure you're happy drawing it on a HR diagram too.*

# Stellar Evolution

## High Mass Stars go out with a Bit of a Bang...

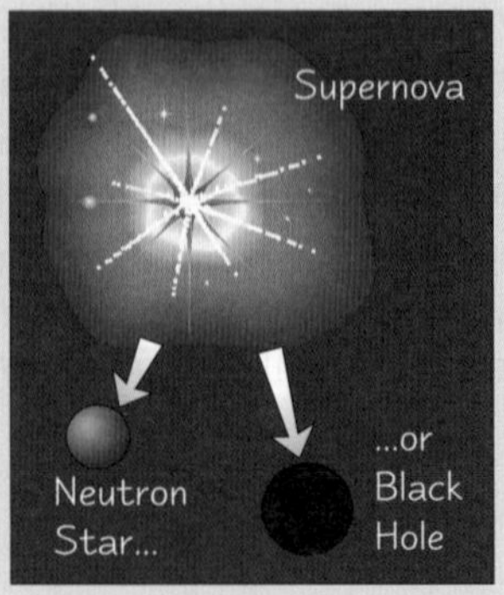


1) Even though stars with a **large mass** have a **lot of fuel**, they use it up **more quickly** and don't spend so long as main sequence stars.
2) When they are **red giants** the **'core burning to shell burning'** process can continue beyond the fusion of helium, building up layers in an **onion-like structure** to become **red supergiants**. For **really massive** stars this can go all the way up to **iron**.
3) Nuclear fusion **beyond iron** isn't **energetically favourable**, though, so once an iron core is formed then very quickly it's goodbye star.
4) The star explodes cataclysmically in a **SUPERNOVA**. For some very massive stars, **bursts** of high energy **gamma rays** are emitted. The gamma burst can go on for minutes or very rarely, hours.
5) Left behind is a **NEUTRON STAR** or (if the star was massive enough) a **BLACK HOLE**.

## ...Leaving Behind Neutron Stars...

1) When the core of a star runs out of fuel, it starts to **contract**.
2) If the star is **massive enough**, **electron degeneracy** (see p.78) can't **stop** the core contracting. This happens when the mass of the core is more than **1.4 times** the mass of the **Sun**.
3) The electrons get **squashed** onto the atomic **nuclei**, combining with protons to form **neutrons** and **neutrinos**.
4) The core suddenly collapses to become a **NEUTRON STAR**, which the outer layers then **fall** onto.
5) When the outer layers **hit** the surface of the **neutron star** they **rebound**, setting up huge **shock waves**, ripping the rest of the old star apart in a **supernova**. The absolute magnitude rapidly increases, meaning light from a supernova can briefly outshine an **entire galaxy**.

1) **Neutron stars** are incredibly **dense** (about $4 \times 10^{17}$ kg m$^{-3}$) stars made up of neutrons.
2) They're **very small**, typically about 20 km across, and they can **rotate very fast** (up to 600 times a second).
3) Some neutron stars emit **radio waves** in two beams as they rotate. These beams sometimes sweep past the Earth and can be observed as **radio pulses** rather like the flashes of a lighthouse. These rotating neutron stars are called **PULSARS**.

## ...Or Black Holes

1) If the **core** of the star remaining after a supernova is more than **3 times** the **Sun's mass**, the **neutrons** can't withstand the gravitational forces.
2) There are **no known mechanisms** left to stop the core collapsing to an **infinitely dense** point called a **singularity**. At that point, the **laws of physics** break down completely. This is called a **black hole**.
3) Up to a certain distance away (called the **Schwarzschild radius**) the gravitational pull is **so strong** that nothing, not even **light**, can escape its grasp. The **boundary** of this region is called the **event horizon**.

**The Schwarzschild radius is the distance at which the escape velocity is the speed of light**

An object moving at the **escape velocity** has **just enough kinetic energy** to overcome the black hole's gravitational field.

From Newton's law of gravitation we get $\frac{1}{2}mv^2 = \frac{GMm}{r}$

Dividing through by $m$ and making $r$ the subject gives: $r = \frac{2GM}{v^2}$

By replacing $v$ with the speed of light, $c$, you get the Schwarzschild radius, $R_S$.

This is a bit of a fudge that happens to give the right answer — we've used Newtonian physics when really general relativity (and some very hard maths) is needed.

$$R_S = \frac{2GM}{c^2}$$

$M$ = mass of black hole, $G = 6.67 \times 10^{-11}$ Nm$^2$kg$^{-2}$ and $c$ is the speed of light in a vacuum

# Stellar Evolution

## Learn the Light Curve for Type 1a Supernovae

The defining characteristic of a supernova is a **rapid**, **massive increase** in **brightness**.

1) Different types of supernovae have characteristic **light curves** — a plot of **absolute magnitude** $M$ against **time** since the supernova began.
2) Type I light curves have two defining features:
   - A **sharp initial peak**
   - Then a **gradually decreasing** curve.

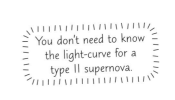

You don't need to know the light-curve for a type II supernova.

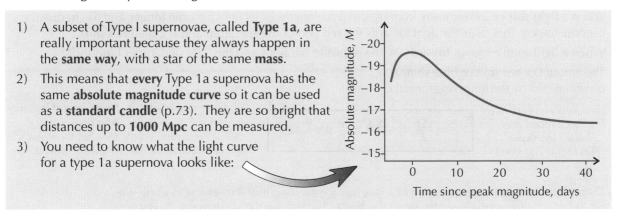

1) A subset of Type I supernovae, called **Type 1a**, are really important because they always happen in the **same way**, with a star of the same **mass**.
2) This means that **every** Type 1a supernova has the same **absolute magnitude curve** so it can be used as a **standard candle** (p.73). They are so bright that distances up to **1000 Mpc** can be measured.
3) You need to know what the light curve for a type 1a supernova looks like:

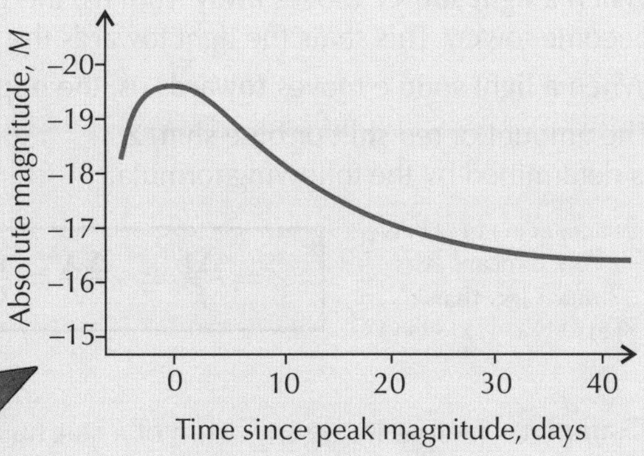


## The Amount of Energy Released in a Supernova is Huge

1) In a type 1a supernova, around $\mathbf{10^{44}}$ **J** of energy is released.
2) This is roughly the **same** as the energy output of the Sun over its **entire lifetime**.
3) Other types of supernova may release **much more** energy than this.
4) Some supernovae release **bursts** of **high energy gamma rays**.

If a supernova was **too close** to Earth and it's energy was directed towards us — it could destroy the ozone layer, leading to possible mass **extinction**.

## Practice Questions

Q1 What is a neutron star?

Q2 What is a pulsar?

Q3 What core condition has to be fulfilled for a star to become a black hole at the end of its life?

Q4 Sketch the light curve of a typical Type 1a supernova.

Q5 How much energy is released by a Type 1a supernova?
How does this compare to the total energy released by the Sun in its lifetime?

**Exam Questions**

Q1 a) What is meant by the Schwarzschild radius of a black hole? [2 marks]

b) Calculate the Schwarzschild radius for a black hole that has a mass of $6.0 \times 10^{30}$ kg. [2 marks]

Q2 a) A star with a core twice the mass of our Sun runs out of fuel.
Describe the process through which it creates a supernova. [3 marks]

b) Very massive stars sometimes emit burst of gamma rays as they turn into supernovae.
Explain why these types of supernova might be dangerous to life on Earth. [2 marks]

## Live fast — die young...

*The more massive a star, the more spectacular its life cycle. The most massive stars burn up the hydrogen in their core so quickly that they only live for a fraction of the Sun's lifetime — but when they go, they do it in style.*

# The Doppler Effect and Red Shift

*Everyone's heard of the Big Bang theory — well here's some evidence for it.*

## The **Doppler Effect** — the **Motion** of a Wave's **Source** Affects its **Wavelength**

1) You'll have experienced the Doppler effect **loads of times** with **sound waves**.
2) Imagine an ambulance driving past you. As it moves **towards you** its siren sounds **higher-pitched**, but as it **moves away**, its **pitch** is **lower**. This change in **frequency** and **wavelength** is called the **Doppler shift**.
3) The frequency and the wavelength **change** because the waves **bunch together** in **front** of the source and **stretch out behind** it. The **amount** of stretching or bunching together depends on the **velocity** of the **source**.
4) When a **light source** moves **away** from us, the wavelengths of its light become **longer** and the frequencies become lower. This shifts the light towards the **red** end of the spectrum and is called **red shift**.
5) When a light source moves **towards** us, the **opposite** happens and the light undergoes **blue shift**.
6) The amount of red shift or blue shift, $z$, is determined by the following formula:

v << c means "v is much less than c"

$$z = \frac{\Delta f}{f} = -\frac{\Delta\lambda}{\lambda} = \frac{v}{c} \text{ if } v \ll c$$

$\lambda$ is the emitted wavelength, $f$ is the emitted frequency
$\Delta\lambda = \lambda_{emitted} - \lambda_{observed}$, $\Delta f = f_{emitted} - f_{observed}$
$v$ is the recessional velocity (how fast the source is moving away from the observer) $c$ is the speed of light.

**Example:** A line in the spectrum of a star has a wavelength of 410 nm. On Earth we observe the wavelength of the line to be 365 nm. Calculate the Doppler shift observed, along with the velocity of the star relative to Earth.

First, calculate the change in wavelength:
$\Delta\lambda = \lambda_{emitted} - \lambda_{observed} = 410 \text{ nm} - 365 \text{ nm} = 45 \text{ nm}$

Then use: $z = -\frac{\Delta\lambda}{\lambda} = -\frac{45}{410} = -0.109... = \mathbf{-0.11}$ **(to 2 s.f.)**

This means that

$\frac{v}{c} = -0.109...$ so $v = -0.109...c$

$= -0.109... \times 3.00 \times 10^8 = -3.29... \times 10^7 \text{ms}^{-1} = \mathbf{-3.3 \times 10^7 ms^{-1}}$ **(to 2 s.f.)**

As the wavelength is getting **shorter** (and the velocity is **negative**), the light is being **blue-shifted**. So the star is moving **towards** Earth.

Velocity has a direction, and here it's defined as positive if the source is moving away from the observer (red shift) and negative if it is moving towards the observer (blue shift).

## The **Red Shift** of Galaxies is **Strong Evidence** for the HBB

1) The **spectra** from **galaxies** (apart from a few very close ones) all show **red shift** — the **characteristic spectral lines** of the elements are all at a **longer wavelength** than you would expect. This shows they're all **moving apart**.
2) The way cosmologists tend to look at this stuff, the galaxies aren't actually moving **through space** away from us. Instead, **space itself** is expanding and the light waves are being **stretched** along with it. This is called **cosmological red shift** to distinguish it from **red shift** produced by sources that **are** moving through space.

Hot big bang — the ultimate firework display?

3) The same formula works for both types of red shift as long as $v$ is **much less** than $c$. If $v$ is close to the speed of light, you need to use a nasty, relativistic formula instead (you don't need to know that one).
4) Hubble realised that the **speed** that **galaxies moved away** from us depended on **how far** they were away. This led to the idea that the universe started out **very hot** and **very dense** and is currently **expanding**.

**THE HOT BIG BANG THEORY (HBB)**: the universe started off **very hot** and **very dense** (perhaps as an **infinitely hot, infinitely dense** singularity) and has been **expanding** ever since.

# The Doppler Effect and Red Shift

## *Doppler Shift* is Used to Study Spectroscopic *Binary Stars*

1) About half of the stars we observe are actually **two stars** that orbit each other. Many of them are too far away from us to be **resolved** with **telescopes** but the **lines** in their **spectra** show a binary star system. These are called **spectroscopic binary stars**.
2) By observing how the **absorption lines** in the spectrum change with **time** the **orbital period** can be calculated:

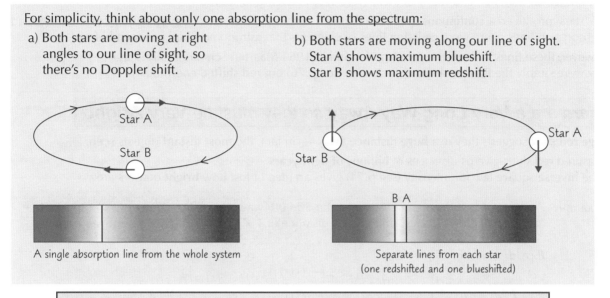

For simplicity, think about only one absorption line from the spectrum:

a) Both stars are moving at right angles to our line of sight, so there's no Doppler shift.

b) Both stars are moving along our line of sight. Star A shows maximum blueshift. Star B shows maximum redshift.

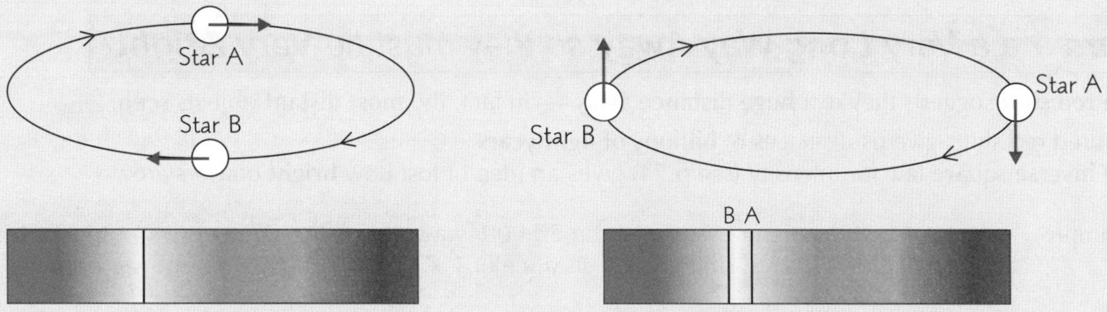


A single absorption line from the whole system

Separate lines from each star (one redshifted and one blueshifted)

As the stars orbit each other, the separation between the lines goes from zero [at a)] up to the maximum separation [at b)] and back to zero again in **half a period**.

3) Astronomers have used a similar method to find **extrasolar planets** (p. 84).

## Practice Questions

Q1 What is the Doppler effect?

Q2 Write down the formula for the red shift and blue shift of light.

Q3 Explain what is meant by the Hot Big Bang. How does Doppler shift support the idea of a Hot Big Bang?

Q4 Explain how the spectra of binary stars can be used to calculate their period of orbit.

**Exam Questions**

Q1 The spectra of two objects have been taken. What can you deduce from each of the following?

a) The absorption lines from object A have been shifted towards the blue end of the spectrum. [1 mark]

b) The absorption lines from object B oscillate back and forth on the spectrum with a period of two weeks. [2 marks]

Q2 The observed wavelength of the hydrogen alpha line of a distant object's spectrum is 667.83 nm. In the laboratory, the wavelength of the same line is measured as 656.28 nm.

a) Calculate the amount of red or blue shift of the spectral line. [1 mark]

b) Calculate the velocity of the object relative to Earth. State and explain whether it is moving towards or away from Earth. [2 marks]

## *Neeeee-Owwww — like my Doppler shift impression?*

*Doppler shift is one of the lovely parts of astrophysics that you can actually see in your daily life (without a big ol' telescope anyway...). The basics of it are pretty simple, but to get all of the marks you've got to be able to explain how its used in astrophysics — to study binary stars or to support the Hot Big Bang. Get that down and you're laughing.*

# Quasars and Exoplanets

*The Doppler effect is handy in explaining quasars and detecting exoplanets too. Read on.*

## Quasars — Quasi-Stellar Objects

1) **Quasars** were discovered in the late 1950s and were first thought to be **stars in our galaxy**.
2) The puzzling thing was that their spectra were **nothing like** normal stars. They sometimes shot out **jets** of material, and many of them were very active **radio sources**.
3) The 'stars' produced a **continuous spectrum** that was nothing like a black body radiation curve and instead of absorption lines, there were **emission lines** of elements that astronomers **had not seen before**.
4) However, these lines looked strangely familiar and in 1963 Maarten Schmidt realised that they were simply the **Balmer series** of hydrogen (see p.76) but **red shifted** enormously.

## Quasars are a Very Long Way Away so they must be Very Bright

This **huge red shift** suggests they're a **huge distance away** — in fact, the **most distant** objects seen.
The measured red shifts give us distances of **billions of light years**.
Using the **inverse square law** for intensity (see p.74) gives an idea of just how **bright** quasars are:

**Example** A quasar has the same intensity as a star 20 000 ly away with the same power output as the Sun ($4 \times 10^{26}$ W). Its red shift gives a distance of $1 \times 10^{10}$ ly. Calculate its power output.

$$P \propto Id^2$$

$$\Rightarrow \frac{P_{quasar}}{P_{star}} = \frac{I_{quasar}\,d_{quasar}^2}{I_{star}\,d_{star}^2} = \frac{d_{quasar}^2}{d_{star}^2}$$

$I_{quasar} = I_{star}$ so they cancel out of the equation.

$$\Rightarrow P_{quasar} = P_{star}\frac{d_{quasar}^2}{d_{star}^2} = 4 \times 10^{26} \times \frac{1 \times 10^{20}}{4 \times 10^{8}} = \mathbf{1 \times 10^{38}\ W}$$

That's bright — about **10 times** the **luminosity** of the **entire Milky Way galaxy**!

1) There's very good evidence to suggest that quasars are only about the size of the **Solar System**.
2) Let me run that past you again. **That's the power of a trillion Suns from something the size of the Solar System.**
3) These numbers caused a lot of controversy in the astrophysics community — they seemed crazy. Many astrophysicists thought there must be a more reasonable explanation. But then evidence for the distance of quasars came when **sensitive CCD** equipment detected the fuzzy cloud of **a galaxy around a quasar**.
4) The current consensus is that a quasar is a very powerful **galactic nucleus**, containing a huge **active black hole** (one which is currently **taking in** matter) at the centre of a distant galaxy. This supermassive black hole has a mass of about $10^6$ times the mass of the Sun.
(Almost all galaxies are thought to have these 'supermassive' black holes at their centres, but most aren't active).
5) This black hole is surrounded by a doughnut shaped mass of **whirling gas** falling into it, which produces the light. In the same way as a pulsar (see p.80), magnetic fields produce jets of radiation streaming out from the poles. The black hole must consume the mass of about **10 Suns per year** to produce the energy observed.

## Exoplanets Are Hard To Find

**Red shift** can also be used to discover other objects like **exoplanets**. An exoplanet (sometimes called an **extrasolar** planet) is any 'planet' not in our solar system — this is because the word **planet** is usually reserved for only things within our solar system, orbiting the **Sun**. They're pretty hard to find though, because:

1) They're orbiting **stars** which are much **brighter** than them. Most exoplanets cannot be seen as the bright light from the stars or other objects they're orbiting drowns out any light from the exoplanet.
2) They're **too small** to distinguish from nearby stars (the subtended angle is too small for the resolving power of most telescopes — see p.67).

Only a few of the largest and hottest exoplanets that are furthest away from their stars can be **seen directly** using specially built telescopes.

# Quasars and Exoplanets

## One Method To **Find Exoplanets** is To Use **Doppler Shift**

Sometimes called the **radial velocity method**, the Doppler shift method measures how much the emissions from stars have been red or blue shifted (similar to binary stars on p.83).

This is sometimes called Doppler spectroscopy.

1) An exoplanet orbiting a star has a small effect on the star's orbit. It causes **tiny variations** (a **wobble**) in the star's **orbit**.
2) This is because the star and the exoplanet are actually orbiting around the **centre of mass** between them — but as the star is so much bigger than the exoplanet, the centre is much closer to the centre of the star.
3) This wobble causes **tiny red** and **blue shifts** in the star's emissions which can be **detected** on Earth and can suggest the presence of an exoplanet.
4) From this, the **minimum mass** of the exoplanet can also be calculated.
5) There are however problems with this method, as the movement needs to be **aligned** with the observer's line of sight — if the planet orbits the star perpendicular to the line of sight then there won't be any detectable shift in the light from the star.

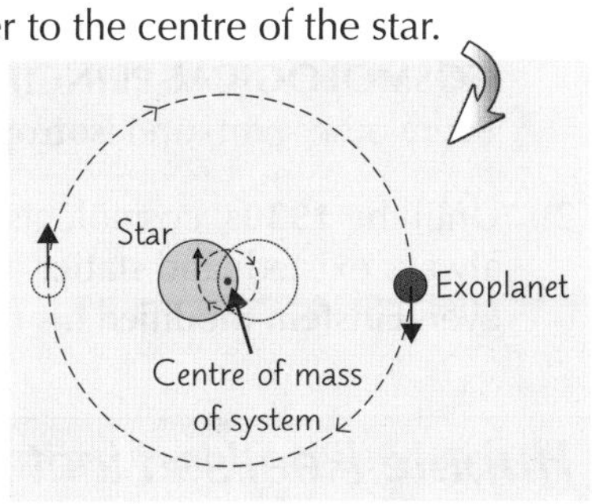


## Another is the **Transit Method**

The **transit** method measures the **change** in **apparent magnitude** as an exoplanet travels in front of a star.

1) As the **exoplanet** crosses in front of the star, some of the light from the star is **blocked** from Earth's view.
2) This leads to a **dip** in the **light curve** observed on Earth.
3) From this, the **radius** of the exoplanet can be found.
4) However, the **chances** of the planet's path being perfectly lined up so that it crosses the line of sight between the star and the Earth is **incredibly low**. This means you can only **confirm** observed exoplanets, not **rule out** the locations of any.

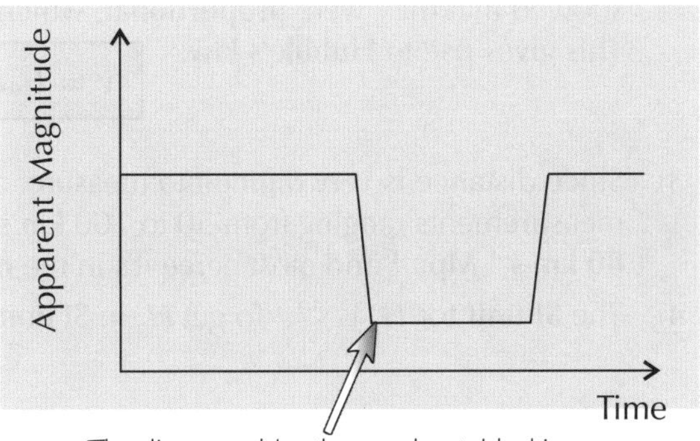

The dip caused by the exoplanet blocking some of the light from the star.

## Practice Questions

Q1 Define an exoplanet.

Q3 Explain two reasons why exoplanets are hard to observe.

Q4 Describe the radial velocity method for observing exoplanets.

Q5 Explain why you cannot use either of the methods above to rule out the presence of exoplanets around a star.

**Exam Questions**

Q1 a) State one piece of evidence that suggests quasars are a very long distance away. [1 mark]

b) Use the concept of the inverse square law to suggest why quasars must be very bright. [2 marks]

c) Describe the main features of a quasar according to the current theory. [2 marks]

Q2 A scientist is confirming the existence of an exoplanet using the transit method.

a) Describe and explain how the transit method can detect exoplanets. [3 marks]

b) Draw the typical light curve for the transit. [2 marks]

## Long ago, in a galaxy far, far away — there was a radio-loud, supermassive black hole with a highly luminous arc...

*Quasars are really weird. There's still some disagreement in the astrophysics community about what they even are. Then you get onto exoplanets — we at least know what they are, but they're really hard to find. Make sure you understand both methods used when trying to find exoplanets and make sure you can draw that light curve.*

# The Big Bang Model of the Universe

*Right, we're moving on to the BIG picture now — we all like a bit of cosmology...*

## The **Universe** is **The Same** in **Every Direction**

When you read that all the **galaxies** in the universe are **moving away** from the **Earth** (see p. 82 and below), it's easy to imagine that the Earth is at the **centre of the universe**, or that there's something really **special** about it. **Earth** is special to us because we **live here** — but on a **universal scale**, it's just like any other lump of rock.

1) The **demotion** of **Earth** from anything special is taken to its logical conclusion with the **cosmological principle**...

> **COSMOLOGICAL PRINCIPLE**: on a **large scale** the universe is **homogeneous** (every part is the same as every other part) and **isotropic** (everything looks the same in every direction) — so it doesn't have a **centre**.

2) Until the **1930s**, cosmologists believed that the universe was **infinite** in both **space** and **time** (that is, it had always existed) and **static**. This seemed the **only way** that it could be **stable** using **Newton's law** of gravitation. Even **Einstein modified** his theory of **general relativity** to make it consistent with the **Steady-State universe**.

## **Hubble** Realised that the **Universe** is **Expanding**

1) The **spectra** from **galaxies** (apart from a few very close ones) all show **red shift**. The amount of **red shift** gives the **recessional velocity** — how fast the galaxy is moving away (see page 82).

> Remember $z = \frac{\Delta f}{f} = -\frac{\Delta\lambda}{\lambda} = \frac{v}{c}$ for v<<c.

2) A plot of **recessional velocity** against **distance** (found using standard candles — see p.73) showed that they were **proportional**, which suggests that the universe is **expanding**. This gives rise to **Hubble's law**:

$$v = H_0 d$$

$v$ = recessional velocity in **kms$^{-1}$**,
$d$ = distance in **Mpc** and
$H_0$ = **Hubble's constant** in **kms$^{-1}$Mpc$^{-1}$**.

3) Since distance is very difficult to measure, astronomers used to **disagree** greatly on the value of $H_0$, with measurements ranging from 50 to 100 km s$^{-1}$ Mpc$^{-1}$. It's now generally accepted that $H_0$ lies **between 65 and 80 km s$^{-1}$ Mpc$^{-1}$** and most agree it's in the **mid to low 70s**. You'll be given a value to use in the exam.

4) The **SI unit** for $H_0$ is s$^{-1}$. To get $H_0$ in SI units, you need $v$ in ms$^{-1}$ and $d$ in m (1 Mpc = $3.08 \times 10^{22}$ m).

## The **Expanding Universe** gives rise to the **Hot Big Bang Model**

1) The universe is **expanding** and **cooling down** (because it's a closed system). So further back in time it must have been **smaller** and **hotter**. If you trace time back **far enough**, you get a **Hot Big Bang** (see page 82).

2) Since the universe is **expanding uniformly** away from **us** it seems as though we're at the **centre** of the universe, but this is an **illusion**. You would observe the **same thing** at **any point** in the universe.

## The **Age** and **Observable Size** of the **Universe** Depend on $H_0$

1) If the universe has been **expanding** at the **same rate** for its whole life, the **age** of the universe is $t = 1/H_0$ (time = distance/speed). This is only an estimate though — see below.

2) Unfortunately, since no one knows the **exact value** of $H_0$ we can only guess the universe's age. If $H_0$ **= 75 kms$^{-1}$Mpc$^{-1}$**, then the age of the universe $\approx 1/(2.4 \times 10^{-18}\ \text{s}^{-1}) = 4.1 \times 10^{17}$ s = **13 billion years**.

3) The **absolute size** of the universe is **unknown** but there is a limit on the size of the **observable universe**. This is simply a **sphere** (with the Earth at its centre) with a **radius** equal to the **maximum distance** that **light** can travel during its **age**. So if $H_0$ **= 75 kms$^{-1}$Mpc$^{-1}$** then this sphere will have a radius of **13 billion light years**. Taking into account the **expansion** of the universe, the radius of the sphere of the observable universe is thought to be more like 46-47 billion light years.

> **THE RATE OF EXPANSION HASN'T BEEN CONSTANT**
>
> 1) All the **mass** in the universe is attracted together by **gravity**. This attraction tends to **slow down** the rate of expansion of the universe. It's thought that the expansion **was** decelerating until about 5 billion years ago.
>
> 2) But in the late 90s, astronomers found evidence that the expansion is now **accelerating**. Cosmologists are trying to explain this acceleration using **dark energy** — a type of energy that fills the whole of space. There's lots of speculation about what dark energy even **is** — no-one knows for sure. This leads to **lots** of new **theories** and mathematical models being proposed to try and explain the accelerating universe.

# The Big Bang Model of the Universe

## Cosmic Microwave Background Radiation — More Evidence for the HBB

1) The Hot Big Bang model predicts that loads of **electromagnetic radiation** was produced in the **very early universe**. This radiation should **still** be observed today (it hasn't had anywhere else to go).
2) Because the universe has **expanded**, the wavelengths of this cosmic background radiation have been **stretched** and are now in the **microwave** region.
3) This was picked up **accidentally** by Penzias and Wilson in the 1960s.

## Properties of the Cosmic Microwave Background Radiation (CMBR)

1) In the late 1980s a satellite called the **Cosmic Background Explorer** (**COBE**) was sent up to have a **detailed look** at the radiation.
2) It found a **perfect black body spectrum** corresponding to a **temperature** of **2.73 K** (see page 74).
3) The radiation is largely **isotropic** and **homogeneous**, which confirms the cosmological principle (see page 86).
4) There are **very tiny fluctuations** in temperature, which were at the limit of COBE's detection. These are due to tiny energy-density variations in the early universe, and are needed for the initial '**seeding**' of galaxy formation.
5) The background radiation also shows a **Doppler shift**, indicating the Earth's motion through space. It turns out that the **Milky Way** is rushing towards an unknown mass (the **Great Attractor**) at over a **million miles an hour**.

## Another Bit of Evidence is the Amount of Helium in the Universe

1) The HBB model also explained the **large abundances of hydrogen and helium** in the universe (around 74% of the universe is hydrogen and 24% is helium).
2) The early universe had been very hot, so at some point it must have been hot enough for **hydrogen fusion** to happen. By studying how much **helium** there is **compared** to **hydrogen**, we can work out a **time frame** for this fusion. Together with the theory of the synthesis of the **heavier elements** in stars, the **relative abundances** of all of the elements can be accounted for.

## Practice Questions

Q1 State the cosmological principle.

Q2 What is Hubble's law? How can it be used to find the age of the universe?

Q3 What is the cosmic background radiation?

Q4 How do the relative amounts of hydrogen and helium in the universe provide evidence for the HBB model?

**Exam Questions**

Q1 a) State Hubble's law, explaining the meanings of all the symbols. [2 marks]

b) State the implications of Hubble's law for the nature of the universe. [2 marks]

c) Assume $H_0 = +50\ \text{kms}^{-1}\text{Mpc}^{-1}$ (*1 Mpc* $= 3.08 \times 10^{22}$ *m*).

i) Calculate $H_0$ in SI units. [2 marks]

ii) Calculate an estimate of the age of the universe, and hence the size of the observable universe. [3 marks]

Q2 a) A certain object has a red shift of 0.37. Estimate the speed the object is moving away from us and the distance (in light years) that the object is away from us.
(*Take* $H_0 = 2.4 \times 10^{-18}\ s^{-1}$, $1\ ly = 9.46 \times 10^{15}\ m$). [3 marks]

b) Explain why this distance is only an estimate. [1 mark]

Q3 Describe the main features of the cosmic background radiation and explain why its discovery was considered strong evidence for the Hot Big Bang model of the universe. [6 marks]

## My brother was a Great Attractor — everyone fell for him...

*The simple Big Bang model doesn't actually work — not quite, anyway. There are loads of little things that don't quite add up. Modern cosmologists are trying to improve the model using a period of very rapid expansion called inflation.*

# Physics of the Eye

*The eye uses lenses, rods and cones to allow you to see all the things around you.*

## The Eyes Contain **Converging Lenses**

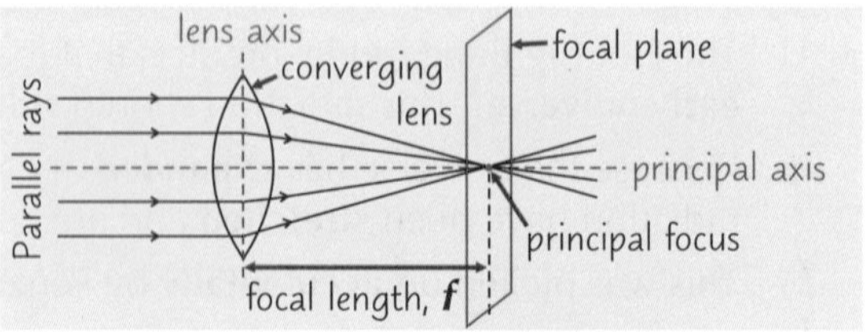


1) **Lenses** change the **direction** of light rays by **refraction**.
2) Rays **parallel** to the **principal axis** of the lens **converge** (are brought together) onto a point called the **principal focus**.
3) The **focal length**, ***f***, is the distance between the **lens axis** and the **principal focus**.
4) The **eye** has a **converging lens** which focuses incoming light to form an image on the **retina**, which is then **interpreted** by the **brain**.
5) The **cornea** is a **transparent** 'window' with a **convex** shape, and a **high refractive index**. The cornea does most of the eye's focusing.
6) The **lens** acts as a **fine focus** and is controlled by muscles which release tension in the lens when **contracted**. The lens then takes on a **fat**, more **spherical** shape. When the muscles **relax**, the lens is pulled into a **thin**, **flatter** shape. This changes the **focal length** of the eye.
7) The **retina** is where images are formed. It contains **light-sensitive cells** called **rods** and **cones** (see below). The **yellow spot** is a particularly sensitive region of the retina. In the centre of the yellow spot is the **fovea**. This is the part of the retina with the highest concentration of **cones**.

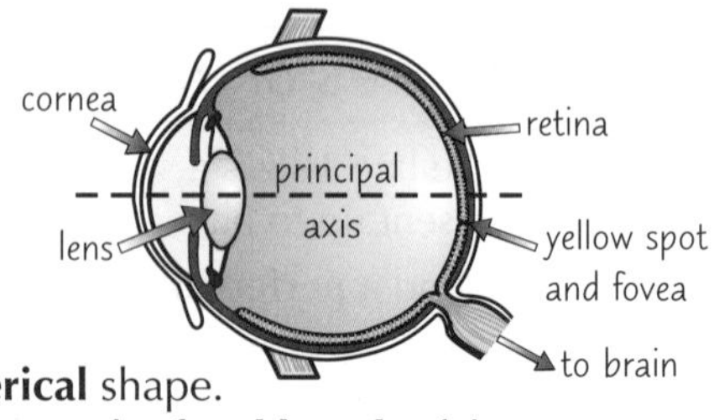


## You can use the **Lens Equation** for **Eyes**

The **lens equation** for **thin lenses** can be applied to the whole eye: $\frac{1}{f} = \frac{1}{u} + \frac{1}{v}$

where $f$ is the focal length (m), $u$ is the object distance (m) and $v$ is the image distance (m).

You can also calculate the **power** of a lens, which tells you the lens' ability to **bend light**. The higher the power, the more the lens will **refract** light. $P = \frac{1}{f}$

where $P$ is the power of the lens in dioptres (D).

## The **Eye** is an **Optical Refracting System**

1) The **far point** is the **furthest distance** that the eye can focus comfortably. For normally sighted people that's **infinity**. When your eyes are focusing at the far point, they're **'unaccommodated'**.
2) The **near point** is the **closest distance** that the eye can focus on. For young people it's about 9 cm.
3) You can **add together** the **powers** of the cornea, lens and other eye parts. That means you can think of the eye as a **single converging lens** of **power 59 D** at the far point. This gives a **focal length** of **1.7 cm**.
4) When looking at nearer objects, the eye's power **increases**, as the lens changes shape and the **focal length decreases** — but the distance between the lens and the image, $v$, stays the same at 1.7 cm.

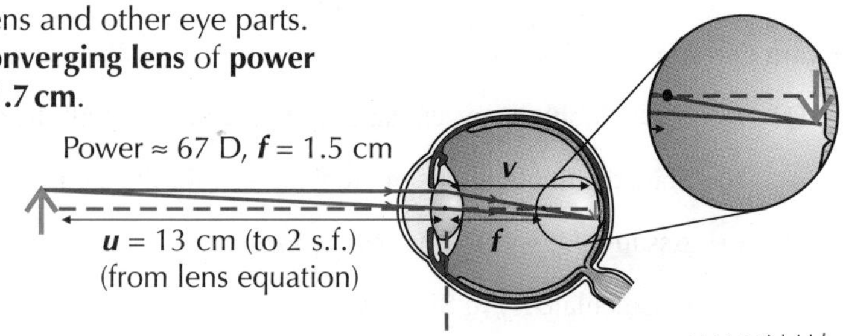


If you don't know how to draw a ray diagram, have a flick to p.66.

## The **Retina** has **Rods and Cones**

1) **Rods** and **cones** are cells at the back of the **retina** that respond to **light**. They're known as **photoreceptors**. Light travels **through the retina** to the rods and cones at the back.
2) Rods and cones all contain chemical **pigments** that **bleach** when **light** falls on them. This bleaching stimulates (or activates) the cell to send signals to the **brain** via the **optic nerve**.
3) The cells are **reset** (i.e. unbleached) by enzymes using **vitamin A** from the blood.
4) There's only **one** type of **rod** but there are **three** types of **cone**, which are sensitive to **red**, **green** and **blue** light.

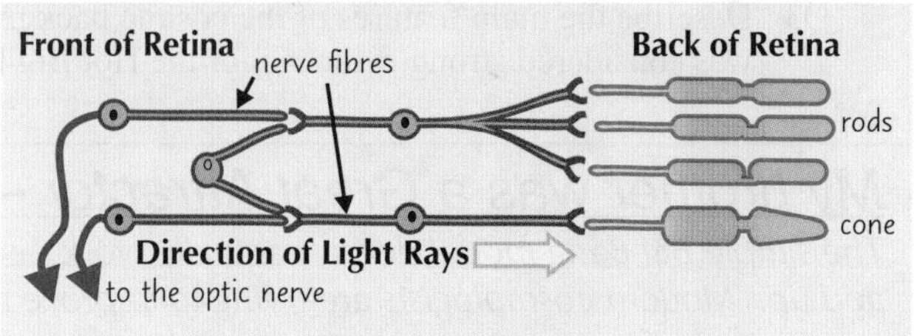

# Physics of the Eye

## The **Cones** let you See in **Full Colour**

1) The red, green and blue **cones** each absorb a **range of wavelengths**.
2) The eye is **less responsive** to blue light than to red or green, so blues often look dimmer.
3) The brain receives signals from the three types of cone and interprets their **weighted relative strengths** as **colour**...

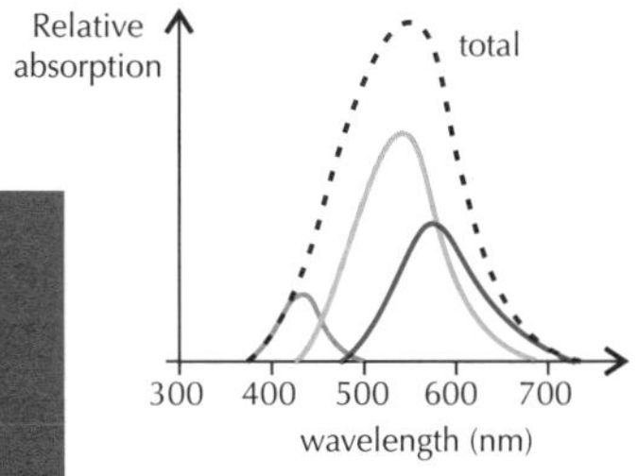


Yellow light produces almost equal responses from the red and green cones. Yellow light can therefore be 'faked' by combining red and green light of almost equal intensity — the electrical signal from the retina will be the same and the brain interprets it as 'yellow'.

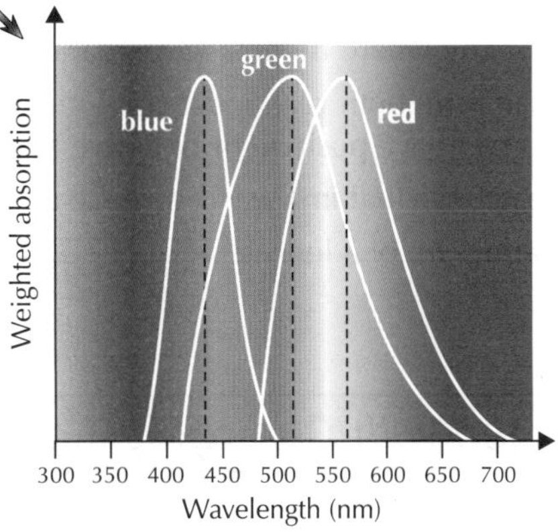

4) **Any** colour can be produced by **combining** different intensities of **red**, **green** and **blue** light. Colour televisions work like this.

## You Need Good **Spatial Resolution** to See **Details**

1) Two objects can only be distinguished from each other if there's **at least one rod** or **cone between** the light from each of them. Otherwise the brain can't **resolve** the two objects and it 'sees' them as one.

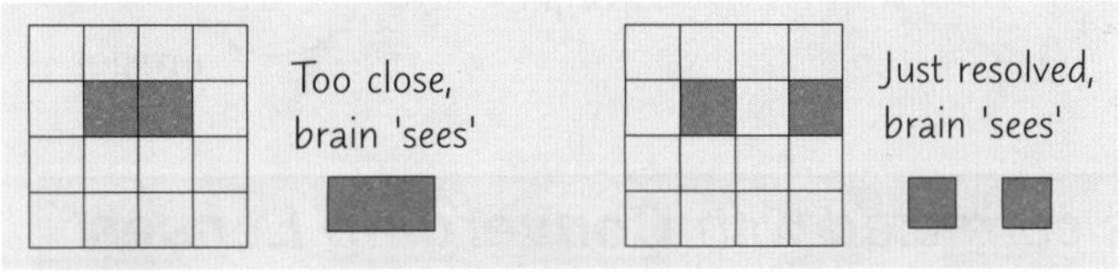


2) **Spatial resolution** is **best** at a certain spot on the retina, called the yellow spot — the **cones** are very **densely packed** here and each cone always has its **own nerve fibre**. There are **no rods in the yellow spot**, though. This means that in **dim light**, when **cones don't work**, resolution is best slightly off the direct line of sight, where the **rods** are more **densely packed**.
3) Away from the yellow spot, resolution is much worse. The light-sensitive cells are **not** as **densely packed** and the rods **share nerve fibres** — there are up to 600 rods per fibre at the edges of the retina.

## Practice Questions

Q1 Briefly describe how the three types of cone cells combine to let you see in colour.

Q2 Sketch a graph showing how the different types of cone cell in the retina respond to different wavelengths of light.

**Exam Question**

Q1 The power of an unaccommodated eye is 60 D (to 2 s.f.).

a) Calculate the image distance, $v$, when the eye focuses at infinity. [2 marks]

b) The eye then focuses on an object 30 cm away (to 2 s.f.). Draw a ray diagram showing the eye focusing on the image, labelling the image and object distances. [2 marks]

c) Calculate the extra power that the lens must produce for the eye to focus on the object. [2 marks]

## The eyes are the window on the soul...

*Or so they said in the 16th century. Sadly, that won't get you far with a question about the power of eye lenses.*

# Defects of Vision

*Plenty of people don't have perfect vision, and need auxiliary lenses to correct their sight.*

## ***Real*** *is* ***Positive, Virtual*** *is* ***Negative***

Lenses can produce **real** or **virtual** images, and you need to follow the "**real** is **positive**, **virtual** is **negative**" rule.

1) A **real image** is formed when light rays from an object are made to **pass through** another point in space. The light rays are **actually there**, and the image can be **captured** on a **screen**.
2) A **virtual image** is formed when light rays from an object **appear** to have come from another point in space. The light rays **aren't really where the image appears to be**, so the image **can't** be captured on a screen.
3) **Converging lenses** can form both **real** and **virtual** images, depending on where the **object** is. So converging lenses can have **positive or negative** focal lengths.
4) **Diverging lenses** create a **virtual image**. They have a **negative focal length**.
5) The **linear magnification**, ***m***, of a lens is:

$$m = \frac{\text{size of image}}{\text{size of object}} = \frac{v}{u}$$

where v is image distance (m) and u is object distance (m)

## ***Myopia*** *is Corrected with* ***Diverging Lenses***

1) **Short-sighted** (myopic) people are unable to focus on distant objects — this happens if their **far point** is **closer** than infinity (see p.88).
2) Myopia occurs when the **cornea** and **lens** are too **powerful** or the **eyeball** is too **long**.
3) The focusing system is **too powerful** and images of distant objects are brought into focus in **front** of the retina.
4) A lens of **negative power** is needed to correct this defect — so a **diverging** lens is placed in front of the eye.

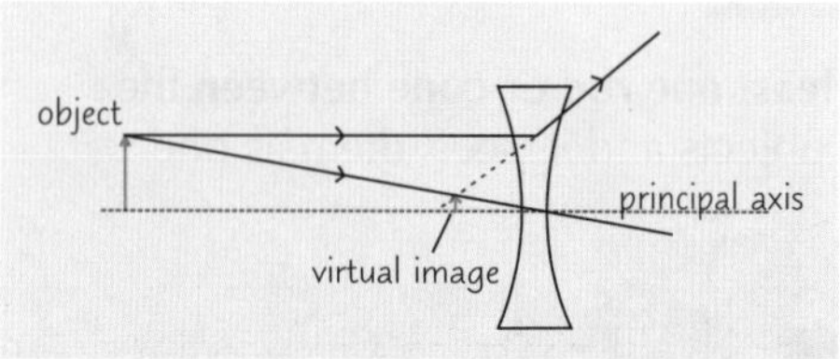


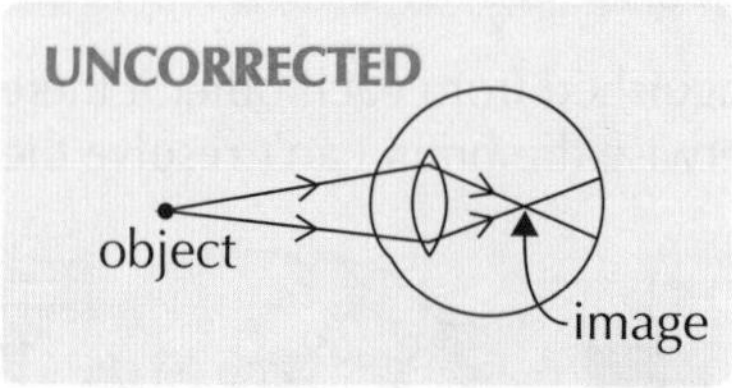


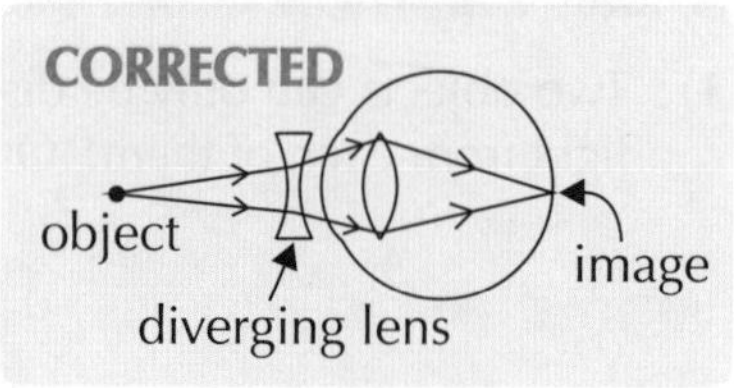


## ***Hypermetropia*** *is corrected with* ***Converging Lenses***

Long-sightedness is common among young children whose lenses have grown quicker than their eyeballs.

1) **Long-sighted** (hypermetropic) people are unable to focus clearly on near objects. This happens if their **near point** is **further** away than normal (25 cm or more).
2) Long sight occurs because the **cornea** and **lens** are too **weak** or the **eyeball** is too **short**.
3) The focusing system is **too weak** and images of near objects are brought into focus **behind** the retina.
4) A lens of **positive power** is needed to correct the defect — so a **converging** lens is placed in front of the eye.

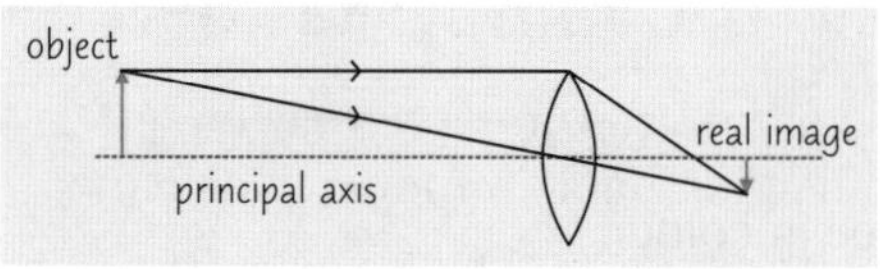


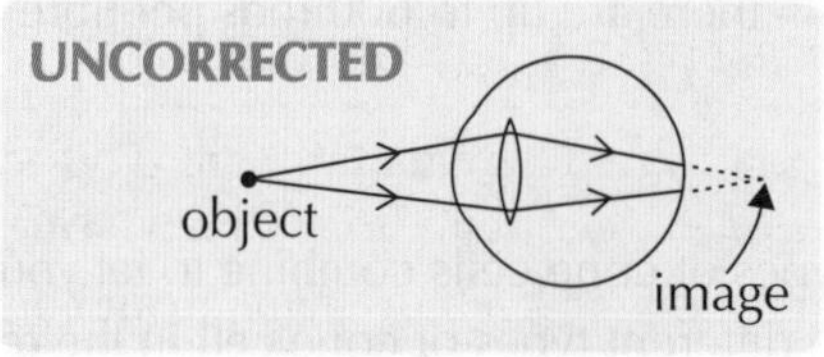


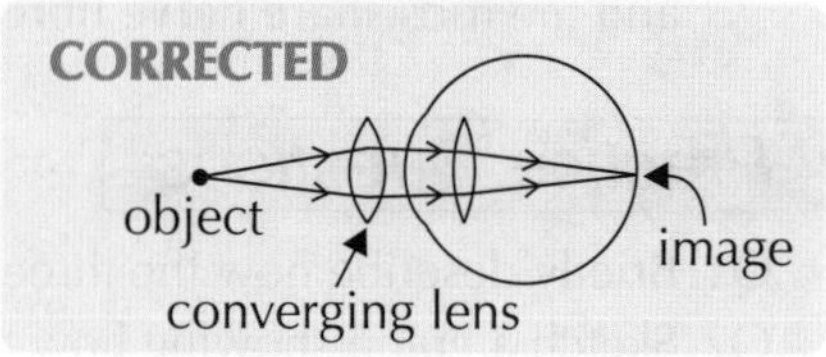


## ***Astigmatism*** *is Corrected with* ***Cylindrical Lenses***

1) **Astigmatism** is caused by an irregularly shaped **cornea** or **lens** which has **different focal lengths** for different **planes**. For instance, when **vertical lines** are in focus, **horizontal** lines might not be.
2) The condition is corrected with **cylindrical lenses.**

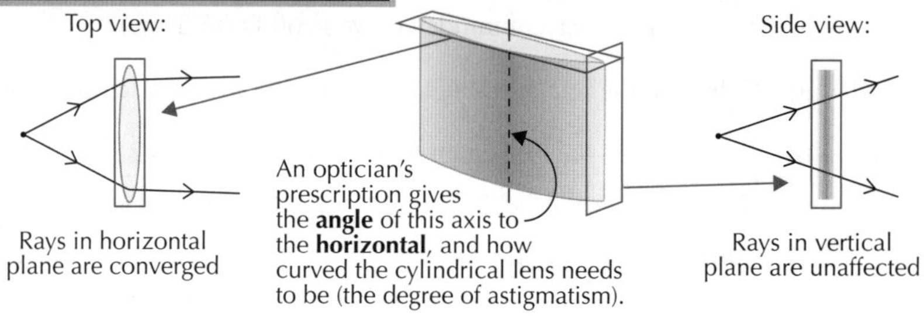


3) A cylindrical lens **prescription** has the **power** needed to correct for the long or short-sightedness, the power needed to **correct** the astigmatism and the **angle** to the **horizontal** of the **plane** that **doesn't** need correcting for astigmatism (shown by the **axis** in the **diagram**).

# Defects of Vision

## Choosing a Lens to Correct for Short Sight Depends on the Far Point

1) To correct for **short sight**, a **diverging** lens is chosen which has its **principal focus** at the eye's **faulty far point**.
2) The **principal focus** is the point that rays from a distant object **appear** to have come from.
3) The lens must have a **negative focal length** which is the same as the **distance to the eye's far point**. This means that objects at **infinity**, which were out of focus, now seem to be in focus at the far point.

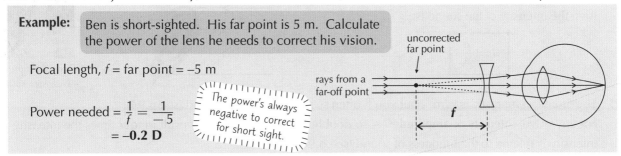

**Example:** Ben is short-sighted. His far point is 5 m. Calculate the power of the lens he needs to correct his vision.

Focal length, $f$ = far point = –5 m

Power needed = $\frac{1}{f} = \frac{1}{-5}$

= **–0.2 D**

The power's always negative to correct for short sight.

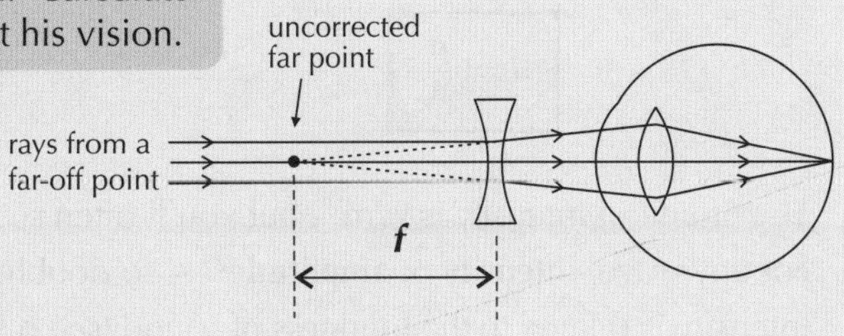


## Calculations Involving Long Sight Use the Lens Equation

1) People with these conditions have a near point which is too far away. An 'acceptable' near point is 25 cm.
2) A **converging lens** is used to produce a **virtual image** of objects 0.25 m away **at the eye's near point**. This means that close objects, which were out of focus, now seem to be in focus at the near point.
3) You can work out the **focal length**, and hence the **power** of lens needed, using the **lens equation**.

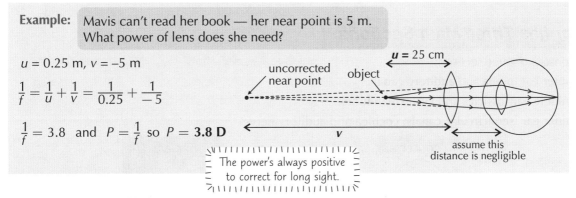

**Example:** Mavis can't read her book — her near point is 5 m. What power of lens does she need?

$u = 0.25$ m, $v = -5$ m

$\frac{1}{f} = \frac{1}{u} + \frac{1}{v} = \frac{1}{0.25} + \frac{1}{-5}$

$\frac{1}{f} = 3.8$ and $P = \frac{1}{f}$ so $P = $ **3.8 D**

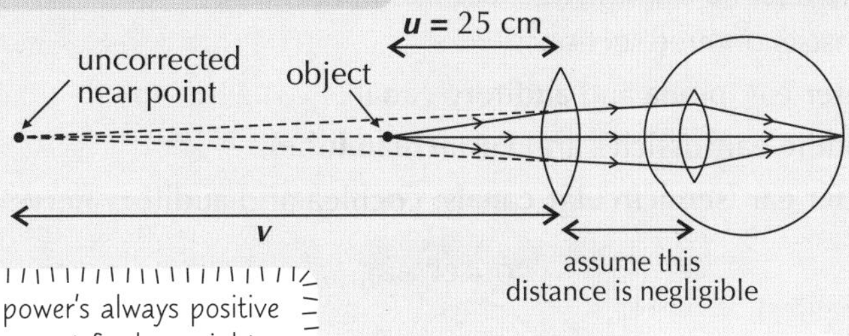


The power's always positive to correct for long sight.

## Practice Questions

Q1 Write down the equation for calculating the linear magnification of a lens.

Q2 Define the terms myopia, hypermetropia and astigmatism.

Q3 What type of auxiliary lenses are used to correct each of these conditions?

**Exam Questions**

Q1 A man with short sight has a far point of 4.0 m.
Calculate the power of auxiliary lens needed to correct his far point. [3 marks]

Q2 A girl has a near point of 2.0 m.
Calculate the power of lens required to correct her near point to 25 cm. [3 marks]

Q3 Claire suffers from astigmatism.

a) State the type of lenses that are used to correct astigmatism. [1 mark]

b) State what information the optician includes in a prescription for lenses which correct astigmatism. [2 marks]

## You can't fly fighter planes if you wear glasses...

*There's a hidden bonus to having dodgy eyes — in the exam, you can take your specs off (discreetly) and have a look at the lenses to remind yourself what type is needed to correct short sight, long sight, or whatever it is you have. Cunning.*

# Physics of the Ear

*Ears are pretty amazing — they convert sound into electrical energy, using some tiny bones and lots of even tinier hairs.*

## The *Intensity* of *Sound* is *Power* per *Unit Area*

The **intensity** of a sound wave is defined as the amount of sound **energy** that passes **per second per unit area** (perpendicular to the direction of the wave). That's **power per unit area.**

1) If the sound energy arriving at the ear per second is ***P***, then the intensity of the sound is:

$$I = \frac{P}{A}$$

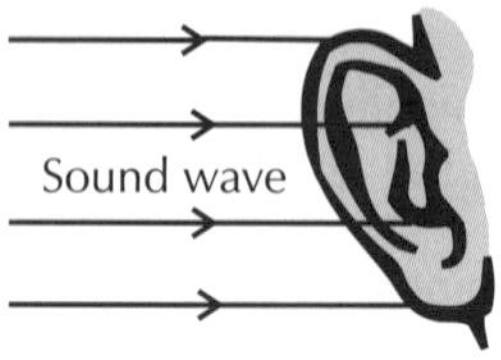

Felicity thought her waves were sound.

2) The SI unit of intensity is $Wm^{-2}$, but you'll often see decibels used instead (see p.94).
3) For any wave, **intensity** $\propto$ **amplitude²** — so doubling the amplitude will result in four times the intensity.
4) Intensity is related to the **loudness** of sound (see p.94).

**Example:** A fire alarm sounds with a power of 4.5 W. Calculate the intensity of sound a person standing 3.0 m away would hear, assuming the sound waves spread equally in all directions.

Surface area of a sphere = $4\pi r^2$ so $A = 4\pi \times 3.0^2 = 36\pi$

Intensity $= I = \frac{P}{A} = \frac{4.5}{36\pi} = 0.03978...\text{Wm}^{-2} =$ **0.040 Wm⁻² (to 2 s.f.)**

## The *Ear* has *Three Main Sections*

The ear consists of three sections:

1) The **outer** ear (**pinna** and **auditory canal**).
2) The **middle ear** (**ossicles** and **Eustachian tube**).
3) The **inner ear** (**semicircular canals**, **cochlea** and **auditory nerve**).

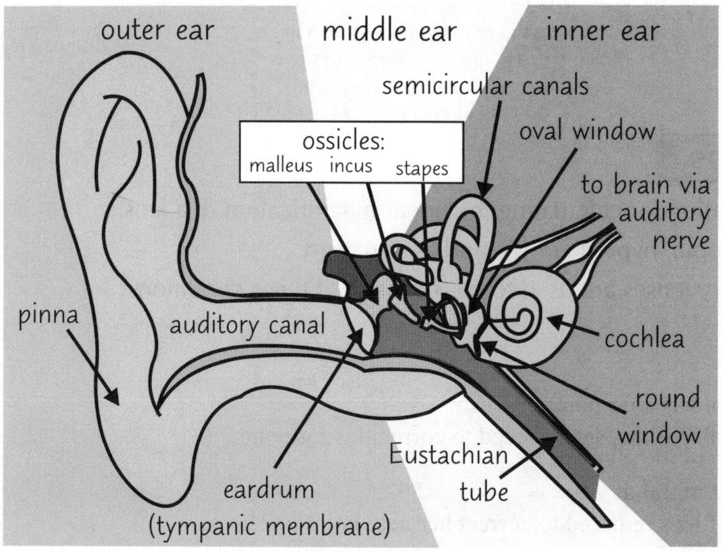


1) The **tympanic membrane** (eardrum) separates the **outer** and **middle** ears.
2) Although separated, the **outer** and **middle** ears both contain **air** at **atmospheric pressure**, apart from slight pressure variations due to sound waves. This pressure is maintained by **yawning** and **swallowing** — the middle ear is opened up to the outside via the **Eustachian tube** (which is connected to the throat).
3) The **oval** and **round windows** separate the **middle** and **inner** ears.
4) The **inner ear** is filled with fluid called **perilymph** (or **endolymph** in the **cochlear duct**). This fluid allows **vibrations** to pass to the basilar membrane in the **cochlea**.
5) The **semicircular canals** are involved with **maintaining balance.**

# Physics of the Ear

## The **Ear** acts as a **Transducer,** converting **Sound Energy**...

1) The **pinna** (external ear) acts like a funnel, channelling sound waves into the auditory canal. The sound energy is now **concentrated** onto a **smaller area**, which increases its **intensity**.
2) The sound waves consist of **variations** in **air pressure**, which make the **tympanic membrane** (eardrum) **vibrate**.
3) The tympanic membrane is connected to the **malleus** — one of the **three tiny bones** (**ossicles**) in the middle ear. The malleus then passes the **vibrations** of the eardrum on to the **incus** and the **stapes** (which is connected to the **oval window**).
4) As well as **transmitting vibrations**, the **ossicles** have **two** other functions — **amplifying** the sound signal and **reducing** the **energy reflected back** from the inner ear.
5) The **oval window** has a much **smaller area** than the **tympanic membrane**. Together with the **increased force** produced by the ossicles, this results in **greater pressure variations** at the oval window.
6) The **oval window** transmits vibrations to the **fluid** in the **inner ear**.
7) As the sound wave travels **through** the ear, its **amplitude decreases**, but its **frequency** remains the **same**.

## ...into **Electrical Energy**

1) Pressure waves in the fluid of the **cochlea** make the **basilar membrane** vibrate. Different regions of this membrane have different **natural frequencies**, from 20 000 Hz near the middle ear to 20 Hz at the other end.
2) When a sound wave of a particular **frequency** enters the inner ear, one part of the basilar membrane **resonates** and so vibrates with a **large amplitude**.
3) **Hair cells** attached to the basilar membrane trigger **nerve impulses** at this point of greatest vibration.
4) These **electrical impulses** are sent, via the **auditory nerve**, to the **brain**, where they are interpreted as **sounds**.

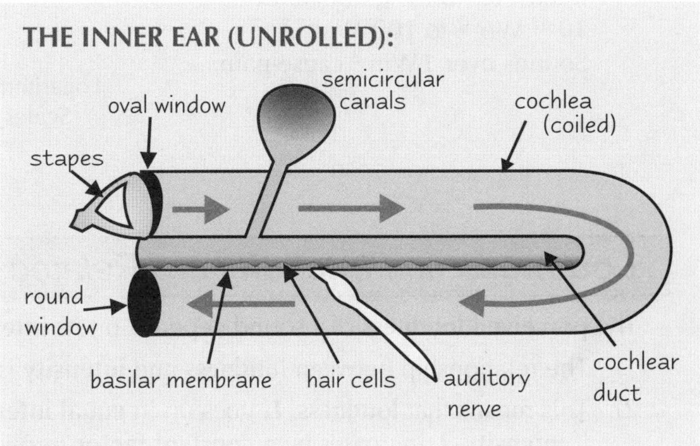


## Practice Questions

Q1 What is meant by the 'intensity' of sound? What is the formula for intensity?

Q2 Sketch a diagram of the ear, labelling the structures within it.

Q3 Describe the function of the ossicles.

Q4 Explain why the relative sizes of the oval window and tympanic membrane are important.

**Exam Question**

Q1 The ear is designed to transduce sound energy into electrical energy.

a) State the function of the pinna. [1 mark]

b) Describe how sound energy is transmitted through the middle ear. [3 marks]

c) The surface area of the tympanic membrane is around 14 times the area of the oval window. Show that this increases the amplitude of vibrations in the ear by a factor of approximately 3.7. [3 marks]

d) Describe how pressure waves in the cochlea are converted to electrical impulses. [2 marks]

e) Explain how the ear is able to encode the frequency of a sound in the information sent to the brain. [2 marks]

## Ears are like essays — they have a beginning, middle and end...

*Or outer, middle and inner, if we're being technical. Learn what vibrates where, and you'll be fine.*

# Intensity and Loudness

*The ear's sensitivity depends on the frequency and intensity of sounds, and deteriorates as you get older.*

## Humans can Hear a Limited Range of Frequencies

1) Young people can hear frequencies ranging from about **20 Hz** (low pitch) up to **20 000 Hz** (high pitch). As you get older, the upper limit decreases.
2) Our ability to **discriminate between frequencies** depends on how **high** that frequency is. For example, between 60 and 1000 Hz, you can hear frequencies 3 Hz apart as **different pitches**. At **higher** frequencies, a **greater difference** is needed for frequencies to be distinguished. Above 10 000 Hz, pitch can hardly be discriminated at all.
3) The **loudness** of sound you hear depends on the **intensity** and **frequency** of the sound waves.
4) The **weakest intensity** you can hear depends on the **frequency** of the sound wave.
5) The ear is **most sensitive** at around **3000 Hz**. For any given intensity, sounds of this frequency will be **loudest**.
6) Humans can hear sounds at intensities ranging from about $10^{-12}$ Wm$^{-2}$ to 100 Wm$^{-2}$. Sounds **over 1 Wm$^{-2}$** cause **pain**.

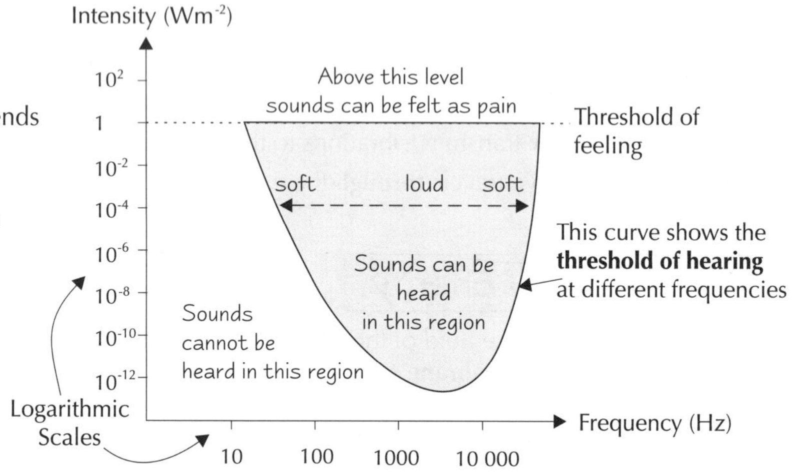


## Loudness and Intensity are Related Logarithmically

The **perceived loudness** of a sound depends on its **intensity** (and its frequency — see above).

1) The relationship between **loudness** and **intensity** is **logarithmic.**
2) This means that **loudness**, $L$, goes up in **equal intervals** if **intensity**, $I$, increases by a **constant factor** (provided the frequency of the sound doesn't change).

$$\Delta L \propto \log\left(\frac{I_2}{I_1}\right)$$

$\Delta L$ is increase in loudness
$I_1$ is the original intensity
$I_2$ is the new intensity

3) E.g. if you **double** the intensity, **double it again** and so on, the **loudness** keeps going up in **equal steps**.

## The Decibel Scale is used for Measuring Relative Intensity

1) You can often measure loudness using a **decibel meter**. The **decibel scale** is a **logarithmic scale** which actually measures **intensity level** — how intense the sound is **compared** to the human **threshold of hearing**.
2) The **intensity level, $IL$,** of a sound of intensity $I$ is defined as:

$$IL = 10\log\left(\frac{I}{I_0}\right)$$

$I$ = intensity
$I_0$ = threshold of hearing

3) $I_0$ is the **threshold of hearing** (the **lowest intensity** of sound that can be heard) at a frequency of **1000 Hz**.
4) The value of $I_0$ is **$1.0 \times 10^{-12}$ Wm$^{-2}$**.
5) The units of $IL$ are **decibels** (dB). Intensity level can be given in **bels** (one decibel is a tenth of a bel) but decibels are usually a more convenient size.

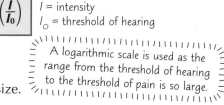

A logarithmic scale is used as the range from the threshold of hearing to the threshold of pain is so large.

## The dBA Scale is an Adjusted Decibel Scale

1) The **perceived loudness** of a sound depends on its **frequency** as well as its intensity. Two different frequencies with the **same loudness** will have **different intensity levels** on the dB scale.
2) The **dBA** scale is an **adjusted decibel scale** which is designed to take into account the **ear's response** to **different frequencies**.
3) On the **dBA scale**, sounds of the **same intensity level** have the **same loudness** for the average human ear.

# Intensity and Loudness

## You can Generate *Curves of Equal Loudness*

1) Start by generating a **control frequency** of **1000 Hz** at a particular **intensity level**.
2) Generate another sound at a different frequency. Vary the volume of this sound until it appears to have the **same loudness** as the 1000 Hz frequency. Measure the **intensity level** at this volume.
3) Repeat this for several different frequencies, and plot the resulting curve on a graph.
4) Change the **intensity level** of the **control frequency** and repeat steps two and three.
5) If you measure **intensity level** in **decibels**, then the **loudness** of the sound is given in **phons**.

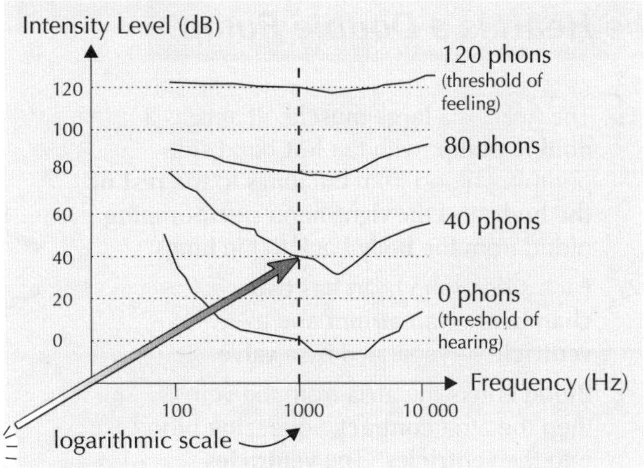


At 1000 Hz, the loudness in phons is the same value as the intensity level in decibels.

## *Hearing Deteriorates with Age and Exposure to Excessive Noise*

1) As you get **older**, your hearing deteriorates **generally**, but **higher frequencies** are affected **most**.
2) Your ears can be damaged by **excessive noise**. This results in general hearing loss, but frequencies around **4000 Hz** are usually worst affected.
3) People who've worked with very **noisy machinery** have most hearing loss at the **particular frequencies** of the noise causing the damage.
4) **Equal loudness curves** can show hearing loss.
5) For a person with hearing loss, **higher intensity levels** are needed for the **same loudness**, when compared to a normal ear. A **peak** in the curve shows damage at a **particular** range of **frequencies**.

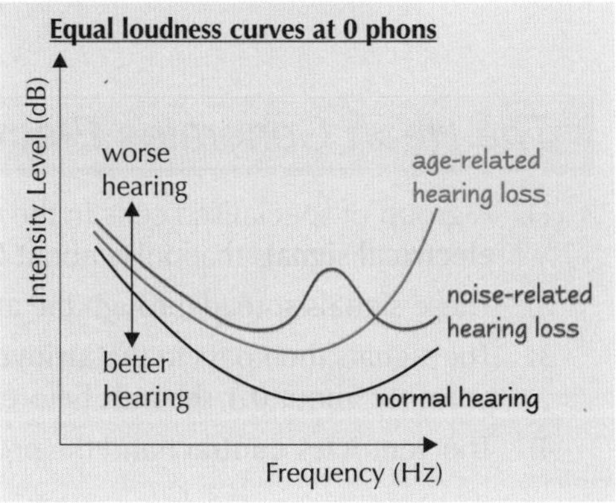


## Practice Questions

Q1 Define the threshold of hearing and sketch a graph that shows how it depends on frequency.

Q2 What is the dB scale? How is the dBA scale different?

Q3 How are curves of equal loudness generated?

**Exam Questions**

Q1 A siren, which can be regarded as a point source, emits sound waves at a frequency of 3000 Hz (to 2 s.f.). The intensity of the sound is 0.94 $Wm^{-2}$ at a distance of 10 m (to 2 s.f.).

a) State the accepted value of the threshold of hearing at 1000 Hz, $I_0$, in $Wm^{-2}$. [1 mark]

b) Calculate the intensity level of the sound of the siren. [1 mark]

c) Explain why the siren uses a frequency of 3000 Hz. [1 mark]

Q2 The diagram shows an equal loudness curve for a person suffering hearing loss and a person with normal hearing. The patient believes his hearing may have been damaged by working with noisy machinery. Does his equal loudness curve support this? Explain your answer. [3 marks]

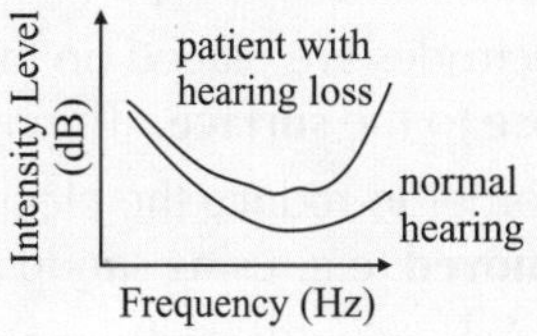


## *Saved by the decibel....*

*It's medical fact that prolonged loud noise damages your hearing, so you should really demand ear protection before you agree to do the housework — some vacuum cleaners are louder than 85 dBA — the 'safe' limit for regular exposure.*

# Electrocardiography (ECG)

*You don't need to know about the structure of the heart or how it actually generates electrical signals for your exam, but you should probably understand the basics before you jump into electrocardiographs.*

## The **Heart** is a **Double Pump**

1) The heart is a **large muscle**. It acts as a **double pump**, with the **left**-hand side pumping blood from the **lungs** to the **rest of the body** and the **right**-hand side pumping blood from the **body** back to the **lungs**.
2) Each side of the heart has **two chambers** — an **atrium** and a **ventricle** — separated by a **valve**.
3) **Blood** enters the **atria** from the veins, then the atria **contract**, squeezing blood into the **ventricles**. The **ventricles** then **contract**, squeezing the blood **out** of the heart into the **arteries**.

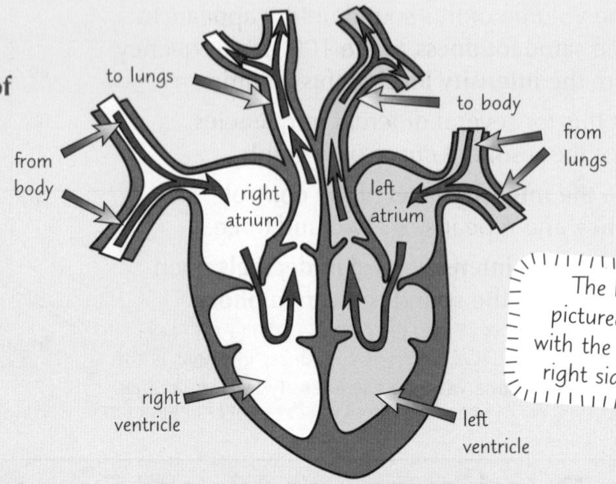

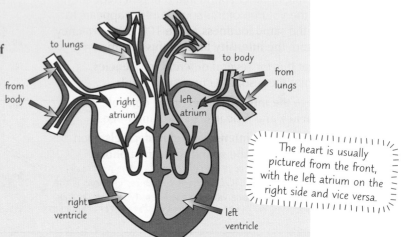

The heart is usually pictured from the front, with the left atrium on the right side and vice versa.

## The Heart Generates **Electrical Signals**

1) A group of specialised cells in the wall of the right atrium produce **electrical signals** that pulse about **70 times a minute**.
2) These signals spread through the **atria** and make them **contract**.
3) The signals then pass to the **atrioventricular node**, which **delays** the pulse for about **0.1 seconds** before passing it on to the **ventricles**.
4) The ventricles **contract** and the process repeats.

Lucy's heart went a bit out of control when she saw Josh.

## The Heart can be **Monitored** by an **Electrocardiograph**

1) The electrical signals of the heart can be detected **weakly** on the surface of the body. A machine called an **electrocardiograph** detects these signals and produces an **ECG** — an **electrocardiogram.**
2) An ECG is a plot of the **potential difference** between electrodes **against time**. They're used to find out about the **condition** of the heart being examined.

### Obtaining an ECG

1) When obtaining an ECG, **electrodes** are placed on the body and the difference in potential difference between the sites is measured.
2) The signal is heavily **attenuated** (absorbed and weakened) by the body and needs to be **amplified** by a **high impedance** amplifier.
3) Electrodes are placed on the chest, which is close to the heart, and the limbs, where the **arteries** are **close** to the **surface**. The right leg is **never** used since it is too far away from the heart.
4) In order to reduce the electrical resistance at the point of contact, **hairs** and dead skin cells are **removed** (e.g. using sandpaper), a **conductive gel** is used and the electrodes are **securely attached**.
5) To reduce unwanted signals, the patient should also remain **relaxed** and **still** during the procedure, and the leads used should be shielded from any possible **interference** from ac sources in the area.

# Electrocardiography (ECG)

## An **Electrocardiogram** Has **Three** Distinct Waves

A normal ECG across one heart beat has a set pattern, split into **three parts**.

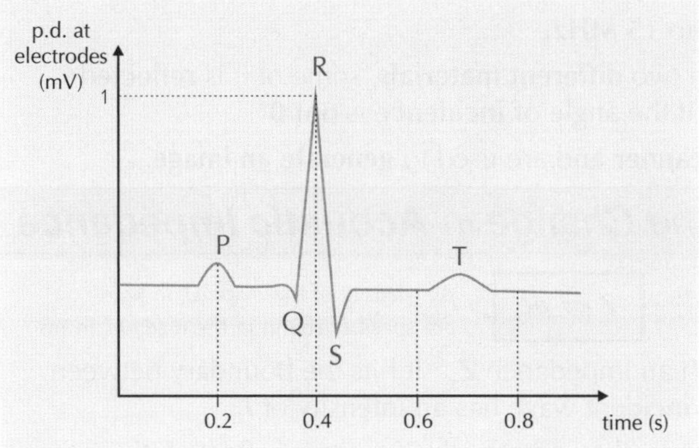

Martin loved distinct waves.

1) **P wave** — this is where a generated signal causes the **atria** to **contract**.
2) **QRS wave** — (about 0.2 seconds later) this is when the **ventricles** are **contracting**. This signal is much greater than the P wave which causes the atria to contract.
3) **T wave** — (another 0.2 seconds later) this corresponds to the **relaxation** of the **ventricles** as they prepare for another heartbeat.

## Practice Questions

Q1 What is an electrocardiograph?

Q2 How many standard ways are there to place electrodes for an ECG?

Q3 What does attenuation mean?

Q4 Why are electrodes never placed on the right leg?

Q5 Why should electrocardiograph leads be shielded if there are sources of ac current nearby?

**Exam Questions**

Q1 A patient has an ECG taken, part of which is shown.

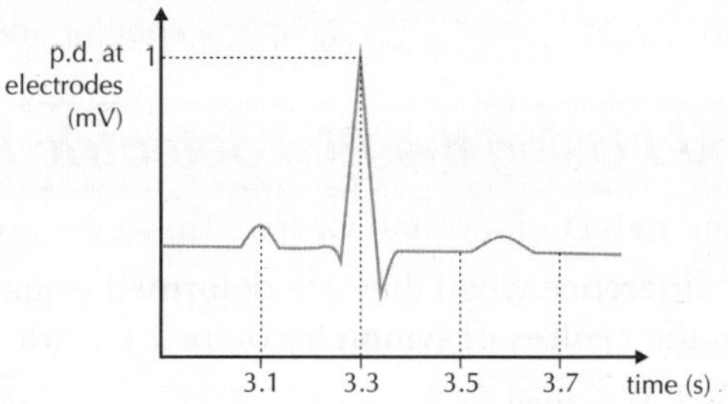


a) State the times that the P, QRS and T wave peaks occur. [1 mark]

b) State which wave corresponds to the atria contracting. [1 mark]

Q2 a) A problem is found on the QRS wave of a patient's ECG. State the area of the heart which could be causing this. [1 mark]

b) The problem arose from intermittent electrical resistance between the electrode and the patient's skin. Suggest one measure which could be taken to prevent this. [1 mark]

## Be still my contracting atria...

*If you rely on the cast of Casualty to get your heart beating faster, console yourself that it's all very educational. Listen out for the machine that goes 'bip, bip, bip', and look for the P waves, QRS waves and T waves on the screen. If there aren't enough waves, the brave docs have to start shouting 'clear' and waving defibrillators around.*

# Ultrasound Imaging

*Ultrasound imaging is a kind of non-invasive diagnostic technique used to avoid having to open you up.*

## *Ultrasound* has a *Higher Frequency* than *Humans* can *Hear*

1) Ultrasound waves are **longitudinal** waves with **higher frequencies** than humans can hear (>20 000 Hz).
2) For **medical** purposes, frequencies are usually from **1** to **15 MHz**.
3) When an ultrasound wave meets a **boundary** between two **different materials**, some of it is **reflected** and some of it passes through (undergoing **refraction** if the **angle of incidence** is **not 0°**).
4) The **reflected waves** are detected by the **ultrasound scanner** and are used to **generate an image**.

## The Amount of *Reflection* depends on the Change in *Acoustic Impedance*

1) The **acoustic impedance**, $Z$, of a medium is defined as: $Z = \rho c$
   $Z$ has units of $kgm^{-2}s^{-1}$.
   $\rho$ = density of the material, in $kgm^{-3}$
   $c$ = speed of sound in the medium, in $ms^{-1}$
2) Say an ultrasound wave travels through a material with an impedance $Z_1$. It hits the boundary between this material and another with an impedance $Z_2$. The incident wave has an intensity of $I_i$.
3) If the two materials have a **large difference** in **impedance**, then **most** of the energy is **reflected** (the intensity of the reflected wave $I_r$ will be high). If the impedance of the two materials is the **same** then there is **no reflection**.
4) The **fraction** of wave **intensity** that is reflected is given by:
   $$\frac{I_r}{I_i} = \left(\frac{Z_2 - Z_1}{Z_2 + Z_1}\right)^2$$
   where $I_r$ is the intensity of the reflected wave.
5) Ultrasound waves undergo **attenuation** (they are **absorbed** and **scattered**) when they travel through a material. The larger the impedance of a material, the greater the attenuation of the ultrasound moving through the material.

## There are *Advantages* and *Disadvantages* to *Ultrasound Imaging*

**ADVANTAGES:**

1) There are **no** known **hazards** — in particular, **no** exposure to **ionising radiation** (p.55).
2) It's good for imaging **soft tissues**, since you can obtain **real-time** images — X-ray fluoroscopy (p.104) can achieve this, but involves a huge dose of radiation.
3) Ultrasound devices are relatively **cheap** and **portable**.
4) The scan is a **quick procedure** (10-15 minutes) and the patient **can move** during the scan.

**DISADVANTAGES:**

1) Ultrasound **doesn't penetrate bone** — so it **can't** be used to **detect fractures** or examine the **brain**.
2) Ultrasound **cannot** pass through **air spaces** in the body (due to the **mismatch** in **impedance**) — so it can't produce images from behind the lungs.
3) The **resolution** is **poor** (about 10 times worse than X-rays), so you **can't see** fine **detail**.
4) Ultrasound can detect **solid masses**, but **can't** give any specific information as to what they are.

## *Ultrasound Images* are *Produced* Using the *Piezoelectric Effect*

1) **Transducers** are used in imaging to **send** and **detect** ultrasound waves. They contain **piezoelectric crystals**.
2) **Piezoelectric crystals** produce a **potential difference** when they are **deformed** (squashed or stretched) — the rearrangement in structure displaces the **centres of symmetry** of their electric **charges**.

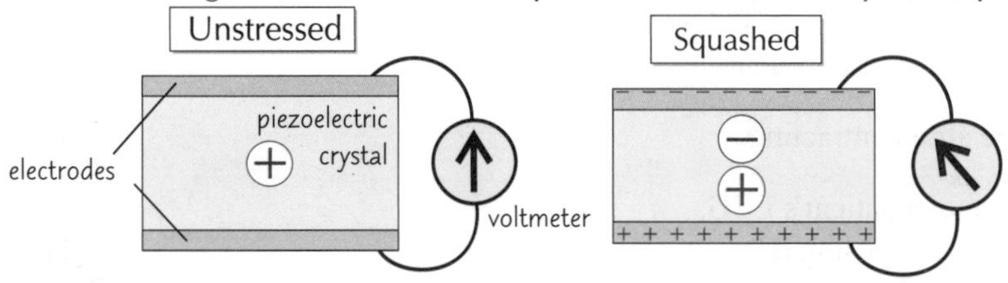

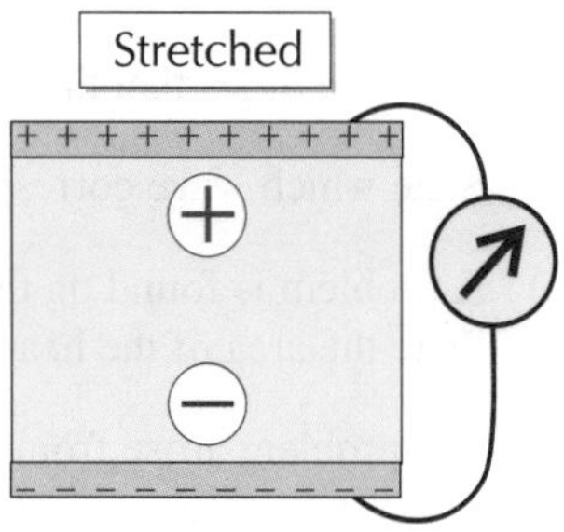


3) When you **apply a p.d.** across a piezoelectric crystal, the crystal **deforms**. If the p.d. is **alternating**, then the crystal **vibrates** at the **same frequency**.
4) A piezoelectric crystal can act as a **receiver** of **ultrasound**, converting **sound waves** into **alternating voltages**, and also as a **transmitter**, converting **alternating voltages** into **sound waves**.
5) Ultrasound devices use **lead zirconate titanate** (**PZT**) crystals. The **thickness** of the crystal is **half the wavelength** of the ultrasound that it produces. Ultrasound of this frequency will make the crystal **resonate** (like air in an open pipe — see p.8) and produce a large signal.
6) The PZT crystal is **heavily damped**, to produce **short pulses** and **increase** the **resolution** of the device.

# Ultrasound Imaging

## You need a Coupling Medium between the Transducer and the Body

1) **Soft tissue** has a very different **acoustic impedance** from **air** (as does the transducer), so almost all the ultrasound **energy** is **reflected** from the surface of the body if there is air between the **transducer** and the **body**.
2) To avoid this, you need a **coupling medium** between the transducer and the body — this **displaces** the **air** and has an impedance much closer to that of body tissue. The use of **coupling media** is an example of **impedance matching**.
3) The coupling medium is usually an **oil** or **gel** that is smeared onto the skin.

## The A-Scan is a Range Measuring System

1) The **amplitude scan** (**A-Scan**) sends a short **pulse** of ultrasound into the body simultaneously with an **electron beam** sweeping across a cathode ray oscilloscope (**CRO**) screen.
2) The scanner receives **reflected** ultrasound pulses that appear as **vertical deflections** on the CRO screen. **Weaker** pulses (that have travelled further in the body and **arrive later**) are **amplified** more to avoid the loss of valuable data — this process is called **time-gain compensation** (**TGC**).

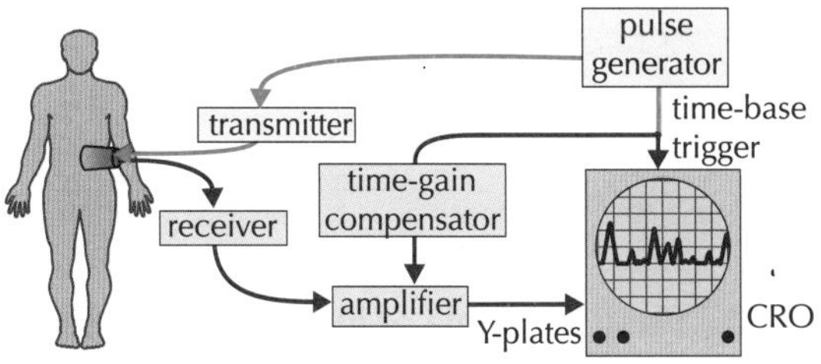


3) The **horizontal positions** of the reflected pulses indicate the **time** the 'echo' took to return, and are used to work out **distances** between structures in the body (e.g. the **diameter** of a **baby's head** in the uterus).
4) A **stream** of pulses can produce the appearance of a **steady image** on the screen, although modern CROs can store a digital image after just one exposure.

## In a B-Scan, the Brightness Varies

1) In a **brightness scan** (**B-Scan**), the electron beam sweeps **down** the screen rather than across.
2) The amplitude of the reflected pulses is displayed as the **brightness** of the spot.
3) You can use a **linear array** of transducers to produce a **two-dimensional** image — for example of a foetus in a womb.

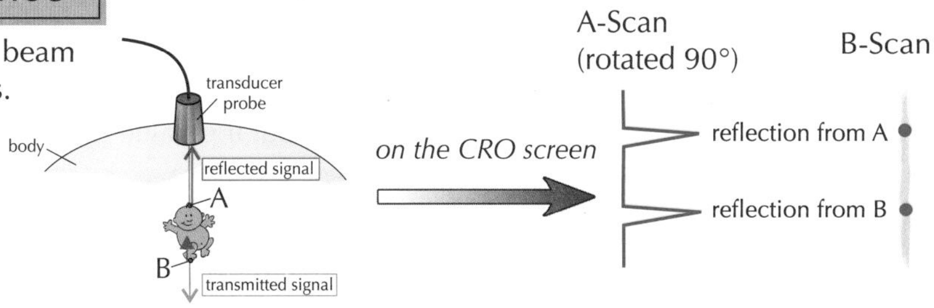


## Practice Questions

Q1 State the equation for acoustic impedance.

Q2 How are ultrasound waves produced and received in an ultrasound transducer?

Q3 What are the two types of ultrasound scan, and what are they both used for?

**Exam Questions**

Q1 a) Calculate what fraction of intensity is reflected when ultrasound waves pass from air to soft tissue.
Use $Z_{air} = 0.430 \times 10^3$ kgm$^{-2}$s$^{-1}$, $Z_{tissue} = 1630 \times 10^3$ kgm$^{-2}$s$^{-1}$. [2 marks]

b) Calculate the ratio between the intensity of the ultrasound that enters the body when a coupling gel is used ($Z_{gel} = 1500 \times 10^3$ kgm$^{-2}$s$^{-1}$) and when none is used. Give your answer to the nearest power of ten. [4 marks]

Q2 The acoustic impedance of a certain soft tissue is $1.63 \times 10^6$ kgm$^{-2}$s$^{-1}$ and its density is $1.09 \times 10^3$ kgm$^{-3}$.
Calculate the velocity the ultrasound waves travel at in this medium. [2 marks]

Q3 State one advantage and one disadvantage of using ultrasound as a medical imaging technique. [2 marks]

## *Ultrasound — Mancunian for 'très bien'*

*You can use ultrasound to make images in cases where other techniques would do too much damage — like to check the development of a baby in the womb. You have to know what you're looking for though, or it just looks like a blob.*

# Endoscopy

*Phew, that ultrasound stuff wasn't exactly a walk in the park — luckily, endoscopes are easier to understand...*

## Optical Fibres Use Total Internal Reflection to Transmit Light

1) **Optical fibres** are a bit like electric wires — but instead of carrying current they **transmit light**.
2) A typical optical fibre consists of a **glass core** (about 5 μm to 50 μm in diameter) **surrounded** by a **cladding**, which has a slightly **lower refractive index**.
3) The **difference** in refractive index means that light travelling along the fibre will be **reflected** at the **cladding-core interface**. If the light ray's **angle of incidence** is **less than or equal** to a **critical angle**, some light will be **lost** out of the fibre.

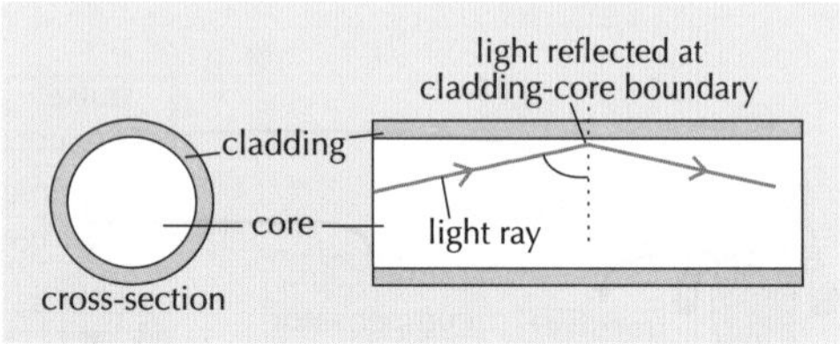


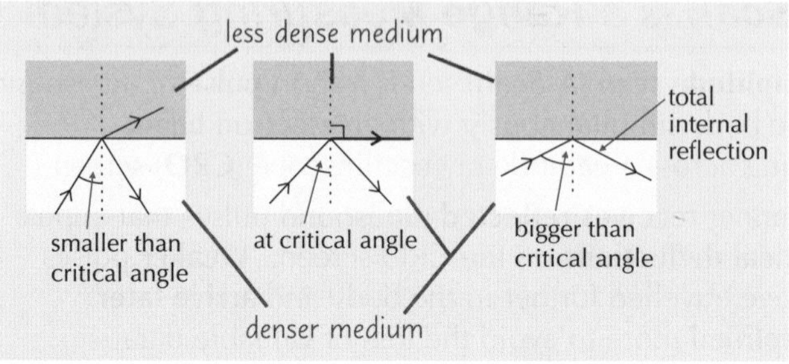


4) But if the **angle of incidence** is **larger** than the **critical angle**, the light ray will be **completely reflected** inside the fibre.
5) This phenomenon is called **total internal reflection** and means that the ray **zigzags** its way along the fibre — so long as the fibre isn't too curved.

## The Critical Angle for an Optical Fibre can be Worked Out

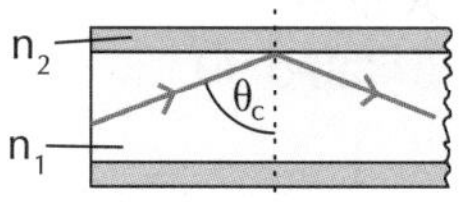


1) The **critical angle**, $\theta_c$, depends on the **refractive index** of the **core**, $n_1$, and **cladding**, $n_2$, in an optical fibre.
2) You can work out this value using the formula:

$$\sin\theta_c = \frac{n_2}{n_1}$$

**Example:** An optical fibre consists of a core with a refractive index of 1.5 and cladding with a refractive index of 1.4. Calculate the critical angle at the core-cladding boundary, and determine whether total internal reflection would occur if the incident angle was 70°.

$$\theta_c = \sin^{-1}\left(\frac{n_2}{n_1}\right) = \sin^{-1}\left(\frac{1.4}{1.5}\right) = 68.96...^\circ = \mathbf{69^\circ\ (to\ 2\ s.f.)}$$

70° > 69°, so total internal reflection would occur.

## Lots of Optical Fibres can be Bundled Together

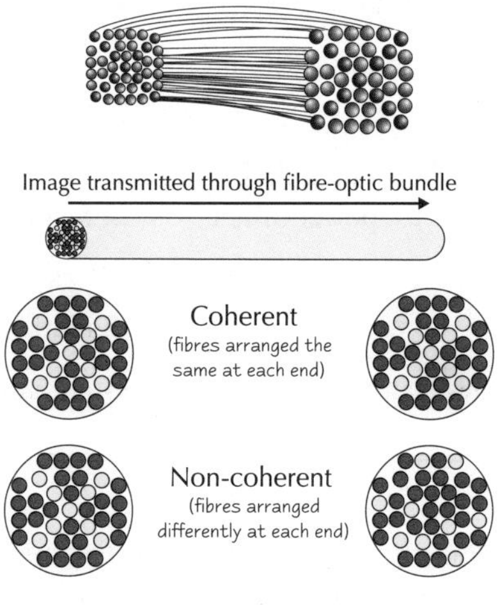


1) An **image** can be transmitted along a **bundle** of optical fibres.
2) This can only happen if the **relative positions** of fibres in a bundle are the **same** at each end (otherwise the image would be jumbled up) — a fibre-optic bundle in this arrangement is said to be **coherent**.
3) The **resolution** (i.e. how much detail can be seen) depends on the **thickness** of the fibres. The thinner the fibres, the **more detail** that can be resolved — but thin fibres are more **expensive** to make.
4) Images can be **magnified** by making the diameters of the fibres get **gradually larger** along the length of the bundle.
5) If the relative **position** of the fibres **does not** remain the same between each end the bundle of fibres is said to be **non-coherent**.
6) **Non-coherent bundles** are much easier and **cheaper** to make. They **can't** transmit an **image** but they can be used to get **light** to hard-to-reach places — kind of like a flexible **torch**.

# Endoscopy

## **Endoscopes** Use Optical Fibres to Create an **Image**

1) An **endoscope** consists of a **long tube** containing **two bundles** of fibres — a **non-coherent** bundle to carry **light** to the area of interest and a **coherent** bundle to carry an **image** back to the eyepiece.
2) Endoscopes are widely used by surgeons to examine inside the body.
3) An **objective lens** is placed at the **distal** end (**furthest from the eye**) of the **coherent** bundle to form an image, which is then transmitted by the fibres to the **proximal** end (**closest to the eye**) where it can be **viewed** through an **eyepiece**.
4) The **endoscope tube** can also contain a **water channel**, for cleaning the objective lens, a **tool aperture** to perform **keyhole surgery** and a **$CO_2$ channel** which allows $CO_2$ to be pumped into the area in front of the endoscope, making more room in the body.

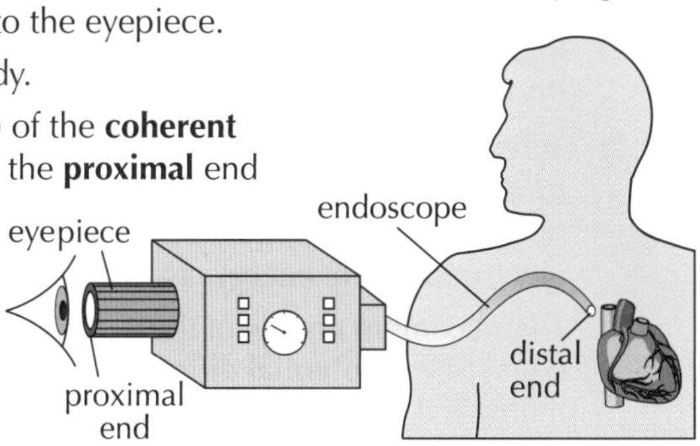


## Endoscopes are Used in **Keyhole Surgery**

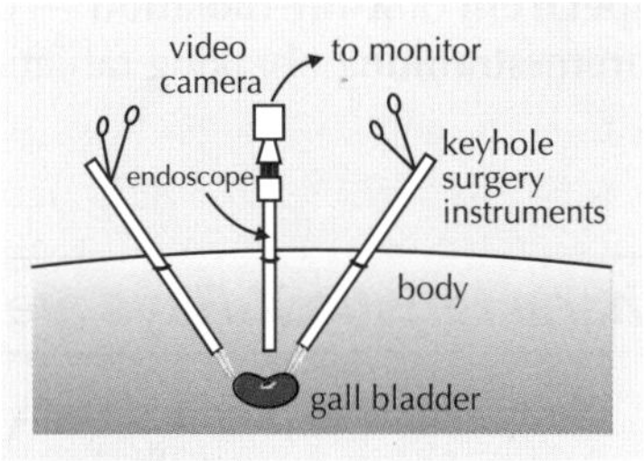


1) **Traditional** surgery needs a **large cut** to be made in the body so that there's **room** for the surgeons to get in and perform an **operation**.
2) This means that there's a **large risk of infection** to the exposed tissues and that permanent **damage** could be done to the patient's **body**.
3) New techniques in **minimally invasive surgery** (MIS or **keyhole surgery**) mean that only a **few small holes** need to be cut into the body.
4) An **endoscope** can be used in keyhole surgery to show the surgeon an **image** of the area of interest. **Surgical instruments** are passed through the endoscope tube, or through additional **small holes** in the body, so that the **operation** can be carried out.
5) **Common procedures** include the removal of the **gall bladder**, investigation of the **middle ear**, and removal of abnormal polyps in the **colon** so that they can be investigated for **cancer**.
6) **Recovery times** tend to be **quicker** for keyhole surgery, so the **patient** can usually **return home** on the **same day** — which makes it much **cheaper** for the hospital and **nicer** for the patient.

## Practice Questions

Q1 What conditions must be satisfied for total internal reflection to occur?

Q2 Describe the difference between a coherent and a non-coherent bundle of fibres.

Q3 Describe the main features of an endoscope.

Q4 How have endoscopes revolutionised some surgical procedures?

**Exam Questions**

Q1 A beam of light is transmitted through an optical fibre.
The refractive index of the fibre's core is 1.35 and the refractive index of its cladding is 1.30.

a) Determine the critical angle for the core-cladding boundary. [2 marks]

b) Explain why the angle of incidence of the beam of light should be kept at or above the critical angle. [2 marks]

Q2 Coherent fibre-optic bundles can be used to transmit images. Describe the main features of the structure of a coherent fibre-optic bundle, and explain why each feature is important for the bundle's function. [4 marks]

## If you ask me, physics is a whole bundle of non-coherentness...

*If this is all getting too much, and your brain is as fried as a pork chipolata, just remember the wise words of revision wisdom from the great Spike Milligan — Ying tong, ying tong, ying tong, ying tong, ying tong, iddly-I-po, iddly-I-po...*

# X-Ray Production

*Now it's time to make some X-rays by firing electrons at some metal.*

## X-Rays are Produced by Bombarding Tungsten with High Energy Electrons

1) In an X-ray tube, **electrons** are emitted from a **heated filament** and **accelerated** through a high **potential difference** (the **tube voltage**) towards a **tungsten anode**.
2) When the **electrons** smash into the **tungsten anode**, they **decelerate** and some of their **kinetic energy** is converted into **electromagnetic energy**, as **X-ray photons**.
3) The **maximum energy** of the X-ray photons is equal to the **potential difference** of the X-ray tube multiplied by the **charge** of an electron. So, if a potential difference of 50 kV is used in the tube, the maximum X-ray energy will be 50 keV.
4) The tungsten anode emits a **continuous spectrum** of **X-ray radiation** — this is called **bremsstrahlung** ('braking radiation').

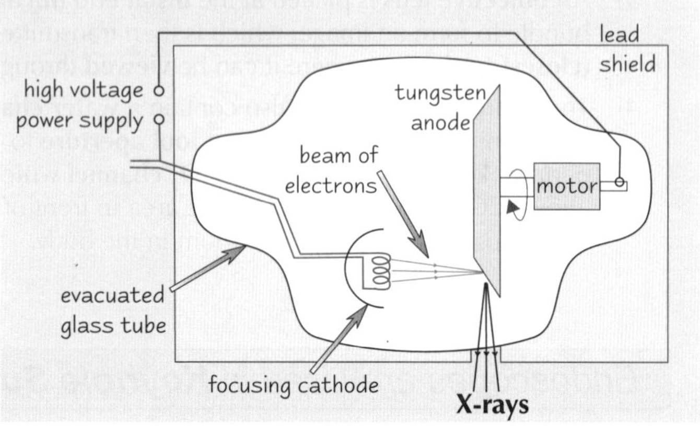


## Characteristic X-Rays are also Produced

1) X-rays are also produced when beam electrons **knock out** other electrons from the **inner shells** of the **tungsten atoms**.
2) Electrons in the atoms' **outer shells** move into the **vacancies** in the **lower energy levels**, and **release energy** in the form of **X-ray photons**.
3) The energies of these X-rays are **known** for a given metal as they relate to the energy between electron shells in tungsten — so they're called **characteristic X-rays**.

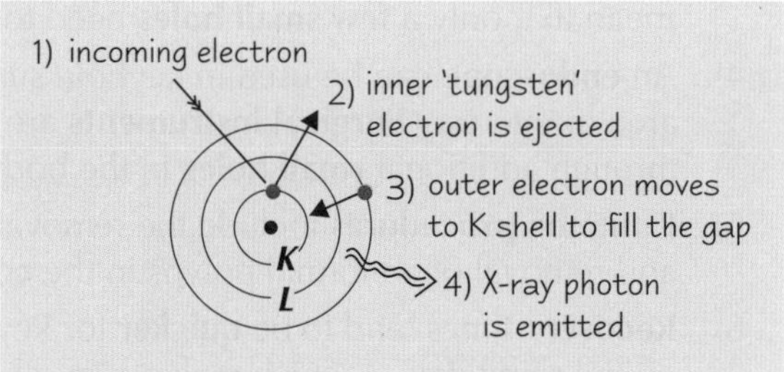


## Combining Both gives the Energy Spectrum of X-Rays Produced

When you combine the **continuous** spectrum from **bremsstrahlung** and the **characteristic** spectrum you see **line spectra** superimposed on a **continuous spectrum**.

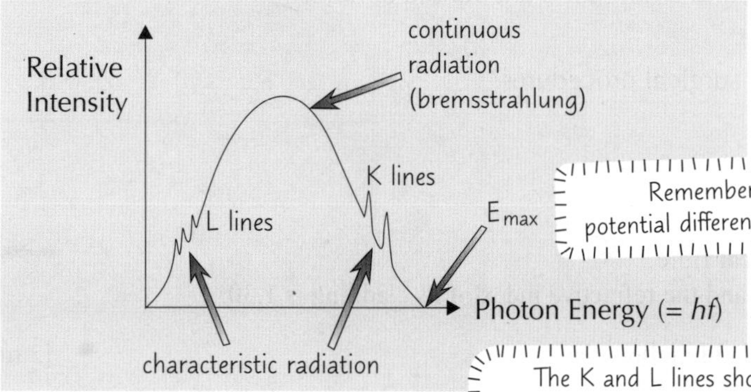

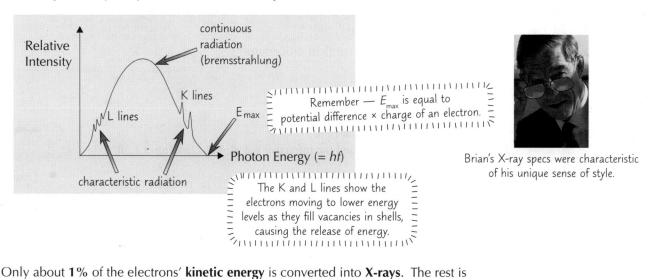

Remember — $E_{max}$ is equal to potential difference × charge of an electron.

The K and L lines show the electrons moving to lower energy levels as they fill vacancies in shells, causing the release of energy.

Brian's X-ray specs were characteristic of his unique sense of style.

Only about **1%** of the electrons' **kinetic energy** is converted into **X-rays**. The rest is converted into **heat**, so, to avoid overheating, the tungsten anode is **rotated** at about 3000 rpm. It's also **mounted** on **copper** — this **conducts** the heat away effectively.

# X-Ray Production

## Beam Intensity and Photon Energy can be Varied

The **intensity** of the X-ray beam is the **energy per second per unit area** passing through a surface (at right angles). There are two ways to increase the **intensity** of the X-ray beam:

1) Increase the **tube voltage**. This gives the electrons **more kinetic energy**. Higher energy electrons can **knock out** electrons from shells **deeper** within the tungsten atoms — giving more 'spikes' on the graphs. Individual **X-ray photons** also have **higher maximum energies**.

   **Intensity** is approximately **proportional** to **voltage squared**.

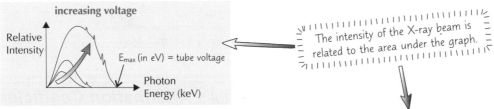

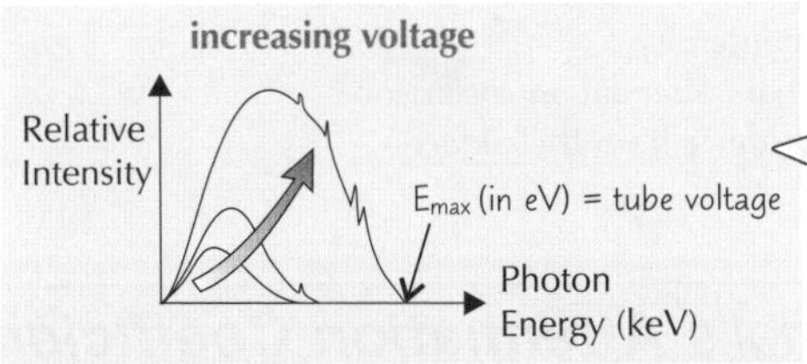


The intensity of the X-ray beam is related to the area under the graph.

2) Increase the **current** supplied to the filament. This liberates **more electrons per second**, which then produce **more X-ray photons per second**. Individual **photons** have the **same energy** as before.

   **Intensity** is approximately **proportional** to **current**.

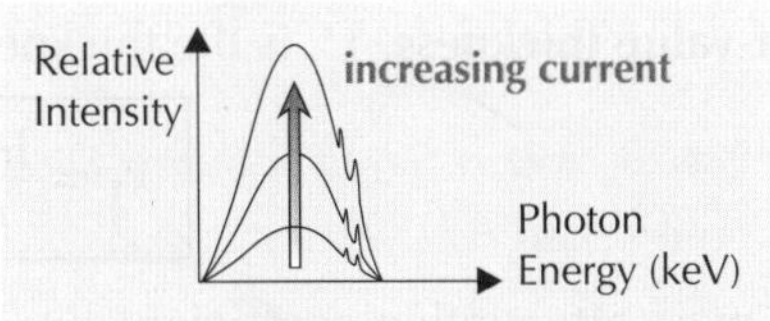


## Radiographers try to Produce a Sharp Image and Minimise the Radiation Dose

Medical X-rays are a compromise between producing really sharp, clear images, whilst keeping the amount of radiation the patient is exposed to as low as possible. To do this, radiographers:

1) Put the **detection plate close** to the patient and the **X-ray tube far** away from the patient to **increase image sharpness**.
2) Make sure the patient **keeps still** — if they move around, the image will be blurred.
3) Put a **lead grid** between the patient and film to **stop** scattered radiation '**fogging**' the film and **reducing contrast**.
4) Use an **intensifying screen** next to the film surface. This consists of crystals that **fluoresce** — they **absorb X-rays** and re-emit the energy as **visible light**, which helps to develop the photograph quickly. A shorter exposure time is needed, keeping the patient's radiation dose lower.

## Practice Questions

Q1 Draw a diagram of an X-ray tube and explain how a typical X-ray spectrum is produced.

Q2 State two methods used to avoid overheating of the anode.

Q3 Give two ways in which the intensity of an X-ray beam can be increased.

Q4 What measures can be taken to produce a high quality X-ray image while reducing the patient's radiation dose?

**Exam Question**

*Charge on an electron (e) = $-1.60 \times 10^{-19}$ J.*

Q1 An X-ray tube is connected to a potential difference of 30 kV.

a) Sketch a graph of relative intensity against photon energy (in eV) for the resulting X-ray spectrum, and indicate its main features. [3 marks]

b) Calculate the maximum energy of the X-ray photons produced. Give your answer in joules. [2 marks]

c) Sketch how the graph in (a) would change if the tube voltage were increased. [2 marks]

## Situation vacant — electron needed for low energy position...

*I have a question — why, when something could have a nice, simple name like 'braking radiation', do scientists insist on giving it a much fancier one? 'Bremsstrahlung' just sounds baffling — well, unless you speak German of course.*

# X-Ray Imaging Techniques

*So, you know how X-rays are produced and what the radiographer does — but why, I hear you cry, do some bits of you (i.e. your bones) show up nicely in an X-ray image, while others fade into the background? Attenuation, that's why...*

## X-Rays are Attenuated when they Pass Through Matter

When X-rays pass through matter (e.g. a patient's body), they are **absorbed** and **scattered**. The intensity of the X-ray beam **decreases** (attenuates) **exponentially** with the **distance from** the **surface**, according to the material's **attenuation coefficient**.

$$I = I_0 e^{-\mu x}$$

Where $I$ is the intensity of the X-ray beam, $I_0$ is the initial intensity, $\mu$ is the material's attenuation coefficient and $x$ is the distance from the surface.

## Half-value Thickness Depends on a Material's Attenuation Coefficient

1) **Half-value thickness**, $x_{\frac{1}{2}}$, is the thickness of material required to **reduce** the **intensity** to **half** its **original value**.

$$x_{\frac{1}{2}} = \frac{\ln 2}{\mu}$$

Where $\mu$ is the material's linear attenuation coefficient.

2) The **mass attenuation coefficient**, $\mu_m$, describes how the intensity of an X-ray beam decreases **per unit mass**. For a material of **density** $\rho$, it is given by:

$$\mu_m = \frac{\mu}{\rho}$$

## X-Rays are Absorbed More by Bone than Soft Tissue

1) X-rays are **attenuated** by **absorption** and **scattering**. How much **energy is absorbed** by a **material** depends on its **atomic number**.
2) So tissues containing atoms with **different atomic numbers** (e.g. **soft tissue** and **bone**) will **contrast** in the X-ray image.
3) If the tissues in the region of interest have similar attenuation coefficients then artificial **contrast media** can be used — e.g. **barium meal**.
4) **Barium** has a **high atomic number**, so it shows up clearly in X-ray images and can be followed as it moves along the patient's digestive tract.

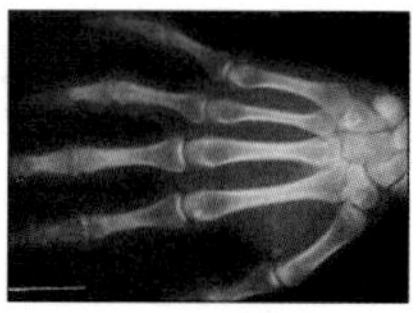

Bones show up brightly in X-ray images because they absorb more X-rays than the surrounding soft tissue.

## CT Scans use X-Rays to Produce High-Quality Images

1) **Computed tomography** (CT) scans produce an image of a **two-dimensional slice** through the body.
2) A narrow **X-ray beam** consisting of a single wavelength (**monochromatic**) **rotates** around the body and is picked up by thousands of **detectors**. The detectors feed the signal to a **computer**.
3) The computer works out how much attenuation has been caused by each part of the body and produces a very **high quality** image.
4) However, the machines are **expensive** and the scans involve a **high radiation dose** for the patient.

## Fluoroscopy is used to Create Moving Images

1) **Moving images** can be created using a **fluorescent screen** and an **image intensifier**. This is useful for **imaging organs** as they **work**.
2) **X-rays** pass through the patient and hit the **fluorescent screen**, which **emits light**.
3) The **light** causes **electrons** to be emitted from the **photocathode**.
4) The **electrons** travel through the **glass tube** towards the **fluorescent viewing screen**, where they form an image. Electrodes in the glass tube **focus** the **image** onto the screen.

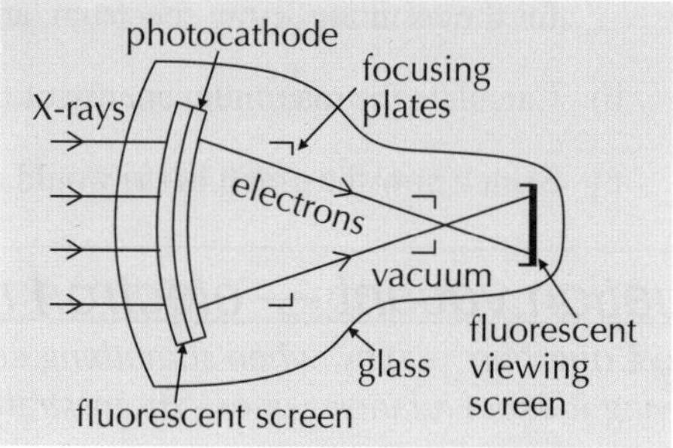

# X-Ray Imaging Techniques

## ***Flat Panel (FTP)*** *Detectors can be used Instead of* ***Photographic*** *Detection*

Flat Panel detectors are a **digital** method of X-ray imaging. X-rays are fired at the patient, who has a FTP detector behind them. The X-rays hit the detector and an **image** is created.

1) X-ray photons excite **scintillator** material in the detector. This produces **light** with intensity proportional to the energy of the incident X-ray photon.
2) **Photodiode pixels** in the detector generate a **voltage** when light hits them. The voltage is **proportional** the intensity of the light.
3) **Thin-film transistors** — one for every pixel — are then used to read the **digital signal**. A **digital image** of inside the patient is then created.

### *FTP Detectors have many* ***Advantages*** *over Photographic Detection*

1) They are more **light-weight** and compact, making them much more convenient as they can be **moved** around a hospital or positioned around an immobile patient.
2) They have a **higher resolution** so can detect finer details.
3) There is **less distortion** of the final image.
4) The digital read out can easily be **copied**, stored or **shared**.
5) They require a **lower exposure** to produce **clear images**.

## *There are* ***Advantages*** *and* ***Disadvantages*** *to* ***X-Ray Imaging***

ADVANTAGES:

1) Good **resolution** and provides clear imaging of **bones**.
2) CT scans are **much quicker** than MR scans (p.106).
3) **Cheaper** than MR scanners.

DISADVANTAGES:

1) X-rays are a form of **ionising radiation** — which can **damage cells** and in rare cases lead to the development of **cancer**.
2) Investigating **soft tissue** with fluoroscopy requires a **larger dose** of radiation.
3) Generally unsuitable for **pregnant** women.

## *Practice Questions*

Q1 Write down the formula which relates the intensity of X-rays at a given point, initial intensity, distance and the attenuation constant.

Q2 State the formula for calculating the half-value thickness of a material.

Q3 Explain how fluoroscopy allows you to see a real-time image.

Q4 State two advantages of using a Flat Panel detector.

**Exam Questions**

Q1 The half-value thickness for aluminium is 3 mm for 30 keV X-ray photons.

a) State what is meant by the term 'half-value thickness'. [1 mark]

b) Calculate the thickness of aluminium needed to reduce the intensity of a homogeneous beam of X-rays at 30 keV to 1% of its initial value. [3 marks]

Q2 a) A patient is going in for a CT scan. Describe briefly how a CT scan works. [3 marks]

b) State one negative aspect of CT scanners. [1 mark]

## *There's more than just the bare bones of X-ray imaging here...*

*I'm afraid you've got to get into the mathsy details of how an X-ray works. Practise using those equations and make some lists weighing up the advantages and disadvantages of using things like CT scanners and fluoroscopy.*

# Magnetic Resonance (MR) Imaging

*Magnetic Resonance (MR) imaging is another form of non-invasive diagnostic imaging — enjoy.*

## Magnetic Resonance can be used to Create Images

1) The MR machine contains a huge **superconducting** magnet which the patient lies in the centre of. This magnet produces a **uniform magnetic field**. The magnet needs to be **cooled** by liquid helium — this is partly why the scanner is so expensive.
2) The uniform magnetic field generated by the machine has an effect on the **protons** (hydrogen nuclei) in the patient's body. **Protons** (and neutrons) possess a quantum property called **spin**, which makes them behave like **tiny magnets**.
3) Initially, all of the protons are orientated **randomly**, but in a uniform magnetic field the protons align themselves with the **magnetic field lines**.
4) Protons in **parallel alignment** point in the **same direction** as the external **magnetic field**. **Antiparallel** alignment means the protons point in the **opposite** direction to the field.
5) As the protons spin, they **precess** (**wobble**) about the magnetic **field lines**.
6) This wobble has an **angular frequency** (p.5) called the **precession frequency**, which is proportional to the magnetic **field strength**.
7) By using smaller electromagnets, smaller magnetic fields can be **superimposed** onto the main one, creating a **gradient** of **magnetic field strength** across the patient. This means the protons in different sections of the body will have **different precession frequencies** and will absorb **different frequencies of radiation** (see below).

Tom and Taylor thought it was never too early to start learning physics.

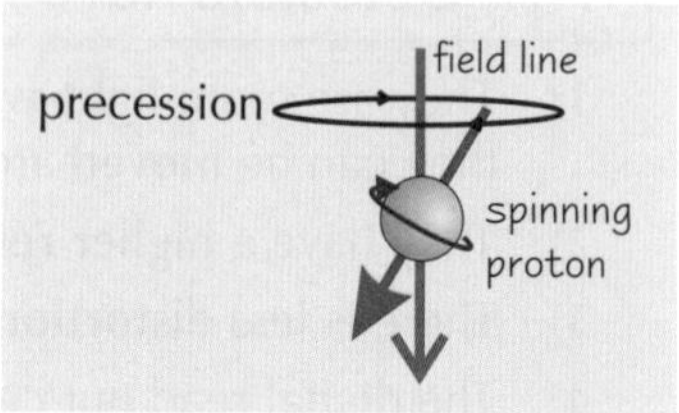


## Radio Waves at the Precession Frequency Excite the Protons

1) Radio frequency (RF) **coils** are used to transmit **pulses** of **radio waves** at the same **frequency** as the **precession frequency**, allowing the protons to **absorb** their energy and become **excited,** causing them to change their **spin state** (**flip** their alignment).
2) **Protons** in different **sections** of the body have different **precession frequencies** (due to the **gradient** of the field) and will absorb **different** RF waves.
3) The RF coils can transmit pulses of **different frequencies** to **excite** protons in successive **small regions** of the body.
4) When the radio waves are switched **off**, the protons **relax** and **re-emit** electromagnetic energy at their **precession frequency**. This is the **MR signal**.
5) As the computer knows the **positions** in the body **relating** to each precession **frequency**, it can then generate an **image** of a **2D cross-section** through the body, or build up a 3D image, by measuring various quantities of the MR signal like amplitude, frequency and phase.

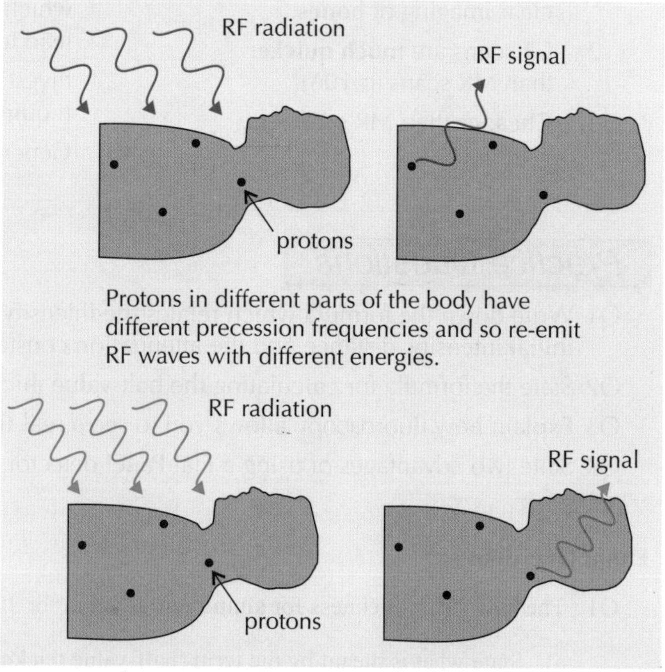


## Contrast can be Controlled by Varying the Pulses of Radio Waves

1) Radio waves are applied in **pulses**. Each short pulse **excites** the hydrogen nuclei and then allows them to **relax** and emit a signal. The response of **different tissue types** can be enhanced by varying the **time between pulses**.
2) Tissues consisting of **large molecules** such as **fat** are best imaged using **rapidly repeated pulses**. This technique is used to image the internal **structure** of the body.
3) Allowing **more time** between pulses enhances the response of **watery** substances. This is used for **diseased** areas.

# Magnetic Resonance (MR) Imaging

## MR scans has Advantages and Disadvantages

ADVANTAGES:
1) There are **no** known **side effects**.
2) An image can be made for any slice in any **orientation** of the body from a single scan.
3) High quality images can be obtained for **soft tissue** such as the **brain**.
4) **Contrast** can be **weighted** in order to investigate different situations.
5) MR imaging can give **real-time** images.

DISADVANTAGES:
1) The imaging of **bones** is very **poor**.
2) Some people suffer from **claustrophobia** in the scanner.
3) Scans can be **noisy** and take a **long time**.
4) MR imaging can't usually be used on people with **pacemakers** or some **metal implants** — the strong magnetic fields would be very harmful.
5) Scanners **cost millions** of pounds.

## Comparing MR, CT Scans and Ultrasound

You need to be able to **compare** imaging techniques — ultrasound (p.98-99), X-rays (p.102-105) and MR scans — and talk about their **convenience**, **safety** and **resolution**.

| | Ultrasound | X-Rays | MR |
|---|---|---|---|
| **Safety** | No known side effects | Uses ionising radiation | No known side effects |
| **Image Resolution for Bones** | Can't penetrate | Very good | Poor |
| **Image Resolution for Soft Tissue** | Poor | Good | Very good |
| **Convenience** | Quick, cheap and portable | Quick, becoming more portable | Expensive and large |

You might also have to include PET scans in your comparisons. They're coming up in a bit (p.109).

## Practice Questions

Q1 Describe what is meant by precession frequency.

Q2 Describe how using a magnetic field gradient can produce a cross-section of a patient.

Q3 What method is used to investigate diseased areas using radio frequency pulses?

Q4 State which imaging method would be best out of ultrasound, X-rays and an MR scan, when trying to take an image of a fracture in a bone.

**Exam Questions**

Q1 Outline how an MR scanner is used to produce an image of a section of a patient's body. The quality of your written answer will be assessed in this question. [6 marks]

Q2 State two advantages and two disadvantages of using MR scanners as an imaging technique. [4 marks]

## *All those radio waves have given me a headache...*

*OK, so these aren't the easiest of pages. Make sure you really understand how MR scanners work — it took me a long time to get my head around it. At least now you know why people sit in vats of baked beans to raise money for their local hospital to buy an MR scanner though... well, maybe not the beans part, best leave that to A-level psychology.*

# Medical Uses of Radiation

*Radiation can be incredibly useful in medicine, but any use of ionising radiation carries some risk.*

## ***Medical Tracers** are Used to **Diagnose** the **Function of Organs***

**Medical tracers** are **radioactive substances** that are used to show tissue or **organ function**. Other types of imaging, e.g. **X-rays** (p.104), only show the **structure** of organs — medical tracers show **structure and function**.

**Medical tracers** usually consist of a **radioactive isotope** — e.g. **technetium-99m, iodine-131** or **indium-111** — bound to a **substance** that is **used** by the **body** — e.g. **glucose** or **water**. The tracer is **injected** into or **swallowed** by the patient and then **moves** through the **body** to the region of interest. **Where** the tracer goes depends on the **substance** the isotope is bound to — i.e. it goes anywhere that the substance would **normally go**, and is used how that substance is **normally used**. The **radiation emitted** is **recorded** (e.g. by a **gamma camera** or **PET scanner**, see p.109) and an **image** of inside the patient produced.

You need to know about three of the main radioactive isotopes used in medical tracing:

1) **Technetium-99m** is a **widely** used isotope, due to its effective half-life — **long enough** that $\gamma$ **radiation** can still be **detected** once it reaches the **organ** and **short enough** that the patient isn't **exposed** to radiation for too long.
2) Iodine is naturally used by the **thyroid**, so **iodine-131** is used to detect and treat problems in the thyroid.
3) **Indium-111** is used to label **antibodies** and **blood cells**, to detect **infections**.

| | Physical half-life | Radiation emitted | Energy of gamma radiation emitted |
|---|---|---|---|
| **Technetium-99m** | 6 hours | Gamma | 140 keV |
| **Iodine-131** | 8 days | Beta and gamma | 360 keV |
| **Indium-111** | 2.8 days | Gamma | 170 or 250 keV |

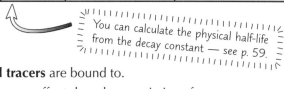

You can calculate the physical half-life from the decay constant — see p. 59.

### *Medical Tracers Have An **Effective Half-Life***

1) Your body **metabolises** (uses up) the substances that **medical tracers** are bound to.
2) The **rate** at which it manages to do this — the rate of excretion — affects how long emissions from the body can be detected for. You can think of this rate in the form of a **biological half-life**, $T_B$.
3) When combined with the **physical half-life**, $T_P$ (which only depends on the decay constant, p.58) you get an **effective half-life**, $T_E$, for the tracer.

$$\frac{1}{T_E} = \frac{1}{T_B} + \frac{1}{T_P}$$

## *Technetium-99m is **Generated** with **Molybdenum***

Technetium-99m has a physical half-life which is **too short** for it to be practically transported.
Instead, hospitals have **Molybdenum-Technetium generators** delivered.
Molybdenum has a much longer half-life — **66 hours**, making it much better for transport.

1) Inside the generator, the molybdenum has been combined with **aluminium oxide**, which it bonds strongly with.
2) Molybdenum then **decays**, producing Technetium-99m which does not bond as strongly with aluminium oxide.
3) A **saline solution** is placed into the generator, washing out any technetium-99m. This solution can then be injected into patients, or combined with a substance to make a specific **tracer**.

## ***Gamma Cameras** Detect **Gamma Radiation***

The $\gamma$**-rays** emitted by **radiotracers** injected into a patient's body are detected using a **gamma camera**. **Gamma cameras** (like the one shown on the right) consist of **five** main parts:

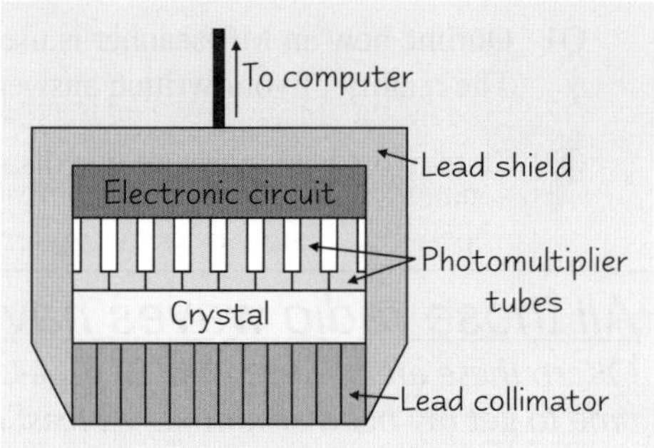


1) **Lead shield** — **stops radiation** from **other sources** entering the camera.
2) **Lead collimator** — a **piece of lead** with thousands of **vertical holes** in it — only $\gamma$-rays **parallel** to the holes can **pass through**.
3) **Sodium iodide crystal** — emits a **flash of light** (**scintillates**) whenever a $\gamma$**-ray** hits it.
4) **Photomultiplier tubes** — turn the flashes of **light** into **pulses of electricity**. Each tube contains a **photocathode** that releases an electron by the **photoelectric effect** when hit by a photon. Each electron is then **multiplied** into a **cascade** of electrons.
5) **Electronic circuit** — **collects** the **signals** from the photomultiplier tubes and sends them to a **computer** for processing into an **image**.

# Medical Uses of Radiation

## PET Scanning Involves Positron/Electron Annihilation

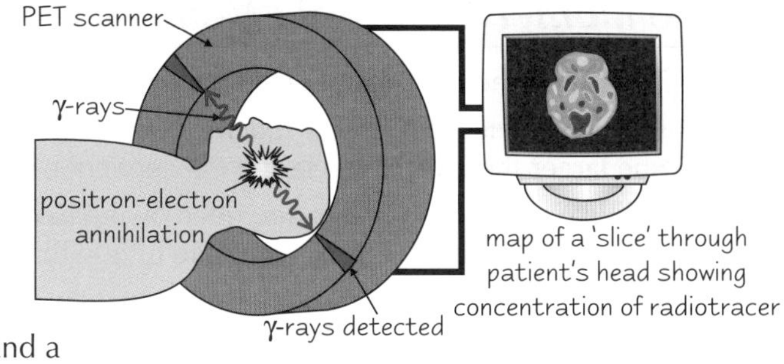


1) The patient is injected with a substance used by the body, e.g. glucose, containing a **positron-emitting** radiotracer with a **short half-life**, e.g. $^{13}N$, $^{15}O$, $^{18}F$.
2) The patient is left for a time to allow the radiotracer to **move through the body** to the organs.
3) **Positrons** emitted by the radioisotope collide with **electrons** in the organs, causing them to **annihilate**, emitting **high-energy gamma rays** in the process.
4) **Detectors** around the body record these **gamma rays**, and a computer builds up a **map of the radioactivity** in the body.
5) The main advantage of PET scans is that the **distribution of radioactivity** matches up with **metabolic activity**. This is because **more** of the radioactive glucose (or whatever) injected into the patient is taken up and **used** by cells that are **doing more work** (cells with an **increased metabolism**, in other words).
6) Another advantage is that **brain activity** can be investigated, whereas some other non-invasive methods cannot **penetrate** the **skull**. It can also give information about the **malignancy** of tumours and whether a tumour is **spreading**.
7) There are **disadvantages** too — **ionising radiation** is used which could **damage** the patient's cells. Scans take a **long time** and require the patient to stay **still**, which can be **uncomfortable** and **claustrophobic**. The machine itself is **expensive** and very **large**, so patients have to **travel** to their nearest hospital which has a PET scanner, which could be **inconvenient** for them.

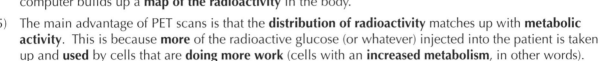

## Radiation Can Also Be Used to Treat Cancer

Ionising radiation **damages cells** — usually a bad thing, but in some cases this property can be helpful.

1) **High energy X-rays** are fired at tumours from outside of the patient's body. This means that surrounding **healthy cells** are also **damaged** — which can lead to **mutations** and even a higher risk of **future cancers**.
2) To **limit** the radiation patients are exposed to, carefully **focussed beams** are controlled by computers to ensure the majority of the radiation is hitting the tumour. **Shielding** is also sometimes used, and the X-ray beam may be **rotated** around the patient to minimise the radiation dose to healthy tissue.
3) Radioactive treatments can also be placed **inside** a patient. Implants containing **beta-emitters** are placed next to or inside of the tumour. Beta radiation is ionising, so damages the cells in the tumour, but has a **short range** so the damage to healthy tissue is **limited**.

## Practice Questions

Q1 List 3 radioactive isotopes which are used in medical tracers.
State the energies of the gamma radiation they emit.

Q2 Which of the three isotopes is primarily used to investigate problems in the thyroid?

Q3 Explain what an effective half-life is and why it must be used when evaluating medical tracers.

Q4 Explain how technetium-99m is generated in hospitals.

Q5 Describe how gamma cameras work.

Q6 Apart from radioactive tracers, what else can nuclear radiation be used for?

**Exam Questions**

Q1 If technetium-99m has a biological half-life of 24 hours, calculate its effective half-life. [2 marks]

Q2 Discuss the advantages and disadvantages of PET scanners. [4 marks]

Q3 A patient has a small, cancerous tumour.
Explain how and why beta-emitters could be used to internally treat it. [2 marks]

## Gamma cameras — for energetic selfies...

*Woo-hoo! Finally, at the end of the section. Doesn't mean you can run off and enjoy yourself just yet though — get the explanations of how tracers, technetium-99m generators, gamma cameras and PET scans work firmly in your head first.*

# Inertia and Kinetic Energy

*The moment of inertia — it sounds weird but it's a fairly simple concept. It's just the rotational equivalent of mass.*

## The Moment of Inertia Measures Resistance to Rotation

1) To make something **start** or **stop moving** requires a **force** to be applied.
2) **Inertia** is a measure of how much an object **resists** a change in velocity (the **larger** the **inertia**, the **larger** the applied **force** needed to change its velocity by a given amount).
3) In **linear** systems, inertia is described by the **mass** of an object, but for **rotating objects** it's described by the **moment of inertia**. This is a measure of how difficult it is to rotate an object, or to change its rotational speed.
4) The **moment of inertia** measures **resistance** to **rotation**, and depends on **mass** and its **distance** from the **axis of rotation** (the point or line around which the object is rotating).

## Moment of Inertia Depends on How the Mass is Distributed

1) For a particle (**point mass**), the moment of inertia is simply:

$$I = mr^2$$

where $I$ is moment of inertia ($kgm^2$), $m$ is the mass of the particle (kg) and $r$ is the distance from the axis of rotation (m).

2) For an **extended object**, like a rod, the moment of inertia is calculated by **adding** up the **individual** moments of inertia of **each point mass** that makes up the object.

$$I = \Sigma mr^2$$

3) This means that the moment of inertia changes depending on the **mass** and how it is **distributed** about the **axis of rotation**. For example, a **hollow** object will have a different moment of inertia to a **solid** one with the same mass.

The moment of inertia for a solid golf ball is $I = \frac{2}{5}mr^2$

But for a hollow tennis ball it's $I = \frac{2}{3}mr^2$

The moment of inertia for a solid wheel is $I = \frac{1}{2}mr^2$

But for a hollow ring or circular hoop it's $I = mr^2$

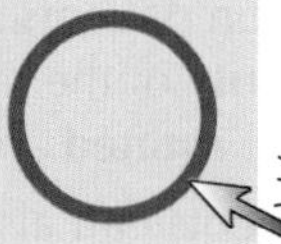

You don't need to learn specific moments of inertia for different shapes — they'll be given in the exam.

The mass is concentrated further from the centre, so its moment of inertia is greater, per unit mass.

4) Similarly, an object rotated about its **centre** will have a different moment of inertia if it is rotated about a point near its **edge**.

## You Can Combine Moments of Inertia

You can **add together** the individual moments of inertia of different objects to find the moment of inertia of the whole system. You'll usually be able to model individual objects as point masses.

**Example:** a) Calculate the moment of inertia of a 750 g bike wheel, which has a radius of 31.1 cm. The moment of inertia for a hollow cylinder (a bike wheel) is $I = mr^2$.

$I = 0.75 \times 0.311^2 = 0.0725... = \mathbf{0.073\ kgm^2}$ **(to 2 s.f.)**

A bicycle wheel can be modelled as a hollow cylinder or a circular hoop — the moment of inertia is the same.

b) A 20.0 g reflector is attached to the wheel 6.0 cm in from the outer edge. Assuming the reflector behaves like a point mass, calculate the new moment of inertia of the wheel.

$I = \Sigma mr^2$, so $I_{new} = I_{initial} + mr^2$ ← This is the MOI of the reflector.

$r = 31.1 - 6.0 = 25.1$ cm $= 0.251$ m and $m = 0.0200$ kg

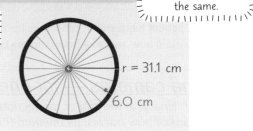

$I_{new} = 0.0725... + 0.0200 \times 0.251^2 = 0.0738...$
$= \mathbf{0.074\ kgm^2}$ **(to 2 s.f.)**

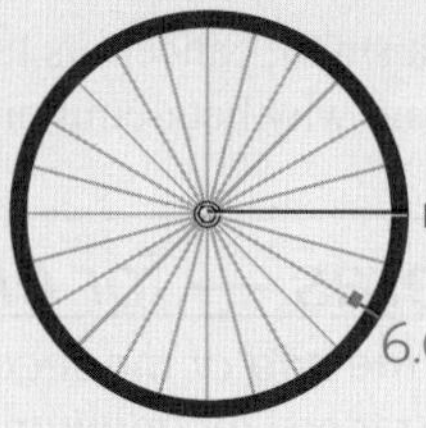

# Inertia and Kinetic Energy

## An Object's **Rotational Kinetic Energy** Depends on its **Moment of Inertia**

Just like you can find the **kinetic energy** of an object with **linear** motion, you can find the kinetic energy of a **rotating object**:

$$E_k = \frac{1}{2}I\omega^2$$

where $I$ is moment of inertia ($kgm^2$), and $\omega$ is the angular speed (rad $s^{-1}$)

The moment of inertia, $I$, is like the rotational equivalent of linear mass, $m$. This means $\frac{1}{2}mv^2$ can be rewritten using $I$ and $\omega$ to get rotational kinetic energy.

**Example:** A dancer adds a 60.0 g mass to each end of her twirling baton. The baton rod is uniform, 70 cm long (to 2 s.f.) and has a mass of 150 g. Assume the added masses act as point masses. Calculate the rotational kinetic energy of the baton as she spins it about its centre at an angular speed of 1.1 rad $s^{-1}$ (to 2 s.f.). The moment of inertia for a rod of length $L$ about its centre is $I = \frac{1}{12}mL^2$.

First, calculate the overall moment of inertia for the object.

$$I = I_{rod} + \Sigma mr^2 = \frac{1}{12}mL^2 + 2 \times \left[m \times \left(\frac{L}{2}\right)^2\right]$$

There are 2 masses, each a distance of $L/2$ from the baton's centre.

$$= \frac{1}{12} \times 0.15 \times 0.7^2 + 2 \times [0.06 \times 0.35^2] = 0.0208...\text{ kgm}^2$$

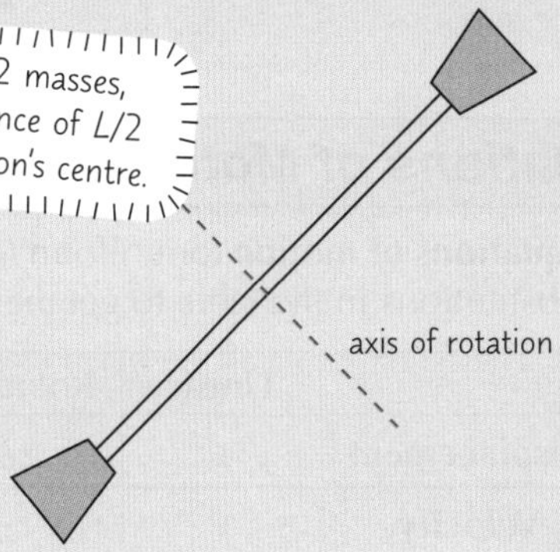


Then substitute this value into the formula for kinetic energy:

$$E_k = \frac{1}{2}I\omega^2 = \frac{1}{2} \times 0.0208... \times 1.1^2 = 0.0125...$$

So the rotational kinetic energy of the baton is **0.013 J (to 2 s.f.)**

## Practice Questions

Q1 What is the moment of inertia?

Q2 What is the formula for calculating the moment of inertia of a point mass?

Q3 Describe how you get the moment of inertia for an extended object.

Q4 State the formula for calculating rotational kinetic energy.

### Exam Questions

Q1 Calculate the moment of inertia for a 30 g point mass 80 cm from the axis of rotation. [1 mark]

Q2 A child jumps onto the edge of a 130 kg roundabout. The moment of inertia of the roundabout with the child is 531 $kgm^2$. Assuming the child is a point mass, calculate the mass of the child. The radius of the roundabout is 2.5 m and the moment of inertia for a solid disc is $I = \frac{1}{2}mr^2$. [3 marks]

Q3 A hollow 500 g ball with a 10 cm radius rolls down a slope with an angular velocity of 1.5 rad $s^{-1}$. $I = \frac{2}{3}mr^2$ for a hollow sphere.

a) Calculate the moment of inertia for the ball. [1 mark]

b) Calculate the rotational kinetic energy of the ball. [2 marks]

c) The ball is replaced with a solid ball of the same mass and radius, travelling at the same angular velocity. Calculate the ratio of the solid ball's kinetic energy to the kinetic energy of the hollow ball. $I = \frac{2}{5}mr^2$ for a solid sphere. [2 marks]

## *I'll give you a moment to let this sink in...*

*It sounds tricky, but really the moment of inertia is pretty simple. You want to make something spin about a point, but it's putting up a bit of a fight. You'll be given any formulas you need in the exam, but make sure you are comfortable using them and you know how to work out the new moment of inertia if a point mass is added to the system.*

# Rotational Motion

*All you could ever want to know about how to describe rotating objects... almost.*

## Angular Displacement is Measured in Radians

You need to be familiar with each of these terms to do with rotational motion:

1) **Angular displacement** is the **angle** through which a point has been rotated.
2) **Angular velocity** is a **vector** quantity describing the **angle** a point rotates through **per second**.

$$\omega = \frac{\Delta\theta}{\Delta t}$$

where $\omega$ is angular velocity (rad $s^{-1}$), $\theta$ is angular displacement (rad) and $t$ is time (s).

3) **Angular speed** is just the **magnitude** of the angular velocity.
4) **Angular acceleration** is the **rate of change** of **angular velocity**.

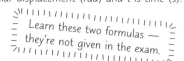

Learn these two formulas — they're not given in the exam.

$$\alpha = \frac{\Delta\omega}{\Delta t}$$

where $\alpha$ is angular acceleration (rad $s^{-2}$), $\omega$ is angular velocity (rad $s^{-1}$) and $t$ is time (s).

## Equations of Motion for Uniform Angular Acceleration

The **equations of motion** for uniform (constant) linear acceleration that you already know can be **rewritten** using the substitutions in the table to get the **equations of motion** for objects **rotating** with **uniform angular** acceleration.

| | Linear | Rotational |
|---|---|---|
| Displacement | $s$ | $\theta$ |
| Velocity | $v$ | $\omega$ |
| Acceleration | $a$ | $\alpha$ |

$$\omega_2 = \omega_1 + \alpha t \qquad \omega_2^2 = \omega_1^2 + 2\alpha\theta$$

$$\theta = \omega_1 t + \frac{1}{2}\alpha t^2 \qquad \theta = \frac{1}{2}(\omega_1 + \omega_2)t$$

where $\omega_1$ is initial angular velocity and $\omega_2$ is final angular velocity

**Example:** A figure skater initially at rest begins to spin with uniform angular acceleration. After 2.5 revolutions, she has an angular velocity of 4.9 rad $s^{-1}$. Calculate her angular acceleration.

First, see what variables you have to tell you which equation to use.

$\alpha = ?$, $\omega_1 = 0$, $\omega_2 = 4.9$ rad $s^{-1}$, $\theta = 2.5$ revolutions — so you should use $\omega_2^2 = \omega_1^2 + 2\alpha\theta$.

Next, make sure all values are in the correct units.

$\theta = 2.5$ revolutions $= 2.5 \times 2\pi = 15.7...$ radians

Rearrange the formula for $\alpha$ and substitute in the given values.

$$\alpha = \frac{\omega_2^2 - \omega_1^2}{2\theta} = \frac{4.9^2 - 0}{2 \times 15.7...} = 0.764... = \mathbf{0.76\ rad\ s^{-2}\ (to\ 2\ s.f.)}$$

Angular displacement might be given in revolutions, and angular velocity in revs $min^{-1}$ or revs $s^{-1}$. So make sure you always convert to radians for displacement and rad $s^{-1}$ for velocity.

## Angular Velocity is the Gradient of an Angular Displacement-Time Graph

When you plot **angular displacement** against **time** for a **constant** angular acceleration, you get a curve showing that **displacement** is **proportional** to $t^2$.

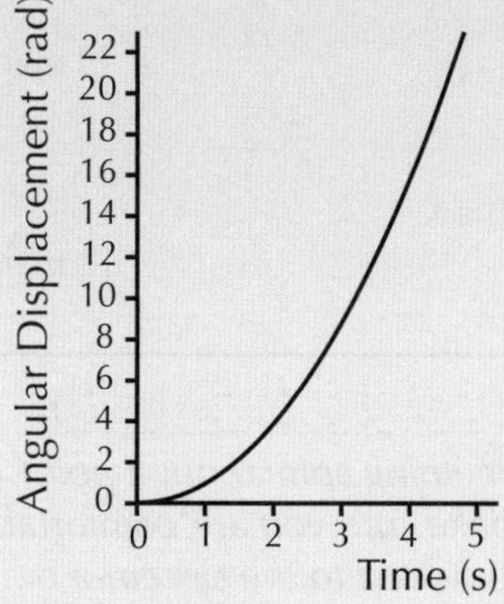


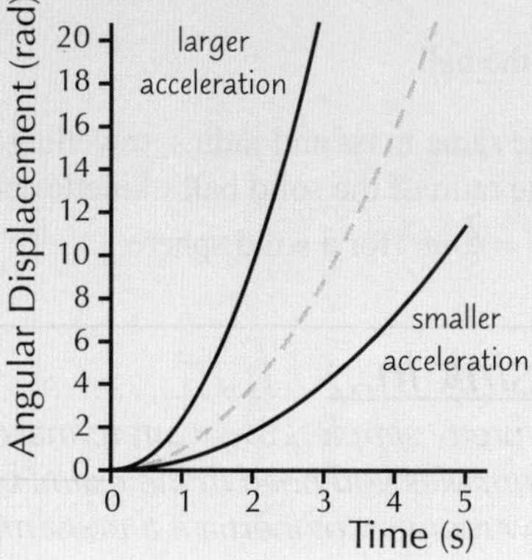


When the angular acceleration is **not constant**, the displacement is no longer proportional to $t^2$.

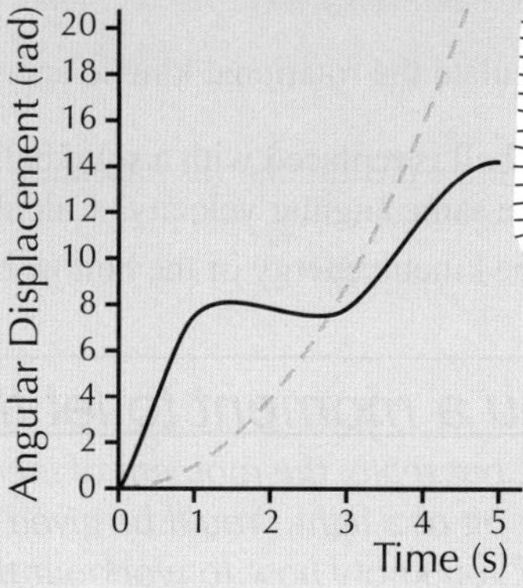

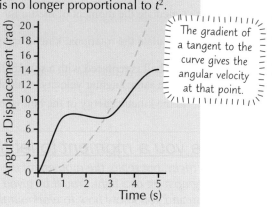

The gradient of a tangent to the curve gives the angular velocity at that point.

# Rotational Motion

## *Angular Acceleration* is the *Gradient* of an *Angular Velocity-Time* Graph

When you plot **angular velocity** against **time** for a **constant** angular acceleration, you get a straight line.

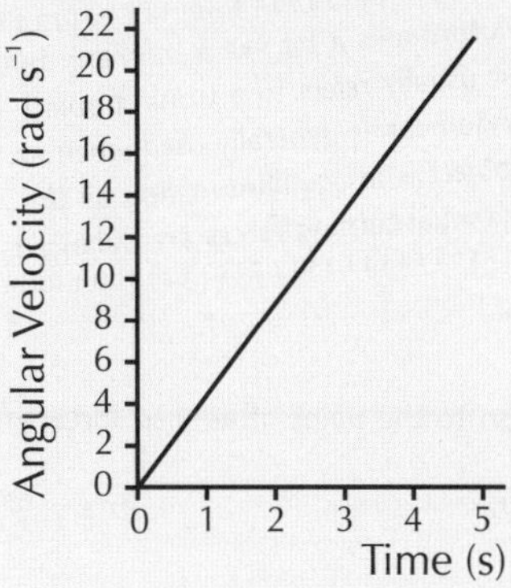


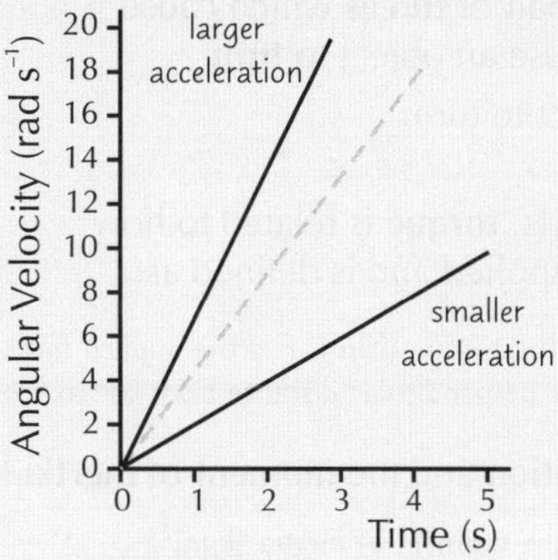


When the angular acceleration is **not constant**, the graph has a changing gradient.

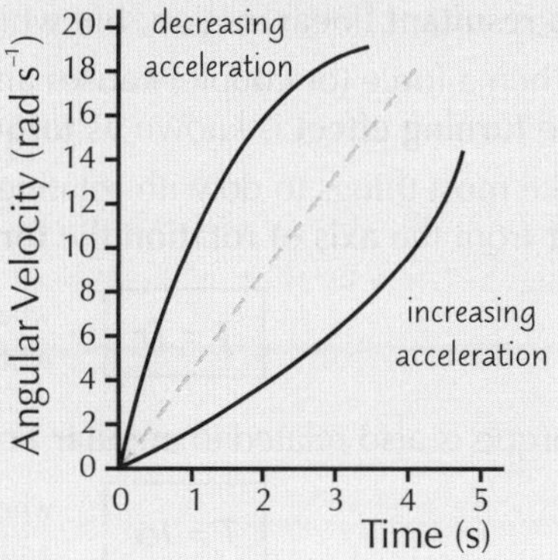


1) For **uniform** angular acceleration, to find the acceleration, you simply find the **gradient** of the **angular velocity-time** graph.
2) For **non-uniform** angular acceleration, to find the acceleration at a **given point**, you find the **gradient** of the **tangent** to the curve at that point.
3) The **area** under the curve between two points gives the **angular displacement** travelled in that time period.
4) A **negative** gradient would show **deceleration**.

## Practice Questions

Q1 What is angular velocity? State the formula for calculating it.

Q2 What is the formula for calculating angular acceleration?

Q3 How do you find angular velocity from an angular displacement-time graph?

Q4 What does the gradient of an angular velocity-time graph describe?

Q5 What does the area under an angular velocity-time graph describe?

**Exam Questions**

Q1 Calculate the angular velocity of Earth spinning about its axis. [1 mark]

Q2 An object is spinning at 30.0 revs min$^{-1}$ at a time $t$. If it has a constant angular acceleration of 1.57 rad s$^{-2}$, calculate its angular velocity 5.00 seconds after time $t$. [3 marks]

Q3 Sketch a graph of angular displacement against time for an object with constant angular acceleration. [2 marks]

Q4 The graph shows the angular velocity against time for a spinning object.

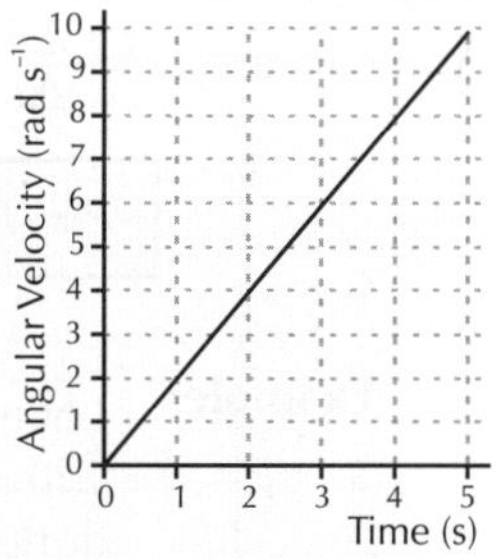


a) State whether the object's angular acceleration is increasing, decreasing or constant. [1 mark]

b) Calculate the angular acceleration of the object. [1 mark]

c) Calculate the angular displacement for the object for the interval 2-5 seconds. [1 mark]

## All this spinning in circles makes my head hurt — or maybe it's the maths...

*They look pretty horrible, but actually the equations on these pages are pretty much the same as the equations of motion that you're used to — only someone's come along and replaced some letters with Greek ones. The only thing that might catch you out is not remembering to convert your angular displacement into radians per second, so beware.*

# Torque, Work and Power

*Again, lots of similarities here between the regular force, work and power that you know. It's just a case of changing those formulas to describe stuff that's rotating instead of moving in a straight line.*

## Torque is the Turning Effect of a Force

1) You should remember that a **couple** is a pair of **forces** which cause **no resultant** linear motion, but which cause an object to **turn**.
2) When a force (or couple) causes an object to turn, the **turning effect** is known as **torque**.
3) Like most things to do with rotating objects, **torque** is related to how **far** from the **axis of rotation** the **force** is applied and is defined as:

A torque is a bit like a moment, but it usually refers to a turning object. 'Moment' is generally used when an object is in equilibrium, and all the potential turning forces are balanced.

$$T = Fr$$

where $T$ is the torque (Nm), $F$ is the applied force (N) and $r$ is the perpendicular distance from the axis of rotation to the point of applied force (m).

4) Torque is also related to **angular acceleration** and the **moment of inertia** (p.110).

$$T = I\alpha$$

where $I$ is the moment of inertia (kgm$^2$) and $\alpha$ is the angular acceleration (rad s$^{-2}$).

**Example:** Four 100 g (to 2 s.f.) masses are suspended from the axle of a wheel, as shown in the diagram. The perpendicular distance from the point of the applied weight to the centre of the axis of rotation is 0.15 m. When the masses are released, the wheel spins with an angular acceleration of 1.3 rad s$^{-2}$. Calculate the moment of inertia of the wheel. Friction is negligible.

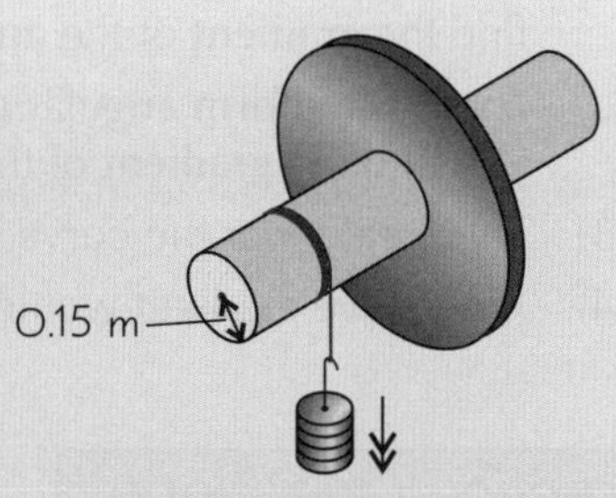

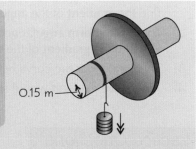


$T = Fr = mgr = 4 \times 0.10 \times 9.81 \times 0.15$
$= 0.5886$ Nm

$T = I\alpha$ so $I = T \div \alpha = 0.5886 \div 1.3$
$= 0.452... =$ **0.45 kgm$^2$ (to 2 s.f.)**

## Torque is also Related to Work and Power

When you rotate an object, you have to do **work** to make it move. Work in a linear system is the **force** multiplied by the **distance**. This can be rewritten for a rotating system using **torque** and **angular displacement** (p.112).

$$W = T\theta$$

where $W$ is the work (J), $T$ is the torque (Nm) and $\theta$ is the angular displacement (rad).

**Power** is the amount of **work done** in a **given time**.
You can use $\omega = \frac{\Delta\theta}{\Delta t}$ to derive an equation for power from the equation for work shown above.

$$P = T\omega$$

where $P$ is the power (W), $T$ is the torque (Nm) and $\omega$ is the angular velocity (rad s$^{-1}$).

Liz had just about had enough of work for the minute.

**Example:** Louise applies a torque of 0.2 Nm to turn a doorknob 90° with an angular speed of 3.1 rad s$^{-1}$. Calculate the work done and the power exerted by Louise to turn the doorknob.

The doorknob is turned $90° = 90 \times \frac{\pi}{180} = \frac{\pi}{2}$ radians.

So $W = T\theta = 0.2 \times \frac{\pi}{2} = 0.314... =$ **0.3 J (to 1 s.f.)**

Power $= T\omega = 0.2 \times 3.1 = 0.62 =$ **0.6 W (to 1 s.f.)**

# Torque, Work and Power

## In **Mechanical Systems** There is **Frictional Torque**

In real-world applications, **friction** has to be taken into account. Machines with rotating parts will experience an opposing **frictional torque**. Some of the **power** of the machine has to be used to overcome this frictional torque.

**Example:** A cog has a moment of inertia of 0.0040 $kgm^2$ and a diameter of 20.0 cm. A force of 0.070 N acts at the edge of the cog in the direction of the motion of the cog at that point, causing it to accelerate. Find the power needed to overcome the frictional torque at the point that the cog has an angular velocity of 120 revs $min^{-1}$, if the angular acceleration at that instant is 1.25 rad $s^{-2}$.

1) First calculate the net torque on the cog: $T_{net} = T_{applied} - T_{frictional} = I\alpha = 0.0040 \times 1.25 = 0.0050$ Nm
2) Then calculate the applied torque: $T_{applied} = Fr = 0.070 \times 0.100 = 0.0070$ Nm
3) Rearrange the equation for net torque to find the frictional torque:
$T_{frictional} = T_{applied} - T_{net} = 0.0070 - 0.0050 = 0.0020$ Nm
4) Finally, calculate the power needed to overcome friction using $P = T\omega$:
$P = T\omega = 0.0020 \times \left(\frac{120 \times 2\pi}{60}\right) = 0.0251... =$ **0.025 W (to 2 s.f.)**

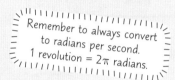

Remember to always convert to radians per second. 1 revolution = $2\pi$ radians.

**Example:** A wheel has four 0.10 kg masses suspended from it. The four masses are released. Just before they hit the ground, the masses have velocity 1.70 $ms^{-1}$ and the wheel has 0.73 J of rotational kinetic energy, having turned through 0.90 radians. There is 0.10 Nm of frictional torque acting upon the system. Calculate the height at which the masses were initially suspended above the ground.

Energy is always conserved, so the gravitational potential energy lost by the masses is equal to the total kinetic energy gained by the masses and the wheel, plus the work done to overcome frictional torque.

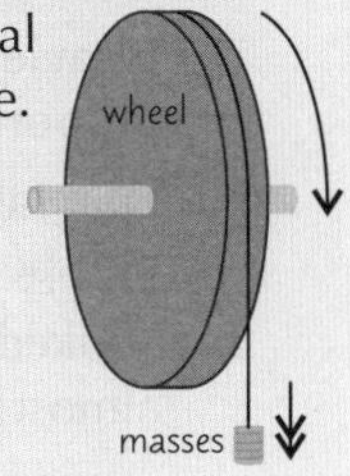


$E_P = E_K + W$ so $mgh = \frac{1}{2}mv^2 + E_{Krotational} + T\theta$

The total KE is the linear KE of the masses, plus the rotational KE of the wheel.

$mgh = \frac{1}{2} \times 0.40 \times 1.70^2 + 0.73 + 0.10 \times 0.90 = 1.398$

$g = 9.81\ ms^{-2}$.

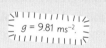

So $h = \frac{1.398}{0.40 \times 9.81} = 0.356... =$ **0.36 m (to 2 s.f.)**

## Practice Questions

Q1 Define torque. State the two formulas for calculating torque.

Q2 What is the formula for calculating the work done turning an object?

Q3 State the formula which relates power, torque and angular velocity.

Q4 What is frictional torque?

**Exam Questions**

Q1 A force of 1 N is applied at the edge of a wheel to make it spin. If the diameter of the wheel is 0.1 m, calculate the torque applied to the wheel. [1 mark]

Q2 A constant force of 140 N is applied at the edge of a park roundabout. The force acts perpendicular to the roundabout's radius of 2.5 m, causing it to complete a full spin. The roundabout has moment of inertia 500 $kgm^2$. Assume there is no frictional torque.

a) Calculate the angular acceleration of the roundabout. [2 marks]

b) Calculate the work done to move the roundabout one full spin. [2 marks]

Q3 Without friction, a torque of 0.45 Nm would be needed to rotate an object at an angular velocity of 3.0 rad $s^{-1}$. A total torque of 0.50 Nm is applied, in order to overcome friction and rotate the object at the required angular velocity. Calculate how much power is lost in overcoming frictional torque. [2 marks]

## *Don't torque to me about work — I had to write all this...*

*Thankfully, most of the equations on these two pages are given to you in the exam — yippee. I know they're not too difficult, but you should still spend some time practising using them. And make sure you understand all of the symbols.*

# Flywheels

*Flywheels are things you've probably not heard much about, but which are used in lots of ingenious ways.*

## Flywheels **Store Energy**

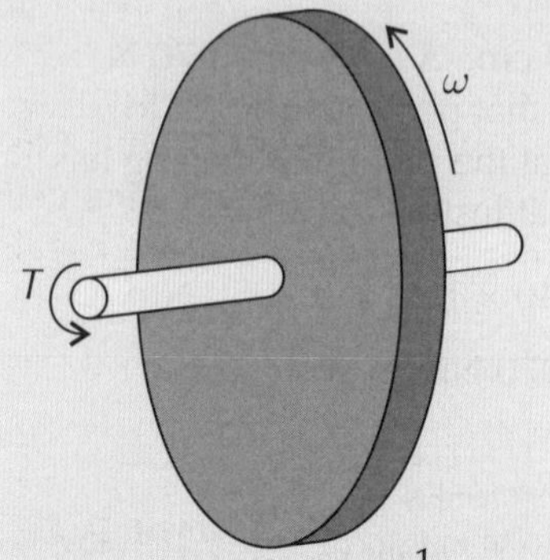

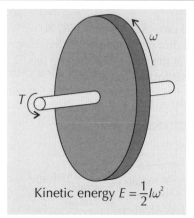


Kinetic energy $E = \frac{1}{2}I\omega^2$

1) A flywheel is a **heavy** wheel with a high **moment of inertia** (p.110) in order to resist changes to its rotational motion.
2) This means that **once** it is spinning, it's hard to make it **stop** spinning (it has a high **angular momentum**).
3) It is 'charged' as it is spun, turning the inputted **torque** (p. 114) into **rotational kinetic energy** (p.111).
4) **Just enough** power is continuously input to overcome **frictional torque**, keeping the flywheel fully charged.
5) When **extra energy** is needed in a machine, the flywheel decelerates, transferring some of its **kinetic energy** to another part of the machine.
6) Flywheels designed to store as much **energy** as possible are called **flywheel batteries**.

## Energy Stored is Affected by Mass, Shape and Angular Speed

**Rotational kinetic energy** is related to the **moment of inertia** and the square of the **angular speed**, which means these both affect how much **energy** a flywheel can store.

To **increase** the energy a flywheel can store, you should make it:

1) **Heavier** — the moment of inertia, and so the kinetic energy stored, is **directly proportional** to the mass. So the heavier the flywheel is, the better.
2) **Spin faster** — the **energy stored** increases with **angular speed squared**, so increasing the speed the flywheel spins at greatly increases the amount of energy it can store.
3) **Spoked** — compared to a solid wheel, a **spoked wheel** of the same mass stores almost **twice** as much energy (assuming everything else is kept constant).

Using a flywheel that is thinner at the centre than the edges also increases energy storage capacity — more of the mass is concentrated further from the axis of rotation.

However, there is a **limit** to how much you can increase these factors before they become impractical — you don't want a giant, heavy wheel taking up half of your machine. And if you increase the **angular velocity**, the **centrifugal force** can increase to a point where it starts **breaking** the flywheel **apart**. Modern flywheels are generally made out of **carbon fibre** to stop this — although it is **lighter** than steel, it is far **stronger** and so the wheel can be spun much **faster**.

## A Flywheel's **Energy** is also Affected by **Friction**

Even though a flywheel is very efficient at storing energy, it still loses some to **air resistance** and **friction** between the wheel and the **bearings** which it spins on. To combat this, modern flywheels can be:

1) **Lubricated** to reduce friction between the bearings and the wheel.
2) **Levitated** with **superconducting magnets** so there is **no** contact between the bearings and the wheel.
3) Operated in **vacuums** or inside **sealed cylinders** to reduce the drag from **air resistance**.

## Flywheels **Smooth Torque** and **Angular Velocity**

1) In systems where the **force supplied** to the system can **vary**, e.g. if an engine only kicks in intermittently, flywheels are used to keep the **angular velocity** of any rotating components **constant**.
2) Flywheels use each spurt of power to **charge up**, then they deliver the stored energy **smoothly** to the rest of the system, instead of in bursts.
3) They are also used when the **force** that the system has to **exert** can **vary**. If at any time the **load torque** is **too high**, then the flywheel **decelerates**, releasing some of its energy to **top-up** the system.
4) When the engine torque is **higher** than the load torque, the flywheel **accelerates** and **stores** the spare energy until it is needed.

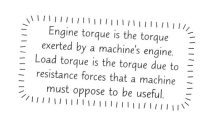

Engine torque is the torque exerted by a machine's engine. Load torque is the torque due to resistance forces that a machine must oppose to be useful.

# Flywheels

## *Flywheels* are used in many *Different Systems*

Flywheels are used in lots of everyday things, with some of the most common examples being:

1) **Potter's wheels** — A potter's wheel is controlled by a foot pedal, making it hard to apply a **constant force** to it. A flywheel is used to keep the speed of the wheel constant in order to make ceramic pots.
2) **Regenerative braking** — In regular cars, when the brakes are applied, friction causes the wheels to slow down, generating lots of heat. However, in some electric vehicles like cars and buses, when the brakes are hit, a **flywheel** is engaged. The flywheel then **charges up** with the energy being lost. When the vehicle is ready to accelerate, the flywheel uses its energy to turn the vehicle's wheels faster, before being disengaged until it's needed again.
3) **Power grids** — When lots of **electricity** is used in an area, the electricity grid sometimes cannot meet that **demand**. Flywheels can be used to provide the **extra energy** needed whilst **backup power stations** are started up.
4) **Wind turbines** — Flywheels can be used to store excess power on windy days or during off-peak times, and to give power on days without wind.
5) **Riveting machines** — An electric motor charges up a flywheel, which then **rapidly transfers** a **burst** of **power** as the machine **presses down** on the rivet and fixes two sheets of material together. This is useful as it stops rapid changes of power going through the motor, which could cause it to **stall**, and means a **less powerful** motor can be used.

## Flywheels have *Advantages* and *Disadvantages*

**Advantages**

1) They are very **efficient**.
2) They last a **long time** without degrading.
3) The **recharge time** is **short**.
4) They can react and **discharge quickly**.
5) They are **environmentally friendly** (they don't rely on chemicals to store energy).

**Disadvantages**

1) They are much **larger** and **heavier** than other storage methods (e.g. batteries).
2) They pose a safety risk as the wheel could **break apart** at high speeds. **Protective casing** to protect against this results in **extra weight**.
3) Energy can be lost through **friction**.
4) If used in **moving objects**, they can **oppose changes in direction**, which can cause problems for **vehicles**.

This feature can also be an advantage as it improves the vehicle's stability.

## Practice Questions

Q1 What is a flywheel?

Q2 How does a flywheel store energy?

Q3 What three properties affect how much energy can be stored in a flywheel?

Q4 How can energy loss through friction be reduced?

Q5 Give two advantages and disadvantages of flywheels.

**Exam Questions**

Q1 Taylor buys a new car with regenerative braking that uses a flywheel.

a) Explain how regenerative braking works in Taylor's car. [3 marks]

b) Give another use for flywheels. [1 mark]

Q2 An engineer is trying to improve a solid flywheel battery and decides to double the mass of the flywheel. Explain what effect this would have on the energy the flywheel could store and suggest one disadvantage of doing this. Suggest another improvement the engineer could make to increase the energy stored by the flywheel battery. [4 marks]

## Time flies when you're doing physics...

*Flywheels are pretty nifty things, used in loads of places you wouldn't even imagine. Make sure you understand and can explain how they work. Then get a few examples of their uses stored in your brain too for good measure.*

# Angular Momentum

*Surprisingly, angular momentum is a lot like regular momentum. Who'd have thought it?*

## Angular Momentum Relates Moment of Inertia and Angular Velocity

You already know that **linear momentum** is equal to mass × velocity. You can replace **mass** with the **moment of inertia**, and **linear velocity** with **angular velocity**, and you get the formula for **angular momentum**:

**angular momentum** $= I\omega$

where $I$ is the moment of inertia ($kgm^2$), $\omega$ is the angular velocity (rad $s^{-1}$) and angular momentum has units Nms.

Billy thinks his dad misunderstood when he asked him to explain angular momentum.

## Angular Momentum is Always Conserved

When **no external forces** are applied (torque, friction, etc.), the total angular momentum of a system remains constant. It's useful to write this as:

$$I_{initial}\omega_{initial} = I_{final}\omega_{final}$$

This is the law of conservation of angular momentum.

This can be seen if you put two objects with **different moments of inertia** or **angular velocities** together.

**Example:** A disc has a moment of inertia $I$ and is rotating at an angular velocity of 4 rad $s^{-1}$. A second identical disc that is not spinning is placed on top of the spinning disc, where it is held in place and begins to spin. Calculate the angular velocity of the combined discs as they spin together at the same speed. Frictional losses are negligible.

Before the discs are put together, angular momentum $= I_1\omega_1 + I_2\omega_2$

Once they are put together, angular momentum $= (I_1 + I_2)\omega$

You can then equate these: $I_1\omega_1 + I_2\omega_2 = (I_1 + I_2)\omega$

So $\omega = \dfrac{I_1\omega_1 + I_2\omega_2}{(I_1 + I_2)}$

The discs are identical, so $I_1 = I_2$ and the equation becomes:

$$\omega = \frac{I \times 4 + I \times 0}{2I} = \frac{4}{2} = \mathbf{2\ rad\ s^{-1}}$$

Another common example is an **ice skater** doing a spin. At the start of the spin, her arms are out **away** from her body. She then pulls her arms **closer** towards her, and begins to **spin faster**. This is due to the **conservation of angular momentum** — as she pulls in her arms, she decreases her **moment of inertia**, so her **angular velocity** must increase in order to conserve angular momentum.

**Example:** An ice skater is spinning with her arms out at an angular velocity of 13 rad $s^{-1}$. With her arms out, her moment of inertia is 3.5 $kgm^2$. She then tucks in her arms, changing her moment of inertia to 1.2 kg $m^2$. Calculate her angular velocity in revolutions per second as she spins with her arms tucked in.

You can write the conservation of angular momentum as:

$I_{initial}\omega_{initial} = I_{final}\omega_{final}$

$\omega_{final} = \dfrac{I_{initial}\omega_{initial}}{I_{final}} = \dfrac{3.5 \times 13}{1.2} = 37.91...$ rad $s^{-1}$

$37.91... \div 2\pi = 6.03...$ = **6.0 revolutions per second (to 2 s.f.)**

# Angular Momentum

## Angular *Impulse* is the *Change* in *Angular Momentum*

You can write the equation of angular impulse as:

$$\textbf{Angular impulse} = \Delta(I\omega)$$

The units are Nms.

However, if the torque (p.114) on the system is constant, this can also be written as:

$$\Delta(I\omega) = T\Delta t$$

where $T$ is torque (Nm) and $\Delta t$ is the time the torque is applied for (s).

**Example:** A spanner, initially at rest, has a constant torque of 0.3 Nm applied to it for 2 seconds. Calculate the angular impulse acting on the spanner and the angular velocity of the spanner at the end of the 2 seconds. The moment of inertia of the spanner is 0.2 kgm$^2$.

The equation for angular impulse is: $\Delta(I\omega) = T\Delta t$

This can also be written as: $I\omega_{final} - I\omega_{initial} = T\Delta t$

Which can then be rearranged to give: $\omega_{final} = \frac{T\Delta t + I\omega_{initial}}{I} = \frac{0.3 \times 2 + 0.2 \times 0}{0.2}$

$= \mathbf{3\ rad\ s^{-1}}$

Luke, Chris and Ben were regretting their impulse buy of matching suits.

## Practice Questions

Q1 Write down the formula for angular momentum.

Q2 What is angular impulse?

Q3 State the formula for angular impulse when the torque isn't constant.

Q4 State the formula relating angular impulse, constant torque and time.

**Exam Questions**

Q1 A ball with a moment of inertia of 0.04 kgm$^2$ is rolling with an angular velocity of 4 rad s$^{-1}$. Calculate its angular momentum. [1 mark]

Q2 Using ideas about angular momentum, explain why divers tuck themselves into a ball to complete fast spins. [3 marks]

Q3 A clutch in a car brings together two rotating shafts. The engine shaft has a moment of inertia of 0.10 kgm$^2$ and spins at 3000 rpm (to 2 s.f.). The second shaft has a moment of inertia of 0.15 kgm$^2$ and an angular velocity of 2000 rpm (to 2 s.f.) in the same direction as the first shaft. Calculate the angular velocity of the system once the two shafts are brought together. [3 marks]

Q4 A bike wheel is spinning at an angular velocity of 2.2 rad s$^{-1}$. A constant torque is applied for 4.0 s until the angular velocity of the wheel is 24 rad s$^{-1}$. The wheel has a moment of inertia of 0.20 kgm$^2$.

a) Calculate the angular impulse applied to the bike wheel over the four seconds during which the torque is applied. [1 mark]

b) Calculate the size of the torque applied to the wheel. [1 mark]

## I have the impulse to take a break...

*All in all, these last two pages haven't been too bad. Mostly just a few equations you've already seen dressed up to look like fancy new ones. Go back over these pages before looking back over the whole of the section so far. Make sure you're set with how to describe rotating things, then have a well-earned break. The joys of thermodynamics await.*

# The First Law of Thermodynamics

*Ah, thermodynamics — it's all about the wonders of heat energy. The first law tells you how adding heat energy can be used to do work or to ramp up the internal energy of the gas particles in your system. Which is surprisingly useful...*

## *The **First Law of Thermodynamics** Describes **Energy Conservation***

1) The **first law of thermodynamics** describes how **energy** is **conserved** in a **system** through heating, cooling and doing work.
2) A **system** is a **volume** of space filled with **gas**.
3) Systems can be either **open** or **closed**.
4) **Open systems** allow gas to **flow** in, out or through them, e.g. water vapour leaving a boiling kettle.
5) **Closed systems don't** allow gas to **enter** or **escape**, e.g. gas in a balloon.

After baked beans, Sgt. Gray was an open system.

## *The **First Law** Links **Heat**, **Work** and **Internal Energy***

1) The first law of thermodynamics can be written as: $Q = \Delta U + W$
2) $Q$ is the **energy transferred** to the system by **heating**. If energy is transferred **away** from the system, this will be **negative**.
3) $\Delta U$ is the **increase** in **internal energy**. Internal energy is the **sum** of the **potential** and **kinetic energies** of all of the particles in a system (see p.10 for more).
4) $W$ is the **work done by** the system (the work the **gas** is **doing**), e.g. gas in a cylinder expanding and moving a piston. If work is done **on** the gas, e.g. by **compressing** it, then the value of $W$ will be **negative**.

**Example:** A cylinder is sealed by a moveable piston. The gas in the cylinder is heated with 60 J of heat to move the piston. The internal energy of the gas increases by 5 J.

a) Calculate the work done by the gas to move the piston.

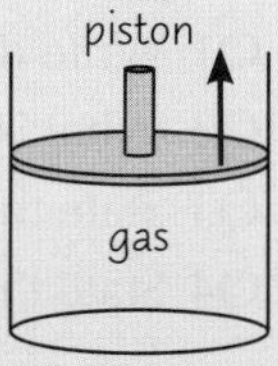


As heat is being inputted and the gas is doing work, both $Q$ and $W$ are positive.
$Q = \Delta U + W$, so $W = Q - \Delta U = 60 - 5 =$ **55 J** of work is done by the gas to move the piston.

b) Now the piston does 60 J of work on the gas to compress it.
No heat is lost. Calculate the change in the internal energy of the gas.

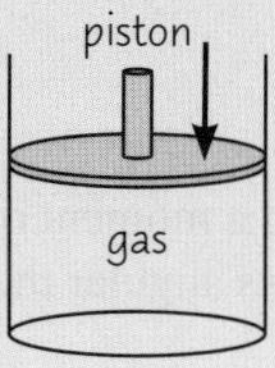


$Q = \Delta U + W = 0$, so $\Delta U = -W$. Work is done **on** the gas, so $W = -60$ J.
$\Delta U = -W =$ **60 J** — the internal energy of the gas increases by 60 J.

## *You Can Use **Ideal Gas Assumptions***

1) You need to know how to **apply** the first law to changes in **closed systems**. These are also known as **non-flow processes** because the gas doesn't go anywhere.
2) To do this, you have to assume that the gas in a system is an **ideal gas**.
3) This means you **assume** that **internal energy** is only dependent on the **temperature** — as the **temperature increases**, the internal energy **increases**.
4) You also assume **work done** causes a **change in volume**.
5) You can use the **ideal gas law** (p.14): $pV = nRT$

   $p$ is the pressure (Pa),
   $V$ is the volume of the system ($m^3$),
   $n$ is the number of moles of gas,
   $R$ is the molar gas constant, 8.31 $JK^{-1}mol^{-1}$,
   $T$ is the absolute temperature (K)

   0 K ≈ −273 °C

6) For a change in a closed system, $n$ is constant, so $\frac{pV}{T}$ = **constant**. You could also write this as:

$$\frac{p_1 V_1}{T_1} = \frac{p_2 V_2}{T_2}$$

This form is really handy to remember for thermodynamics questions.

# The First Law of Thermodynamics

## *Isothermal* Changes Happen at a **Constant Temperature**

1) The **internal energy** of a gas, $U$, only depends on the **temperature**. The temperature during an isothermal change remains **constant**, which means that for an **isothermal** process: $\Delta U = 0$
2) Using the first law of thermodynamics, $Q = 0 + W$, which means that: $Q = W$

   That means the amount of **work** a system **does** will be **equal** to the amount of **heat energy supplied** (here $Q$ and $W$ will both be **positive**). It also means that any work done **on** the system will cause the system to **lose** that amount of **heat energy** ($Q$ and $W$ will both be **negative**).

3) Using the **ideal gas law** (see p.14), you can see that a constant temperature $T$ means that:

$$pV = \text{constant} \quad \text{and} \quad p_1V_1 = p_2V_2$$

## In **Adiabatic Processes Q = 0**

1) An **adiabatic** process is one where **no heat** is **lost** or **gained** by the system: $Q = 0$.
2) Using the first law, if $Q = 0$ then $\Delta U = -W$. This means that any change in the **internal energy** of the system is **caused** by **work** done by/on the system. E.g. if work is done by the system (it expands), $W$ will be positive, and so the **internal energy** of the system will **decrease**.
3) As internal energy only depends on **temperature**, this means a **change** in **temperature** occurs.
4) The maths behind this process is pretty hard, but thankfully you just need to know that for an adiabatic change:

$$pV^\gamma = \text{constant} \quad \text{and} \quad p_1V_1^\gamma = p_2V_2^\gamma$$

$\gamma$ is the adiabatic constant, which depends on the type of gas in the system. For a monatomic gas, $\gamma = \frac{5}{3}$.

**Example:** A container full of helium (a monatomic gas) is sealed by a moveable piston (so gas cannot escape). The container is cylindrical, with a radius of 20 cm and a height of 60 cm. The initial pressure inside the container is $1.2 \times 10^5$ Pa. The piston moves downwards by 15 cm, adiabatically compressing the gas. Calculate the pressure inside the container after the piston has moved.

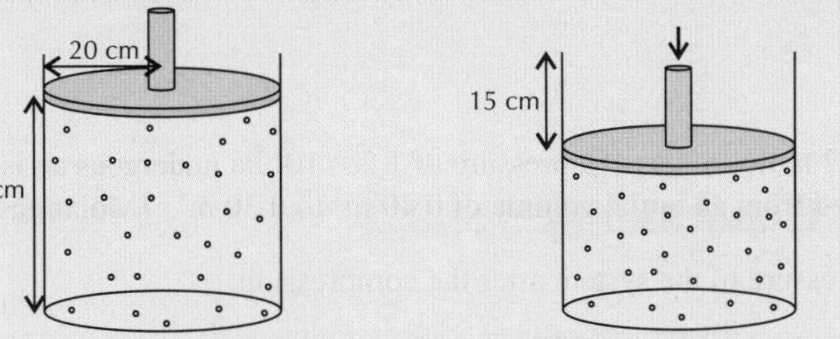


1) The volume of a cylinder is given by $V = \pi r^2 h$. As the gas is compressed, $r$ stays **constant** so the change in volume **only depends** on the **change in height**.
2) This means you can rearrange $p_1V_1^\gamma = p_2V_2^\gamma$ to give:

$$p_2 = \frac{p_1V_1^\gamma}{V_2^\gamma} = p_1\left(\frac{h_1}{h_2}\right)^\gamma = (1.2 \times 10^5) \times \left(\frac{60}{45}\right)^{\frac{5}{3}} = 193\,826.1...$$

Helium is monatomic so $\gamma = \frac{5}{3}$.

So the final pressure inside the container is **$1.9 \times 10^5$ Pa (to 2 s.f.)**.

Don't worry if you didn't spot that you could do it this way — you'd still get all of the marks if you calculated each volume separately and then substituted them into the equation for $p_2$.

# The First Law of Thermodynamics

## $W = p\Delta V$ for Changes at a Constant Pressure

1) For processes where the **pressure doesn't change**, you can calculate work done by using: $W = p\Delta V$

   $W$ is the work done by a system (J), $p$ is the pressure of the system (Pa), $\Delta V$ is the change in the volume of the system ($m^3$)

2) You can easily see where this equation comes from. Work = force × distance, $W = F\Delta x$. Pressure = force ÷ area, so force is pressure times area, $F = pA$. Substituting $pA$ for $F$ in the work done equation gives you $W = pA\Delta x$. $A\Delta x$ is simply the change in volume, which gives $W = p\Delta V$.

3) For an expansion, the change in volume and work done **by** the system are **positive**. For a compression, both are **negative**.

4) From the ideal gas law (see page 14), if $p$ is constant then: $\frac{V_1}{T_1} = \frac{V_2}{T_2}$ (where $T$ is the absolute temperature (see page 12)).

To maintain a constant pressure, a change in temperature must cause a change in volume. (E.g. heating a gas will cause it to expand.)

## Processes at a Constant Volume do No Work

1) In changes where the **volume** of the system is kept **constant**, the **work done** is **zero**. $W = 0$

2) From the first law, if $W = 0$, then: $Q = \Delta U$

3) This means that by transferring **heat energy** to the system, you only increase the **internal energy** $U$ of the system.

4) You can also see this by using $pV = nRT$ for a system. If $V$ is **constant** and you increase the **pressure**, only the **temperature** increases, which will increase the internal energy.

Remember that for an ideal gas the internal energy only depends on the temperature.

## Practice Questions

Q1 Define an open and a closed system.

Q2 Give the equation for the first law of thermodynamics and the meanings of the symbols used.

Q3 Write down the ideal gas equation.

Q4 What is an isothermal process?

Q5 What is an adiabatic process?

Q6 State the rule relating pressure and volume for an adiabatic process. Define gamma.

Q7 How would you calculate the work done in a non-flow process that occurs at a constant pressure?

Q8 How much work is done in a non-flow process where the volume doesn't change?

**Exam Questions**

Q1 A system containing 0.82 moles of gas at a pressure of $1.2 \times 10^4$ Pa undergoes an isothermal compression. The system is compressed from an initial volume of 0.40 $m^3$ to 0.30 $m^3$. (Molar gas constant, $R = 8.31$ $JK^{-1}mol^{-1}$)

a) Calculate the new pressure of the system after the compression. [2 marks]

b) Calculate the temperature of the system. [2 marks]

Q2 A closed system at 300 K has a pressure of $1.1 \times 10^4$ Pa. 3000 J of heat is transferred to the system while the pressure is kept constant. The internal energy of the system increases by 300 J. The volume of the system after this heat transfer is 0.360 $m^3$. Calculate the final temperature of the gas. [4 marks]

Q3 A closed system undergoes three thermodynamic processes. From 0-3 s, it is heated at a constant volume. The volume of the system is then increased isothermally from 3-8 s, before being left to compress adiabatically from 8-15 s. Explain whether the temperature is increasing, decreasing or constant for each stage. [5 marks]

## If only keeping your belly volume constant in real-life took no work...

*Whew, that's a lot to take in. Make sure you know the definitions of all the symbols in the first law — and know when they're negative and when they're not. Then get your head around all the different processes a system can undergo.*

# P-V Diagrams

*P-V diagrams are really useful as all of the non-flow processes you've just met can be plotted on them. You can use them to calculate work done for any process and they're super handy once you get to the section about engines...*

## You can use P-V Diagrams to Represent Non-flow Processes

1) As well as using equations, all of the different **non-flow** processes (see page 121-122) that can happen to a system can be **represented** on a ***p-V* diagram** — a graph of pressure against volume.
2) An **arrow** is put on a *p-V* curve to show the **direction** the change is happening in.
3) The **area under a line** on a *p-V* diagram represents the **work done** during that process.
4) You need to be able to **estimate** the **work done** from a given ***p-V* diagram**. You can estimate area by **counting squares** (like in the example below) or by using the **trapezium rule**.

'The trapezium rule' sounds pretty fancy, but all it means is estimating the area of the curve by splitting it into trapeziums. Calculate the area of each trapezium and then add them all together. The more trapeziums you create, the more accurate your answer will be.

## p-V Curves for Isothermal Processes are Called Isotherms

1) A *p-V* diagram for an **isothermal process** (p.121) will be a smooth curve — remember $p_1V_1 = p_2V_2$.
2) The *p-V* diagram for an isothermal **compression** is shown on the right. The **arrow** shows the direction the change happens in *(V* decreases and *p* increases).
3) A *p-V* diagram for an **isothermal expansion** at the same **temperature** will look almost **identical** to the compression *p-V* diagram. The only difference would be that the **arrow** would point in the **other direction** (as *V* would increase and *p* would decrease).
4) The **area under the curve** (shaded in blue) is the **magnitude** of the **work done** during the process. (Remember, the sign will depend on whether the work is done **by** or **on** the system.)
5) *p-V* curves for isothermal processes are called **isotherms**.
6) The **position** of an isotherm on a *p-V* diagram depends on the **temperature** the process happens at. The **higher** the temperature of the system, the **further** from the **origin** the isotherm will be.

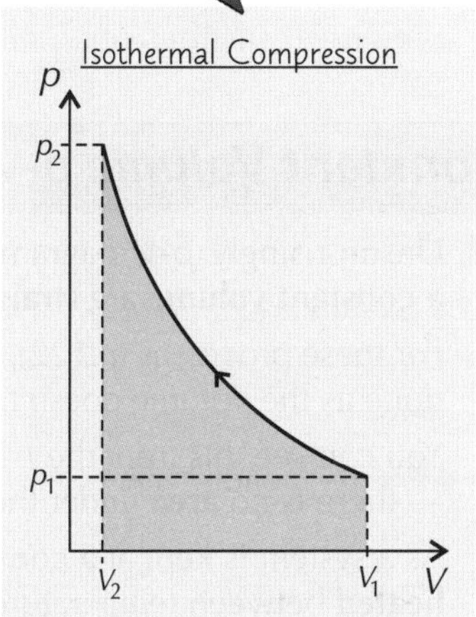


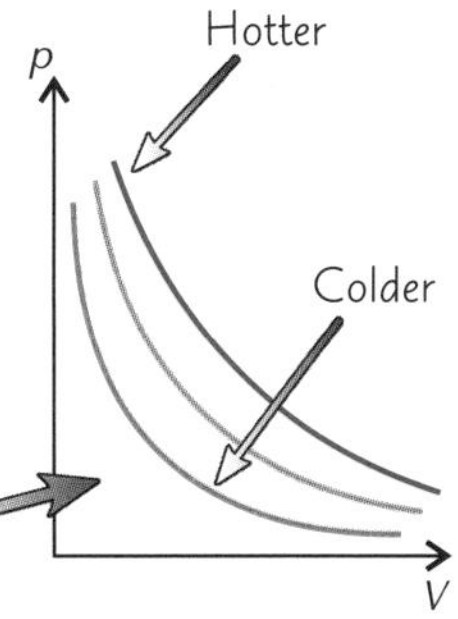


**Example:** The *p-V* diagram below shows the isothermal expansion of a system. Calculate the work done by the system as it expands between pressures A and B.

The work done is equal to the **area** under the graph.

You can estimate the area by counting the **total number of squares** under the curve. To find the work done between A and B, go across from the vertical axis to the curve and find the value of *V* at each of those points. Then find the area under the graph between these two values of *V*.

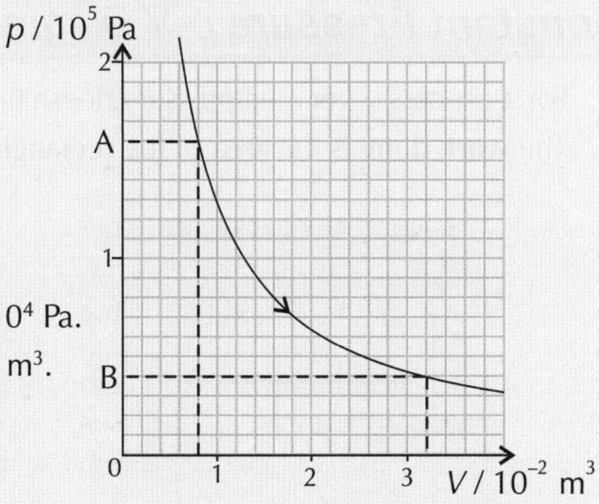


First find out how much energy each square is worth:

1) The height of each square represents $(1 \times 10^5) \div 10 = 1 \times 10^4$ Pa.
2) The width of each square represents $(1 \times 10^{-2}) \div 5 = 0.002$ m$^3$.
3) $W = p\Delta V$, so work done represented by each square is $0.002 \times 1 \times 10^4 = 20$ J.

Next count the number of squares under the curve and multiply it by the work per square.

The number of squares under the line between the values of *V* that correspond to pressures A and B is around 89.

So about $89 \times 20 \approx$ **1780 J** of work is done between pressures A and B.

# P-V Diagrams

## p-V Diagrams for **Adiabatic** Processes are Similar to **Isotherms**

1) The $p$-$V$ curves for **adiabatic** processes (p.121) are similar to those for **isothermal** processes, but they have a **steeper gradient**.
2) The graph below shows how an **isothermal** and **adiabatic compression** between two volumes would look if they had the **same initial temperature**.
3) The **area** under the **adiabatic curve** is **larger** than the area under the **isothermal curve**, so **more work** is done to **compress gas adiabatically** than isothermally.
4) The gas does **less work** if it **expands adiabatically instead** of isothermally.

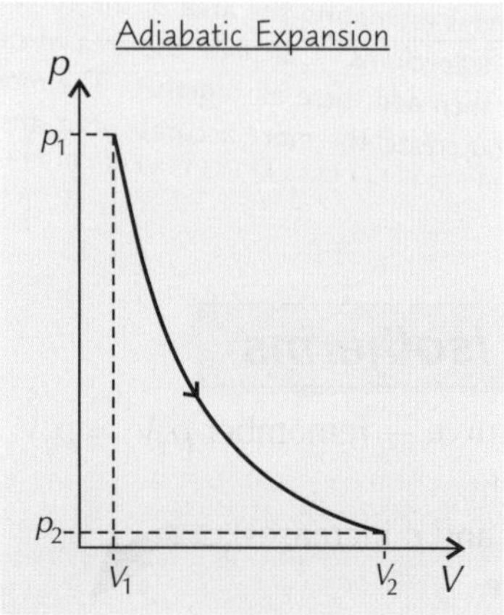


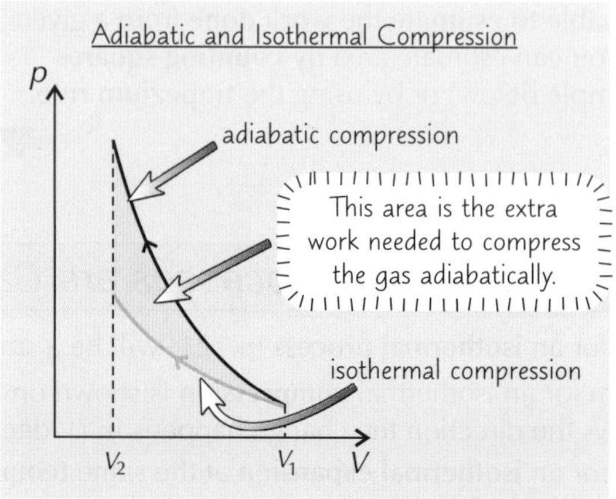


## **Constant Volume** p-V Diagrams are **Straight Vertical Lines**

1) Unsurprisingly, $p$-$V$ diagrams for changes with a **constant volume** are **straight vertical lines**.
2) For these processes (p.122), there is **no work** done as the volume doesn't change.
3) You can see this from the $p$-$V$ diagram — there is no **area** under the line.
4) As a system is kept at a constant volume but **heated** between temperatures $T_1$ and $T_2$, its pressure will **increase**. If it is **cooled** at a constant volume, the pressure will **decrease**.

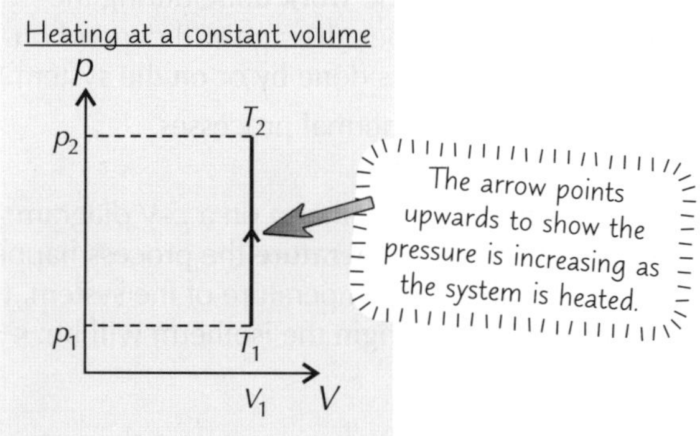


## **Constant Pressure** p-V Diagrams are **Straight Horizontal Lines**

1) For a process where the pressure doesn't change, the $p$-$V$ diagram is a **horizontal straight** line.
2) The **work done** is the **area** of the **rectangle** under the graph — work done $W = p\Delta V$.

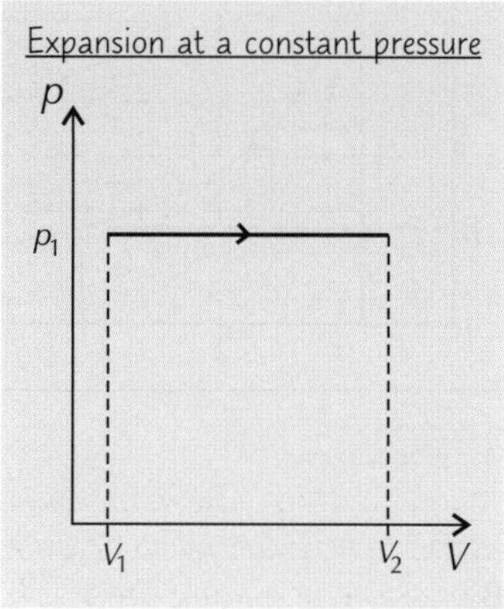


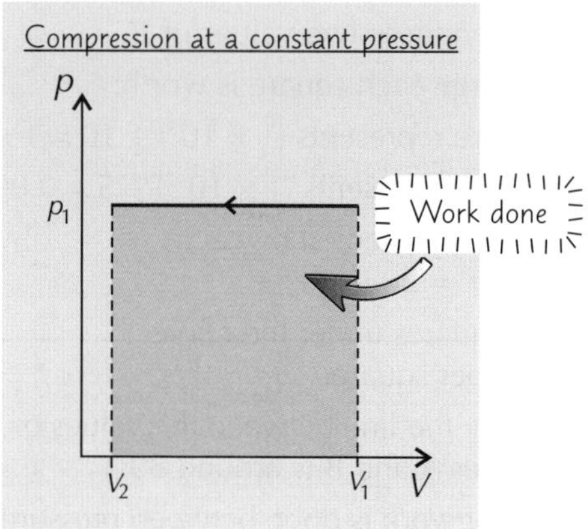

Louise worked best when she was under constant pressure.

# P-V Diagrams

## Cyclic Processes Create a Loop on a p-V Diagram

1) A system can undergo **different processes one after another** which form a **cycle** (loop). They start at a certain **pressure** and **volume** and return to them at the end of each **cycle**.
2) To find the **net work** of the cyclic process, you find the **difference** between the **work** done **by** a system and the work done **to** the system. This equals the **area of the loop** created by the cyclic process.

**Work done per cycle = Area of loop**

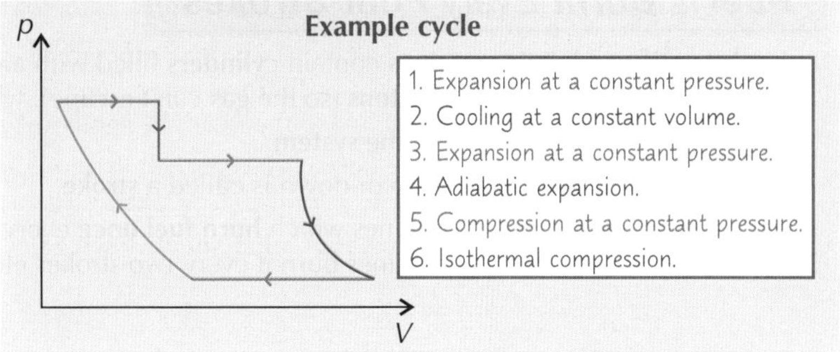

Example cycle
p
V
1. Expansion at a constant pressure.
2. Cooling at a constant volume.
3. Expansion at a constant pressure.
4. Adiabatic expansion.
5. Compression at a constant pressure.
6. Isothermal compression.


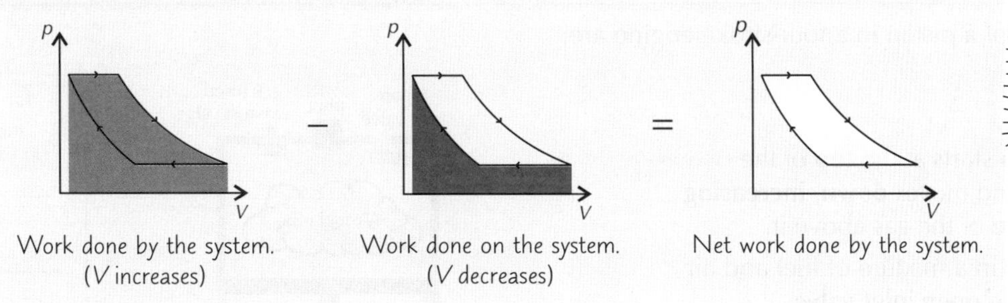


The operation of an engine is one example of a cyclic process (see p.126).

## Practice Questions

Q1 How would you calculate work done from a *p-V* diagram showing an adiabatic expansion between two volumes?

Q2 What are the *p-V* curves for isothermal processes called?

Q3 Sketch the *p-V* diagrams for a change where the pressure is constant and a change where the volume is constant.

Q4 What is a cyclic process?

Q5 How would you calculate the work done for one cycle of a cyclic process from a *p-V* diagram?

### Exam Questions

Q1 A system undergoes a cyclic process made up of four stages, A, B, C and D, described below.
Stage A: heated at a constant volume, $V_1$. Stage B: expansion at a constant pressure until the system reaches a volume of $V_2$. Stage C: adiabatic expansion. Stage D: isothermal compression until it reaches volume $V_1$.
Draw the *p-V* diagram for this cycle, labelling stages A, B, C and D. [4 marks]

Q2 The *p-V* diagram on the right is for a cyclic process where the system undergoes an isothermal expansion, an isothermal compression, and an expansion and compression at a constant pressure.

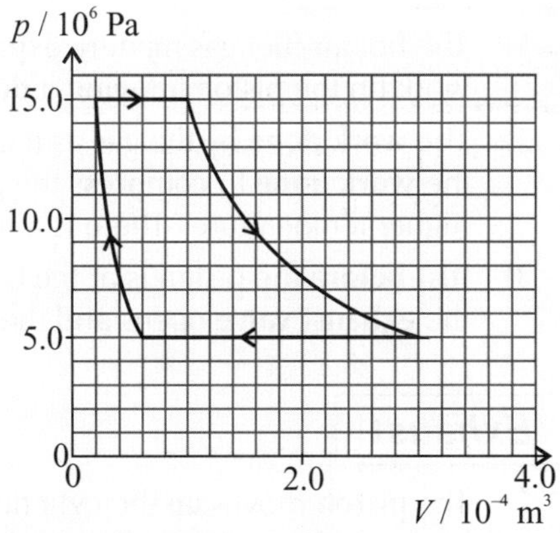


a) Calculate the work done during the expansion at a constant pressure. [1 mark]

b) Estimate the net work done by the process per cycle. [3 marks]

c) Explain whether the net work done per cycle would increase, decrease or stay the same if the system was adiabatically expanded instead of isothermally expanded to $4 \times 10^6$ Pa. No other changes are made to the cycle processes. [2 marks]

## Become a cyclic process — reread the last three pages...

*Seriously, this stuff is really helpful for understanding what's actually happening to a system. Go back and make sure you've got it all in your head. The big things to remember are what each line looks like and how to calculate the work done by each process. Then have a good practice at actually drawing the graphs and calculating the work from them.*

# Four-Stroke Engines

*Ever wondered how a car engine actually works? Well, now you get to find out...*

## Fuel is Burnt Every Four Strokes

1) **Internal combustion engines** contain **cylinders** filled with air. The air in these cylinders is trapped by tight-fitting **pistons** (so the gas can't escape), which move up and down.
2) The **gas** inside a cylinder is the **system**.
3) Each time a piston moves up or down is called a **stroke**.
4) **Four-stroke engines** are engines which **burn fuel once** every **four strokes** of a piston. (Two-stroke engines burn it every two strokes etc.)

Bailey thought that four strokes wasn't nearly enough.

## You Need to Understand Indicator Diagrams for Four-Stroke Petrol Engines

The four strokes of a piston in a four-stroke engine are:

The p-V diagrams for engines are called indicator diagrams.

### Induction

1) The **piston** starts at the **top** of the cylinder and moves **down**, **increasing** the **volume** of the gas above it.
2) This sucks in a mixture of fuel and air through the **open inlet valve**.
3) The **pressure** of the gas in the cylinder remains **constant**, **just below** atmospheric pressure.

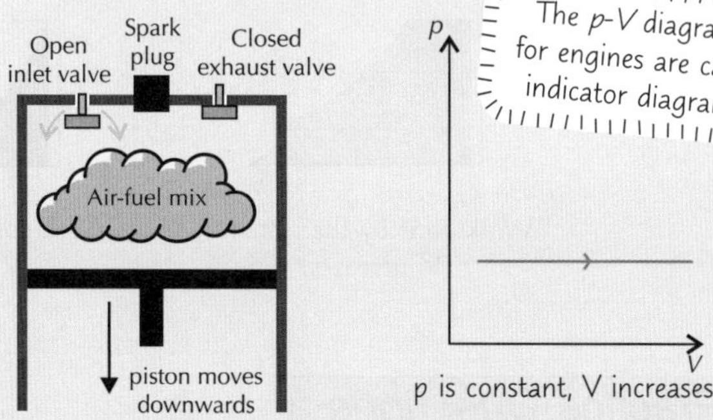


p is constant, V increases.

### Compression

1) The inlet valve is **closed**.
2) The piston moves back **up** the cylinder and does work on the gas, **increasing** the **pressure**.
3) **Just before** the piston is at the end of this stroke, the **spark plug** creates a spark which **ignites** the **air-fuel mixture**.
4) The **temperature** and **pressure** suddenly increase at an almost **constant volume**.

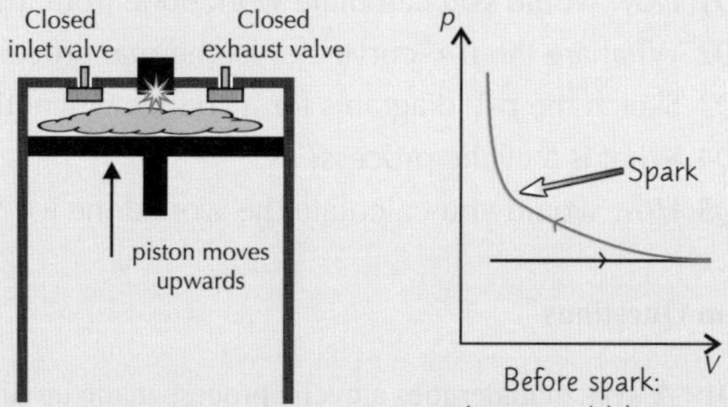


Before spark: *p* increases, *V* decreases.
After spark: *T* and *p* increase, *V* is roughly constant.

### Expansion

1) The hot air-fuel gas mixture **expands** and does work on the piston, moving it **downwards**.
2) The **work done** by the gas as it **expands** is **more** than the **work done** to **compress** the gas, as it is now at a higher temperature. There is a **net output of work**.
3) **Just before** the piston is at the bottom of the stroke, the **exhaust valve** opens and the **pressure** reduces.

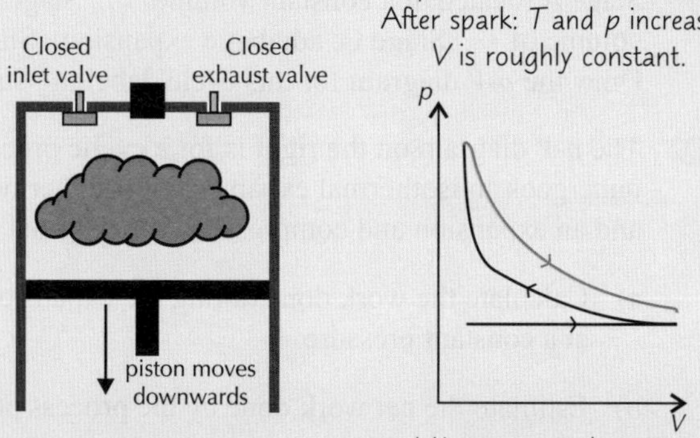


*V* increases, *p* decreases.

### Exhaust

1) The **piston** moves **up** the cylinder, and the burnt gas leaves through the **exhaust valve**.
2) The pressure remains almost **constant**, **just above** atmospheric pressure.

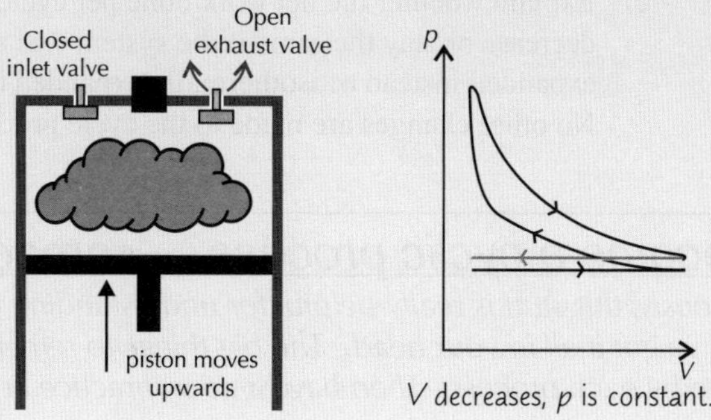


*V* decreases, *p* is constant.

# Four-Stroke Engines

## Four-Stroke Diesel Engines Use Compressed Air to Ignite Fuel

1) Whilst four-stroke **diesel engines** undergo the same **four strokes**, they work slightly differently to four-stroke petrol engines.
2) The **induction stroke**: here **only air** is pulled into the cylinder, not an air-fuel mixture.
3) The **compression stroke**: the air is compressed so it reaches a **temperature** high enough to **ignite diesel fuel**. Just before the end of the stroke, **diesel** is **sprayed** into the cylinder through a fuel injector and ignites.
4) The **expansion** and **exhaust strokes** are then the **same** as for a petrol engine.
5) The **indicator diagram** for a diesel engine is also slightly different — there is no **sharp peak** at the start of the **expansion stroke** — as you can see in the diagram on the right.

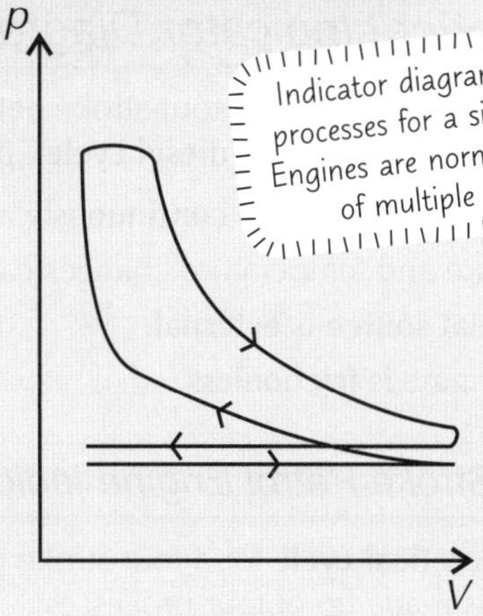


Indicator diagrams show the processes for a single cylinder. Engines are normally made up of multiple cylinders.

## Practice Questions

Q1 What is meant by the term 'four-stroke engine'?

Q2 Name the four strokes of a four-stroke engine.

Q3 What is the function of the inlet valve in a four-stroke petrol engine?

Q4 What is the function of the spark plug in a four-stroke petrol engine?

Q5 Explain why there is a net output of work by a four-stroke engine.

Q6 Sketch the indicator diagram for a four-stroke diesel engine.

**Exam Questions**

Q1 The sketched indicator diagram below shows the pressure and volume changes for the first two strokes in the cycle of a four-stroke petrol engine.

a) Describe what happens during the two strokes shown by the indicator diagram. [4 marks]

b) Complete the indicator diagram to show a complete cycle of a four-stroke engine. [2 marks]

c) Mark a cross at the point on the $p$-$V$ diagram where the spark plug ignites the gas in the engine cycle. [1 mark]

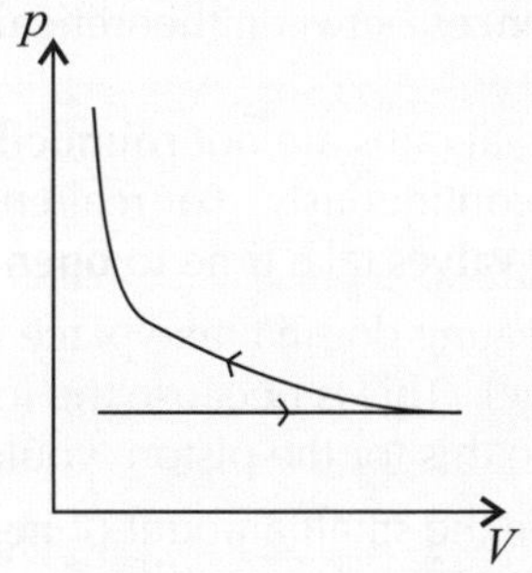


Q2 Describe the differences between how a four-stroke petrol engine and a four-stroke diesel engine operate. [3 marks]

### Show examiners you're a bright spark...

*Four-stroke engines have four different strokes — sorted. Unfortunately, you have to delve a bit deeper to get all the marks. Learn each of the four strokes and make sure you can describe what happens in them. Then make sure you know what the indicator diagrams look like for both petrol and diesel engines, and what each line shows.*

# Using Indicator Diagrams

*By comparing an ideal p-V diagram to a real one for an engine, you can see how well it's performing. You can find out all kinds of things, like how much friction there is and how much power the engine actually produces.*

## ***Theoretical*** *Indicator Diagrams* ***Assume Perfect Conditions***

The **theoretical cycle** for a four-stroke **petrol engine** is called the **Otto cycle**. The theoretical cycle for a four-stroke **diesel engine** is called the **diesel cycle**. Both of these **theoretical models** make the following **assumptions**:

1) The **same gas** is taken **continuously** around the cycle. The gas is **pure air**, with an adiabatic constant $\gamma = 1.4$.
2) Pressure and temperature changes can be **instantaneous**.
3) The **heat source** is **external**.
4) The engine is **frictionless**.

### *Four-Stroke Petrol Engine Indicator Diagrams*

The **theoretical cycle** for a four-stroke **petrol engine** is made up of four processes:

**A** First, it is assumed that the gas is compressed **adiabatically** (p.121), so no heat is transferred.

**B** Heat is supplied whilst the **volume** is kept **constant**.

**C** The gas is allowed to cool **adiabatically**.

**D** The system is cooled at a **constant volume**.

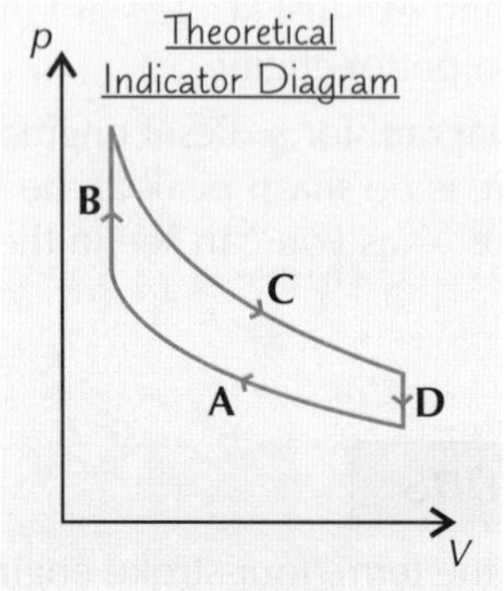


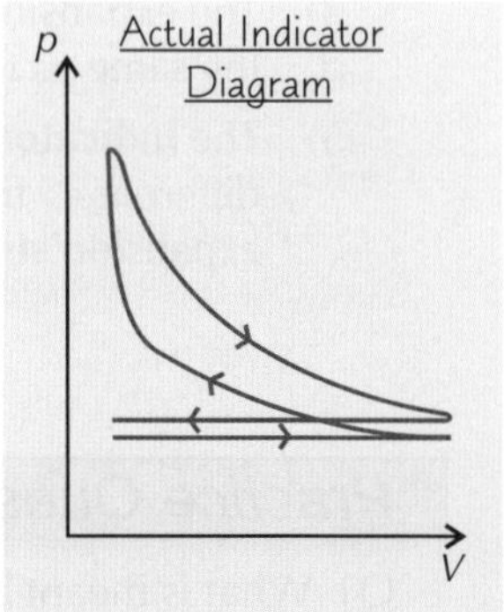


### *Four-Stroke Diesel Engine Indicator Diagrams*

The four processes in the **theoretical cycle** for a four-stroke **diesel engine** are:

**A** The gas is **adiabatically** compressed.

**B** Then heat is supplied, but this time **pressure** is kept **constant**.

**C** The gas is allowed to cool **adiabatically**.

**D** Then the system is cooled at a **constant volume**.

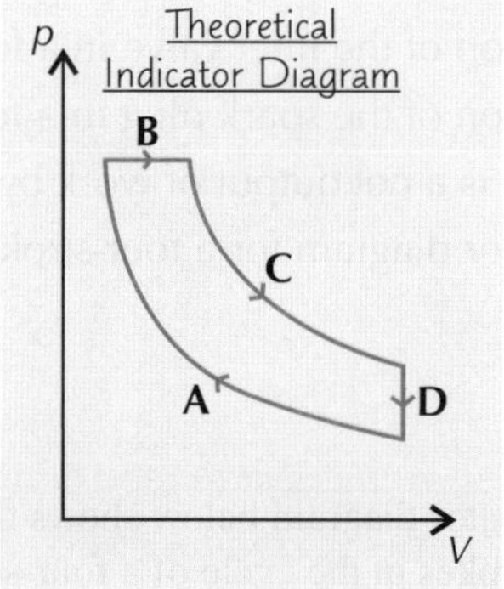


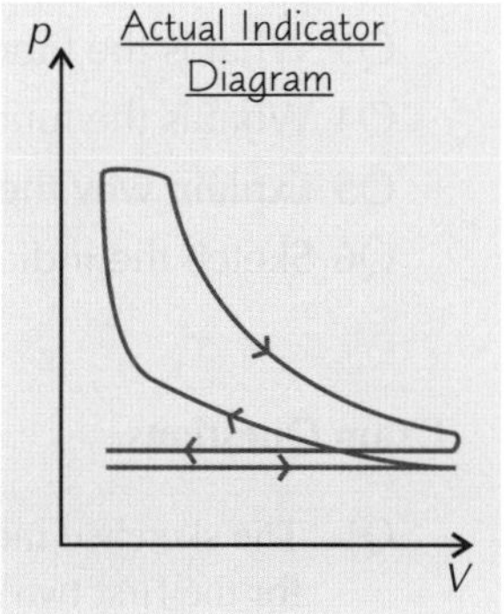


## *You Can* ***Compare Theoretical Diagrams*** *to* ***Real Engines***

Engineers **compare** indicator diagrams of **real** engines to **theoretical** models in order to see how well they are **performing**. The main **differences** between theoretical and real-life diagrams are:

1) The **corners** of theoretical indicator diagrams are not **rounded**. This is because it is assumed that the **same air** is used continuously. For real engines, these corners are rounded as the **inlet** and **exhaust valves** take time to **open** and **close**.
2) In a real four-stroke **petrol engine**, heating doesn't take place at a **constant volume** (process B on the petrol engine indicator diagram above). This is because the increase in **pressure** and **temperature** would have to be **instantaneous** to do this (or the piston would have to pause for a moment).
3) The theoretical model doesn't include the small amount of **negative work** caused by the loop between the **exhaust** and the **induction lines** because it assumes the **same air** cycles around the system **continuously**.
4) Engines have an **internal heat source** (the burning air-fuel mixture), not an external one. This means the **temperature rise** is not as large as in the theoretical model because the fuel used to heat the gas is **never completely burned** in the cylinder, so you can never get the **maximum energy** out of it. This means that **theoretical engines** can achieve **higher pressures** (and so have a higher **peak**).
5) Energy is needed to overcome **friction** caused by the **moving parts** of a real engine, so the **net work** done will always be less than for a theoretical engine. This means that the **area** inside the **loop** is **smaller** for real four-stroke engines.

# Using Indicator Diagrams

## You Can Calculate **Engine Power** from **Indicator Diagrams**

1) You know that the **area** of a **loop** for a cyclic process gives the work done (p.125). For engines, the small amount of **negative work** (see previous page) is **negligible**, so the **net work done** by an engine cylinder for one cycle is the **area** of the **loop** on the indicator diagram.
2) The **indicated power** is the **net work done** by the **engine cylinder** in **one second** (work done in one cycle × number of cycles per second).
3) If an engine has more than one cylinder, multiply the **cylinder's** indicated power by the **number of cylinders** to get the **engine's indicated power**.

**Indicated power = (area of *p-V* loop) × (number of cycles per second) × (number of cylinders)**

## **Friction Reduces** the **Output Power** of an Engine

1) **Friction** occurs between **moving parts** of an engine, e.g. between the **piston** and the **cylinder**, at the **bearings** and when the **valves** are opened or closed.
2) **Work** needs to be done to **overcome friction** in the engine. The power needed to do this is called the **friction power**. This means that the **brake power** (or **output** power) of the engine is **less** than the **indicated power** that was calculated for the engine.

**friction power = indicated power – brake power**

3) The **output** (or **brake**) **power** can be calculated using the equation from p.114:

$P = T\omega$ where $T$ is the engine torque (Nm) and $\omega$ is the angular velocity (rad $s^{-1}$) of the crankshaft.

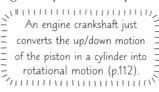

An engine crankshaft just converts the up/down motion of the piston in a cylinder into rotational motion (p.112).

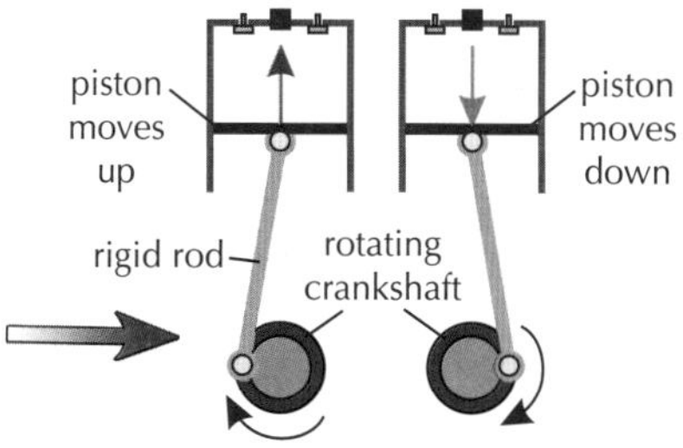


## Practice Questions

Q1 Sketch the theoretical *p-V* diagrams for four-stroke petrol and diesel engines. Explain what processes are represented by them.

Q2 Why are the corners of real-life four-stroke engine indicator diagrams rounded?

Q3 Where does the negative work in an indicator diagram come from?

Q4 Describe and explain any other differences between theoretical and real-life indicator diagrams for four-stroke engines.

**Exam Questions**

Q1 A four-stroke petrol engine operates at 29 cycles per second. The engine has eight identical cylinders. The area of a *p-V* loop on an indicator diagram for one cylinder is 120 J.

a) Calculate the indicated power of the engine. [1 mark]

b) The angular velocity of the engine's crankshaft is $58\pi$ rad $s^{-1}$ and the engine torque is 130 Nm. Calculate the friction power of the engine. [2 marks]

Q2 Indicator diagrams for two real, single-cylinder engines with identical cylinders are shown on the right. The cylinders are powered by crankshafts with the same angular velocity and both engines have the same friction power. Use these indicator diagrams to compare the torque of engine A and engine B. [3 marks]

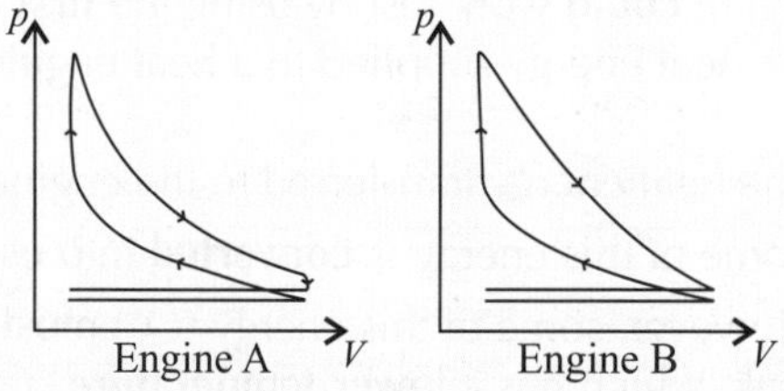


## Assuming I can sing, in theory, I'm a world-famous rock star...

*Unfortunately, theoretical models are generally too good to be true. Still, you have to know them. Learn the theoretical diagrams for petrol and diesel engines and the reasons why the real-life versions are different. Then make sure you know the equations for calculating the indicated, friction and output power and get some practice actually using them.*

# Engine Efficiency

*Efficiency is how much bang for your buck (or work for your energy) your engine is giving you.*

## There are Three Types of Engine Efficiency You Need to Know...

All **efficiencies** are just a measure of how much of the input power is **transferred usefully**. An engine's **input power** is the amount of **heat energy** per unit time it could **potentially** gain from **burning fuel**. The **calorific value** of the fuel tells you how much **energy** the fuel has **stored** in it per unit volume. So the **input power** is the rate fuel is supplied multiplied by its calorific value.

**input power = calorific value × fuel flow rate**

You might be given the calorific value in terms of energy per unit mass. If this happens, you'll need the flow rate to be in terms of mass per second rather than volume per second.

There are three kinds of **engine efficiency** you need to know:

1) The **mechanical efficiency** of an engine is affected by the amount of energy lost through **moving parts** (for example, through friction).

$$\text{mechanical efficiency} = \frac{\text{brake power}}{\text{indicated power}}$$

2) **Thermal efficiency** describes how well **heat** energy is **transferred** into **work**.

$$\text{thermal efficiency} = \frac{\text{indicated power}}{\text{input power}}$$

3) The equation for the **overall efficiency** is:

$$\text{overall efficiency} = \frac{\text{brake power}}{\text{input power}}$$

**Example:** An engine with an overall efficiency of 36% has an input power of 123 kW. The indicator diagram shows the engine has an indicated power of 53 kW. Calculate the mechanical efficiency of the engine.

$$\text{overall efficiency} = \frac{\text{brake power}}{\text{input power}} \text{ so brake power} = \text{overall efficiency} \times \text{input power}$$

brake power = 0.36 × 123 000 = 44 280 W

$$\text{mechanical efficiency} = \frac{\text{brake power}}{\text{indicated power}} = \frac{44\ 280}{53\ 000} = 0.835... = \mathbf{84\%\ (to\ 2\ s.f.)}$$

## The Second Law of Thermodynamics — No Engine is 100% Efficient

1) **Heat engines** convert **heat** energy into **work**. No engine can transfer **all** the heat energy it is supplied with into useful work though — some heat always ends up **increasing** the **temperature** of the **engine**.
2) If the engine temperature reaches that of the **heat source**, then no heat **flows** and no **work** is done. This means that **no** heat engine can operate by using only the **first law of thermodynamics** (p.120).
3) Engines also have to obey the **second law of thermodynamics**: that heat engines **must** operate between a **heat source** and a **heat sink** (a region which **absorbs** heat from the engine).

### The Second Law of Thermodynamics

If an engine **could** work just by using the **first law** of thermodynamics, theoretically **all** of the heat energy supplied to a heat engine could be transferred into **useful work**.

1) The heat energy transferred to the engine from the **heat source** is $Q_H$.
2) Some of this energy is **converted** into **useful work**, $W$.
3) However, some of this energy ($Q_C$) **must** be **transferred** to a **heat sink**, which has a **lower temperature** ($T_C$) than the heat **source**.
4) This means engines can **never** be **100%** efficient.

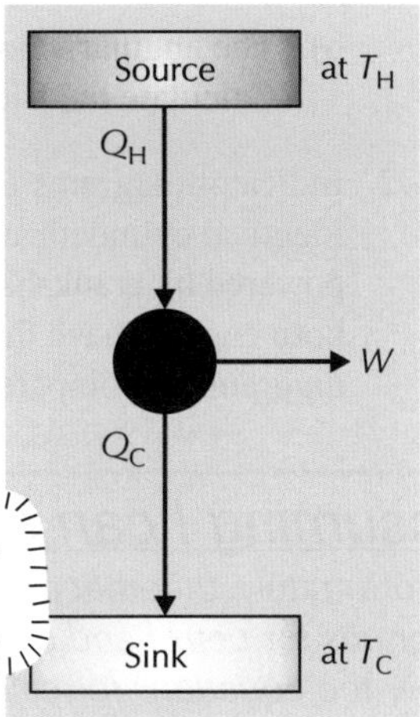


$T_H$ is the temperature of the heat source, $T_C$ is the temperature of the heat sink and $W$ is the work done by the engine.

# Engine Efficiency

## You Can Use the Second Law to Calculate **Efficiency**

You can calculate the **efficiency** of a heat engine using this equation:

$$\text{efficiency} = \frac{W}{Q_H} = \frac{Q_H - Q_C}{Q_H}$$

$Q_H$ is the heat transferred from the heat source (J),
$Q_C$ is the heat transferred to the heat sink (J),
$W$ is work output of the engine (J)

By assuming **perfect conditions**, you can also calculate the **maximum theoretical efficiency**:

$$\text{maximum theoretical efficiency} = \frac{T_H - T_C}{T_H}$$

$T_H$ is the temperature of the heat source (K),
$T_C$ is the temperature of the heat sink (K)

**Real** heat engine's efficiencies are **lower** than their theoretical maximum for multiple reasons:

1) There are **frictional** forces inside the engine (p.129).
2) **Fuel** doesn't burn **entirely**.
3) Energy is needed to **move internal components** of the engine.

## **Waste Heat** is Reused in **CHP Plants**

1) To **maximise** the efficiency of an engine, as much as possible of the inputted heat energy must be transferred usefully.
2) Engines are very **inefficient** — there is usually a lot of **waste heat** from heat engines, which is transferred to the **surrounding area** and lost.
3) **Combined heat and power** (CHP) plants try to limit **energy waste** by using this waste heat for other purposes — e.g. heating houses and businesses nearby.
4) For example, the Markinch Biomass CHP plant was recently built in Fife, Scotland. It generates **electricity** which it supplies to a **local papermaker** and the National Grid. The excess **heat** is then used to create **steam** to dry paper in the **paper mill**.

## Practice Questions

Q1 State the equation for calculating the input power of an engine.

Q2 What are the equations for calculating overall, thermal and mechanical efficiency?

Q3 Why can heat engines never be 100% efficient?

Q4 Draw a diagram to show the second law of thermodynamics being applied to a heat engine.

Q5 Name a system which tries to maximise the work done from the heat input of an engine.

**Exam Questions**

Q1 Petrol has a calorific value of 44.8 $\text{MJkg}^{-1}$. A petrol engine burns petrol at a rate of 2.8 g per second. The brake power of the engine is 44.7 kW. Calculate the overall efficiency of the engine. [3 marks]

Q2 A heat engine has 1000 J of energy transferred to it from a heat source at 1200 K. The engine is also in contact with a heat sink at a temperature of 290 K. The engine transfers 550 J of the supplied energy to the heat sink.

a) Calculate the maximum theoretical efficiency of the engine. [2 marks]

b) Calculate the efficiency of the engine. [2 marks]

c) Suggest one reason for the difference between the efficiencies calculated in a) and b). [1 mark]

## The second law of thermodynamics — not an excuse to do less work...

*First things first, learn that diagram. Not only do you need to know it, but it'll help you remember all of the efficiency stuff that goes with it. Then get to learning and practising the equations for overall, thermal and mechanical efficiency. Then it's just a case of remembering ways that useful work out can be maximised to make an efficient engine.*

# Reversed Heat Engines

*Normal heat engines do work, so reversed heat engines have work done to them.*

## Refrigerators and Heat Pumps are Reversed Heat Engines

1) **Reversed** heat engines operate between **hot** and **cold reservoirs** like other engines.
2) The big difference is the direction of energy transfer — **heat energy** is taken **from** the **cold** reservoir and transferred **to** the **hot** reservoir. For reversed heat engines, we call these reservoirs **spaces** (instead of **sources** and **sinks**).
3) Heat naturally flows from **hotter to colder** spaces. To transfer heat from a **colder** space to a **hotter** space, **work** ($W$) must be done.
4) **Heat pumps** and **refrigerators** are both reversed heat engines, but they have **different functions**.

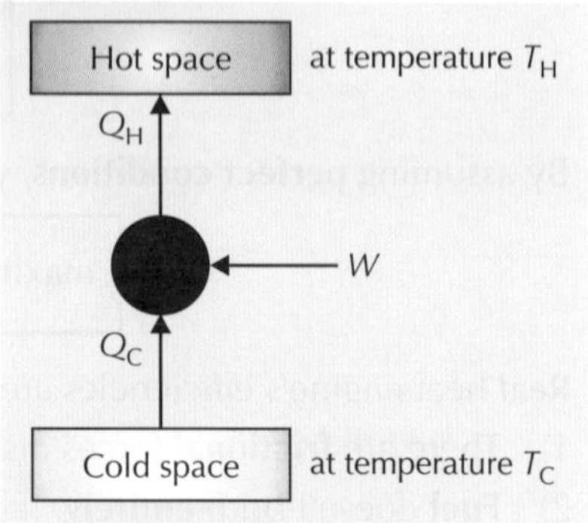


### Refrigerators

1) A refrigerator aims to **extract** as much heat energy from the **cold space** as possible for each joule of **work done**.
2) The **cold space** is the **inside** of the refrigerator, whilst the **hot space** is the **room** the refrigerator is in.
3) Refrigerators keep enclosed spaces cool that can be used to store **perishable food** fresh for longer.

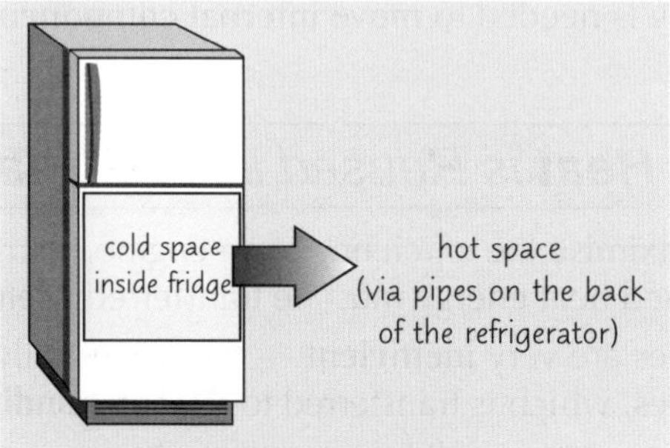


### Heat Pumps

1) A **heat pump** aims to **pump** as much heat as possible into the **hot** space **per joule of work done**.
2) Here, the **cold space** is usually the **outdoors** and the **hot space** is the **inside** of a **house**.
3) They are used to **heat rooms** and **water** in homes.

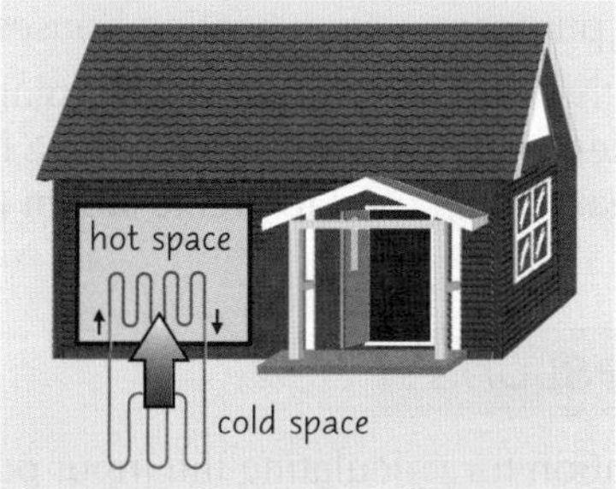


## Coefficient of Performance (COP) Describes How Well Work is Converted

1) Heat engines are judged on how well they can **transfer heat** based on the **amount of work done** on them.
2) The **coefficient of performance** is a measure of how well this **work** is **converted** into **heat transfer**. E.g. a heat pump with a coefficient of performance of **4** transfers **4 J** of energy for every **1 J** of **work** done.
3) It can be thought of like **efficiency** (see page 130), but it's not called that as the **coefficient of performance** can be **above 1**.

## You Can Calculate the Coefficient of Performance (COP) for Refrigerators

As it's the **heat removed** from the **cold** space that's important for a refrigerator, its **coefficient of performance** is:

$$COP_{ref} = \frac{Q_C}{W} = \frac{Q_C}{Q_H - Q_C}$$

$Q_H$ is the heat transferred to the hot space (J),
$Q_C$ is the heat transferred from the cold space (J),
$W$ is work done (J)

If it is running at the **maximum theoretical** efficiency, the coefficient of performance becomes:

$$COP_{ref} = \frac{T_C}{T_H - T_C}$$

$T_H$ is the temperature of the hot space (K),
$T_C$ is the temperature of the cold space (K)

# Reversed Heat Engines

## Coefficient of Performance (COP) is Similar for a Heat Pump

As it's the heat transferred to the hot space that's important for a heat pump, its **coefficient of performance** is:

$$COP_{hp} = \frac{Q_H}{W} = \frac{Q_H}{Q_H - Q_C}$$

Dave's heat pump performance wasn't much cop...

The **maximum theoretical coefficient of performance** is:

$$COP_{hp} = \frac{T_H}{T_H - T_C}$$

**Example:** A house installs a heat pump to keep its rooms at 23 °C by pumping heat in from the outside. In theory, how much does the coefficient of performance change if the outside temperature rises from 2 °C to 10°C?

If the outside temperature is 2 °C, the theoretical coefficient of performance is:

$$COP_{hp} = \frac{T_H}{T_H - T_C} = \frac{296}{296 - 275} = \frac{296}{21} = 14.09...$$

If the outside temperature is 10 °C, the theoretical coefficient of performance is:

$$COP_{hp} = \frac{T_H}{T_H - T_C} = \frac{296}{296 - 283} = \frac{296}{13} = 22.76...$$

So the coefficient of performance increases by:

22.76... – 14.09... = 8.67... = **8.7 (to 2 s.f.)**

Remember to convert to Kelvin for calculating the coefficient of performance. 0 K ≈ –273 °C

## Practice Questions

Q1 Describe how reversed heat engines work.

Q2 Give two examples of reversed heat engines.

Q3 What is the function of a refrigerator, and how does it differ from the function of a heat pump?

Q4 What is a coefficient of performance of a reversed heat engine?

Q5 State the equations for the coefficient of performance for a refrigerator and a heat pump.

Q6 State the maximum theoretical coefficient of performance for a heat pump.

### Exam Questions

Q1 In one hour, a refrigerator extracts 5.66 MJ of heat energy from the cold space in the fridge and transfers it to the air surrounding the fridge. An input of 2.02 MJ of work is needed for this energy transfer to take place.

a) Calculate the amount of heat energy leaving the refrigerator. [1 mark]

b) Calculate the coefficient of performance for this refrigerator. [1 mark]

Q2 a) A heat pump is used to warm a room to 25 °C by transferring heat energy from outside the house to inside. The outside temperature is 3.0 °C. Calculate the maximum theoretical coefficient of performance. (0 °C = 273 K) [1 mark]

b) The heat pump has an actual coefficient of performance of 3.5. It pumps 4.10 MJ of energy into the room. Show that 1.2 MJ of work is done to transfer this energy to the room. [2 marks]

## *It's the end of the section — don't COP out now...*

*So a fridge is just an engine turned on its head. Good to know. Although the diagram and equations are pretty similar to the ones you've already seen before, don't get lazy now. Practise using them and make sure you learn the maximum theoretical coefficients of performance — you won't be given them. Then kick back and relax — you've earned it.*

# Specific Charge of the Electron

*$e/m_e$ was known for quite a long time before anyone came up with a way to measure e or $m_e$ separately.*

## *Cathode Ray is an Old-Fashioned name for a Beam of Electrons*

1) The phrase '**cathode ray**' was first used in 1876, to describe the **glow** that appears on the wall of a **discharge tube** like the one in the diagram, when a **potential difference** is applied across the terminals.
2) The **rays** seemed to come from the **cathode** (hence their name) and there was a lot of argument about **what** the rays were made of.
3) **J. J. Thomson** ended the debate in 1897, when he demonstrated (see next page) that cathode rays:

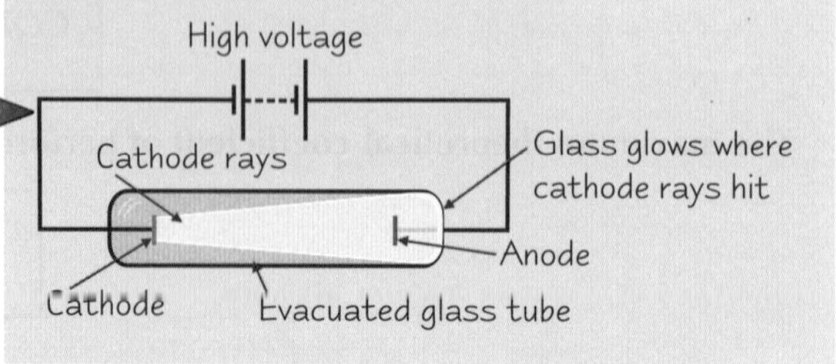


Cathode rays were used in TV and computer screens before LCD, plasma and LED screens came along.

- have **energy**, **momentum** and **mass**,
- have a **negative charge**,
- have the **same properties**, no matter **what gas** is in the tube and what the **cathode** is made of,
- have a **charge to mass ratio** much **bigger** than that of **hydrogen** ions. So they either have a **tiny mass**, or a much higher charge — Thomson assumed they had the same size charge as hydrogen ions.

Thomson concluded that **all atoms** contain these 'cathode ray particles', or **electrons** as they were soon known. He had discovered the **first subatomic particle**.

A particle's charge to mass ratio is called its specific charge (p.135).

## *Electron Beams are Produced by Thermionic Emission*

1) When you **heat** a **metal**, its **free electrons** gain a load of **kinetic energy**.
2) Give them **enough energy** and they'll **break free** from the surface of the metal — this is called **thermionic emission**. (Try breaking the word down — think of it as '**therm**' [to do with heat] + '**ionic**' [to do with charge] + '**emission**' [giving off] — so it's 'giving off charged particles when you heat something'.)
3) Once they've been emitted, the electrons can be **accelerated** by an **electric field** in an **electron gun**:

- A **heating coil** heats the metal cathode. The electrons that are emitted are **accelerated** towards the **cylindrical anode** by the electric field set up by the high voltage.
- Some electrons pass through a **little hole** in the **anode**, making a narrow electron beam. The electrons in the beam move at a **constant velocity** because there's **no field** beyond the anode — i.e. there's **no force**.

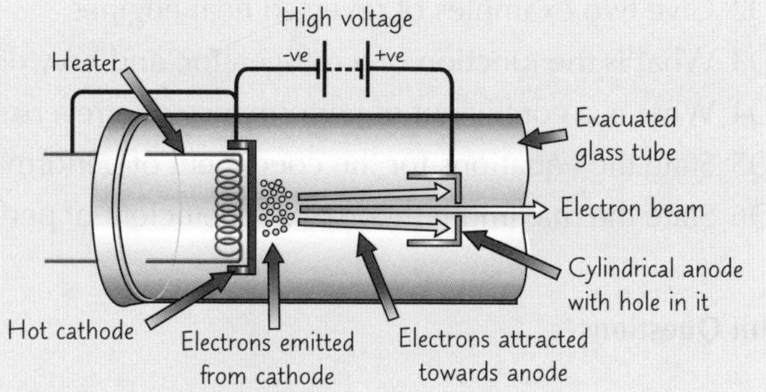


## *The Electronvolt is Defined Using Accelerated Charges*

1) The **work done** on a particle with charge **$Q$** when it's **accelerated** through a p.d. of **$V$** volts is **$QV$** joules. This just comes from the definition of the **volt** ($JC^{-1}$). This energy is converted into the **kinetic energy** of the particle.
2) If you replace **$Q$** in the equation with the magnitude of the charge of a **single electron**, **e**, you get:

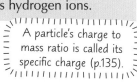

$$\textbf{work done} = \frac{1}{2}mv^2 = eV$$

3) From this you can define a new **unit of energy** called the **electronvolt** (**eV**):

> 1 electronvolt is the **kinetic energy carried** by an **electron** after it has been **accelerated** through a **potential difference** of **1 volt**.

The unit MeV is the mega-electronvolt (equal to $1.6 \times 10^{-13}$ J) and GeV is the giga-electronvolt ($1.6 \times 10^{-10}$ J).

4) So, the **energy gained**, in **electronvolts**, by an electron accelerated through a potential difference is:

**energy gained by electron (eV) = accelerating voltage (V) (work done)**

**Conversion factor:** $1 \text{ eV} = 1.6 \times 10^{-19}$ J

# Specific Charge of the Electron

## **Thomson** Measured the **Specific Charge** of the **Electron**

specific charge = $\frac{e}{m_e}$

1) The **specific charge** of a charged particle is just its **charge** per unit **mass.**
2) There are a **few different ways** of measuring it, and you need to know about **one** of them. This isn't the method that Thomson used, but that's not important.

### Measuring the Specific Charge of an Electron:

Check out Section 11 — Magnetic Fields if you're having trouble with this experiment.

1) Electrons are charged particles, so they can be deflected by an **electric** or a **magnetic field.** This method uses a magnetic field in a piece of apparatus called a **fine beam tube.**
2) When the beam of electrons from the **electron gun** (see previous page) passes through the low-pressure gas, hydrogen atoms along its path **absorb energy**. As the electrons in these **excited hydrogen atoms** fall back to the ground state, they **emit light**. The electron beam is seen as a **glowing trace** through the gas.

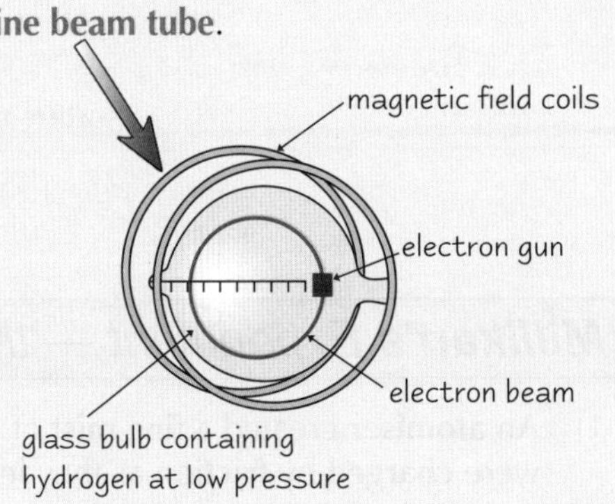


3) Two circular **magnetic field coils** either side generate a **uniform magnetic field** inside the tube.
4) The electron beam is initially fired at **right angles** to the **magnetic field**, so the beam curves round in a **circle.**
5) This means that the **magnetic force** on the electron (see p.40) is acting as a **centripetal force** (see p.3). So the radius of the circle is given by:

$$\frac{m_e v^2}{r} = Bev$$

Where $m_e$ is the mass of an electron, $e$ is the magnitude of the charge on an electron, $B$ is the magnetic field strength, $v$ is the velocity of the electron and $r$ is the radius of the circle.

6) You can **rearrange** this equation to give $v$ in terms of $B$, $e$, $m_e$ and $r$. Then you can substitute that expression into $\frac{1}{2} m_e v^2 = eV$ and tidy it all up a bit to get:

$$\frac{e}{m_e} = \frac{2V}{B^2 r^2}$$

Where $V$ is the accelerating potential.

You can **measure** all the quantities on the **right-hand side** of the equation using the **fine beam tube**, leaving you with the **specific charge, $e/m_e$**. It turns out that $e/m_e$ ($1.76 \times 10^{11}$ Ckg$^{-1}$) is about **1800 times greater** than the **specific charge of a hydrogen ion** or **proton** ($9.58 \times 10^7$ Ckg$^{-1}$). And the **mass** of a **proton** is about **1800 times greater** than the **mass** of an **electron**. **Thomson was right** — electrons and protons do have the **same size charge.**

## Practice Questions

Q1 What is meant by thermionic emission? Describe how this is relevant to cathode ray tube televisions.

Q2 Sketch a labelled diagram of an electron gun that could be used to accelerate electrons.

Q3 What was Thomson's main conclusion following his measurement of $e/m_e$ for electrons?

Q4 How does the specific charge of the electron compare with the specific charge of the proton?

**Exam Questions**

Q1 An electron of mass $9.11 \times 10^{-31}$ kg and charge $-1.60 \times 10^{-19}$ C is accelerated from rest through a potential difference of 1.00 kV.

a) State its energy in eV. [1 mark]

b) Calculate its energy in joules. [1 mark]

c) Calculate its speed in ms$^{-1}$ and express this as a percentage of the speed of light ($3.00 \times 10^8$ ms$^{-1}$). [3 marks]

Q2 Explain the main features of an experiment to determine the specific charge of the electron. The quality of your written answer will be assessed in this question. [5 marks]

## New Olympic event — the electronvault...

*Electronvolts are really handy units — they crop up all over the rest of this book, particularly in nuclear and particle physics. They save you having to mess around with a load of nasty powers of ten. Cathode ray tubes (CRTs) used to be in every TV and computer monitor, but now you'll probably only find them in museums (or in my flat...).*

# Millikan's Oil-Drop Experiment

*Thomson had already found the specific charge of the electron in 1897 — now it was down to Robert Millikan, experimenter extraordinaire, to find the absolute charge...*

## ***Millikan's*** *Experiment used* ***Stokes' Law***

1) Before you start thinking about Millikan's experiment, you need a bit of **extra theory**.
2) When you drop an object into a fluid, like air, it experiences a **viscous drag** force. This force acts in the **opposite direction** to the velocity of the object, and is due to the **viscosity** of the fluid.
3) You can calculate this viscous force on a spherical object using **Stokes' law**:

$$F = 6\pi\eta rv$$

where $\eta$ is the viscosity of the fluid, $r$ is the radius of the object and $v$ is the velocity of the object.

## ***Millikan's*** *Experiment — the* ***Basic Set-Up***

1) An **atomiser** created a **fine mist** of oil drops that were **charged** by **friction** as they left the atomiser (positively if they lost electrons, negatively if they gained electrons).
2) Some of the drops fell through a **hole** in the top plate and could be viewed through the **microscope**. (The eyepiece carried a **scale** to measure distances — and so **velocities** — accurately.)

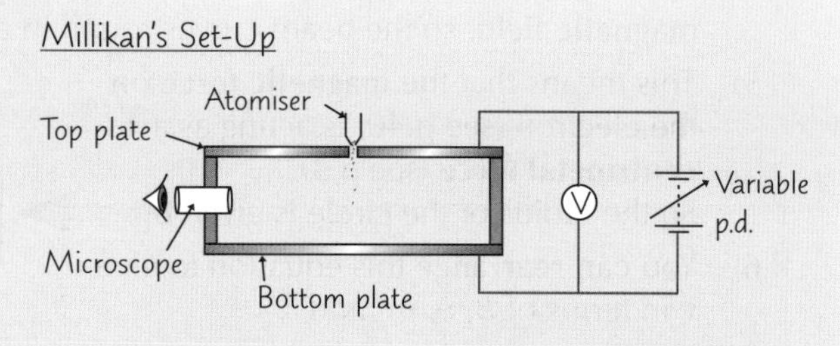


3) When he was ready, Millikan could apply a **potential difference** between the two plates, producing a **field** that exerted a **force** on the charged drops. By **adjusting** the p.d., he could vary the strength of the field.
4) To give you a feel for the **size** of the apparatus, Millikan's plates were circular, with a diameter of about the width of this page. They were separated by about 1.5 cm.

## ***Before*** *the* ***Field*** *is Switched on, there's only* ***Gravity*** *and the* ***Viscous Force***

1) With the electric field turned off, the forces acting on each oil drop are:

   a) the **weight** of the drop — acting downwards
   b) the **viscous force** from the air — acting upwards

Millikan had to take account of things like upthrust as well, but you don't have to worry about that — keep it simple.

2) The drop will reach **terminal velocity** (i.e. it will stop accelerating) when these two forces are equal. So, from Stokes' law (see above):

$$mg = 6\pi\eta rv$$

3) Since the **mass** of the drop is the **volume** of the drop multiplied by the **density**, $\rho$, of the oil, this can be rewritten as:

$$\frac{4}{3}\pi r^3\rho g = 6\pi\eta rv \text{ so } r^2 = \frac{9\eta v}{2\rho g}$$

Millikan measured $\eta$ and $\rho$ in separate experiments, so he could now calculate $r$ — ready to be used when he **switched on** the electric field...

field switched off

field switched on

# Millikan's Oil-Drop Experiment

## Then he **Turned On** the **Electric Field**...

1) The field introduced a **third major factor** — an **electric force** on the drop.
2) Millikan adjusted the applied p.d. until the drop was **stationary**. Since the **viscous force** is proportional to the **velocity** of the object, once the drop stopped moving, the viscous force **disappeared**.
3) Now the only two forces acting on the oil drop were:

   a) the **weight** of the drop — acting downwards
   b) the force due to the **uniform electric field** — acting upwards

4) The **electric force** is given by: $F = \frac{QV}{d}$ where $Q$ is the charge on the oil drop, $V$ is the p.d. between the plates and $d$ is the distance between the plates.
5) Since the drop is **stationary**, this electric force must be equal to the weight, so: $\frac{QV}{d} = mg = \frac{4}{3}\pi r^3 \rho g$

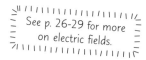

See p. 26-29 for more on electric fields.

   The first part of the experiment gave a value for $r$, so the **only unknown** in this equation is $Q$.
6) So Millikan could find the **charge on the drop**, and repeated the experiment for hundreds of drops. The charge on any drop was always a **whole number multiple** of **$-1.60 \times 10^{-19}$ C**.

## These Results Suggested that **Charge** was **Quantised**

1) This result was **really significant**. Millikan concluded that charge can **never exist** in **smaller** quantities than $1.60 \times 10^{-19}$ C. He assumed that this was the **charge** carried by an **electron**.
2) Later experiments confirmed that **both** these things are true.

> Charge is "**quantised**". It exists in "packets" of size **$1.60 \times 10^{-19}$ C** — the **fundamental unit of charge**. This is the size of the charge carried by **one electron**.

3) This meant that the mass of an electron could be calculated exactly, proving that it was the lightest particle ever discovered (at the time).

## Practice Questions

Q1 Write down the equation for Stokes' law, defining any variables.

Q2 List the forces that act on the oil drop in Millikan's experiment:
  a) with the drop drifting downwards at terminal velocity but with no applied electric field,
  b) when the drop is stationary, with an electric field applied.

Q3 Briefly explain the significance of Millikan's oil-drop experiment in the context of quantum physics.

**Exam Question**

Q1 An oil drop of mass $1.63 \times 10^{-14}$ kg is held stationary in the space between two charged plates 3.00 cm apart. The potential difference between the plates is 4995 V. The density of the oil used is 885 $kgm^{-3}$.

  a) Describe the relative magnitude and direction of the forces acting on the oil drop. [2 marks]
  b) Calculate the charge on the oil drop using $g = 9.81$ $Nkg^{-1}$. Give your answer in terms of $e$, the charge on an electron. [3 marks]

  The electric field is switched off and the oil drop falls towards the bottom plate.

  c) Explain why the oil drop reaches terminal velocity as it falls. [3 marks]
  d) Calculate the terminal velocity of the oil drop using $\eta = 1.84 \times 10^{-5}$ $kgm^{-1}s^{-1}$. [3 marks]

## So next time you've got a yen for $1.59 \times 10^{-19}$ coulombs — tough...

*This was a huge leap. Along with the photoelectric effect (see p.141), this experiment marked the beginning of quantum physics. The world was no longer ruled by smooth curves — charge now jumped from one allowed step to the next...*

# Light — Particles vs Waves

*Newton was quite a bright chap really, but even he could make mistakes — and this was his biggest one. The trouble with being Isaac Newton is that everyone just assumes you're right...*

## Newton had his Corpuscular Theory and Thought Light was Particles

1) In 1671, Newton published his **theory of colour**. In it he suggested that **light** was made up of **tiny particles** that he called '**corpuscles**'.
2) One of his major arguments was that light was known to travel in **straight lines**, yet waves were known to **bend** in the shadow of an **obstacle** (diffraction). Experiments weren't **accurate enough** then to detect the diffraction of light. Light was known to **reflect** and **refract**, but that was it.
3) His theory was based on the principles of his **laws of motion** — that all particles, including his 'corpuscles', will 'naturally' travel in **straight lines**.
4) Newton believed that **reflection** was due to a force that **pushed** the particles away from the surface — just like a ball bouncing back off a wall.
5) He thought **refraction** occurred because the corpuscles travelled **faster** in a **denser** medium like glass.

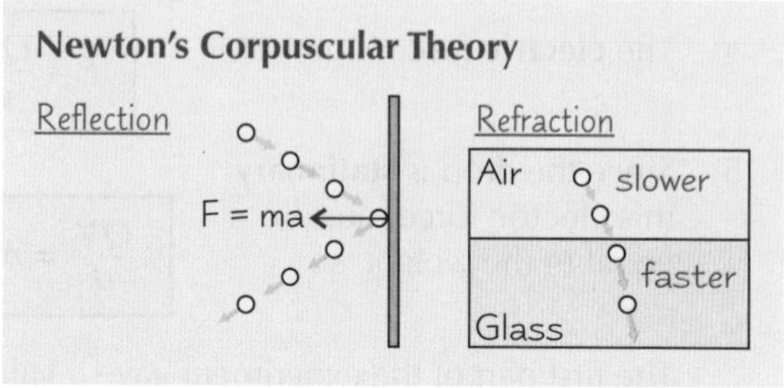


## Huygens thought Light was a Wave

1) The idea that light might be a **wave** had existed for some time before it was formalised by Huygens in 1678 — not long after Newton first publicly stated his belief that light was a particle.
2) Huygens developed a **general model** of the propagation of **waves** in what is now known as **Huygens' principle**:

> **HUYGENS' PRINCIPLE**: Every point on a wavefront may be considered to be a **point source** of **secondary wavelets** that spread out in the forward direction at the speed of the wave. The **new wavefront** is the surface that is **tangential** to all of these **secondary wavelets**.

This diagram shows how this works:

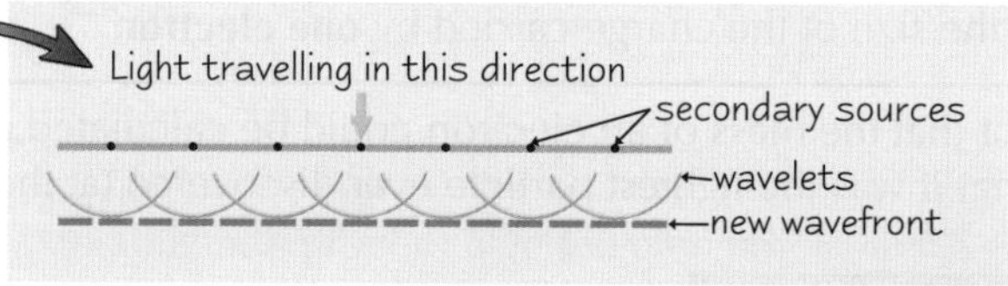


3) By applying his theory to **light**, he found that he could explain **reflection** and **refraction** easily.
   Huygens predicted that light should **slow down** when it entered a **denser medium**, rather than speed up.
4) Huygens also predicted that light should **diffract** around tiny objects and that two coherent light sources should **interfere** with each other.

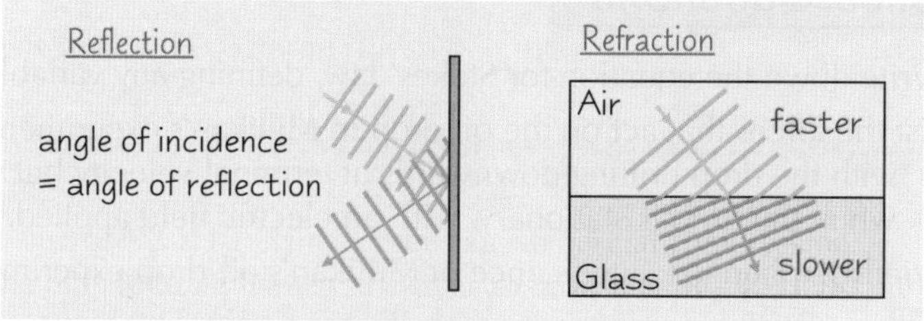


## Scientists of the Period Preferred Newton's Theory

Newton's corpuscular theory was much more popular because:

- Imagining light as a stream of particles explained **reflection** and **refraction** in a way that more intuitively fitted in with the existing understanding of physics. It couldn't explain **diffraction**, but the equipment of the time wasn't capable of demonstrating diffraction in light.
- There was **no experimental evidence** to support Huygens' theory that light was a wave until Young's interference experiments more than 100 years later.
- Scientists thought **double refraction** (a polarisation effect, where shining light through certain crystals makes two images instead of one) couldn't be explained by thinking of light as a wave. Newton's corpuscular theory explained it in terms of the corpuscles having '**sides**'.
- Over time, Newton's **reputation** grew as his ideas on maths, gravity, forces and motion **revolutionised physics**. By the time of Thomas Young a century later, he was a figure scientists didn't want to disagree with.

# Light — Particles vs Waves

## **Young** Proved **Huygens Right** with his **Double-Slit Experiment**

1) **Diffraction** and **interference** are both uniquely **wave** properties. If it could be shown that **light** showed **interference** patterns, that would help decide once and for all between corpuscular theory and wave theory.
2) The problem with this was getting two **coherent** light sources, as **light** is emitted in **random bursts**.
3) In 1802, Thomas Young solved this problem by using only **one point source of light** (a light source behind a narrow slit). In front of this was a **screen** with **two narrow slits** in it. Light spreading out by **diffraction** from the slits was equivalent to **two coherent point sources**.
4) In the area on the screen where light from the two slits **overlapped**, bright and dark '**fringes**' were formed. This was **proof** that light could both **diffract** (through the narrow slits) and **interfere** (to form the interference pattern on the screen) — **Huygens** was right all along.

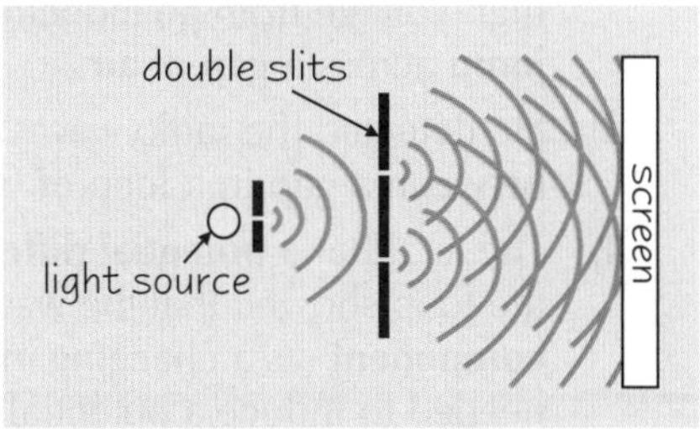


- Even then, Huygens' and Young's ideas weren't widely accepted. Newton's work had **revolutionised physics**, and by this point he was an established historical figure who other scientists didn't want to contradict.
- Huygens had proposed that light was a **longitudinal wave** (like sound), but this couldn't explain **double refraction**.
- It took more than a decade before Young (at about the same time as the French scientist **Fresnel**) realised that **transverse waves** could explain the behaviour of light. Following this, other scientists soon started **agreeing** with Huygens that light was a wave.

## **Fizeau** Measured the Speed of Light

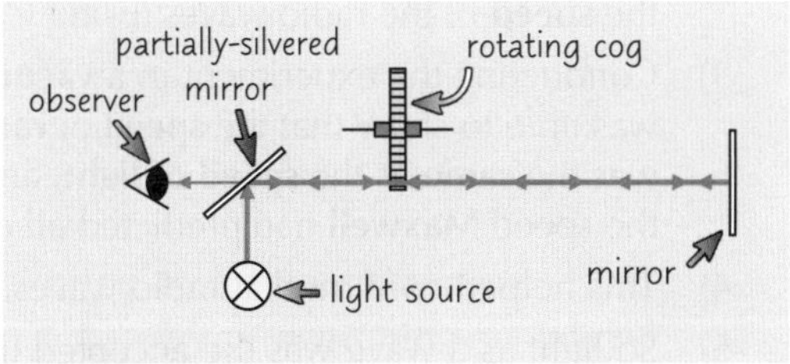


1) In the mid 1800s, a French physicist called Hippolyte Fizeau measured the **speed of light** by passing a **beam** of light through the gap between two **cog teeth** to a **reflector** about 9 km away. The cog was rotated at exactly the right speed so that the reflected beam passed through the **next gap** in the cog teeth.
2) Using the **frequency of rotation** and the **number of gaps**, Fizeau was able to calculate the **time taken** for the light to travel to the reflector and back.
3) So Fizeau could use the time taken and the **distance travelled** to calculate the speed of light.

This **estimate** of the speed of light was **really significant** because **Maxwell** was able to use this value to support his theory that **light** is an electromagnetic wave...

## **Maxwell** Predicted **EM Waves** and their **Speed**

1) In the second half of the 19th century, James Clerk Maxwell was trying to unite the ideas of magnetism and electricity. He created a **mathematical model** of magnetic and electric fields. This model said that a change to these fields would create an **electromagnetic** (EM) **wave**, radiating out from the source of the disturbance. Maxwell's prediction came before any experimental evidence for the existence of EM waves. He predicted that there would be a **spectrum** of EM waves, travelling at the same speed with different **frequencies**.
2) Maxwell showed theoretically that **all electromagnetic waves** should travel at the same speed in a vacuum, **c**:

**Maxwell** calculated the **speed of electromagnetic waves** in a vacuum using:

$$c = \frac{1}{\sqrt{\mu_0 \varepsilon_0}} = 2.998... \times 10^8 \text{ ms}^{-1}$$

$c$ is the speed of the wave in $ms^{-1}$, $\mu_0$ is the permeability of free space ($4\pi \times 10^{-7}$ $Hm^{-1}$), and $\varepsilon_0$ is the permittivity of free space ($8.85 \times 10^{-12}$ $Fm^{-1}$).

You can think of $\varepsilon_0$ as relating the electric field strength to the charge on the object producing it. You can think of $\mu_0$ as relating the magnetic flux density produced by a wire to the current flowing through it.

3) Maxwell's value of $c$ was very close to the value measured by Fizeau. So this provided strong evidence that **light**, as well as ultraviolet and infrared radiation beyond the visible spectrum, is an **electromagnetic wave**.
4) Maxwell was proved right by modern measurements of the speed of light and by the discovery of **radio waves** and other **EM waves**.

# Light — Particles vs Waves

## Heinrich Hertz Discovered Radio Waves...

1) In 1887, **Heinrich Hertz** produced and detected **radio waves** using electric sparks.
2) He showed that radio waves were produced when a high voltage from an induction coil caused sparks to **jump** across a **gap of air**.
3) He detected the radio waves by watching for sparks between a gap in a **loop of wire**.
4) The fact that a **potential difference** was induced in the loop showed that the waves had a **magnetic component** (as a changing magnetic field is needed to induce a potential difference, see p.42).
5) Hertz later went on to show that radio waves could be reflected, refracted, diffracted and polarised, and show interference.

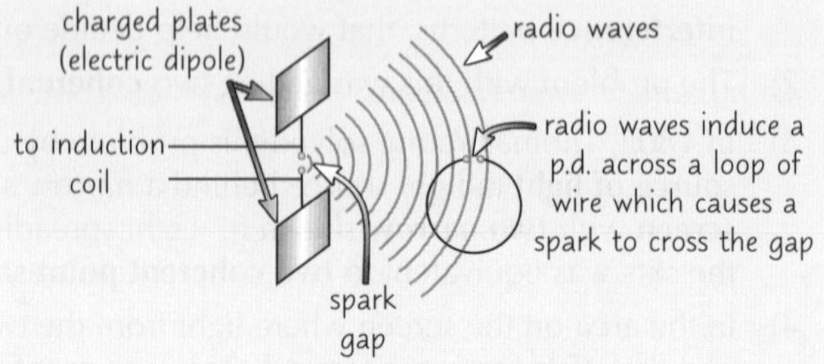


You can show that radio waves have an electric component by replacing the wire loop with a second dipole parallel to the first. The radio waves will create an alternating current in the second dipole.

## ...and Measured their Speed

Hertz set up stationary radio waves at a fixed resonant frequency to measure their speed.

1) He found the **wavelength** $\lambda$ by measuring the **distance** between the **nodes**.
2) Using the **frequency**, Hertz was able to calculate the **speed** of the radio waves (using $v = f\lambda$).
3) Conducting the experiment in a **vacuum**, Hertz was able to show that the **speed** of **radio waves** was the **same** as the **speed of light**, and matched the speed **Maxwell** had predicted all electromagnetic waves would travel at.
4) This helped confirm that radio waves, like light, are **electromagnetic waves**.
5) So light as a wave was the accepted theory up until the very end of the 19th century, when the **photoelectric effect** was discovered. Then the particle theory had to be resurrected, and it was all up in the air again...

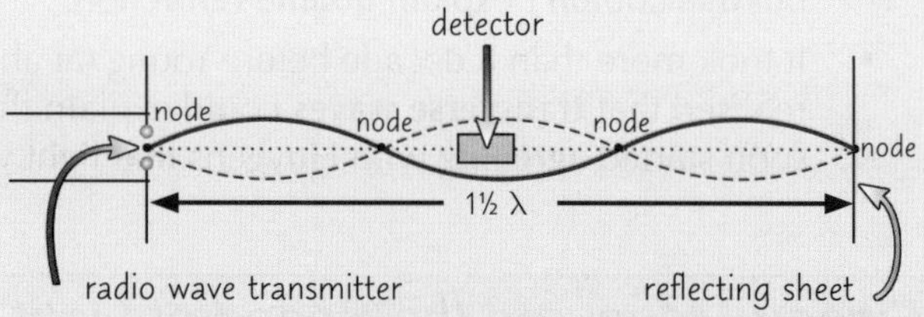

By moving the detector horizontally between the transmitter and the reflecting sheet, Hertz could locate the nodes and measure the distance between them.

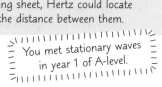

You met stationary waves in year 1 of A-level.

## Practice Questions

Q1 What was the main argument that Newton used to support his corpuscular theory of light?

Q2 What part does diffraction play in Young's double-slit experiment?

Q3 Sketch a diagram showing an experiment to demonstrate Young's fringes for white light in a laboratory.

Q4 What do $\mu_0$ and $\varepsilon_0$ refer to in Maxwell's speed of light calculation?

Q5 Describe an experiment you could do to investigate the speed of electromagnetic waves using stationary waves.

**Exam Questions**

Q1 a) Describe Newton's corpuscular theory of light. [2 marks]

b) Explain why Newton's corpuscular theory was more widely accepted than Huygens' wave theory. [4 marks]

Q2 Explain how the work of Young, Fizeau, Maxwell and Hertz provided evidence to support the wave theory of light. Include descriptions of the experimental evidence they produced in your answer. [4 marks]

## *This isn't a light debate — the physics is so heavy it Hertz... (sorry)*

*Now then young 'un, these three pages might look like one huge-ens history lesson but there's still a new ton of fizeaucs for you to slit down and learn on the double. Don't waver, but if you're wondering how to boost your marks to the max — well, you have to learn it particle-ularly thoroughly so the full corpus(cle) is stored behind your fringe.*

# The Photoelectric Effect and the Photon Model

*You did the photoelectric effect in the first year of A-Level, so it should be familiar. You need it again though, so here it is...*

## ***High Frequency Light** can **Release Electrons** from **Metals***

If you shine **light** of a **high enough frequency** onto the **surface of a metal**, the metal will **emit electrons**. For **most** metals, this **frequency** falls in the **UV** range.

1) **Free electrons** on the **surface** of the metal can sometimes **absorb energy** from the light.
2) If an electron **absorbs enough** energy, the **bonds** holding it to the metal can be **broken** and the electron **released.**
3) This is called the **photoelectric effect** and the electrons emitted are called **photoelectrons.**

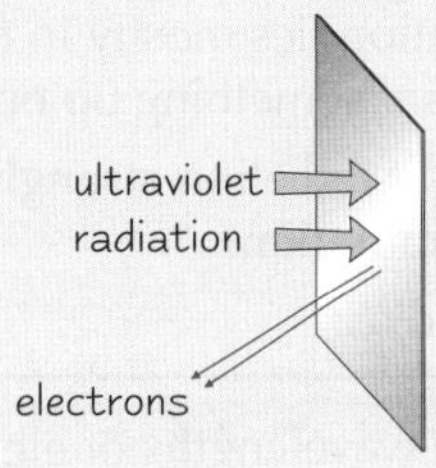


You don't need to know the details of any experiments on this — you just need to learn the three main conclusions:

**Conclusion 1**

For a given metal, **no photoelectrons are emitted** if the radiation has a frequency **below** a certain value — called the **threshold frequency**.

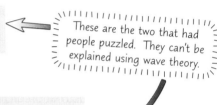

*These are the two that had people puzzled. They can't be explained using wave theory.*

**Conclusion 2**

The photoelectrons are emitted with a variety of kinetic energies ranging from zero to some maximum value. This value of **maximum kinetic energy** increases with the **frequency** of the radiation, and is **unaffected** by the **intensity** of the radiation.

**Conclusion 3**

The **number** of photoelectrons emitted per second is **directly proportional** to the **intensity** of the radiation.

## *Remember that Wave Theory **Can't Explain** the **Photoelectric Effect***

**According to wave theory**:

1) For a particular frequency of light, the **energy** carried is **proportional** to the **intensity** of the beam.
2) The energy carried by the light would be **spread evenly** over the wavefront.
3) **Each** free electron on the surface of the metal would gain a **bit of energy** from each incoming wave.
4) Gradually, each electron would gain **enough energy** to be able to leave the metal.

Theory and practice — two very different things.

SO... The **higher the intensity** of the wave, the **more energy** it should transfer to each electron — so the kinetic energy should increase with **intensity**.
There's **no explanation** for the **kinetic energy** depending only on the **frequency**.

There is **no explanation** for the **threshold frequency**. According to wave theory, electrons should be emitted eventually, no matter what the frequency is.

# The Photoelectric Effect and the Photon Model

## The **Ultraviolet Catastrophe** was about **Black-Body Radiation**

A bit of background, then we'll crack on with something else wave theory couldn't explain...

### A **Black Body** is a **Perfect Absorber** and **Emitter**

1) Objects emit **electromagnetic radiation** due to their **temperature**. At everyday temperatures this radiation lies mostly in the **infrared** part of the spectrum (which we can't see) — but heat something up enough and it will start to **glow**.
2) **Pure black** surfaces emit radiation **strongly** and in a **well-defined way**. We call it **black body radiation**.
3) A black body is defined as:

> A body that **absorbs all wavelengths** of electromagnetic radiation (that's why it's called a **black** body) and can **emit all wavelengths** of electromagnetic radiation.

4) The graph of **intensity** against **wavelength** for black body radiation shows that power radiated varies with wavelength.
5) But wave theory **couldn't explain** all of this graph — catastrophe!

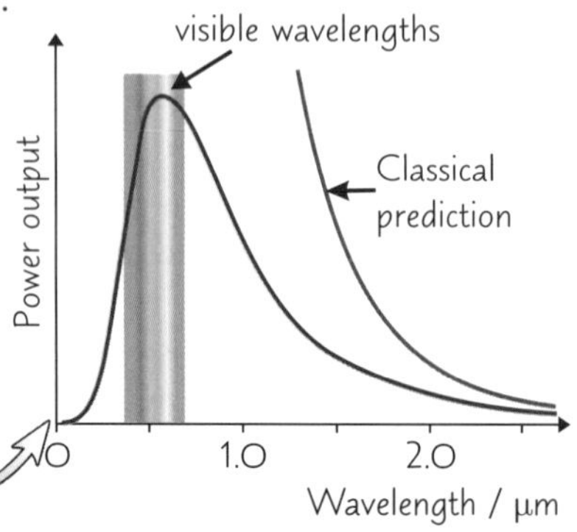

Radiation graph for a very hot black body (e.g. a star).

### **Wave Theory** Predicted an **Infinitely High Peak**

1) Wave theory could explain the slope of the black body radiation graph at long wavelengths (low frequencies), but predicted an **infinitely high** peak towards the ultraviolet region.
2) This was the **ultraviolet catastrophe** — wave theory, then widely accepted, had predicted something that was **impossible**, and nobody could work out how to adapt the theory to explain it.
3) It wasn't until **Einstein** built on **Max Planck's** interpretation of radiation in terms of **quanta** and came up with the **photon model of light** that physics was able to **explain** black body curves — even though Planck wasn't actually trying to solve the ultraviolet catastrophe at the time.

## **Einstein** came up with the **Photon Model of Light**...

1) When Max Planck was investigating **black body radiation** he suggested that **EM waves** can **only** be **released** in **discrete packets**, or **quanta**.
2) The **energy carried** by one of these **wave-packets** had to be:

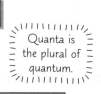

Quanta is the plural of quantum.

$$E = hf = \frac{hc}{\lambda}$$

where $h$ = Planck's constant = $6.63 \times 10^{-34}$ Js and $c$ = speed of light in a vacuum = $3.00 \times 10^{8}$ ms$^{-1}$

3) **Einstein** went **further** by suggesting that **EM waves** (and the energy they carry) can only **exist** in discrete packets. He called these wave-packets **photons**.
4) He saw these photons of light as having a **one-on-one**, **particle-like** interaction with **an electron** in a **metal surface**. It would **transfer all** its **energy** to that **one**, **specific electron**.

Popular new model at the physicists' fashion show.

## ... which **Explained** the **Photoelectric Effect** Nicely

1) According to the photon model, when light hits a metal surface, the metal is **bombarded** by photons.
2) If one of these photons **collides** with a free electron, the electron will gain energy equal to $hf$. If $hf$ is greater than the **work function** (see below), the electron can be emitted.
3) Each electron only absorbs **one photon at a time**, so all the energy the electron needs to be emitted must come from a **single photon**.

**Before** an electron can **leave** the surface of the metal, it needs enough energy to **break the bonds holding it there**. This energy is called the **work function** (symbol $\phi$) and its **value** depends on the **metal**.

# The Photoelectric Effect and the Photon Model

## The **Photon Model** Explains the Photoelectric Effect's **Threshold Frequency**...

1) If the energy **gained** from a photon is **greater** than the **work function**, the electron can be **emitted**.
2) If the energy **isn't** greater than the work function, the metal will heat up, but **no electrons** will be emitted.
3) The threshold frequency is the **minimum frequency** a photon can have and still cause a photoelectron to be emitted. The **energy** of a photon at the threshold frequency is equal to the **work function**.

## ... and the **Maximum Kinetic Energy**

1) The **energy transferred** to an electron by a photon depends on the photon's **frequency**.
2) The **kinetic energy** the electron will be carrying when it **leaves** the metal is the energy it gained from the **photon minus** any energy it's **lost** on the way out.
3) Electrons from deeper down in the metal lose more energy than electrons on the **surface**, so the photoelectrons have a **range** of energies. Photoelectrons have a **maximum kinetic energy** — electrons have this energy when they are on the surface of the metal and the only energy lost is in escaping from the material (i.e. the **work function**).
4) The **kinetic energy** of the photoelectrons is **independent of intensity**, as they **only absorb one photon** at a time. However, increasing the intensity increases the **number** of photons hitting the metal, so increases the number of photoelectrons emitted.

Einstein's work was hugely significant:

- He'd demonstrated that light is a stream of particles called **photons**, and that photons are the **smallest possible** unit of electromagnetic radiation — a **quantum**.
- As well as winning him the **Nobel Prize** in 1921, Einstein's photon model opened up a whole **new branch** of physics called **quantum theory**.

## Practice Questions

Q1 Explain how light can eject electrons from a metal.

Q2 What is a black body?

Q3 What was Max Planck's suggestion about electromagnetic radiation?

Q4 Briefly describe Einstein's photon model and its significance to physics.

**Exam Questions**

Q1 a) State the two results of experiments investigating the photoelectric effect that contradicted wave theory, and describe what physicists would have expected to observe instead if wave theory was correct. [4 marks]

b) Explain these two results in terms of the photon model of electromagnetic radiation. [4 marks]

Q2 Explain the 'ultraviolet catastrophe' and its implications for wave theory. [3 marks]

## Avoid ultraviolet catastrophes — don't play with black-lights...

*So as it turns out, everybody was equally right because light is a wave AND a particle. Or maybe everybody was equally wrong... Anyway — learn why the wave theory can't explain the photoelectric effect, and how photon theory does — then tell someone else to make sure you've learnt it all. Then go and make yourself a nice cup of tea.*

# Wave-Particle Duality

*If you're not very good at making decisions, consider a career as an electron. Wave? Particle? I dunno, let's be both.*

## **Light** Behaves as a **Wave** in **Interference** and **Diffraction**

Give us a wave.

1) Light produces **interference** and **diffraction** patterns — **alternating bands** of **dark** and **light**.
2) These can **only** be explained using **waves interfering constructively** (when two waves overlap in phase) or **interfering destructively** (when two waves are out of phase).

## **Light** Behaves as a **Particle** in the **Photoelectric Effect**

1) **Einstein** explained the results of **photoelectricity experiments** (see p. 141) by thinking of the **beam of light** as a series of **particle-like "photons"**.
2) If a **photon** of light is a **discrete** bundle of energy, then it can **interact** with an **electron** in a **one-to-one way**.
3) **All** the **energy** in the **photon** is **given** to one **electron**.

Neither the **wave theory** nor the **particle theory** describe what light actually **is**. They're just two different **models** that help to explain the way light behaves.

## **De Broglie** came up with the **Wave-Particle Duality Theory**

1) Louis de Broglie made a **bold suggestion** in his **PhD thesis**:

> If "**wave-like**" **light** showed **particle properties** (photons), "**particles**" like **electrons** should be expected to show **wave-like properties**.

2) The **de Broglie equation** relates a **wave property** (**wavelength**, $\lambda$) to a **moving particle property** (**momentum**, $p$). $h$ = Planck's constant = $6.63 \times 10^{-34}$ Js.

$$p = \frac{h}{\lambda}$$

Remember that momentum ($p$) is just mass × velocity.

3) The **de Broglie wave** of a particle can be interpreted as a "**probability wave**". The **probability** of finding a particle at a point is **directly proportional** to the **square of the wave's amplitude** at that point.
4) Many physicists at the time **weren't very impressed** — his ideas were just **speculation**. But later experiments **confirmed** the wave nature of electrons.

## **Electron Diffraction** shows the **Wave Nature** of **Electrons**

1) De Broglie's suggestions prompted a lot of experiments to try to show that **electrons** can have **wave-like** properties. In **1927**, Davisson and Germer succeeded in **diffracting electrons**.
2) They saw **diffraction patterns** when **accelerated electrons** in a vacuum tube **interacted** with the **spaces** in a graphite **crystal**.
3) According to wave theory, the **spread** of the **lines** in the diffraction pattern **increases** if the **wavelength** of the wave **increases**.
4) In electron diffraction experiments, a **small accelerating voltage**, i.e. **slow** electrons, gives **widely spaced** rings.
5) **Increase** the **electron speed** and the diffraction pattern circles **squash together** towards the **middle**. This fits in with the **de Broglie** equation above — if the **velocity** is **higher**, the **wavelength** is **shorter** and the **spread** of the lines is **smaller**.

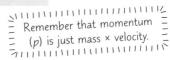

Electron diffraction patterns look like this.

For astrophysics students, this circle is called the Airy disc (see p. 67).

> In general, $\lambda$ for **electrons** accelerated in a **vacuum tube** is about the **same size** as $\lambda$ for **electromagnetic waves** in the **X-ray** part of the spectrum.

6) The de Broglie wavelength of an electron ($\lambda$) is related to the **accelerating voltage** ($V$) by:

$$\lambda = \frac{h}{\sqrt{2meV}}$$

where $e$ is the charge on the electron and $m$ is its mass

# Wave-Particle Duality

## Particles Don't Show Wave-Like Properties All the Time

You **only** get **diffraction** if a particle interacts with an object of about the **same size** as its **de Broglie wavelength**.
A **tennis ball**, for example, with **mass 0.058 kg** and **speed 100 ms$^{-1}$** has a **de Broglie wavelength** of **$10^{-34}$ m**.
That's **$10^{19}$ times smaller** than the **nucleus** of an **atom**! There's nothing that small for it to interact with.

**Example:** An electron of mass $9.11 \times 10^{-31}$ kg is fired from an electron gun at $7.00 \times 10^{6}$ ms$^{-1}$. What size object will the electron need to interact with in order to diffract? What anode voltage will emit electrons with this wavelength?

$p = mv = 6.377 \times 10^{-24}$ kg ms$^{-1}$   $\lambda = h/p = 6.63 \times 10^{-34} \div 6.377 \times 10^{-24} = 1.039... \times 10^{-10}$ m

So the electron must interact with an object with a size of around **$1.04 \times 10^{-10}$ m (to 3 s.f.)** to diffract.

Only crystals with atom layer spacing around this size will diffract this electron.

Calculate the anode voltage needed to emit electrons with this wavelength using the formula at the bottom of the previous page: $\lambda = \frac{h}{\sqrt{2meV}}$ so $V = \frac{h^2}{2me\lambda^2}$ = **139 V (to 3 s.f.)**

A **shorter wavelength** gives **less diffraction**. This is important in **microscopes**, where diffraction **blurs out details**.
The **tiny** wavelength of electrons means an **electron microscope** can resolve **finer detail** than a **light** microscope.

## Electron Microscopes use Electrons Instead of Light

In electron microscopes:

1) A **stream of electrons** is accelerated towards the sample using a **positive electric potential** — an **electron gun**.
2) To **resolve detail** around the size of an **atom**, the **electron wavelength** needs to be similar to the **diameter** of an **atom** (**0.1 nm**) or smaller. From the equation on the previous page this means an **anode voltage** of **at least 150 V**.
3) The **stream of electrons** from the electron gun is confined into a thin **beam** using a **magnetic** (or electric) **field**.
4) The beam is focused onto the sample and any interactions are transformed into an **image**.
The sort of image you get depends on the **type of microscope** you're using:

A **transmission electron microscope** (**TEM**) works a bit like an old-fashioned **slide** projector, but uses electrons instead of light. A **very thin** specimen is used and the parts of the beam that pass through the specimen are projected onto a **screen** to form an image.

A **scanning tunnelling microscope** (**STM**) is a different kind of microscope that uses principles of **quantum mechanics**. A very fine **probe** is moved over the surface of the sample and a **voltage** is applied between the probe and the surface. Electrons "**tunnel**" from the probe to the surface, resulting in a weak **electrical current**. The smaller the **distance** between the probe and the surface, the **greater the current**. By scanning the probe over the surface and measuring the current, you can produce an **image** of the **surface** of the sample.

## Practice Questions

Q1 What name is normally given to "particles" of light?
Q2 What observation showed that electrons could behave as waves?
Q3 What is the advantage of an electron microscope over a light microscope?

**Exam Questions**   *Use $h = 6.63 \times 10^{-34}$ Js, $e = 1.60 \times 10^{-19}$ C, $m_e = 9.11 \times 10^{-31}$ kg.*

Q1 An electron is accelerated from rest through a p.d. of 515 V.
a) Calculate:
i) the velocity of the electron,   ii) its de Broglie wavelength. [4 marks]
b) In which region of the electromagnetic spectrum does this fall? [1 mark]

Q2 a) Describe how a transmission electron microscope (TEM) uses a beam of electrons to produce an image. [3 marks]
b) Show that an anode voltage of at least 150 V is needed for a TEM to resolve detail around the size of an atom (0.100 nm). [3 marks]

## Wave-Particle duelity — pistols at dawn...

*You're getting into the weird bits of quantum physics now — light isn't a wave, and it isn't a particle: it's both... at the same time. And if you think that's confusing, just wait till you get onto relativity — not that I want to put you off.*

# The Speed of Light and Relativity

*First — a bit of a history lesson. Then a really good bit about trains.*

## *Michelson* and *Morley* tried to find the *Absolute Speed* of the Earth

1) During the 19th century, most physicists believed in the idea of **absolute motion**. They thought everything, including light, moved relative to a **fixed background** — something called the **ether**.
2) **Michelson** and **Morley** tried to measure the **absolute speed** of the **Earth** through the ether using a piece of apparatus called an **interferometer**.
3) They expected the motion of the Earth to affect the **speed of light** they measured in **certain directions**. According to Newton, the speed of light measured in a **lab** moving parallel to the light would be ($\mathbf{c} + \mathbf{v}$) or ($\mathbf{c} - \mathbf{v}$), where $v$ is the speed of the lab. By measuring the speed of light **parallel** and **perpendicular** to the motion of the Earth, Michelson and Morley hoped to find $v$, the absolute speed of the Earth.

## They used an *Interferometer* to Measure the Speed of the Earth

The interferometer was basically **two mirrors** and a **partial reflector** (a beam-splitter). When you shine light at a partial reflector, some of the light is **transmitted** and the rest is **reflected**, making **two separate beams**.

The mirrors were at **right angles** to each other, and an **equal distance**, ***L***, from the beam-splitter.

**The Michelson-Morley Interferometer**

1) **Monochromatic light** is sent towards the **partial reflector**.
2) The light is split into **two beams** travelling at **right angles** to each other.
3) The beams are reflected at **mirrors M1** and **M2**.
4) When the reflected beams meet back at the partial reflector, they form an **interference pattern**.
5) This interference pattern is **recorded** by the observer.
6) Then the whole interferometer is **rotated** through **90°** and the experiment **repeated**.

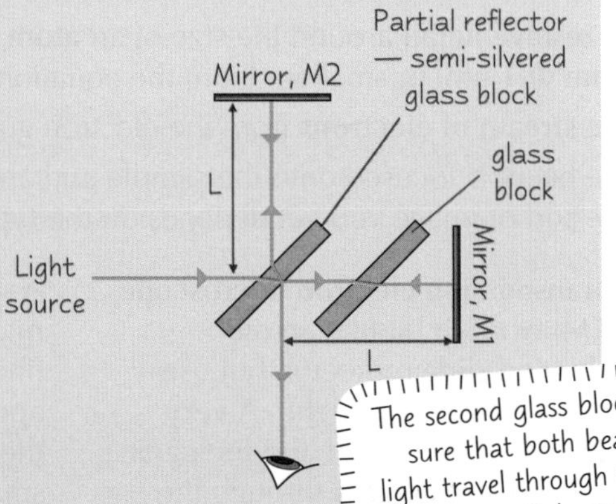


The second glass block makes sure that both beams of light travel through the same amount of air and glass.

**EXPECTED OUTCOME**

According to Newton's laws, light moving **parallel** to the motion of the Earth should take **longer** to travel to the mirror and back than light travelling at **right angles** to the Earth's motion. So **rotating** the apparatus should have changed the **travel time** for the two beams. This would cause a **tiny shift** in the **interference pattern**.

## They *Didn't* get the *Result* they were *Expecting*

They **repeated** the experiment **over** and **over** again — at different **times of day** and at different points in the **year**. Taking into account any **experimental errors**, there was **absolutely no shift** in the interference pattern.

The time taken by each beam to travel to each mirror was **unaffected** by rotating the apparatus.

So, Newton's laws **didn't work** in this situation.

Most scientists were really puzzled by this "null result". Eventually, the following **conclusions** were drawn:

a) It's **impossible** to detect **absolute motion** — the ether doesn't exist.
b) The **speed of light** has the **same value** for all observers.

# The Speed of Light and Relativity

## *Anything Moving with a **Constant Velocity** is in an **Inertial Frame***

The **invariance** of the speed of light (see previous page) is one of the cornerstones of special relativity.

The other is based on the concept of an **inertial frame of reference**. A reference frame is just a **space** that we decide to use to describe the **position of an object** — you can think of a reference frame as a **set of coordinates**.

An **inertial reference frame** is one in which **Newton's 1st law** is obeyed. (Newton's 1st law says that objects won't accelerate unless they're acted on by an external force.)

1) Imagine sitting in a carriage of a train **waiting at a station**. You put a **marble** on the table. The marble **doesn't move**, since there aren't any horizontal **forces** acting on it. **Newton's 1st law** applies, so it's an **inertial frame**.
2) You'll get the **same result** if the carriage moves at a **steady speed** (as long as the track is **smooth, straight and level**) — another inertial frame.
3) As the train **accelerates** out of the station, the marble **moves** without any force being applied. Newton's 1st law **doesn't apply**. The accelerating carriage **isn't an inertial frame**.
4) **Rotating** or **accelerating** reference frames **aren't** inertial. In most cases, though, you can think of the **Earth** as an inertial frame — it's near enough.

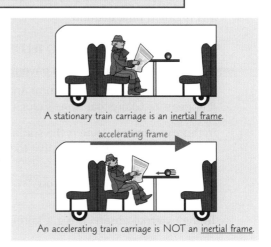

A stationary train carriage is an <u>inertial frame</u>.

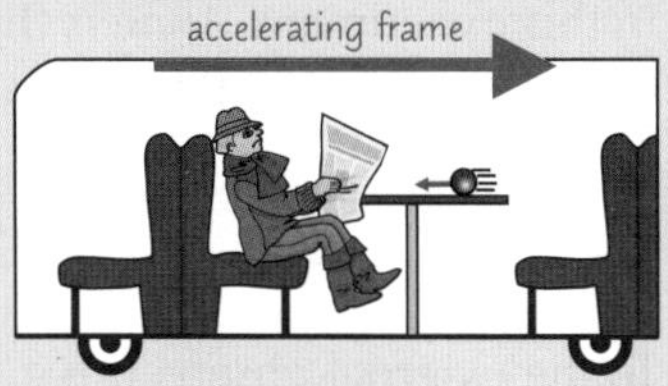


An accelerating train carriage is NOT an <u>inertial frame</u>.

## *Einstein's **Postulates** of **Special Relativity***

Einstein's theory of **special relativity** only works in **inertial frames** and is based on **two postulates** (assumptions):

1) **Physical laws have the same form in all inertial frames.**
2) **The speed of light in free space is invariant.**

1) The first postulate says that if we do **any physics experiment** in any inertial frame we'll always get the **same result**. That means it's **impossible** to use the result of **any experiment** to work out if you're in a **stationary reference frame** or one moving at a **constant velocity**.
2) The second postulate says that the **speed of light** (in a vacuum) always has the **same value**. It isn't affected by the **movement** of the **person measuring it** or by the movement of the **light source**.

## *Practice Questions*

Q1 Draw a labelled diagram showing the apparatus used by Michelson and Morley to determine the absolute speed of the Earth. Include the light source, mirrors, partial reflector, glass block and the position of the observer.

Q2 State the postulates of Einstein's theory of special relativity.

Q3 Explain why a carriage on a rotating Ferris wheel is not an inertial frame.

**Exam Questions**

Q1 In the Michelson-Morley interferometer experiment, interference fringes were observed. When the apparatus was rotated through 90 degrees the expected result was not observed.

a) State the result that was expected. [1 mark]

b) Describe the conclusions that were eventually drawn from these observations. [2 marks]

Q2 a) Using a suitable example, explain what is meant by an inertial reference frame. [2 marks]

b) Explain what is meant by the invariance of the speed of light. [2 marks]

## *<u>The speed of light is always the same — whatever your reference frame...</u>*

*Michelson and Morley showed that Newton's laws didn't always work. This was a huge deal. Newton's laws of motion had been treated like gospel by the physics community since the 17th century. Then along came Herr Einstein...*

# Special Relativity

*Special relativity ONLY WORKS IN INERTIAL FRAMES — it doesn't work in an accelerating frame.*

## A Moving Clock Runs Slow

1) Time runs at **different speeds** for two observers **moving relative** to each other.
2) A **stationary** observer measures the interval between two events as $t_0$, the **proper time**.
3) An observer moving at a **constant velocity**, ***v***, will measure a **longer** interval, ***t***, between the two events. ***t*** is given by the equation:
   The bottom part of this equation is called the **Lorentz factor**.

$$t = \frac{t_0}{\sqrt{1 - \frac{v^2}{c^2}}}$$

4) This is called **time dilation**.

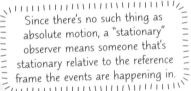

Since there's no such thing as absolute motion, a "stationary" observer means someone that's stationary relative to the reference frame the events are happening in.

**A THOUGHT EXPERIMENT TO ILLUSTRATE TIME DILATION:**

Anne is on a high-speed train travelling at 0.90*c*. She switches on a torch for exactly 2 seconds.
Claire is standing on the platform and sees the same event, but records a longer time.
It appears to Claire that Anne's clock is running slow.

In this experiment, **Anne** is the **stationary observer**, so she measures the **proper time**, $t_0$.
Claire is **moving** at 0.90*c* **relative to the events**, and so measures a time *t* given by:

$$t = \frac{t_0}{\sqrt{1 - \frac{v^2}{c^2}}} = \frac{2}{\sqrt{1 - \frac{(0.90c)^2}{c^2}}} = \frac{2}{\sqrt{1 - 0.90^2}} = 4.5883... = \mathbf{4.6\ s\ (to\ 2\ s.f.)}$$

To the **external observer** (e.g. Claire) **moving clocks** run **slowly**.

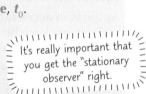

It's really important that you get the "stationary observer" right.

## There's Proof of Time Dilation from Muon Decay

1) **Muons** are **particles** created in the **upper atmosphere** that move towards the ground at speeds close to **c**.
2) In the laboratory (**at rest**) they have a **half-life** of less than **2 μs**. From this half-life, you would expect most muons to **decay** between the top of the atmosphere and the Earth's surface, but that **doesn't happen**.

**Experiment to Measure Muon Decay**

1) Measure the **speed**, ***v***, of the muons (this is about 0.99*c*).
2) Place a **detector** (MR1) at **high altitude** and measure the muon count rate.
3) Use another detector (MR2) to measure the count rate at **ground level**.
4) **Compare** the two figures.

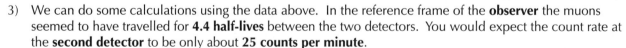

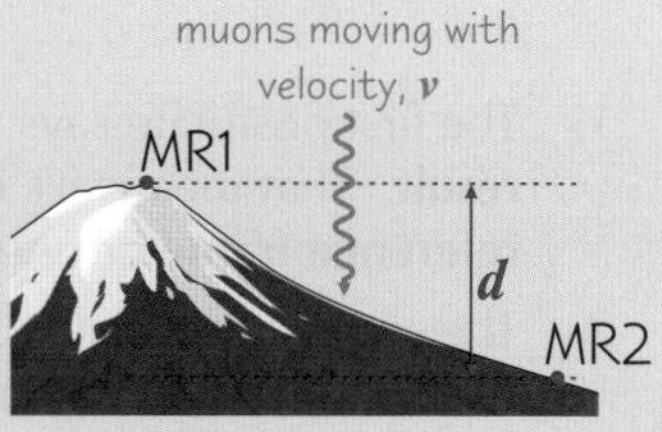


Here are some typical results:
MR1 = 500 per minute MR2 = 325 per minute Distance between detectors (*d*) = 2000 m
Time as measured by an observer = *d*/*v* = 6.73 μs Half-life of muons at rest = 1.53 μs

3) We can do some calculations using the data above. In the reference frame of the **observer** the muons seemed to have travelled for **4.4 half-lives** between the two detectors. You would expect the count rate at the **second detector** to be only about **25 counts per minute**.
4) However, in a **muon's reference frame**, travelling at 0.99*c*, the time taken for the journey is just $t_0$ **= 0.95 μs**. From the point of view of the muons, the time elapsed is **less** than their **half-life**. But from the point of view of the **observer**, it appears that the half-life of the muons has been **extended**.

## A Moving Rod Looks Shorter

1) A **rod** moving in the **same direction** as its **length** looks **shorter** to an external observer.
2) A **stationary** observer measures the length of an object as $l_0$. An observer moving at a **constant velocity**, ***v***, will measure a **shorter** length, ***l***. ***l*** is given by the equation:
   This is called **length contraction**.

$$l = l_0\sqrt{1 - \frac{v^2}{c^2}}$$

**A LENGTH CONTRACTION THOUGHT EXPERIMENT:**

Anne (still in the train moving at 0.90*c*) measures the length of her carriage as 25 m.
Claire, on the platform, measures the length of the carriage as it moves past her.

Length measured by Claire, $l = l_0\sqrt{1 - \frac{v^2}{c^2}} = 25\sqrt{1 - \frac{(0.90c)^2}{c^2}} = 25\sqrt{1 - 0.90^2} = 10.897... = \mathbf{11\ m\ (2\ s.f.)}$

# Special Relativity

## The **Mass** and **Energy** of an Object **Increase** with **Speed**

1) The **faster** an object **moves**, the **more massive** it gets.
2) An object with rest mass $m_0$ moving at a **velocity** $v$ has a **relativistic mass** $m$ given by the equation:

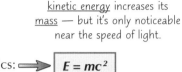

$$m = \frac{m_0}{\sqrt{1 - \frac{v^2}{c^2}}}$$

3) As the relative speed of an object approaches **c**, the mass approaches **infinity**. So, in practice, no massive object can accelerate to a speed **greater than** or **equal to** the speed of light.

So increasing an object's kinetic energy increases its mass — but it's only noticeable near the speed of light.

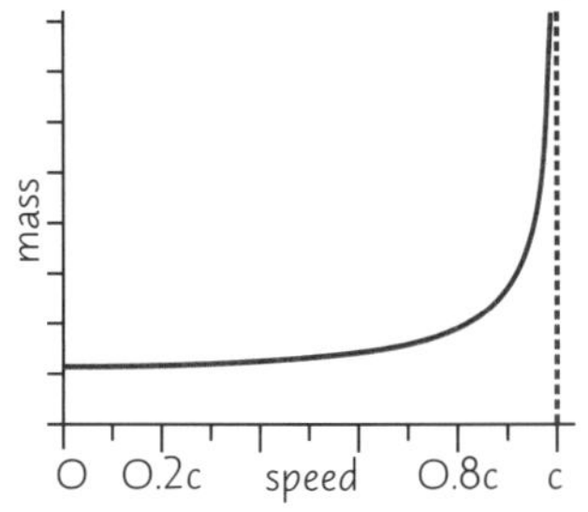


4) Einstein extended his idea of **relativistic mass** to write down the most famous equation in physics: $E = mc^2$
This means that **mass** and **energy** are **equivalent**.
5) This equation says that **mass** can be **converted** into **energy** and vice versa. Or, alternatively, **any energy** you supply to an object **increases** its **mass** — it's just that the increase is usually **too small** to measure.
6) The **total energy** of a relativistic object is given by this equation:

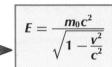

$$E = \frac{m_0c^2}{\sqrt{1 - \frac{v^2}{c^2}}}$$

Equating this with $E = mc^2$ and cancelling the $c^2$'s gives the formula for relativistic mass.

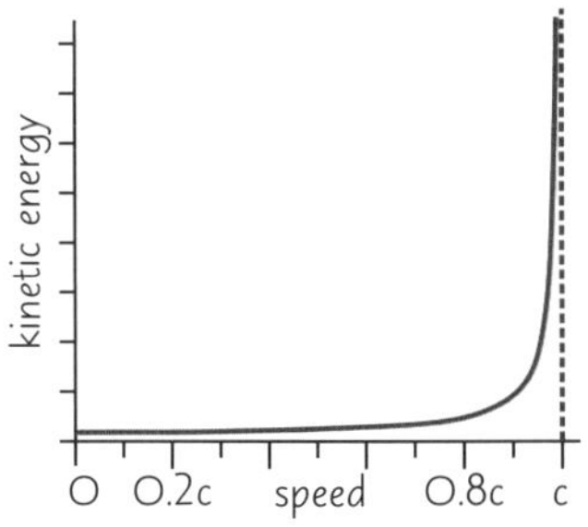


## **Bertozzi Demonstrated** that Mass **Increases** with Speed

1) In the 1960s **Bertozzi** used **linear particle accelerators** to accelerate pulses of electrons to a range of energies from 0.5 MeV to 15 MeV. The particles were **smashed** into an **aluminium disc** a set distance away.
2) The **time** taken by electrons of each energy to reach the aluminium disc was measured so that their speeds could be calculated. As the energy of the electrons was **increased**, the **speed** of the electron's didn't increase as you would expect from $E = ½mv^2$, but instead tailed off towards a **maximum value** approaching $3 \times 10^8$ ms$^{-1}$ ($c$). This showed that as the **energy** increased, the **mass increased** (as the velocity didn't increase past $c$).
3) Bertozzi used the **heat** generated by these collisions at each energy to calculate the **kinetic energy** of the particles immediately before impact.

Bertozzi found that plotting a graph of kinetic energy against **speed** gave a **curve** that **closely matched** that predicted by **Einstein's formula**. This was the **first direct evidence** for special relativity.

## Practice Questions

Q1 State the equations for time dilation and length contraction, carefully defining each symbol.

Q2 Using the results from the muon experiment (page 148), show that the time elapsed in the reference frame of the muon is 0.95 μs.

Q3 A particle accelerated to near the speed of light gains a very large quantity of energy. Sketch a graph and describe how the mass and the energy of the particle change as its speed increases.

Q4 Describe an experiment that provides evidence that mass increases with speed.

**Exam Questions**

Q1 A subatomic particle has a half-life of 20.0 ns when at rest. If a beam of these particles is moving at 0.995$c$ relative to an observer, calculate the half-life of these particles in the frame of reference of the observer. [3 marks]

Q2 Describe a thought experiment to illustrate time dilation. [4 marks]

Q3 For a proton ($m_0 = 1.67 \times 10^{-27}$ kg) travelling at $2.80 \times 10^8$ ms$^{-1}$ calculate:
a) the relativistic mass, [2 marks]
b) the total energy. [1 mark]

## Have you ever noticed how time dilates when you're revising physics...

*In a moving frame, time stretches out, lengths get shorter and masses get bigger. One of the trickiest bits is remembering which observer's which — $t_0$, $m_0$ and $l_0$ are the values you'd measure if the object was at rest.*

# Experiment Design

*Science is all about getting good evidence to test your theories... so you need to be able to spot a badly designed experiment or study a mile off, and be able to interpret the results of an experiment or study properly. Here's a quick reference section to show you how to go about designing experiments and doing data-style questions.*

## Planning Experiments to Solve Problems

Scientists solve problems by **asking** questions, **suggesting** answers and then **testing** them to see if they're correct. Planning an experiment is an important part of this process to help get accurate and precise results (see p. 155).

1) Make a **prediction** or **hypothesis** — a **specific testable statement**, based on theory, about what will happen in the experiment.
2) Think about the aims of the experiment and identify the **independent**, **dependent** and other **variables.**
3) Make a **risk assessment** and plan any safety precautions.
4) Select **appropriate equipment** that will give you accurate and precise results.
5) Decide what **data** to collect and how you'll do it.
6) Write out a **clear** and **detailed method** — it should be clear enough that **anyone** could follow it and exactly repeat your experiment.
7) Carry out **tests** — to provide **evidence** that will support the prediction or refute it.

## Make Sure Your Experiment is a Fair Test

It's important to **control** the **variables** (any quantity that can change) in an experiment. Keeping all variables **constant** (apart from the independent and dependent variables) means that the experiment is a **fair test**. This means you can be more confident that any effects you see are **caused** by changing the independent variable.

**Independent variable**
The thing that you **change** in an experiment.

**Dependent variable**
The thing that you **measure** in an experiment.

**Example:** The pendulum on the right is a simple harmonic oscillator. The length of the light, stiff rod is varied to see how it affects the period of the oscillations. State the independent and dependent variables in this experiment. Suggest how you would make this experiment a fair test.

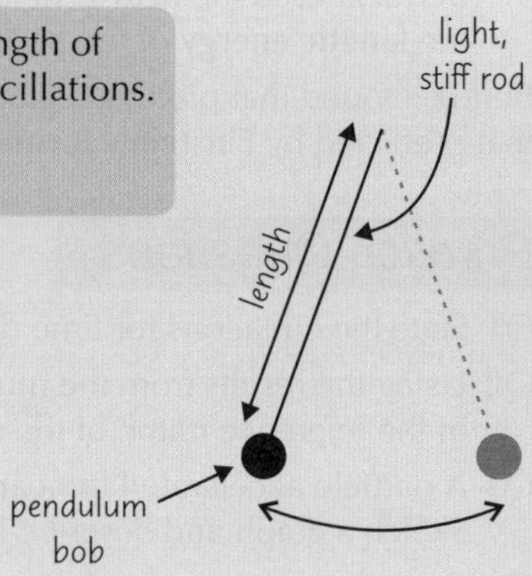


The **independent** variable will be the **length** of the light, stiff rod and the **dependent** variable will be the **period**.

To be a **fair test**, all the other variables must be kept the **same**. You'd use the same pendulum bob throughout the experiment so that the mass of the bob and any friction from air resistance remained the same. You would also make sure the experiment was always carried out in the same way, e.g. by starting the pendulum oscillating with the same amplitude each time.

## Your Experiment Must Be Safe and Ethical

1) You'll be expected to show that you can identify any **risks** and **hazards** in an experiment.
2) You'll need to take appropriate **safety measures** depending on the experiment. For example, anything involving **lasers** will usually need special laser **goggles** and to work with **radioactive substances** you'll probably need to wear **gloves**.
3) You need to make sure you're working **ethically** too — you've got to look after the **welfare** of any people or animals in an experiment to make sure they don't become **ill**, **stressed** or **harmed** in any way.
4) You also need to make sure you're treating the **environment ethically** too, e.g. making sure to not destroy habitats when doing **outdoor** experiments.

It was a little late to start worrying, but Holly wasn't sure her lab partner had carried out a full risk assessment.

# Experiment Design

## Nothing is Certain

1) **Every** numerical measurement you take has an **experimental uncertainty**. If you measured a piece of string with a ruler, you might think you've measured its length as 30 cm, but at **best** you've probably measured it to be 30 **± 0.5** cm. And that's without taking into account any other errors that might be in your measurement.
2) The ± sign gives you the **range** in which the **true** length (the one you'd really like to know) probably lies — 30 ± 0.5 cm tells you the true length is very likely to lie in the range of 29.5 to 30.5 cm.
3) There are **two types** of **error** that cause experimental uncertainty:

### Random errors

1) Random errors affect **precision** (see p. 155). No matter how hard you try, you **can't get rid** of all random errors.
2) They can just be down to **noise**, or that you're measuring a **random process** such as nuclear radiation emission.
3) You get random error in **any** measurement. If you measured the length of a wire 20 times, the chances are you'd get a **slightly different** value each time, e.g. due to your head being in a slightly different position when reading the scale.
4) It could be that you just can't keep controlled variables **exactly** the same throughout the experiment.

### Systematic errors

1) You get systematic errors not because you've made a mistake in a measurement — but because of the **apparatus** you're using, or your experimental method, e.g. using an inaccurate clock.
2) The problem is often that you **don't know they're there**. You've got to spot them first to have any chance of correcting for them.
3) Systematic errors usually **shift** all of your results to be too high or too low by the **same amount**.
4) Reducing systematic errors will **increase** the **accuracy** of your results.

## There are Loads of Ways You Can Reduce Uncertainties

1) One of the easiest things you can do is **repeat** each measurement **several times**. The **more repeats** you do, and the more **similar** the results of each repeat are, the more precise the data.
2) By taking an average of your repeated measurements, you will reduce the **random error** in your result. The **more** measurements you average over, the **less random error** you're likely to have.
3) The **smaller the uncertainty** in a result or measurement, the **smaller the range** of possible values that result could have and the more **precise** your data can be. E.g. two students each measure a length of wire three times. Student A measures the wire to be 30 cm ± 1 cm each time. Student B measures the wire to be 29 cm ± 0.5 cm each time. The **range** that student A's values could take is **larger** than student B's, so student B's data is more **precise**.
4) You should check your data for any **anomalous** results — any results that are **so different** from the **rest of the data** they cannot be explained as variations caused by random uncertainties. For example, a measurement that is ten times smaller than all of your other data values. You should not include anomalous results when you take averages.
5) You can also cut down the **uncertainty** in your measurements by using the most **appropriate** equipment. E.g. a micrometer scale has **smaller intervals** than a millimetre ruler — so by measuring a wire's diameter with a micrometer instead of the ruler, you instantly cut down the **random error** in your experiment.
6) **Computers** and **data loggers** can often be used to measure smaller intervals than you can measure by hand and reduce random errors, e.g. timing an object's fall using a light gate rather than a stop watch. You also get rid of any **human error** that might creep in while taking the measurements.
7) There's a limit to how much you can reduce the random uncertainties in your measurements, as all measuring equipment has a **resolution** — the smallest change in what's being measured that can be detected by the equipment.
8) You can calibrate your apparatus by measuring a **known value**. If there's a **difference** between the **measured** and **known** value, you can use this to **correct** the inaccuracy of the apparatus, and so reduce your **systematic error**.

For example, to calibrate a set of **scales** you could weigh a 10.0 g mass and check that it reads 10.0 g. If these scales measure to the nearest 0.1 g, then you can only **calibrate** to within 0.05 g. Any measurements taken will have an **uncertainty** of ± 0.05 g.

## Reducing uncertainty in your exam results — make sure you revise...

*There's a lot to take in here. Make sure you remember the different kinds of errors and how you can avoid them — like using the right equipment, repeating and averaging measurements and getting rid of any funky-looking anomalies.*

# Uncertainty and Errors

*Physicists are never truly certain of anything.*
*Significant figures, uncertainties and error bars are all ways of saying how almost-sure you are about stuff.*

## Uncertainties Come in Absolute Amounts, Fractions and Percentages

**Absolute uncertainty** is the uncertainty of a measurement given as certain fixed quantity.
**Fractional** uncertainty is the uncertainty given as a **fraction** of the measurement taken.
**Percentage** uncertainty is the uncertainty given as a **percentage** of the measurement.

**Example:** The temperature of a gas is given as 250 ± 5 °C. Give the absolute, fractional and percentage uncertainties for this measurement.

1) The **absolute uncertainty** is given in the question — it's **5 °C**.
2) To calculate **fractional uncertainty**, divide the uncertainty by the measurement and simplify. The **fractional uncertainty** is $\frac{5}{250} = \mathbf{\frac{1}{50}}$
3) To calculate **percentage uncertainty**, divide the uncertainty by the measurement and **multiply** by **100**. The **percentage uncertainty** is $\frac{1}{50} \times 100 = \mathbf{2\%}$

You can **decrease** the **percentage uncertainty** in your data by taking measurements of **large** quantities.
Say you take measurements with a ruler which measures to the nearest **± 0.5 mm**.
The **percentage error** in measuring a length of **10 mm** will be **± 5%**, but using the same ruler to measure a distance of **20 cm** will give a percentage error of only **± 0.25%**.

## Sometimes You Need to Combine Uncertainties

When you do calculations involving values that have an uncertainty, you have to **combine** the uncertainties to get the **overall** uncertainty for your result.

### Adding or Subtracting Data — ADD the Absolute Uncertainties

**Example:** The pressure of a gas increases from 124 ± 0.5 kPa to 127 ± 0.5 kPa. Calculate the increase in pressure of the gas.

1) First subtract the pressures without the uncertainty values: 127 – 124 = 3 kPa
2) Then find the total uncertainty by adding the individual absolute uncertainties: 0.5 + 0.5 = 1 kPa
So, the pressure has increased by **3 ± 1 kPa**.

### Multiplying or Dividing Data — ADD the Percentage Uncertainties

**Example:** A potential difference (p.d.) of 240 ± 3% V is applied across two parallel plates that are a distance, $d$, 0.0075 ± 0.0005 m apart. Calculate the electric field strength between the two plates and state the percentage uncertainty in this value.

1) First calculate the electric field strength without uncertainty: $E = V \div d = 240 \div 0.0075 = 32\,000\ \text{Vm}^{-1}$
2) Next, calculate the percentage uncertainty in the distance: % uncertainty in $d = \frac{0.0005}{0.0075} \times 100 = 6.7\%$
3) Add the percentage uncertainties in the p.d. and distance values to find the total uncertainty in the electric field strength: Total uncertainty = 3% + 6.7% = 9.7%
So, $E$ = **32 000 ± 9.7% Vm$^{-1}$**

### Raising to a Power — MULTIPLY the Percentage Uncertainty by the Power

**Example:** The radius of a sphere is $r$ = 6.5 ± 2.5% fm. What will the percentage uncertainty be in the volume of this sphere, i.e. $\frac{4}{3}\pi r^3$?

The radius will be raised to the power of **3** to calculate the volume.
So, the percentage uncertainty will be 2.5% × 3 = **7.5%**

# Uncertainty and Errors

## **Error Bars** Show the **Uncertainty** of **Individual Points**

1) Most of the time, you work out the **uncertainty** in your **final** result using the uncertainty in **each measurement** you make.
2) When you're plotting a **graph**, you show the uncertainty in **each measurement** by using **error bars** to show the **range** the point is likely to lie in.
3) In exams, you might have to **analyse data** from graphs **with** and **without** error bars — so make sure you really understand what error bars are showing.
4) The **error** of **each measurement** of time for a graph of ln($I$) against time for a discharging capacitor is shown by the **error bars** in the graph to the right.

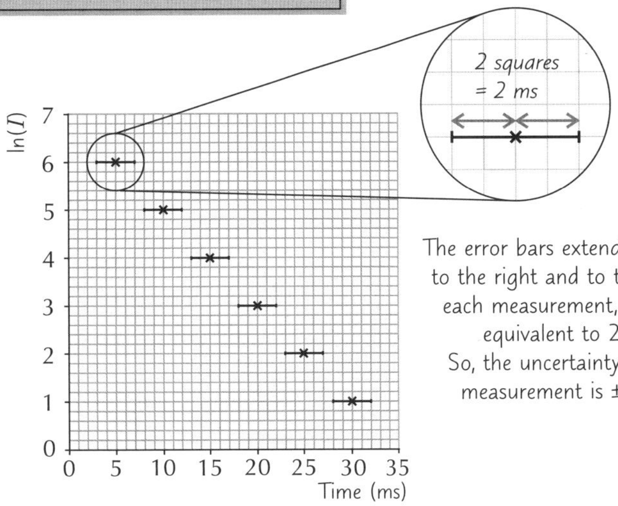


The error bars extend 2 squares to the right and to the left for each measurement, which is equivalent to 2 ms. So, the uncertainty in each measurement is ± 2 ms.

There's more on discharging capacitors on page 35.

## You Can **Calculate** the **Uncertainty** of **Final Results** from a **Line of Best Fit**

Normally when you draw a graph you'll want to find the **gradient** or **intercept**. For example, you can calculate $\tau$, the **time constant**, from –1 divided by the **gradient** of the graph on the right — here that gives a value of about 0.005 s. You can find the **uncertainty** in that value by using **worst lines**:

1) Draw lines of best fit which have the **maximum** and **minimum** possible slopes for the data and which should go through all of the **error bars** (see the pink and blue lines on the right). These are the **worst lines** for your data.
2) Calculate the **gradients** of these slopes — this gives the **maximum** and **minimum** values the true **gradient** is likely to lie between. Here, the gradient of the blue line is about –240 s$^{-1}$ and the gradient of the pink line is about –170 s$^{-1}$, so the true gradient probably lies between –240 s$^{-1}$ and –170 s$^{-1}$. Therefore the true value of $\tau$ probably lies between 0.0042 s and 0.0058 s.
3) This range gives you the **uncertainty** in $\tau$, which for this capacitor is 0.005 ± 0.0008 s (or 0.005 s ± 16%).

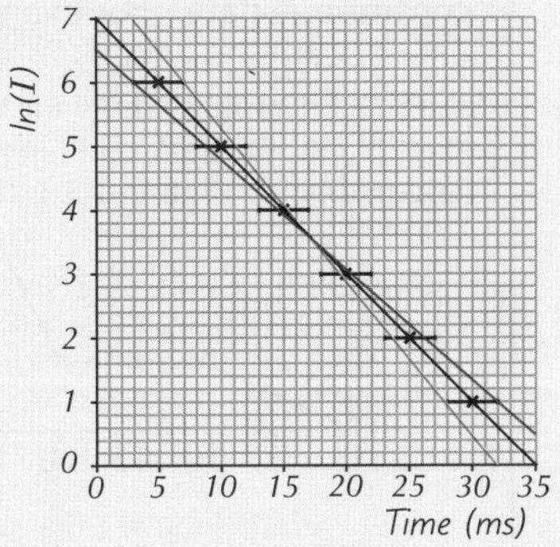


If a graph passes through the origin, then the point at (0, 0) has no uncertainty and so all lines of best fit must pass through it.

## **Significant Figures** Can Show **Uncertainty**

1) You always have to assume the **largest** amount of uncertainty in data.
2) Whether you're looking at experimental results or just doing a calculation question in an exam, you must round your results to have the **same number** of significant figures as the given data value with the **least** significant figures. Otherwise you'd be saying there is less uncertainty in your result than in the data used to calculate it.
3) If no uncertainty is given for a value, the number of **significant figures** a value has gives you an estimate of the **uncertainty**. For example, 2 N only has **1 significant figure**, so without any other information you know this value must be 2 **± 0.5 N** — if the value was less than 1.5 N it would have been rounded to 1 N (to 1 s.f.), if it was greater than 2.5 N it would have been rounded to 3 N (to 1 s.f.).

## Consolidate all your uncertainties into one, easy-to-manage uncertainty...

*There's lots of maths to get your head around here, but just keep practising calculating uncertainties and you'll learn the rules in no time. Well... t = 0 ± 4 hours, sorry. Have another read and flip the book over, then scribble down the key points you can remember. Keep doing it until you can remember all the uncertainty joy without having to sneak a look.*

# Presenting and Evaluating Data

*Once you've got results, you have to present them in a sensible way using a graph. Then it's time to evaluate them and use them to form a conclusion that is supported by your results.*

## Data can be **Discrete, Continuous, Categoric** or **Ordered**

Experiments always involve some sort of measurement to provide data.
There are different types of data — and you need to know what they are.

1) **Discrete data** — you get discrete data by **counting**. E.g. the number of weights added to the end of a spring would be discrete. You can't have 1.25 weights.
2) **Continuous data** — a continuous variable can have **any value** on a scale. For example, the extension of a spring or the current through a circuit. You can never measure the exact value of a continuous variable.
3) **Categoric data** — a categoric variable has values that can be **sorted** into **categories**. For example, types of material might be brass, wood, glass, steel.
4) **Ordered (ordinal) data** — ordered data is similar to **categoric**, but the categories can be put **in order**. For example, if you classify frequencies of light as 'low', 'fairly high' and 'very high' you'd have ordered data.

## **Graphs** — Use the **Best Type** for the Data You've Got

You'll usually be expected to make a **graph** of your results. Not only are graphs **pretty**, they make your data **easier to understand** — so long as you choose the right type. No matter what the type though, make sure you always **label your axes** — including **units**. Choose a **sensible scale** for your axes and **plot points accurately** using a sharp pencil.

Line graphs can be used for **two sets of continuous data**. For example:

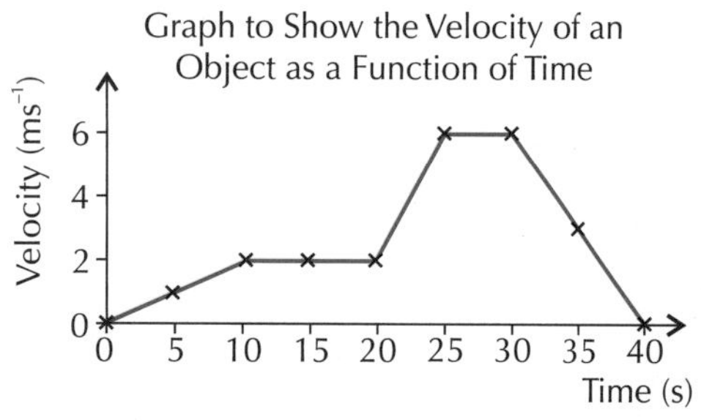


You can also make bar and pie charts — they're normally used to display categoric data.

**Scatter plots** are great for showing how two sets of data are related (or **correlated**). Don't try to join all the points — draw a **line of best fit** to show the **trend**.

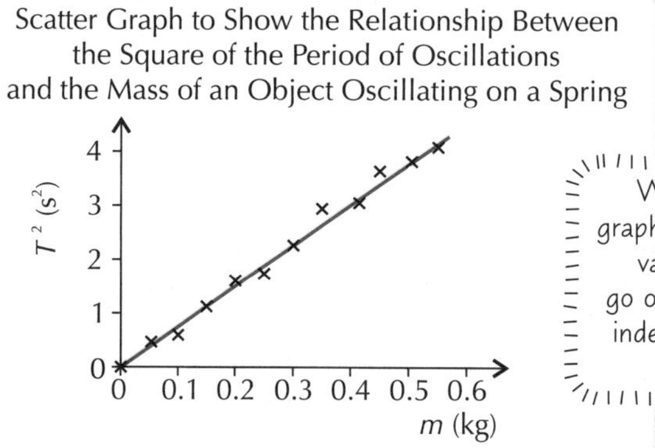


When drawing graphs, the dependent variable should go on the $y$-axis, the independent on the $x$-axis.

## **Correlation** Shows **Trends** in Data

1) **Correlation** describes the relationship between **two variables** — usually the **independent** and **dependent** ones.
2) Data can show **positive**, **negative** or **no correlation**. An easy way to see correlation is to plot a **scatter graph** of your data. If you can, draw a **line of best fit** to help show the **trend**.

**Positive correlation** — as one variable **increases**, the other also **increases**.

**Negative correlation** — as one variable **increases**, the other **decreases**.

**No correlation** — there is **no relationship** between the variables.

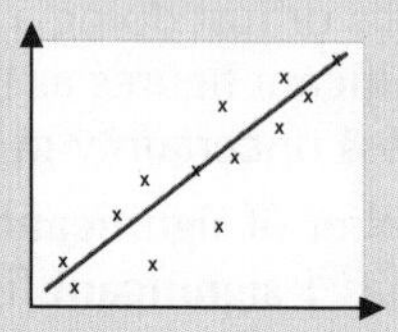

**Positive correlation**

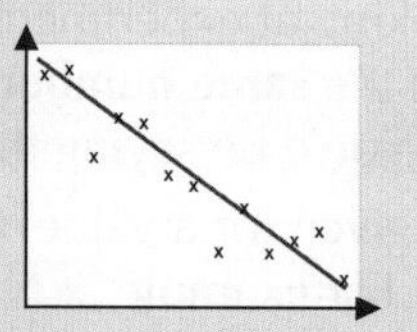

**Negative correlation**

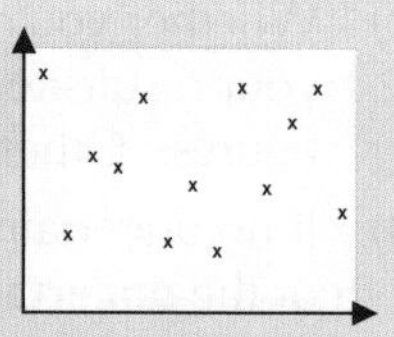

**No correlation**

3) If you've done a **controlled** experiment in a lab and can see **correlation** in your results, you can be fairly certain there's a **causal relationship** between the **independent** and **dependent variables**. This means that a **change** in one **causes** a change in the other.
4) But in experiments or studies **outside** the lab, you can't usually control all the variables. So even if two variables are **correlated**, the change in one may not be causing the change in the other. Both changes might be caused by a **third** variable.

# Presenting and Evaluating Data

## Evaluating Your Data

Once an experiment's over, you have to **explain** what the data shows.
There are some key words you need to know about (and use) when evaluating data:

1) **Precision** — the smaller the **range** that your data spreads, the more precise it is. Experimental data and results are precise if they are **repeatable** and **reproducible**.

Precision is sometimes called reliability.

- **Repeatable** — **you** can **repeat** an experiment multiple times and get the **same results**.
- **Reproducible** — if **someone else** can recreate your experiment using different equipment or methods, and gets the **same results** you do, the results are reproducible.

2) **Valid** — the **original question** is **answered** using **precise** data. If you don't keep all variables apart from the one you're testing **constant**, you haven't **only** tested the variable you're investigating and so the results **aren't valid**.
3) **Accurate** — the result is really close to the **true answer**. You can only comment on how accurate a result is if you know the true value of the result.

There's normally loads of stuff to say when you're looking at data. Have a think about...

1) What **patterns** or trends, if any, the results show.
2) Whether the experiment managed to **answer** the question it set out to answer. If it did, is this a **valid** experiment and if not, why not? How **precise** was the data?
3) How close the results are to the **true value**.
4) Did the measuring instruments have enough **resolution**?
5) Any **anomalies** in the results and the possible causes of them.
6) How **large** the **uncertainties** are. If the percentage uncertainty is large, this suggests the data is not precise and a strong conclusion cannot be made.

A couple of penguins had noticed a slight anomaly when doing the morning register.

If you're asked to analyse data in the exam, look at how many marks the question is worth — the more **marks** allocated to the question in the exam, the **more detail** you have to go into.

## Drawing **Conclusions** From Your **Data**

You need to make sure your conclusion is **specific** to the data you have and is **supported** by the data — don't go making any sweeping generalisations.

**Example:** The amplitude of the oscillations of a mass on a spring was measured at driving frequencies of 2, 4, 6, 8 and 10 Hz. Each driving frequency reading had an error of ±1 Hz. All other variables were kept constant. A physicist drew the graph below from the data and concluded from it that the spring's resonant frequency is 5 Hz. Explain whether or not you agree with this conclusion.

Their conclusion **could** be true — but the **data doesn't support this**. You can't tell **exactly** where the maximum amplitude is from the data because the driving frequency was increased in intervals of 2 Hz. The amplitude at in-between driving frequencies wasn't measured — so all you know is that the peak is somewhere **between** 4 and 8 Hz, as the maximum amplitude recorded (at 6 Hz) lies between these values.

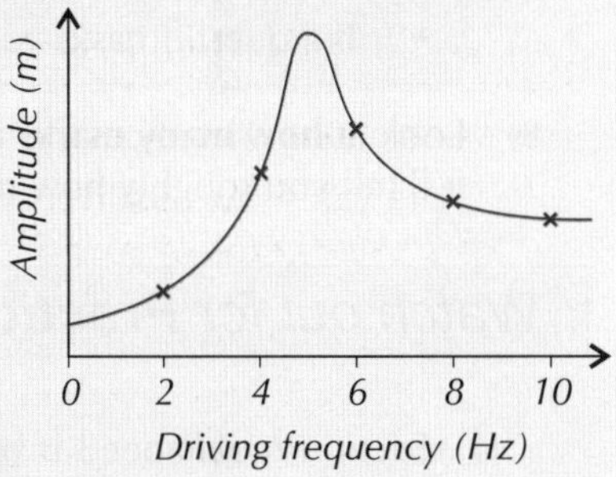


Also, the graph only gives information about this particular experiment. You can't conclude that the resonant frequency would be in this range for **all experiments** — only this one. And you can't say for sure that the spring is **undamped**, which will have an effect on the resonant frequency (p.9).

The error in each reading is 1 Hz, which gives a **percentage uncertainty** of 50% for the lowest driving frequency reading. This is very large and could mean the results are not valid, so no definite conclusions can be drawn from them.

## *I have evaluated all the data and concluded that Physics can be tricky...*

*Remember to evaluate the data thoroughly and when you make your conclusions, always back up your points using those evaluations. Use the checklist above to give you an idea of what to say. Suggest ways in which the experiment could be improved — there's some overlap here with how to improve uncertainties, so practising this is extra useful.*

# Exam Structure and Technique

*Good exam technique can make a big difference to your mark, so make sure you read this stuff carefully.*

## Get Familiar With the **Exam Structure**

For A-level Physics, you'll be sitting **three papers**.
Each paper will be **2 hours** long.

You'll also do a Practical Endorsement as part of your A-level. It'll involve doing practicals throughout the course, and will be reported separately from your exam results.

| | |
|---|---|
| **Paper 1** 34% of your A-level<br>**85** marks: **60** for **Section A** (**short and long answer** questions) **25** for **Section B** (**multiple choice** questions) | Covers everything from **year 1 of A-level** and **section 1** of this book. |
| **Paper 2** 34% of your A-level<br>**85** marks: **60** for **Section A** (**short and long answer** questions) **25** for **Section B** (**multiple choice** questions) | The questions will be on **sections 2** to **6** of this book, but the examiners will assume you know the content from **year 1 of A-level** and **section 1** too. |
| **Paper 3** 32% of your A-level<br>**80** marks: **45** for **Section A** (all **short and long answer** questions). **35** for **Section B** (all **short and long answer** questions). | **Section A** is on **practical skills and data analysis** (pages 150-155), but the questions could be based on **any** of the content from both years of A-level.<br>**Section B** will be on the optional topic you've chosen to study. Options A-D are covered in sections 7 A-D of this book. Option E (electronics) is not covered in this book. |

Find out your **exam timetable** and **plan** your revision carefully. And remember, the Paper 1 material could come up in Paper 2, and anything from either of the first two papers could crop up in Paper 3.

## Make Sure You **Read the Question**

1) It sounds obvious, but it's really important you read each question **carefully**, and give an answer that fits.
2) Look for **command words** in the question — they'll give you an idea of the **kind of answer** you should write. Commonly used command words for written questions are **state**, **describe**, **discuss** and **explain**:
    - If a question asks you to **state** something you just need to give a **definition**, **example** or **fact**.
    - If you're asked to **describe** what happens in a particular situation, don't waste time explaining why it happens — that's not what the question is after.
    - For **discuss** questions, you'll need to include more **detail** — depending on the question you could need to cover what happens, what the effects are, and perhaps include a brief explanation of why it happens.
    - If a question asks you to **explain** why something happens, you must give **reasons**, not just a description.
3) Look at **how many marks** a question is worth before you answer it. It'll tell you roughly **how much information** you need to include.

## Watch out for **Practical Questions**

1) Section A of Paper 3 is based on practical skills. You may have to **describe an experiment** to investigate something, or **answer questions** on an experiment you've been given.
2) These could be experiments you've **met before**, or they could be **entirely new** to you. All the questions will be based on physics that you've **covered**, but may include bits from different topics put together in ways you haven't seen before. Don't let this put you off, just **think carefully** about what's going on.
3) Make sure you know the difference between **precision**, **accuracy** and **validity** (page 155). Learn what **uncertainty**, **random errors** and **systematic errors** are (page 151) and make sure you can give some examples of where each might come from.
4) You need to be able to **calculate errors** and **plot** and **interpret graphs** too — anything on pages 152-153 could come up.

# Exam Structure and Technique

## Be *Careful* With *Calculations*

At least **40%** of the marks up for grabs in A-level physics will require maths skills, so make sure you know your stuff.

1) In calculation questions you should always **show your working** — you may get some marks for your **method** even if you get the answer wrong.
2) Don't **round** your answer until the **very end**. A lot of calculations in A-level physics are quite **long**, and if you round too early you could introduce errors to your final answer.
3) Be careful with **units**. Lots of formulas require quantities to be in specific units (e.g. time in seconds), so its best to **convert** any numbers you're given into these before you start. And obviously, if the question **tells** you which units to give your **answer** in, don't throw away marks by giving it in different ones.
4) You should give your final answer to the same number of **significant figures** as the data that you use from the question with the **least number** of significant figures. If you can, write out the **unrounded answer**, then your **rounded** answer with the number of significant figures you've given it to — it shows you know your stuff.

## *Manage* Your *Time* Sensibly

1) The **number of marks** tells you roughly **how long** to spend on a question. You've got just over a minute per mark, so if you get stuck on a question for too long, it may be best to **move on**.
2) The **multiple choice questions** are only worth **one mark each**, so it's not worth stressing over one for ages if you get stuck — **move on** and come back to it later.
3) You don't have to work through the paper **in order** — you could do all the multiple choice questions first, or leave questions on topics you find harder until the end.

Giles didn't like to brag, but his time-management skills were excellent.

## Don't be *Put Off* if a Question Seems *Strange*

1) You may get some weird questions that seem to have nothing to do with anything you've learnt. **DON'T PANIC.** Every question will be something you can answer **using physics you know**, it just may be in a new **context**.
2) Check the question for any **keywords** that you recognise. For example, if a question talks about acceleration, think about the rules and equations you know, and whether any of them apply to the situation in the question.
3) Sometimes you might have to **pull together** ideas from different parts of physics, like this:

**Example:** A windmill is being used to turn a generator. The generator contains of a coil of wire of 32 turns, each with an area of 0.22 m$^2$, held in a uniform 1.5 ×10$^{-3}$ T magnetic field. The arms of the windmill are 0.50 m long. A point on the end of one of the arms of the windmill is found to be travelling at 3.4 ms$^{-1}$. Calculate the maximum e.m.f. induced in the coil.

This question looks ghastly, but there are only two bits of theory you need to use — **electromagnetic induction** and **circular motion** (the windmill).

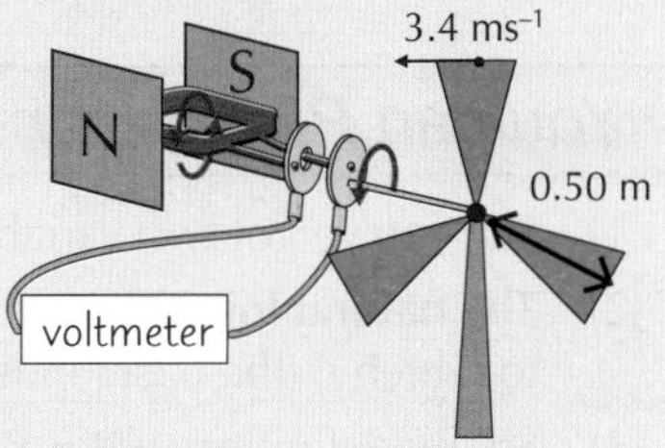


From page 45, you know that the e.m.f. induced in a coil of wire turning in a uniform magnetic field at a given time is given by: $\varepsilon = BAN\omega \sin \omega t$.

The question tells you $B = 1.5 \times 10^{-3}$ T, $A = 0.22$ m$^2$, and $N = 32$ turns. You want the **maximum e.m.f.**, which will happen when $\sin \omega t = 1$, so the only variable you don't know is $\omega$, the **angular velocity**.

$$\varepsilon = BAN\omega \sin \omega t = 1.5 \times 10^{-3} \times 0.22 \times 32 \times \omega \times 1$$

You've been given the **velocity** of a point at the end of one of the windmill's arms (3.4 ms$^{-1}$), and the **length** of the arm (0.50 m), so you can find out the **angular velocity** of the windmill (and hence the coil) using the equation from page 2: $\omega = \frac{v}{r}$.

$$\omega = \frac{3.4}{0.50} = 6.8 \text{ rad s}^{-1} \qquad \text{so: } \varepsilon = 1.5 \times 10^{-3} \times 0.22 \times 32 \times 6.8 \times 1 = 0.071808 = \mathbf{0.072\ V\ (to\ 2\ s.f.)}$$

## *Just follow the scouts' motto — if in doubt, tie a knot...*

*Making sure you're prepared for what the exams will be like. Reading questions carefully and managing your time all sounds like pretty basic advice, but you'd be surprised how many people don't follow it. Make sure you do...*

# Working with Exponentials and Logarithms

*As well as being given some tricky calculations, you could be asked to work with exponentials and logarithms and work out values from log graphs. And it's easy when you know how...*

## Many Relationships in Physics are **Exponential**

A fair few of the relationships you need to know about in A-level Physics are **exponential** — where the **rate of change** of a quantity is **proportional** to the **amount** of the quantity left. Here are a couple that crop up in the A-level course (if they don't ring a bell, go have a quick read about them)...

**Charge on a capacitor** — the decay of charge on a discharging capacitor is proportional to the amount of charge left on the capacitor: $Q = Q_0 e^{\frac{-t}{RC}}$ (see p.36)

There are also exponential relationships for $I$ and $V$ and for charging capacitors.

**Radioactive decay** — the rate of decay of a radioactive sample is proportional to the **number of undecayed nuclei** in the sample: $N = N_0 e^{-\lambda t}$ (see p.59)

The activity of a radioactive sample behaves in the same way.

## You can **Model Exponential Relationships** using a **Spreadsheet**

You've seen that for exponential relationships, the **rate of change** of a quantity is proportional to the amount of that quantity left. Rates of change like this can be modelled using an **iterative spreadsheet** that works out the amount of the quantity left over regular time intervals (or intervals of another variable). Models like this make it easier to plot graphs of exponential relationships.

For example, radioactive decay can be described using the formula $\frac{\Delta N}{\Delta t} = -\lambda N$ (see page 58).

If you know the **decay constant**, $\lambda$, and the **number of undecayed nuclei** in the initial sample, $N_0$, you can model $\Delta N$ over small intervals of $\Delta t$:

1) Set up a spreadsheet with column headings for **total time ($t$)**, **$\Delta N$** and **$N$**, and a data input cell for each of **$\Delta t$** and **$\lambda$**.

A data input cell is separate from the table and is used to refer to a fixed value that's used throughout your calculations, e.g. decay constant.

| | |
|---|---|
| $\lambda$ in $s^{-1}$ | $1 \times 10^{-4}$ |
| $\Delta t$ in s | 1000 |

| $t$ / s | $\Delta N$ | $N$ |
|---|---|---|
| $t_0 = 0$ | | $N_0$ |
| $t_1 = t_0 + \Delta t$ | $(\Delta N)_1 = -\lambda \times N_0 \times \Delta t$ | $N_1 = N_0 + (\Delta N)_1$ |
| $t_2 = t_1 + \Delta t$ | $(\Delta N)_2 = -\lambda \times N_1 \times \Delta t$ | $N_2 = N_1 + (\Delta N)_2$ |
| $t_3 = ...$ | $(\Delta N)_3 = ...$ | $N_3 = ...$ |

2) Decide on a **$\Delta t$** that you want to use — this is the **time interval** between the values of $N$ to be calculated.
3) Enter formulas to calculate the number of undecayed nuclei left in the sample after each time interval, as shown. You'll need to use **$\Delta N = -\lambda \times N \times \Delta t$** (rearranged from the equation above).
   If you write the formulas properly, the spreadsheet can automatically fill in as many rows as you want, but make sure that the references to the data input cells stay fixed as you do.
4) Plot a graph of the number of undecayed nuclei against time. It should look like this:
   (You may have to fiddle with your value for $\Delta t$ to get a graph with a nice shape.)
   This is an **exponential graph** — it's a graph of the equation $N = N_0 e^{-\lambda t}$ above.

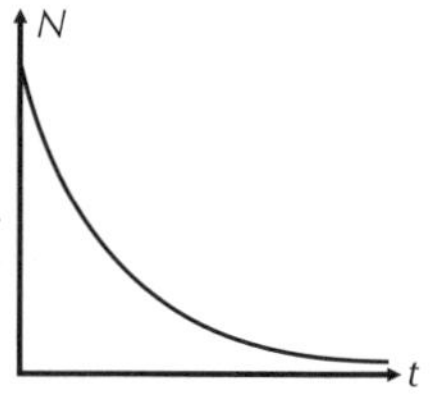


## You can **Plot** Exponential Relations Using the **Natural Log, ln**

1) Say you've got two variables, $x$ and $y$, which are related by $y = ke^{-ax}$ (where $k$ and $a$ are constants).
2) The **natural logarithm** of $x$, **ln $x$**, is the power to which e (the base) must be raised to to give $x$.
3) So, by definition, $e^{\ln x} = x$ and $\ln(e^x) = x$.
   So far so good... now you need some **log rules**:

A logarithm can be to any base you want. Another common one is 'base 10' which is usually written as '$\log_{10}$' or just 'log'.

$\ln(AB) = \ln A + \ln B$ $\quad$ $\ln\left(\frac{A}{B}\right) = \ln A - \ln B$ $\quad$ $\ln x^n = n \ln x$

These log rules work for all logs (including the natural logarithm). You won't be given them in the exam — so make sure you learn them.

4) So, for $y = ke^{-ax}$, if you take the natural log of both sides of the equation you get:
   $\ln y = \ln(ke^{-ax}) = \ln k + \ln(e^{-ax})$ → $\ln y = \ln k - ax$
5) This is of the form of an equation of a straight line ($y = mx + c$), so all you need to do is plot ($\ln y$) against $x$, and Eric's your aunty:

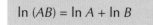

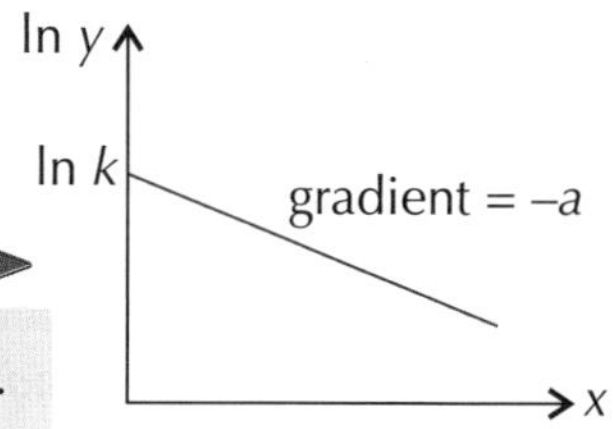

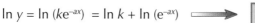

You get a **straight-line** graph with (**ln $k$**) as the **vertical intercept**, and **$-a$** as the **gradient**.

# Working with Exponentials and Logarithms

## You Might be Asked to find the **Gradient** of a Log Graph

This log business isn't too bad when you get your head around which bit of the log graph means what.

**Example:** The graph shows the radioactive decay of isotope $X$.

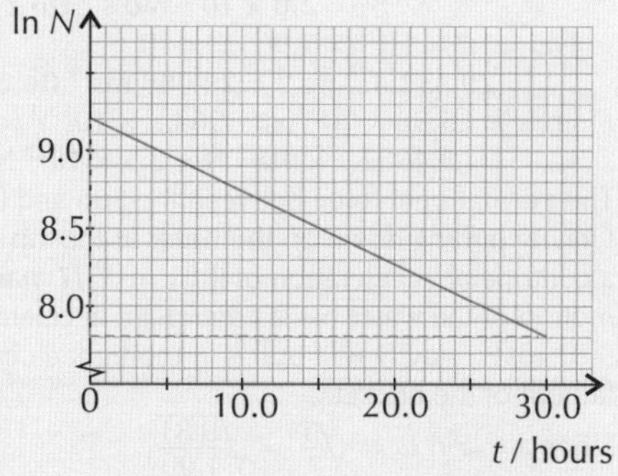


a) Find the initial number of undecayed nuclei, $N_0$, in the sample.

You know that the number of undecayed nuclei in a sample, $N$, is related to the initial number of undecayed nuclei, $N_0$, by the equation $\mathbf{N = N_0 e^{-\lambda t}}$.

So: $\ln N = \ln N_0 - \lambda t$

The $y$-intercept of the graph is $\ln N_0 = 9.2$

$N_0 = e^{9.2} = 9897.129... = 9900$ nuclei (to 2 s.f.)

b) Find the decay constant $\lambda$ of isotope $X$.

$-\lambda$ is the gradient of the graph, so:

$$\lambda = \frac{\Delta \ln N}{\Delta t} = \frac{9.2 - 7.8}{30.0 \times 60 \times 60} = 1.296... \times 10^{-5} = 1.3 \times 10^{-5}\ \text{s}^{-1}\ \text{(to 2 s.f.)}$$

## You can Plot **Any Power Law** as a **Log-Log Graph**

You can use logs to plot a straight-line graph of **any power law** — it doesn't have to be an exponential.

Say the relationship between two variables $x$ and $y$ is:

$$y = kx^n$$

Take the **log** (base 10) of both sides to get:

$$\log y = \log k + n \log x$$

So $\log k$ will be the ***y*-intercept** and $n$ will be the **gradient** of the graph.

When it came to logs, Geoff always took time to smell the flowers...

**Example:** A physicist carries out an experiment to determine the nuclear radius $R$ (in m) of various elements, which have nucleon number $A$. She plots a line of best fit for her results on a graph of $\log R$ against $\log A$. Part of the graph is shown. Using the equation $R = R_0 A^{1/3}$, find the value of the constant $R_0$ from the graph.

First take logs of both sides:

$\log R = \log (R_0 A^{1/3}) = \log R_0 + \log A^{1/3}$

$= \log R_0 + \frac{1}{3} \log A$

Look back at pages 52-53 for more on nuclear radius.

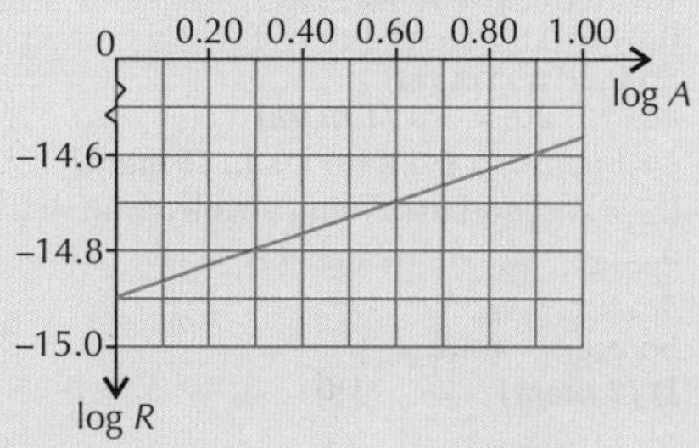


Comparing this to the equation of a straight line (in the form $y = mx + c$), you can see that the gradient of the graph is $\frac{1}{3}$ and the vertical intercept is $\log R_0$.

So, reading from the graph, the vertical intercept is about $-14.9$.

$\log R_0 = -14.9$, so $R_0 = 10^{-14.9} = 1.258... \times 10^{-15} = 1.3$ fm (to 2 s.f.)

If $a = \log_{10} b$, then $b = 10^a$.

## Lumberjacks are great musicians — they have a natural logarhythm...

*Well, that's it folks. Crack open the chocolate bar of victory and know you've earned it. Only the tiny detail of the actual exam to go... ahem. Make sure you know which bit means what on a log graph and you'll pick up some nice easy marks. Other than that, stay calm, be as clear as you can and good luck — I've got my fingers, toes and eyes crossed for you.*

# Answers

## Section 1 — Further Mechanics

### Page 3 — Circular Motion

1 a) $\omega = \frac{\theta}{t}$ ***[1 mark]***

so $\omega = \frac{2\pi}{3.2 \times 10^7} = 1.963... \times 10^{-7}$
$= \mathbf{2.0 \times 10^{-7}\ rad\ s^{-1}}$ **(to 2 s.f.)** ***[1 mark]***

b) $v = r\omega = 1.5 \times 10^{11} \times 1.963... \times 10^{-7}$
$= 29\ 452.4...\ ms^{-1} = \mathbf{29\ 000\ ms^{-1}}$ **(to 2 s.f.)** ***[1 mark]***

c) $F = m\omega^2 r = 5.98 \times 10^{24} \times (1.963... \times 10^{-7})^2 \times 1.5 \times 10^{11}$ ***[1 mark]***
$= 3.4582... \times 10^{22}\ N = \mathbf{3.5 \times 10^{22}\ N}$ **(to 2 s.f.)** ***[1 mark]***

d) The gravitational force between the Sun and the Earth ***[1 mark]***.

2 a) Gravity pulling down on the water at the top of the swing gives a centripetal acceleration of 9.81 $ms^{-2}$ ***[1 mark]***. If the circular motion of the water has a centripetal acceleration of less than 9.81 $ms^{-2}$, gravity will pull it in too tight a circle. The water will fall out of the bucket.

Since $a = \omega^2 r$, $\omega = \sqrt{\frac{a}{r}} = \sqrt{\frac{9.81}{1.00}}$,

so $\omega = 3.13...\ rad\ s^{-1} = \mathbf{3.13\ rad\ s^{-1}}$ **(to 3 s.f.)** ***[1 mark]***

$\omega = 2\pi f$, so $f = \frac{\omega}{2\pi} = \frac{3.13...}{2\pi} = \mathbf{0.498\ rev\ s^{-1}}$ **(to 3 s.f.)** ***[1 mark]***

b) Centripetal force $= m\omega^2 r = 10.0 \times (5.00)^2 \times 1.00 = 250$ N ***[1 mark]***
This force is provided by both the tension in the rope, $T$, and gravity acting on the water and the bucket (their weight).
$T + (10.0 \times 9.81) = 250$ ***[1 mark]***
So $T = 250 - (10.0 \times 9.81) = 151.9\ N = \mathbf{152\ N}$ **(to 3 s.f.)** ***[1 mark]***
Remember, $W = mg$.

### Page 5 — Simple Harmonic Motion

1 a) Simple harmonic motion is an oscillation in which the acceleration of an object is directly proportional to its displacement from the midpoint ***[1 mark]***, and is directed towards the midpoint ***[1 mark]***.
(The SHM equation would get you the marks if you defined all the variables).

b) Acceleration during free fall is constant, not proportional to displacement, which is a requirement of SHM ***[1 mark]***.

2 E.g. The total energy of the mass-spring system is constant ***[1 mark]***. At the midpoint, the mass's $E_p$ is zero and its $E_k$ is maximum ***[1 mark]***. At the maximum displacement (the amplitude) on both sides of the midpoint, the mass's $E_k$ is zero and its $E_p$ is at its maximum ***[1 mark]***. As the mass moves away from the midpoint, $E_k$ is transferred into $E_p$ in the spring. As it moves towards the midpoint, $E_p$ in the spring is transferred into $E_k$ ***[1 mark]***.

3 a) Maximum speed $= \omega A = (2\pi f)A = 2\pi \times 1.5 \times 0.05$ ***[1 mark]***
$= 0.471...\ ms^{-1} = \mathbf{0.5\ ms^{-1}}$ **(to 1 s.f.)** ***[1 mark]***

b) $x = A\cos(\omega t) = A\cos(2\pi ft)$
$= 0.05 \times \cos(2\pi \times 1.5 \times 0.1) = 0.05 \times \cos(0.94...)$ ***[1 mark]***
$= 0.0294...\ m = \mathbf{0.03\ m}$ **(to 1 s.f.)** ***[1 mark]***
Remember to make sure your calculator is in radian mode.

c) $x = A\cos(\omega t) = A\cos(2\pi ft)$
$0.01 = 0.05 \times \cos(2\pi \times 1.5t)$
So $0.20 = \cos(3\pi t)$
$\cos^{-1}(0.20) = 3\pi t$ ***[1 mark]***
$t = 0.145... = \mathbf{0.1\ s}$ **(to 1 s.f.)** ***[1 mark]***

4 $\omega_C = 2\omega_D$ and maximum acceleration $= \omega^2 A$.
$a_{max(C)} = \omega_C{}^2 A = (2\omega_D)^2 A = 4\omega_D{}^2 A$
$a_{max(D)} = \omega_D{}^2 A$
So $a_{max(C)} = 4a_{max(D)}$
**D** ***[1 mark]***

### Page 7 — Simple Harmonic Oscillators

1 a) Extension of spring, $x = 0.20 - 0.10 = 0.10$ m ***[1 mark]***
Force = –weight = – 9.81 $Nm^{-1} \times 0.10$ m = –0.981 N
$F = -kx$ so $k = -F \div x = -(-9.81 \times 0.10) \div (0.20 - 0.10)$
$= 9.81 = \mathbf{9.8\ Nm^{-1}}$ **(to 2 s.f.)** ***[1 mark]***

b) $T = 2\pi\sqrt{\frac{m}{k}} = 2\pi\sqrt{\frac{0.10}{9.81}} = 0.634...$ s
$= \mathbf{0.63\ s}$ **(to 2 s.f.)** ***[1 mark]***

c) $m \propto T^2$ so if $T$ is doubled, $T^2$ is quadrupled and $m$ is quadrupled ***[1 mark]***.
So mass needed $= 4 \times 0.10 = \mathbf{0.40\ kg}$ ***[1 mark]***

2 E.g. $5T_{short\ pendulum} = 3T_{long\ pendulum}$ ***[1 mark]*** and $T = 2\pi\sqrt{\frac{l}{g}}$
Let length of long pendulum = $l$
So $5\left(2\pi\sqrt{\frac{0.20}{g}}\right) = 3\left(2\pi\sqrt{\frac{l}{g}}\right)$ ***[1 mark]***
Dividing by $2\pi$ and squaring gives: $25 \times \frac{0.2}{g} = 9 \times \frac{l}{g}$
Which simplifies to $5 = 9l$
So length of long pendulum = 5/9 = 0.555...
$= \mathbf{0.56\ m}$ **(to 2 s.f.)** ***[1 mark]***

### Page 9 — Free and Forced Vibrations

1) a) When a system is forced to vibrate at a frequency that's close to, or the same as its resonant frequency ***[1 mark]*** and oscillates with a much larger than usual amplitude ***[1 mark]***.

b)

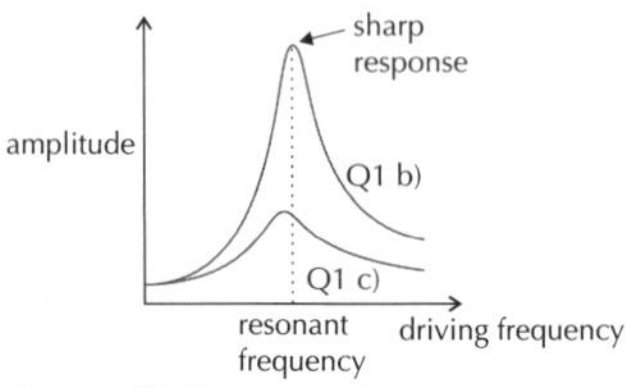


***[1 mark]*** for a peak at the resonant frequency,
***[1 mark]*** for a sharp peak.

c) See graph. ***[1 mark]*** for a smaller peak around the resonant frequency.

2 a) A critically damped system returns to rest in the shortest time possible when displaced from equilibrium and released ***[1 mark]***.

b) E.g. suspension in a car ***[1 mark]***.

## Section 2 — Thermal Physics

### Page 11 — Thermal Energy Transfer

1 Electrical energy supplied: $Q = 90 \times 3 \times 60 = 16\ 200$ J ***[1 mark]***
The temperature rise is 12.7 – 4.5 = 8.2 °C
$c = \frac{Q}{m\Delta\theta}$ so $c = \frac{16\ 200}{2.0 \times 8.2}$ ***[1 mark]***
$= 987.8... = \mathbf{990\ Jkg^{-1}°C^{-1}}$ **(to 2 s.f.)**
***[1 mark for correct number, 1 mark for correct unit.]***
You need the right unit for the fourth mark — $Jkg^{-1}K^{-1}$ would be right too.

2 a) Energy required to heat water to boiling point $= Q = mc\Delta\theta$,
$Q = 0.500 \times 4180 \times (100 - 20) = 1.672 \times 10^5$ J ***[1 mark]***
Energy required to boil dry $= Q = ml = 0.500 \times 2.26 \times 10^6$
$= 1.13 \times 10^6$ J ***[1 mark]***

So time to boil dry:
$\frac{\text{energy required to heat to 100°C and boil dry}}{\text{energy supplied per second}}$ ***[1 mark]***
$= \frac{(1.672 \times 10^5) + (1.13 \times 10^6)}{3.00 \times 10^3}$ ***[1 mark]***

$= 432.4 = \mathbf{432\ s}$ **(to 3 s.f.)** ***[1 mark]***

b) B ***[1 mark]***

### Page 13 — Gas Laws

1 $107.89 + 273.15 = \mathbf{381.04\ K}$ ***[1 mark]***

2 $V_1 = 2.42\ m^3$, $V_2 = 6.43\ m^3$, $T_2 = 293$ K.
Charles's Law: $\frac{V}{T}$ = constant so $\frac{V_2}{T_2} = \frac{6.43}{293} = 0.02194...$ ***[1 mark]***
$T_1 = \frac{V_1}{\text{constant}} = \frac{2.42}{0.02194...} = 110.273...$
$= \mathbf{110\ K}$ **(to 3 s.f.)** ***[1 mark]***

3 a) E.g. Connect a tube containing only oil and air to a Bourdon gauge and a bike pump ***[1 mark]***. Measure the dimensions of the tube and the depth of the oil, then increase the pressure in the tube using the bike pump ***[1 mark]***. Note down the pressure from the Bourdon gauge and measure the depth of the oil again ***[1 mark]***. Repeat for different pressures then use your measurements to calculate the volume of the air in the tube. The results should show that as pressure increases, air volume decreases by the same proportion, and vice versa — i.e. $pV$ = constant ***[1 mark]***.

# Answers

b) $V_1 = 0.460 \text{ m}^3$, $p_1 = 1.03 \times 10^5$ Pa, $p_2 = 3.41 \times 10^5$ Pa.
$p_1 \times V_1$ = constant
$(1.03 \times 10^5) \times 0.460 = 47\,380$ ***[1 mark]***
$V_2$ = constant $\div p_2 = 47\,380 \div (3.41 \times 10^5)$
$= 0.13894... =$ **0.139 m³ (to 3 s.f.)** ***[1 mark]***

## *Page 15 — Ideal Gas Equation*

1 a) i) Number of moles $= \dfrac{\text{mass of gas}}{\text{molar mass}} = \dfrac{0.014}{0.028} =$ **0.50** ***[1 mark]***
ii) Number of molecules = number of moles × Avogadro's constant
$= 0.50 \times 6.02 \times 10^{23} =$ **$3.0 \times 10^{23}$ (to 2 s.f.)** ***[1 mark]***
b) $pV = nRT$, so $p = \dfrac{nRT}{V}$. $T = 27.2 + 273.15 = 300.35$ K ***[1 mark]***
$p = \dfrac{0.50 \times 8.31 \times 300.35}{0.0130} = 95\,996.4...$
**= 96 000 Pa (to 2 s.f.)** ***[1 mark]***
c) The pressure would also halve ***[1 mark]*** because it is proportional to the number of molecules — $pV = NkT$ ***[1 mark]***.

2 At ground level, $\dfrac{pV}{T} = \dfrac{1.00 \times 10^5 \times 10.0}{293} = 3412.9...$ ***[1 mark]***
$pV/T$ is constant, so higher up $pV/T = 3412.9...$ JK$^{-1}$ ***[1 mark]***
Higher up, $p = \dfrac{3412.9... \times T}{V} = \dfrac{3412.9... \times 261}{25.0}$
$= 35\,631.3... =$ **35 600 Pa (to 3 s.f.)** ***[1 mark]***

3 Work done $= p\Delta V = p(V_2 - V_1)$
so $V_1 = V_2 - \dfrac{\text{work done}}{p}$
$= 10.3 - \dfrac{470 \times 10^3}{1.12 \times 10^5} = 6.1035...$ ***[1 mark]***
**= 6.10 m³ (to 3 s.f.)** ***[1 mark]***

## *Page 17 — The Pressure of an Ideal Gas*

1 a) $pV = \frac{1}{3}Nm(c_{rms})^2$ Rearrange the equation: $(c_{rms})^2 = \dfrac{3pV}{Nm}$
$(c_{rms})^2 = \dfrac{3 \times (1.03 \times 10^5) \times (7.00 \times 10^{-5})}{(2.17 \times 10^{22}) \times (6.65 \times 10^{-27})}$ ***[1 mark]***
$= 149\,890.8... =$ **150 000 m²s⁻² (to 3 s.f.)** ***[1 mark]***
b) r.m.s. speed $= \sqrt{(c_{rms})^2} = \sqrt{149\,890.8...} = 387.15....$
**= 387 ms⁻¹ (to 3 s.f.)** ***[1 mark]***
c) $pV$ is proportional to $T$, so doubling $T$ will double $pV$ ***[1 mark]***.
r.m.s. speed $= \sqrt{(c_{rms})^2} = \sqrt{\dfrac{3pV}{Nm}}$, so doubling $pV$ will increase the r.m.s. speed by a factor of $\sqrt{2}$.
r.m.s. speed $= 387.15... \times \sqrt{2}$
$= 547.5... =$ **548 ms⁻¹ (to 3 s.f.)** ***[1 mark]***

## *Page 19 — Kinetic Energy and the Development of Theories*

1 $\frac{1}{2}m(c_{rms})^2 = \dfrac{3kT}{2}$
Rearranging gives: $(c_{rms})^2 = \dfrac{3kT}{m}$ ***[1 mark]***
$m$ = mass of 1 mole $\div N_A$
$= 2.80 \times 10^{-2} \div 6.02 \times 10^{23}$
$= 4.651... \times 10^{-26}$ kg ***[1 mark]***
$(c_{rms})^2 = \dfrac{3 \times (1.38 \times 10^{-23}) \times 308}{4.651... \times 10^{-26}} = 274\,150.8$ ***[1 mark]***
Typical speed = r.m.s. speed $= \sqrt{274\,150.8}$
$= 523.59... =$ **524 ms⁻¹ (to 3 s.f.)** ***[1 mark]***

2 a) Time = distance ÷ speed = 8.19 m ÷ 395
$= 0.02073...$
**= 0.0207 s (to 3 s.f.)** ***[1 mark]***
b) Although the particles move at 395 ms$^{-1}$ on average, they frequently collide with fast-moving molecules ***[1 mark]***. So the particles move randomly in a zigzag motion — this is Brownian motion ***[1 mark]***. So their motion in any one direction is limited and they only move slowly from one end of the room to another ***[1 mark]***.

# *Section 3 — Gravitational and Electric Fields*

## *Page 21 — Gravitational Fields*

1 a) $g = \dfrac{GM}{r^2}$ so $M = \dfrac{gr^2}{G}$
$M = \dfrac{9.81 \times (6400 \times 1000)^2}{6.67 \times 10^{-11}}$ ***[1 mark]***
$= 6.024... \times 10^{24} =$ **$6.0 \times 10^{24}$ kg (to 2 s.f.)** ***[1 mark]***
b) $F = \dfrac{Gm_1m_2}{r^2} = \dfrac{6.67 \times 10^{-11} \times 1.99 \times 10^{30} \times 6.024... \times 10^{24}}{(1.5 \times 10^{11})^2}$
***[1 mark]***
$F = 3.55... \times 10^{22} =$ **$3.6 \times 10^{22}$ N (to 2 s.f.)** ***[1 mark]***

2 $g = \dfrac{GM}{r^2} = \dfrac{6.67 \times 10^{-11} \times 7.35 \times 10^{22}}{(1740 \times 1000)^2}$
$= 1.619... = 1.62$ Nkg$^{-1}$ (to 2 s.f.) ***[1 mark]***
$F = mg = 25 \times 1.619... = 40.48... =$ **40 N (to 2 s.f.)** ***[1 mark]***

3 E.g. $r$ is the distance between A and B. $r_1$ is three quarters of $r$. $r_2$ is one quarter of $r$. $r_1 = 3r_2$

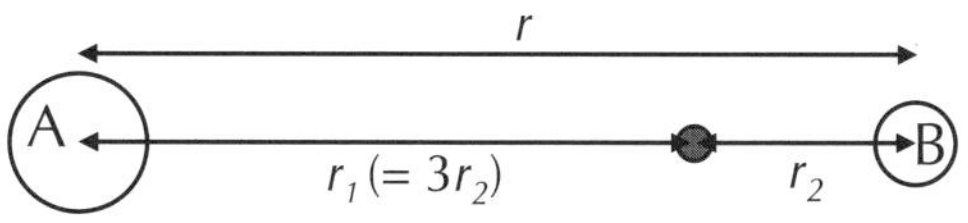


You can write an equation for $g$ due to each planet:
$g = \dfrac{GM_A}{r_1^2}$ and $g = \dfrac{GM_B}{r_2^2}$
The force on the object is 0, so $g = 0$.
This means you can equate the two equations for $g$:
$\dfrac{GM_A}{r_1^2} = \dfrac{GM_B}{r_2^2}$
Then replace $r_1$ with $3r_2$ and simplify:
$\dfrac{GM_A}{(3r_2)^2} = \dfrac{GM_B}{r_2^2}$
$\dfrac{M_A}{9r_2^2} = \dfrac{M_B}{r_2^2}$
$M_B = \frac{1}{9}M_A$
Answer = **A** ***[1 mark]***

## *Page 23 — Gravitational Potential*

1 a) $\Delta V = (-1.52 \times 10^4) - (-1.50 \times 10^4) = 0.02 \times 10^4$
$g = \dfrac{-\Delta V}{\Delta r} = \dfrac{-0.02 \times 10^4}{1540}$ ***[1 mark]***
$= -0.1298... =$ **$-1.30$ ms⁻² (to 3 s.f.)** ***[1 mark]***
Note: $g$ is negative because it points 'down' towards the asteroid.
b) At the surface:
$V = \dfrac{-GM}{r}$ so $r = \dfrac{-GM}{V}$
$r = \dfrac{-6.67 \times 10^{-11} \times 2.67 \times 10^{19}}{-1.52 \times 10^4}$
$= 117163.8... =$ **117 000 m (to 3 s.f.)** ***[1 mark]***
c) $v = \sqrt{\dfrac{2GM}{r}} = \sqrt{\dfrac{2 \times 6.67 \times 10^{-11} \times 2.67 \times 10^{19}}{117\,163.8...}}$
$v = 174.3...... =$ **174 ms⁻¹ (to 3 s.f.)** ***[1 mark]***
d) $V$ at 2020 m above the surface $= \dfrac{-GM}{r}$
$= \dfrac{-6.67 \times 10^{-11} \times 2.67 \times 10^{19}}{(117\,163.8... + 2020)}$
$= -1.49423... \times 10^4$ ***[1 mark]***
$\Delta W = m\Delta V$
so $\Delta W = 300 \times (-1.49423... \times 10^4 - (-1.52 \times 10^4))$ ***[1 mark]***
$= 7.728... \times 10^4 =$ **$7.73 \times 10^4$ J (to 3 s.f.)** ***[1 mark]***

## *Page 25 — Orbits and Gravity*

1 $v \propto \dfrac{1}{\sqrt{r}}$ so if $r$ is doubled, $v$ increases by a factor of $\dfrac{1}{\sqrt{2}}$
$\dfrac{1}{\sqrt{2}} = 0.707... = 0.71$ (to 2 s.f.)
So the answer is C ***[1 mark]***

# Answers

2 $v \propto \frac{1}{\sqrt{r}}$ and $T^2 \propto r^3$ ***[1 mark]***
So $r \propto \frac{1}{v^2}$ meaning $T \propto \sqrt{\left(\frac{1}{v^2}\right)^3}$ ***[1 mark]***

If $v$ becomes $\frac{v}{2}$, then $T \propto \sqrt{\left(\frac{2^2}{v^2}\right)^3}$ ***[1 mark]***

So $T$ increases by a factor of $\sqrt{4^3} = 8$
The new orbital period is 8 × 3 = **24 hours** ***[1 mark]***

## Page 27 — Electric Fields

1 Charge on alpha particle, $Q_1 = +2e = 2 \times 1.60 \times 10^{-19}$
$= \mathbf{3.20 \times 10^{-19}}$ **C**
Charge on gold nucleus, $Q_2 = +79e = 79 \times 1.60 \times 10^{-19}$ C
$= 1.264 \times 10^{-17}$ C ***[1 mark for both]***
$F = \frac{1}{4\pi\varepsilon_0}\frac{Q_1Q_2}{r^2} = \frac{1}{4\pi\varepsilon_0}\frac{3.20 \times 10^{-19} \times 1.264 \times 10^{-17}}{(5.0 \times 10^{-12})^2}$ ***[1 mark]***
$= 1.4548... \times 10^{-3} = \mathbf{1.5 \times 10^{-3}}$ **N (to 2 s.f.)** ***[1 mark]***
away from the gold nucleus ***[1 mark]***

2 a) $E = V/d = 1500/(4.5 \times 10^{-3}) = 3.33... \times 10^5$
$= \mathbf{3.3 \times 10^5}$ $\mathbf{Vm^{-1}}$ **(to 2 s.f.)** ***[1 mark]***
The field is perpendicular to the plates ***[1 mark]***.

b) $d = 2 \times (4.5 \times 10^{-3}) = 9.0 \times 10^{-3}$ m
$E = V/d \Rightarrow V = Ed = 3.33... \times 10^5 \times 9 \times 10^{-3} =$ **3000 V** ***[1 mark]***

## Page 29 — Electric Potential and Work Done

1 $V = \frac{1}{4\pi\varepsilon_0}\frac{Q}{r} = \frac{1}{4\pi \times 8.85 \times 10^{-12}} \times \frac{-1.6 \times 10^{-19}}{6.0 \times 10^{-10}}$ ***[1 mark]***
$V = -2.397... =$ **–2.4 V (to 2 s.f.)** ***[1 mark]***

2 $\Delta W = Q\Delta V$ and $F = \Delta W \div d$ so $F = \frac{Q\Delta V}{d}$ ***[1 mark]***
$E = \frac{F}{Q} = \frac{\Delta V}{d}$ ***[1 mark]***

3 a) $\Delta W = Q\Delta V = 1.6 \times 10^{-19} \times 200 = \mathbf{3.2 \times 10^{-17}}$ **J** ***[1 mark]***

b) It is moving along an equipotential and so $\Delta V$ is 0 ***[1 mark]***.

## Page 31 — Comparing Electric and Gravitational Fields

1 a) Gravitational:
$F = \frac{Gm_1m_2}{r^2} = \frac{6.67 \times 10^{-11} \times (9.11 \times 10^{-31})^2}{(8.00 \times 10^{-10})^2}$
$= -8.649... \times 10^{-53} = \mathbf{-8.65 \times 10^{-53}}$ **N (to 3 s.f.)** ***[1 mark]***
Electric:
$F = \frac{1}{4\pi\varepsilon_0}\frac{Q_1Q_2}{r^2} = \frac{1}{4\pi\varepsilon_0}\frac{(1.6 \times 10^{-19})^2}{(8.00 \times 10^{-10})^2}$
$= 3.596... \times 10^{-10} = \mathbf{3.60 \times 10^{-10}}$**N (to 3 s.f.)** ***[1 mark]***

The force caused by gravity is a factor of $10^{43}$ smaller than the electrostatic force ***[1 mark]***. The gravitational force is attractive (it's negative) and the electrostatic force is repulsive (it's positive) ***[1 mark]***.

b) The electric force on each electron is much larger than the gravitational force, by a factor of over $10^{40}$ — so the gravitational forces are so small they can be ignored ***[1 mark]***.

# Section 4 — Capacitors

## Page 33 — Capacitors

1 a) Capacitance is the amount of charge stored per unit potential difference ***[1 mark]***.

b) $C = \frac{Q}{V} = \frac{660 \times 10^{-6}}{3}$ ***[1 mark]***
$= 220 \times 10^{-6} =$ **220 μF** ***[1 mark]***

2 Before the dielectric is removed:
$V = \frac{Q}{C} = \frac{2.47 \times 10^{-9}}{137 \times 10^{-12}} = 18.0...$ V ***[1 mark]***
When the dielectric is removed, $A$, $d$ and $\varepsilon_0$ remain constant:
$C_{original} = \frac{A\varepsilon_0\varepsilon_r}{d} = 137 \times 10^{-12}$ F

$C_{new} = \frac{A\varepsilon_0}{d} = C_{original} \times \frac{1}{\varepsilon_r}$

$C_{new} = \frac{137 \times 10^{-12}}{3.1} = 4.41... \times 10^{-11}$F ***[1 mark]***

$V_{new} = \frac{Q}{C_{new}} = \frac{2.47 \times 10^{-9}}{4.41... \times 10^{-11}} = 55.8...$V ***[1 mark]***
So the change in potential difference is 55.8... – 18.0...
= **38 V (to 2 s.f.)** ***[1 mark]***

3 $Q = CV = 8.0 \times 10^{-6} \times 12 = 9.6 \times 10^{-5}$ C ***[1 mark]***
$E = ½\, QV = ½ \times 9.6 \times 10^{-5} \times 12$ ***[1 mark]***
$= 5.76 \times 10^{-4}$ J $= \mathbf{5.8 \times 10^{-4}}$ **J (to 2 s.f.)** ***[1 mark]***

## Page 35 — Charging and Discharging

1 a) $E = \frac{1}{2}\frac{Q^2}{C} = \frac{1}{2} \times \frac{(1.5 \times 10^{-6})^2}{250 \times 10^{-6}} = \mathbf{4.5 \times 10^{-9}}$ **J** ***[1 mark]***

b) $E = \frac{1}{2}QV$ so $V = \frac{2E}{Q}$

$V = \frac{2 \times 4.5 \times 10^{-9}}{1.5 \times 10^{-6}}$ ***[1 mark]***
$V = 6.0 \times 10^{-3} =$ **6.0 mV** ***[1 mark]***

c) 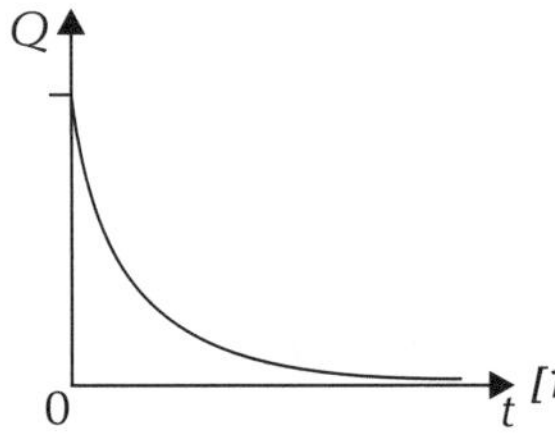

***[1 mark]***

2 The current decreases exponentially because as charge builds on the plates of the capacitor, it becomes harder and harder to overcome the electrostatic repulsion and deposit electrons onto the plate ***[1 mark]***

3 C ***[1 mark]***

## Page 37 — More Charging and Discharging

1 a) The charge falls to 37% after $RC$ seconds ***[1 mark]***,
so $\tau = 1000 \times 2.5 \times 10^{-4} =$ **0.25 seconds** ***[1 mark]***

b) $Q = Q_0e^{\frac{-t}{RC}}$, so after 0.7 seconds:

$Q = Q_0e^{\frac{-0.7}{0.25}} = 0.06Q_0$ (to 1 s.f.) ***[1 mark]***
6% of the initial charge is left on the capacitor after 0.7 s ***[1 mark]***.

c) The total charge stored doubles: $V$ is proportional to $Q$ ***[1 mark]***.
The capacitance wouldn't change — this is a fixed property of the capacitor ***[1 mark]***.
The time taken to charge wouldn't change, as the charging time depends only on the capacitance of the capacitor and the resistance of the circuit, which don't change ***[1 mark]***.

2 $T_{½} = 0.69RC$
$= 0.69 \times 1.6 \times 10^3 \times 320 \times 10^{-6}$ ***[1 mark]*** = 0.353... s
= **0.35 s (to 2 s.f.)** ***[1 mark]***

# Section 5 — Magnetic Fields

## Page 39 — Magnetic Fields

1 a) $F = BIl = 2.00 \times 10^{-5} \times 3.00 \times 0.0400$ ***[1 mark]***
$= \mathbf{2.40 \times 10^{-6}}$ **N** ***[1 mark]***

b) The force is zero ***[1 mark]*** because there is no component of the current that is perpendicular to the external magnetic field ***[1 mark]***.

2 C ***[1 mark]***

# Answers

## Page 41 — Charged Particles in a Magnetic Field

1 $F = BQv$ so $v = \frac{F}{BQ} = \frac{4.91 \times 10^{-15}}{1.10 \times 1.60 \times 10^{-19}}$ ***[1 mark]***

$= 27897.7... =$ **27900 ms⁻¹ (to 3 s.f.)** ***[1 mark]***

2 Horizontally from south to north ***[1 mark]***.

3 a) The particle has a charge and is moving in a magnetic field so $F = BQv$, and the particle is moving in a circle so $F = \frac{mv^2}{r}$

So $BQv = \frac{mv^2}{r}$ ***[1 mark]*** which gives $r = \frac{mv^2}{BQv} = \frac{mv}{BQ}$ ***[1 mark]***

b) $r = \frac{mv}{BQ}$ so $v = \frac{rBQ}{m} = \frac{(3.52 \times 10^{-2}) \times 0.00510 \times (1.6 \times 10^{-19})}{9.11 \times 10^{-31}}$

$= 3.512... \times 10^7 =$ **$3.51 \times 10^7$ ms⁻¹ (to 3 s.f.)** ***[1 mark]***

## Page 43 — Electromagnetic Induction

1 a) $\phi = BA = (2.00 \times 10^{-3}) \times 0.230 =$ **$4.60 \times 10^{-4}$ Wb** ***[1 mark]***

b) Flux linkage $= BAN = (2.00 \times 10^{-3}) \times 0.230 \times 151 = 0.06946$

$=$ **0.0695 Wb (to 3 s.f.)** ***[1 mark]***

c) $\varepsilon = -\frac{\Delta(N\phi)}{\Delta t} = -\frac{\Delta(NBA)}{\Delta t} = -\frac{NA\Delta B}{\Delta t}$ ***[1 mark]***

$= -\frac{151 \times 0.230 \times (1.50 \times 10^{-3} - 2.00 \times 10^{-3})}{2.5}$ ***[1 mark]***

$= 6.946 \times 10^{-3} =$ **$6.95 \times 10^{-3}$ V (to 3 s.f.)** ***[1 mark]***

2 a) Flux linkage $= BAN = 0.92 \times 0.010 \times 550 =$ **5.06 Wb** ***[1 mark]***

b) Flux linkage after movement

$= BAN \cos\theta = 550 \times 0.92 \times 0.010 \times \cos 90° = 0$ Wb ***[1 mark]***

$\varepsilon = -\frac{\Delta(N\phi)}{\Delta t} = -\frac{0 - 5.06}{0.5} = 10.12 =$ **10 V (to 2 s.f.)** ***[1 mark]***

3

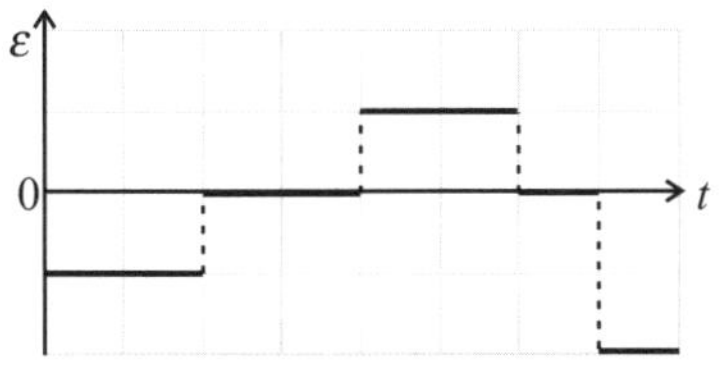


Step graph ***[1 mark]*** with the first and fifth steps negative and third step positive ***[1 mark]*** and the last step twice as negative as the others ***[1 mark]***.

## Page 45 — Induction Laws and Alternators

1 a) The distance travelled by the aeroplane is $v\Delta t$ so area cut, $A = lv\Delta t$

flux linkage $= BA$ so $\Phi = Blv\Delta t$

$\varepsilon = N\frac{\Delta\Phi}{\Delta t} = 1 \times \frac{Blv\Delta t}{\Delta t}$ ***[1 mark]*** $= Blv$

$= 6.00 \times 10^{-5} \times 33.9 \times 148$ ***[1 mark]*** $= 0.3010...$

$=$ **0.301 V (to 3 s.f.)** ***[1 mark]***

b)

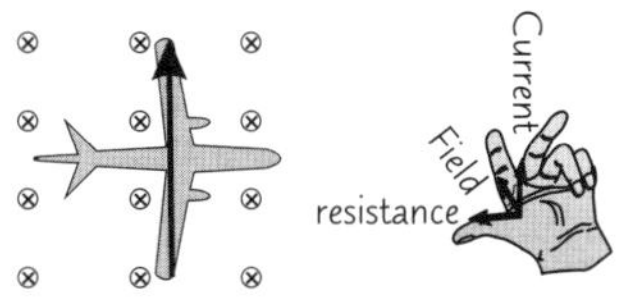


***[1 mark]***

2 a) $N\Phi = BAN \cos\theta = 0.900 \times 0.0105 \times 521 \times \cos 60.0° = 2.4617...$

$=$ **2.46 Wb (to 3 s.f.)** ***[1 mark]***

b) Peak e.m.f. when $\sin \omega t = \pm 1$,

giving $\varepsilon = \pm BAN\omega$ ***[1 mark]***

So, peak e.m.f. is:

$\varepsilon = \pm 0.900 \times 0.0105 \times 521 \times 40\pi$ ***[1 mark]***

$= \pm 618.698... =$ **± 619 V (to 3 s.f.)** ***[1 mark]***

## Page 47 — Alternating Currents

1 a) Turn on the time base ***[1 mark]***.

b) He has used a direct current (d.c.) / non-alternating power supply ***[1 mark]***.

2 a) $I_{rms} = \frac{I_0}{\sqrt{2}} = \frac{9.13}{\sqrt{2}} = 6.4558... =$ **6.46 A (to 3 s.f.)** ***[1 mark]***

b) $V_{rms} = \frac{V_0}{\sqrt{2}}$ so $V_0 = V_{rms} \times \sqrt{2} = 119 \times \sqrt{2} = 168.29...$ ***[1 mark]***

$V_{peak\ to\ peak} = 2 \times V_0 = 2 \times 168.29... = 336.58...$

$=$ **337 V (to 3 s.f.)** ***[1 mark]***

## Page 49 — Transformers

1 a) $\frac{N_s}{N_p} = \frac{V_s}{V_p}$ so, $N_s = \frac{V_s \times N_p}{V_p} = \frac{45.0 \times 158}{9.30} = 764.51...$

$=$ **765 turns** ***[1 mark]***

b) $\frac{I_s}{I_p} = \frac{V_p}{V_s}$ ***[1 mark]*** so, $I_s = \frac{V_p \times I_p}{V_s} = \frac{9.30 \times 1.50}{45.0}$

$=$ **0.310 A** ***[1 mark]***

c) efficiency $= \frac{I_s V_s}{I_p V_p} = \frac{P_s}{I_p V_p} = \frac{10.8}{1.5 \times 9.3} = 0.7741...$

$=$ **77.4% (to 3 s.f.)** ***[1 mark]***

You could also give your answer as a decimal — efficiency = 0.774.

d) Laminating the core with layers of insulation would reduce the effect of eddy currents and improve the efficiency of the transformer ***[1 mark]***.

2 power transmitted = power received + power wasted ***[1 mark]***

power transmitted $= 943\,000 + I^2 \times R$

$= 943\,000 + 15.6^2 \times 132 = 975\,123.52$

$=$ **975 kW (to 3 s.f.)** ***[1 mark]***

# Section 6 — Nuclear Physics

## Page 51 — Rutherford Scattering and Atomic Structure

1 a) The majority of alpha particles are not scattered because the nucleus is a very small part of the whole atom and so the probability of an alpha particle getting near it is small [1 mark]. Most alpha particles pass undeflected through the empty space around the nucleus [1 mark].

b) Alpha particles and atomic nuclei are both positively charged [1 mark]. If an alpha particle travels close to a nucleus, there will be a significant electrostatic force of repulsion between them [1 mark]. This force deflects the alpha particle from its original path [1 mark].

c) $\frac{Q_{gold} Q_{alpha}}{4\pi\varepsilon_0 r} = E_k$ so $r = \frac{Q_{gold} Q_{alpha}}{4\pi\varepsilon_0 E_k}$

$r = \frac{79 \times (1.60 \times 10^{-19}) \times 2 \times (1.60 \times 10^{-19})}{4\pi \times (8.85 \times 10^{-12}) \times (4.8 \times 10^6 \times 1.60 \times 10^{-19})}$ ***[1 mark]***

$r = 4.735... \times 10^{-14}$ m $=$ **$4.7 \times 10^{-14}$ m (to 2 s.f.)** ***[1 mark]***

d) 0 J ***[1 mark]***

At the distance of closest approach, all of the kinetic energy has been transferred into electric potential energy, so kinetic energy is zero.

## Page 53 — Nuclear Radius and Density

1 a) $\theta \approx \sin^{-1}\left(\frac{1.22\lambda}{2r}\right) = \sin^{-1}\left(\frac{1.22 \times (3.0 \times 10^{-15})}{2 \times (2.7 \times 10^{-15})}\right)$ ***[1 mark]***

$= 42.67...° =$ **43° (to 2 s.f.)** ***[1 mark]***

b)

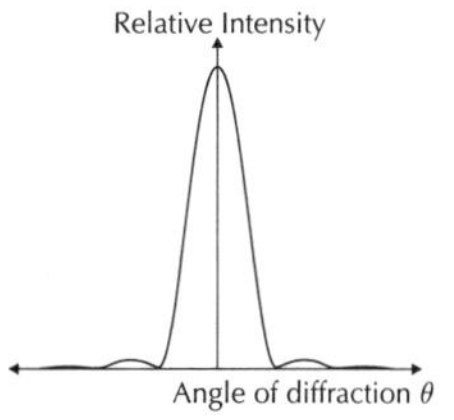


***[1 mark for general shape, 1 mark for a central maximum with significantly larger intensity]***

2 For carbon, $A = 12$ so $R = R_0 A^{\frac{1}{3}} = 1.4 \times 10^{-15} \times 12^{\frac{1}{3}}$

$R = 3.205... \times 10^{-15}$ m ***[1 mark]***

Volume $= \frac{4}{3}\pi R^3 = \frac{4}{3}\pi(3.205... \times 10^{-15})^3 = 1.379... \times 10^{-43}\text{m}^3$

$\rho = \frac{m}{V} = \frac{2.00 \times 10^{-26}}{1.379... \times 10^{-43}} = 1.45... \times 10^{17}\text{kgm}^{-3}$ ***[1 mark]***

For gold, $A = 197$ so $R = R_0 A^{\frac{1}{3}} = 1.4 \times 10^{-15} \times 197^{\frac{1}{3}}$

$R = 8.146... \times 10^{-15}$ m ***[1 mark]***

Volume $= \frac{4}{3}\pi R^3 = \frac{4}{3}\pi(8.416... \times 10^{-15})^3 = 2.264... \times 10^{-42}\text{m}^3$

$\rho = \frac{m}{V} = \frac{3.27 \times 10^{-25}}{2.264... \times 10^{-42}} = 1.44... \times 10^{17}\text{kgm}^{-3}$ ***[1 mark]***

# Answers

## Page 55 — Radioactive Emissions

1 Put paper then a sheet of aluminium between source and detector and measure the amount of radiation getting through each time ***[1 mark]***. Alpha radiation will be stopped by paper, beta will be stopped by aluminium and gamma isn't stopped by either.

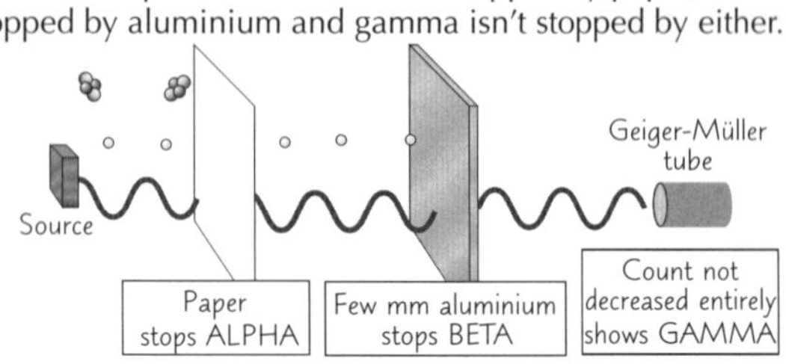


***[1 mark for each material stopping its corresponding radiation]***

2 E.g. gamma rays are used in the treatment of cancerous tumours ***[1 mark]***. The radiation damages cells, including the cancerous ones within the body and can sometimes lead to the patient being cured of cancer ***[1 mark]***. However, exposure to gamma radiation can lead to long term side effects like infertility ***[1 mark]***.

## Page 57 — Investigations of Radioactive Emissions

1 a) Background radiation = 60 cpm = 1 cps
$20.0 \div 10.0 = 2$
So count rate at 20 cm = $(240 - 1) \div 2^2 = 59.75$ cps ***[1 mark]***
Now add back on the contribution of background radiation:
$59.75 + 1 = 60.75$ cps = **61 cps (to 2 s.f.)** ***[1 mark]***

b) 35.0 cm is 3.5 times further away than 10.0 cm, so the count rate will be $(240 - 1) \div 3.5^2 = 19.5102...$
Now add back on the contribution from background radiation:
$19.5102... + 1 = 20.5102...$ = **21 cps (to 2 s.f.)** ***[1 mark]***

2 At 40 cm, $x = 0.4$ so $k = Ix^2 = 30 \times 0.4^2 = 4.8$ ***[1 mark]***
At A, a distance $x$ times away from the starting position,
$I = 4.8$ cps so $x = \sqrt{\frac{k}{I}} = \sqrt{\frac{4.8}{4.8}} = 1$
So the Geiger counter is 1 m away from the source at A ***[1 mark]***.

## Page 59 — Exponential Law of Decay

1 Any one of: You can't say which atom/nucleus in a sample will decay next. / You can only estimate the fraction of nuclei that will decay or the probability an atom/nucleus will decay in a given time. / You cannot say exactly how many atoms will decay in a given time. ***[1 mark]***

2 a) Activity, $A$ = measured activity – background activity
= 750 – 50 = 700 Bq ***[1 mark]***
Number of particles = number of moles × $N_A$
$N = 8.3 \times 10^{-20} \times 6.02 \times 10^{23} = 49\,966$ ***[1 mark]***
$A = \lambda N \Rightarrow 700 = 49\,996\,\lambda$ ***[1 mark]***
So $\lambda = 700 \div 49\,996$ = **0.014... s$^{-1}$** ***[1 mark]***
$T_{½} = \frac{\ln 2}{\lambda} = \frac{0.693...}{0.014...} = 49.4... =$ **49 s (to 2 s.f.)** ***[1 mark]***

b) $N = N_0 e^{-\lambda t} = 49\,996 \times e^{-0.014... \times 300}$
$= 747.5... =$ **750 (to 2 s.f.)** ***[1 mark]***

3 Some parts of radioactive waste have a very long half-life ***[1 mark]*** so it must be stored safely and securely to prevent as much damage as possible to people, animals and the environment ***[1 mark]***.

## Page 61 — Nuclear Decay

1 a) ${}^{226}_{88}\text{Ra} \rightarrow {}^{222}_{86}\text{Rn} + {}^{4}_{2}\alpha$ ***[1 mark for alpha particle, 1 mark for proton and nucleon number of radon.]***

b)

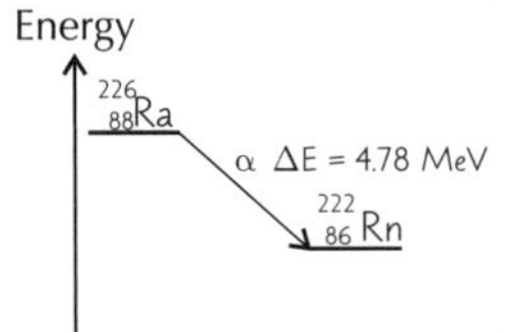


***[1 mark]***

2 ${}^{40}_{19}\text{K} \rightarrow {}^{40}_{20}\text{Ca} + {}^{0}_{-1}\beta + {}^{0}_{0}\bar{\nu}_e$ ***[1 mark for beta particle, 1 mark each for proton and nucleon number of calcium.]***

## Page 63 — Nuclear Fission and Fusion

1 a) Nuclear fission can be induced by neutrons and produces more neutrons during the process ***[1 mark]***. This means that each fission reaction induces more fission reactions, resulting in an ongoing chain of reactions ***[1 mark]***. The critical mass is the amount of fuel needed to sustain a chain reaction at a steady rate ***[1 mark]***.

b) E.g. control rods limit the rate of fission by absorbing neutrons ***[1 mark]***. The number of neutrons absorbed by the rods is controlled by varying the amount they are inserted into the reactor ***[1 mark]***. A suitable material for the control rods is boron ***[1 mark]***.

c) In an emergency shut-down, the control rods are released into the reactor ***[1 mark]***. The control rods absorb the neutrons, and stop the reaction as quickly as possible ***[1 mark]***.

2 E.g. advantages: nuclear power produces less greenhouse gases than burning fossil fuels ***[1 mark]*** / nuclear power produces huge amounts of energy ***[1 mark]***.
Any two disadvantages from e.g.: danger of the reactor getting out of control ***[1 mark]*** / risks of radiation from radioactive materials used ***[1 mark]*** / having to store waste products safely ***[1 mark]***.

## Page 65 — Binding Energy

1 a) Binding energy = $931.5 \times m$
$= 931.5 \times 1.864557 = 1736.8...$ MeV ***[1 mark]***
$1736.8... \times 1.60 \times 10^{-13} = 2.77893... \times 10^{-10}$ J
= **2.78 × 10$^{-10}$ J (to 3 s.f.)** ***[1 mark]***

b) Average binding energy per nucleon
$= 1736.8... \div 235 = 7.3907...$ MeV = **7.39 MeV (to 3 s.f.)** ***[1 mark]***

2 a) Fusion ***[1 mark]***

b) The increase in binding energy per nucleon is about 0.86 MeV ***[1 mark]***. There are 2 nucleons in ${}^{2}_{1}\text{H}$, so the increase in binding energy is about $2 \times 0.86 = 1.72$ MeV — so about 1.7 MeV (to 2 s.f.) is released (ignoring the positron) ***[1 mark]***.

# Section 7: Option A — Astrophysics

## Page 68 — Optical Telescopes

1 a) $\theta \approx \frac{\lambda}{D} = \frac{620 \times 10^{-9}}{1.6} = 3.875 \times 10^{-7}$
= **3.9 × 10$^{-7}$ rad (to 2 s.f.)** ***[1 mark]***

b) A smaller dish means a larger minimum angular resolution. As the resolving power is dependent on the minimum angular resolution (the smaller the minimum angular resolution, the better the resolving power), the resolving power of the telescope decreases. ***[1 mark]***

2 a) Separation of lenses must be $f_o + f_e = 5.0 + 0.10$ = **5.1 m** ***[1 mark]***

b) Angular magnification = angle subtended by image at eye / angle subtended by object at unaided eye ***[1 mark]***
$M = f_o/f_e = 5.0 / 0.10$ = **50** ***[1 mark]***

## Page 71 — Non-Optical Telescopes

1 The collecting power of the telescope is proportional to the area of the objective dish or mirror ***[1 mark]***. As both of the dishes have equal areas, their collecting powers are the same ***[1 mark]***. Resolving power depends on the wavelength of the radiation and the diameter of the dish ***[1 mark]***. Since UV radiation has a much smaller wavelength than radio, UV telescopes have a better resolving power ***[1 mark]***.

2 a) The telescope emits infrared radiation, which masks the infrared it is trying to detect ***[1 mark]***. The colder the telescope, the less infrared it emits ***[1 mark]***.

b) They are set up at high altitude in dry places ***[1 mark]***.

3 a) On high altitude aeroplanes / weather balloons ***[1 mark]***, to get above the level of the atmosphere that absorbs the radiation ***[1 mark]***.

b) A UV telescope uses a single parabolic mirror, whereas an X-ray telescope uses a series of nested 'grazing' mirrors ***[1 mark]***. This is because UV reflects in the same way as visible light ***[1 mark]*** but X-rays can only be reflected at very shallow angles / would be absorbed by a parabolic mirror ***[1 mark]***.

# Answers

4 a) power $\propto$ diameter$^2$ ***[1 mark]***.

b) $\frac{\text{power of Arecibo}}{\text{power of Lovell}} = \frac{300^2}{76^2}$ ***[1 mark]***
Ratio = 15.6 : 1 = **16 : 1 (to 2 s.f.)** ***[1 mark]***

## *Page 73 — Distances and Magnitude*

1 The absolute magnitude is the apparent magnitude ***[1 mark]*** that the object would have if it were 10 pc away from Earth ***[1 mark]***.

2 Distance to Sun in pc = $1/(2.1 \times 10^5) = 4.76... \times 10^{-6}$ pc ***[1 mark]***
$m - M = 5 \log (d/10)$
$-27 - M = 5 \log (4.76... \times 10^{-6}/10)$ ***[1 mark]***
$= 5 \log (4.76... \times 10^{-7})$
$= -31.61... \Rightarrow M = 4.611... =$ **4.6 (to 2 s.f.)** ***[1 mark]***

3 a) Sirius ***[1 mark]***

b) For Sirius, $m - M = -1.46 - 1.4 = -2.86$
For Canopus, $m - M = -0.72 - (-5.5) = 4.78$
Canopus has the larger difference between apparent and absolute magnitudes, so it is further away ***[1 mark]***.
$m - M = 5 \log (d/10)$
$4.78 = 5 \log (d/10) \Rightarrow \log (d/10) = 0.956$
$d/10 = 10^{0.956}$ ***[1 mark]***
So $d = 90.3... =$ **90 pc (to 2 s.f.)** ***[1 mark]***

## *Page 75 — Stars as Black Bodies*

1 a) According to Wien's displacement law $\lambda_{max} \times T = 2.9 \times 10^{-3}$, so for this star
$\lambda_{max} = 2.9 \times 10^{-3} \div 4000 = 7.25 \times 10^{-7}$ m ***[1 mark]***
Curve Y peaks at around 0.7 $\mu$m (= $7 \times 10^{-7}$ m), so could represent the star ***[1 mark]***.

b) Star X is the larger ***[1 mark]***.
From $P = \sigma A T^4$, power output is proportional to temperature ($T^4$) and to area. Given that the power output of both stars is the same, if one star has a higher temperature than the other, it must have a smaller surface area. The Sun has a higher temperature than star X, so it must have a smaller surface area ***[1 mark]***.

2 $\lambda_{max} T = 2.9 \times 10^{-3}$
So $T = (2.9 \times 10^{-3})/(436 \times 10^{-9}) = 6651.37...$ K ***[1 mark]***
$P = \sigma A T^4$
So $2.3 \times 10^{27} = 5.67 \times 10^{-8} \times A \times 6651.37...^4$ ***[1 mark]***
which gives $A = 2.07... \times 10^{19}$ m$^2$
= **$2.1 \times 10^{19}$ m$^2$ (to 2 s.f.)** ***[1 mark]***

## *Page 77 — Spectral Classes and the H-R Diagram*

1 a) To get strong Balmer lines, the majority of the electrons need to be at the $n = 2$ level ***[1 mark]***. At low temperatures, few electrons have enough energy to be at the $n = 2$ level ***[1 mark]***. At very high temperatures, most electrons are at $n = 3$ or above, both of which lead to weak Balmer lines ***[1 mark]***.

b) Spectral classes A ***[1 mark]*** and B ***[1 mark]***

c) Class F stars are white ***[1 mark]***, have a temperature of 6000 – 7500 K ***[1 mark]*** and show prominent absorption lines from metal ions ***[1 mark]***.

2 Molecules are only present in the lowest temperature stars as these are the only stars that are cool enough for molecules to form ***[1 mark]***.

3

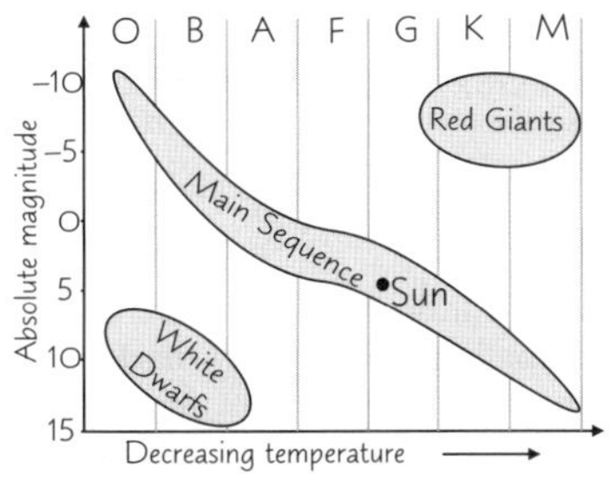


***[1 mark for correct axes, 1 mark each for each correctly located and labelled section, 1 mark for correct position of the Sun]***

## *Page 79 — Stellar Evolution*

1 Clumps of dust and gas begin to contract under gravity. Eventually, the clumps become dense enough that the cloud of dust and gas breaks into separate regions called protostars ***[1 mark]***. As a protostar becomes denser, the temperature increases, until hydrogen nuclei are fused into helium. This releases lots of energy ***[1 mark]***. The radiation and gas pressure are now so large that it stops the gravitational collapse, and the protostar becomes a stable main sequence star ***[1 mark]***.

2 a) When a star runs out of hydrogen fuel to fuse in the core, the outward radiation pressure stops, so the core of the star begins to contract, causing a rise in temperature ***[1 mark]***. The outer layers expand and begin to cool ***[1 mark]***.

b) Red giant ***[1 mark]***

c) a white dwarf ***[1 mark]***

## *Page 81 — Stellar Evolution*

1 a) The Schwarzschild radius is the distance ***[1 mark]*** from the black hole singularity to where the escape velocity is the speed of light (to the event horizon) ***[1 mark]***.

b) $R_s = \frac{2GM}{c^2} = \frac{2 \times 6.67 \times 10^{-11} \times 6.0 \times 10^{30}}{(3.00 \times 10^8)^2}$ ***[1 mark]***
= 8.89... km = **8.9 km (to 2 s.f.)** ***[1 mark]***

2 a) For a star of that mass, the electron degeneracy is not large enough to stop the core contracting ***[1 mark]***. The electrons and protons in the core are forced to combine, forming neutrons and neutrinos. The core collapses into a neutron star ***[1 mark]***. The outer layers of the star collapse and rebound off the core, leading to massive shock waves which cause the supernova ***[1 mark]***.

b) E.g. they could destroy the ozone layer and cause mass extinction ***[1 mark]*** if they were directed towards Earth ***[1 mark]***.

## *Page 83 — The Doppler Effect and Red Shift*

1 a) Object A is moving towards us ***[1 mark]***.

b) Object B is part of a binary star system (or is being orbited by a planet) ***[1 mark]*** with a period of two weeks ***[1 mark]***.

2 a) $z = -\frac{\Delta\lambda}{\lambda} = -\left(\frac{656.28 \times 10^{-9} - 667.83 \times 10^{-9}}{656.28 \times 10^{-9}}\right)$
= 0.0175991... = **0.017599 (to 5 s.f.)** ***[1 mark]***

b) $v = 0.175991... \times 3.00 \times 10^8 = 5.279... \times 10^6$ ms$^{-1}$
= **$5.28 \times 10^6$ ms$^{-1}$ (to 3 s.f.)** ***[1 mark]***
Object C is moving away from Earth as the observed wavelength has been stretched / the velocity is positive ***[1 mark]***.

## *Page 85 — Quasars and Exoplanets*

1 a) Their spectra show an enormous red shift ***[1 mark]***.

b) Intensity is proportional to 1/distance$^2$ ***[1 mark]***. So, e.g., if a quasar is 500 000 times further away than, but just as bright as, a star in the Milky Way it must be 500 000$^2$ times brighter than the star ***[1 mark]***.

c) A supermassive, active black hole ***[1 mark]*** surrounded by a doughnut-shaped mass of whirling gas ***[1 mark]***.

2 a) The transit method detects an exoplanet through a change in the apparent magnitude of a star ***[1 mark]***. As an exoplanet's path crosses in front of a star relative to Earth, it blocks some of the light ***[1 mark]***. This causes a dip in the star's light curve, which can be used to confirm the existence of an exoplanet and measure its radius ***[1 mark]***.

b)

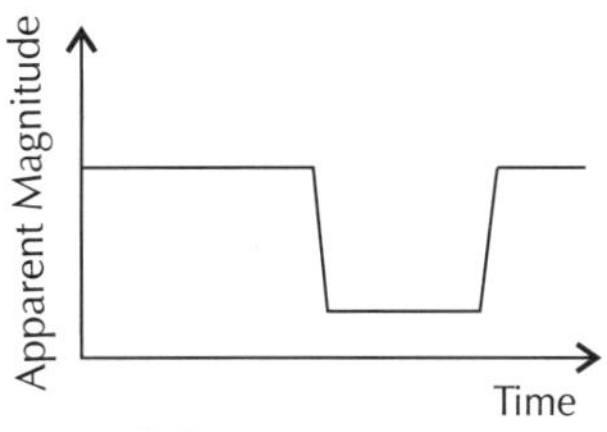


***[1 mark for correct axes, 1 mark for dip in apparent magnitude]***

# Answers

## Page 87 — The Big Bang Model of the Universe

1 a) $v = H_0 d$ ***[1 mark]*** where $v$ is recessional velocity (in $\text{kms}^{-1}$), $d$ is distance (in Mpc) and $H_0$ is Hubble's constant in ($\text{kms}^{-1}\text{Mpc}^{-1}$) ***[1 mark]***.

b) Hubble's law suggests that the Universe originated with the Big Bang ***[1 mark]*** and has been expanding ever since ***[1 mark]***.

c)i) $H_0 = v \div d = 50 \text{ kms}^{-1} \div 1 \text{ Mpc}^{-1}$.
$50 \text{ kms}^{-1} = 50 \times 10^3 \text{ ms}^{-1}$ and $1 \text{ Mpc}^{-1} = 3.08 \times 10^{22}$ m
So, $H_0 = 50 \times 10^3 \text{ ms}^{-1} \div 3.08 \times 10^{22}$ m
$= 1.623... \times 10^{-18} \text{ s}^{-1} = \mathbf{2 \times 10^{-18} \text{ s}^{-1}}$ **(to 1 s.f.)**
***[1 mark for the correct value, 1 mark for the correct unit]***

ii) $t = 1/H_0 = 1/1.623... \times 10^{-18} = 6.16 \times 10^{17}$ s ***[1 mark]***
$\approx \mathbf{2 \times 10^{10}}$ **years (to 1 s.f.)** ***[1 mark]***
The observable Universe has a radius of ~20 billion light years. ***[1 mark]***

2 a) $z = v/c$, so $v = 0.37 \times 3.00 \times 10^8 = 1.11 \times 10^8 \text{ ms}^{-1}$ ***[1 mark]***
$d = v/H_0 \approx 1.11 \times 10^8 / 2.4 \times 10^{-18} = 4.625 \times 10^{25}$ m ***[1 mark]***
$= 4.625 \times 10^{25} / 9.46 \times 10^{15}$ ly = **4.9 billion ly (to 2 s.f.)** ***[1 mark]***

b) $z = v/c$ is only valid if $v << c$ — it isn't the case here ***[1 mark]***

3 ***5-6 marks:***
The answer describes fully how the cosmic microwave background is strong evidence for the HBB.
The answer has a clear and logical structure.
***3-4 marks:***
Cosmic microwave background radiation is fully described, with some correct attempts made at explaining why it is evidence for the HBB. Most of the information given is relevant.
***1-2 marks:***
Some mention of what the cosmic background radiation is with no explanation as to why it supports the HBB. The information given is basic and lacking in detail. It may not all be relevant.
***0 marks:***
No relevant information is given.
**Here are some points your answer may include:**
The cosmic background radiation is microwave radiation showing a perfect black body spectrum of a temperature of about 2.73 K. It is very nearly isotropic and homogeneous. This is consistent with the Big Bang model of the universe, which suggests the early universe would have been filled with gamma radiation, that would have been stretched into the microwave region of the electromagnetic spectrum over time due to the expansion of the universe.

# Section 7: Option B — Medical Physics

## Page 89 — Physics of the Eye

1 a) The distance will be the focal length of the lens ***[1 mark]***
$v = f = 1/\text{power} = 1/60 =$ **0.017 m (to 2 s.f.)** ***[1 mark]***

b)

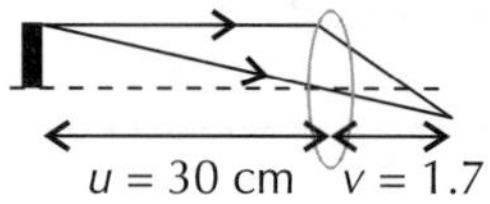


***[1 mark for correct rays, 1 mark for correctly labelling distances]***

c) $1/u + 1/v = 1/f$, $u = 0.30$ m, $v = 1/60$ m.
$1/f = 63.33...$ D ***[1 mark]***.
So the extra power needed = 63.33... – 60
= 3.33... D = **3.3 D (to 2 s.f.)** ***[1 mark]***.

## Page 91 — Defects of Vision

1 Focal length of diverging lens needs to be –4.0 m ***[1 mark]***.
Power = $1/f$ = **–0.25 D**
***[1 mark for value, 1 mark for negative sign]***

2 Lens equation $1/u + 1/v = 1/f$. When $u = 0.25$ m, $v = -2.0$ m
$1/f = 1/0.25 - 1/2.0$ ***[1 mark]*** = 3.5. Power = **+3.5 D**
***[1 mark for value, 1 mark for sign]***

3 a) Cylindrical lenses ***[1 mark]***.

b) The optician gives the angle between the horizontal axes and the vertical lens axis ***[1 mark]*** and how curved the lens needs to be / the power of the lens needed to correct the astigmatism ***[1 mark]***.

## Page 93 — Physics of the Ear

1 a) The pinna concentrates the sound energy entering the ear into the auditory canal, increasing its intensity ***[1 mark]***.

b) Sound energy entering the ear causes the tympanic membrane (eardrum) to vibrate ***[1 mark]***. The vibrations are transmitted through the middle ear by the malleus, incus and stapes in turn ***[1 mark]***. The stapes is connected to the oval window, so causes it to vibrate ***[1 mark]***.

c) The amplitude of a sound is proportional to the square root of its intensity, and the intensity is inversely proportional to the area ***[1 mark]***. This means that the amplitude is inversely proportional to the square root of the area ***[1 mark]***, so if the area is decreased by a factor of 14, the amplitude is increased by a factor of $\sqrt{14} = 3.7$ (to 2 s.f.) ***[1 mark]***.

d) Pressure waves in the cochlea cause the basilar membrane to vibrate ***[1 mark]***, which causes hair cells on the membrane to trigger electrical impulses ***[1 mark]***.

e) Different regions of the basilar membrane have different natural frequencies ***[1 mark]***. When the frequency of a sound wave matches the natural frequency of a part of the membrane, that part resonates, causing the hair cells in that area to trigger impulses, so different frequencies trigger different nerve cells ***[1 mark]***.

## Page 95 — Intensity and Loudness

1 a) $1.0 \times 10^{-12} \text{ Wm}^{-2}$ ***[1 mark]***

b) $IL = 10\log\left(\frac{I}{I_0}\right) = 10\log\left(\frac{0.94}{1.0 \times 10^{-12}}\right) = 119.7... \text{dB}$
= **120 dB (to 2 s.f.)** ***[1 mark]***

c) The ear is most sensitive at about 3000 Hz, so the siren will sound as loud as possible ***[1 mark]***.

2 The patient has suffered hearing loss at all frequencies, but the loss is worst at high frequencies ***[1 mark]***. If the patient's hearing had been damaged by excessive noise, you would expect to see a peak at a particular frequency ***[1 mark]***. This isn't present, so the patient's hearing loss is more likely to be age-related ***[1 mark]***.

## Page 97 — Electrocardiography (ECG)

1 a) Peaks of the waves occur at:
P wave: 3.1 s, QRS wave: 3.3 s, T wave: 3.6 s ***[1 mark]***

b) The P wave ***[1 mark]***

2 a) The QRS wave is when the ventricles are contracting, so there may be a problem with the ventricles ***[1 mark]***.

b) Any one from: removed hair and dead skin, apply conductive gel, make sure electrodes are attached securely. ***[1 mark]***

## Page 99 — Ultrasound Imaging

1 a) $\left(\frac{Z_{tissue} - Z_{air}}{Z_{tissue} + Z_{air}}\right)^2 = \left(\frac{1630 \times 10^3 - 0.430 \times 10^3}{1630 \times 10^3 + 0.430 \times 10^3}\right)^2$ ***[1 mark]***
= 0.9989... = **0.999 (to 3 s.f.)** ***[1 mark]***

b) From part a), 1.00 – 0.998... = 0.1% enters the body when no gel is used ***[1 mark]***.
$\left(\frac{Z_{tissue} - Z_{gel}}{Z_{tissue} + Z_{gel}}\right)^2 = \left(\frac{1630 \times 10^3 - 1500 \times 10^3}{1630 \times 10^3 + 1500 \times 10^3}\right)^2$
= 0.0017... ***[1 mark]***,
1 – 0.0017... = 0.9982...
So 99.82...% of the ultrasound is transmitted ***[1 mark]***.
99.82...% ÷ 0.1% ≈ 1000, so the ratio is **1000:1** ***[1 mark]***.

2 $Z = \rho c$, $c = (1.63 \times 10^6)/(1.09 \times 10^3)$ ***[1 mark]***
$= 1495 \text{ ms}^{-1} = \mathbf{1.50 \text{ kms}^{-1}}$ **(to 3 s.f.)** ***[1 mark]***.

3 Advantages: e.g. there are no known hazards / they can obtain real-time images of soft tissue / ultrasound devices are cheap and portable / they are quick and patient can move ***[1 mark]***
Disadvantages: e.g. they cannot penetrate bone / ultrasound cannot pass through air spaces / images have a poor resolution / they can't give any information on any solid masses found (i.e. what the solid mass is) ***[1 mark]***

# Answers

## Page 101 — Endoscopy

1 a) $\sin \theta_c = n_2/n_1 = 1.30/1.35$ ***[1 mark]***
$\theta = 74.35... =$ **74.4° (to 3 s.f.)** ***[1 mark]***

b) When the angle of incidence is greater than or equal to the critical angle, the beam of light will undergo total internal reflection ***[1 mark]***. If the angle of incidence falls below the critical angle, then some light will be lost ***[1 mark]***.

2 A coherent fibre-optic bundle consists of a large number of very thin fibres ***[1 mark]***, arranged in the same way at either end of the bundle ***[1 mark]***. Lots of thin fibres are used to increase the resolution of the image ***[1 mark]***. The relative positions of the fibres must remain constant or the image would be jumbled up ***[1 mark]***.

## Page 103 — X-Ray Production

1

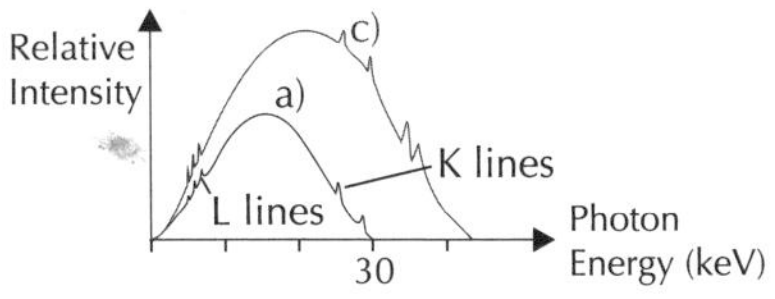


a) See graph ***[1 mark for shape of graph, 1 mark for 30 keV maximum energy and 1 mark for correct labelling of line spectrum]***

b) Maximum energy = Voltage × $e$
$= 30 \times 10^3 \times 1.60 \times 10^{-19}$ ***[1 mark]*** = **$4.8 \times 10^{-15}$ J** ***[1 mark]***

c) See graph ***[1 mark for higher intensity and higher maximum energy and 1 mark for a few extra lines in the line spectrum]***

## Page 105 — X-Ray Imaging Techniques

1 a) The half-value thickness is the thickness of material that reduces the intensity of an X-ray beam to half its original value ***[1 mark]***.

b) $\mu = \frac{\ln 2}{x_{\frac{1}{2}}} = \frac{\ln 2}{3} = 0.231...\text{mm}^{-1}$ ***[1 mark]***, $\frac{I}{I_0} = e^{-\mu x}$

So, $0.01 = e^{-0.231...x}$ for the beam to reach 1% of its initial value.
Take the natural log of both sides: $\ln(0.01) = -0.231...x$ ***[1 mark]***,
$x = 19.9...$ mm = **20 mm (to 1 s.f.)** ***[1 mark]***

2 a) A narrow beam of monochromatic X-rays is rotated and fired at a patient ***[1 mark]***. Some X-rays are absorbed by bones and soft tissue. Thousands of detectors pick up the X-rays which haven't been absorbed ***[1 mark]***. A computer calculates the attenuation caused by each part of the body and builds a 2D slice ***[1 mark]***.

b) Either: the patient is subjected to a high dose of ionising radiation or the machines are expensive ***[1 mark]***

## Page 107— Magnetic Resonance (MR) Imaging

1 ***5-6 marks:***
All steps are covered in detail, with correct usage of terminology. Explanation is clear and concise.
***3-4 marks:***
The majority of steps are covered with an attempt made to use appropriate terminology. The explanation is legible and logical.
***1-2 marks:***
Two steps are explained briefly. Explanation is not clear.
***0 marks:***
No relevant information is given.
**Points your answer should include:**
The patient lies in the centre of a large superconducting magnet, which produces a magnetic field. The magnetic field aligns hydrogen protons in the patient's body. The protons precess about the magnetic field lines with a precession frequency. The precession frequency of the proton depends on its location within the body. Radio frequency coils are used to transmit radio waves which, if they have the same frequency as the precession frequency of a proton, will cause the aligned protons to absorb energy and change their spin state. When the radio waves stop, the protons emit the stored energy as radio waves with frequency the same as the precession frequency of the proton. These radio waves are recorded by the scanner. A computer analyses the received radio waves to produce a cross-section of the patient's body.

2 E.g. there are no known side effects, so patients have a lower risk when using a MR scanner (unlike with ionising radiation) ***[1 mark]***. You can also take a slice at any orientation of the body — saving the patient's and doctor's time ***[1 mark]***. A disadvantage is that their imaging of bones is very poor, so alternative methods have to be used which have a higher risk attached to them ***[1 mark]***. They're also incredibly expensive, so some hospitals cannot afford them ***[1 mark]***.

## Page 109 — Medical Uses of Radiation

1 $\frac{1}{T_E} = \frac{1}{T_B} + \frac{1}{T_P} = \frac{1}{24} + \frac{1}{6} = \frac{5}{24}$ ***[1 mark]***
So $T_E = 24 \div 5 = 4.8$ hours = **5 hours (to 1 s.f.)** ***[1 mark]***

2 E.g. PET scanners give information about the metabolic activity of a patient ***[1 mark]*** and can be used to monitor brain activity. Some other imaging techniques are unable to penetrate bone, so this is particularly useful ***[1 mark]***. One disadvantage is that PET scanners use ionising radiation, which can damage healthy cells inside a patient ***[1 mark]***. PET scanners are also very large, which means they cannot easily be transported. Patients have to travel to their nearest hospital with a PET scanner, which can be difficult for some people / The scans can be uncomfortable and claustrophobic ***[1 mark]***.

3 Implants containing beta-emitters could be placed either inside or next to the tumour ***[1 mark]***. The ionising radiation would kill off the cancerous cells, but due to the short range of beta radiation, damage to nearby healthy cells would be limited ***[1 mark]***.

# Section 7: Option C — Engineering Physics

## Page 111 — Inertia and Kinetic Energy

1 $I = mr^2 = 0.03 \times 0.8^2 = 0.0192 =$ **0.02 kgm² (to 1 s.f.)** ***[1 mark]***

2 Without the child, the moment of inertia of the roundabout is:
$I = \frac{1}{2}mr^2 = 0.5 \times 130 \times 2.5^2 = 406.25$ ***[1 mark]***
Subtract this from the moment of inertia with the child
$531 - 406.25 = 124.75$
As the child is a point mass, $I = mr^2 = 124.75$ ***[1 mark]***
So $m = 124.75 \div 2.5^2 = 19.96 =$ **20 kg (to 2 s.f.)** ***[1 mark]***

3 a) $I = \frac{2}{3}mr^2 = \frac{2}{3} \times 0.5 \times 0.1^2 = 0.0033...$
= **0.003 kgm² (to 1 s.f.)** ***[1 mark]***

b) $E_k = \frac{1}{2}I\omega^2 = \frac{1}{2} \times 0.0033... \times 1.5^2$ ***[1 mark]*** $= 0.00375$
= **0.004 J (to 1 s.f.)** ***[1 mark]***

c) $\frac{E_{k solid}}{E_{k hollow}} = \frac{\frac{1}{2}I_{solid}\omega^2}{\frac{1}{2}I_{hollow}\omega^2} = \frac{I_{solid}}{I_{hollow}}$ ***[1 mark]*** $= \frac{\frac{2}{5}mr^2}{\frac{2}{3}mr^2}$
$= \frac{3}{5}$, so the ratio is 3:5 [1 mark].

## Page 113 — Rotational Motion

1 $\omega = \frac{\Delta\theta}{\Delta t} = \frac{2\pi}{24 \times 60 \times 60} = 0.000072...$
= **$7.3 \times 10^{-5}$ rad s⁻¹ (to 2 s.f.)** ***[1 mark]***

2 Its initial angular velocity is
$\omega_1 = \frac{30.0 \times 2\pi}{60} = \pi = 3.14...\text{rad s}^{-1}$ ***[1 mark]***
$\omega_2 = \omega_1 + \alpha t = 3.14... + 1.57 \times 5.00$ ***[1 mark]***
$= 10.99... =$ **11.0 rad s⁻¹ (to 3 s.f.)** ***[1 mark]***

3

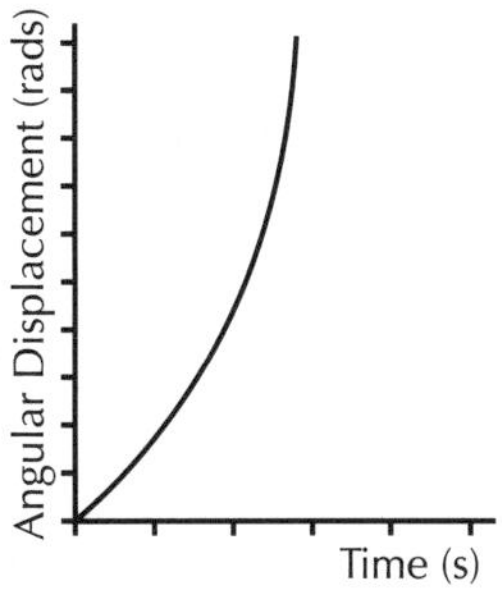


***[1 mark for correct axes, 1 mark for correct curved shape]***

# Answers

4 a) The angular acceleration is constant ***[1 mark]*** as the graph is a straight line.

b) Calculate the gradient of the line
E.g. $\alpha = \frac{\Delta\omega}{\Delta t} = \frac{4}{2} = \mathbf{2\ rad\ s^{-2}}$ ***[1 mark]***

c) The displacement is the area under the graph.
Area of a trapezium = $\frac{a+b}{2}h = \frac{4+10}{2} \times 3$
So Area = Angular displacement = **21 radians** ***[1 mark]***

## Page 115 — Torque, Work and Power

1 $T = Fr = 1 \times (0.1 \div 2) = \mathbf{0.05\ Nm}$ ***[1 mark]***

2 a) $Fr = I\alpha$ so $\alpha = \frac{Fr}{I} = \frac{140 \times 2.5}{500}$ ***[1 mark]*** = **0.7 rad s$^{-2}$** ***[1 mark]***

b) $W = T\theta = Fr\theta = 140 \times 2.5 \times 2\pi$ ***[1 mark]***
= 2199.1... = **2200 J (to 2 s.f.)** ***[1 mark]***

3 $T_{friction} = T_{applied} - T_{required} = 0.50 - 0.45 = 0.05$ Nm ***[1 mark]***
Power = $T\omega = 0.05 \times 3.0 = \mathbf{0.15\ W}$ ***[1 mark]***

## Page 117 — Flywheels

1 a) When Taylor's car uses its brakes, a flywheel is engaged. The kinetic energy from the car is transferred to the flywheel, charging it up ***[1 mark]***. When the car then next accelerates, the flywheel decelerates and gives kinetic energy back to the car, meaning it needs less energy from the motor to accelerate ***[1 mark]***. The flywheel is then disengaged until the car brakes again ***[1 mark]***.

b) E.g. in a potter's wheel to keep the angular speed smooth, even though the applied torque varies ***[1 mark]***.

2 Increasing the mass would increase the maximum amount of energy the flywheel could store, as it would increase the moment of inertia of the flywheel ***[1 mark]***. The moment of inertia is proportional to the flywheel's mass, so the maximum energy the flywheel could store would double if its mass was doubled ***[1 mark]***. One disadvantage of this is that the flywheel would now be twice as heavy and would need stronger bearings to support it ***[1 mark]***. A different improvement which could be made is to use a spoked wheel of the same mass instead of a solid wheel. This also increases the moment of inertia (and thus energy stored) whilst the mass of the flywheel stays the same ***[1 mark]***.

## Page 119 — Angular Momentum

1 Angular momentum = $I\omega = 0.04 \times 4 = \mathbf{0.16\ Nms}$ ***[1 mark]***

2 A diver tucks into a ball to bring their limbs closer to the axis of rotation, which reduces their moment of inertia ***[1 mark]***. As no external forces are being applied, the angular momentum remains constant ***[1 mark]***. As the angular momentum remains constant, the diver's angular velocity must increase ***[1 mark]***.

3 Angular momentum before = Angular momentum after
$I_1\omega_1 + I_2\omega_2 = (I_1 + I_2)\omega$ so $\omega = \frac{I_1\omega_1 + I_2\omega_2}{(I_1 + I_2)}$ ***[1 mark]***

$$\omega = \frac{0.10 \times \left(\frac{3000 \times 2\pi}{60}\right) + 0.15 \times \left(\frac{2000 \times 2\pi}{60}\right)}{0.25}$$ ***[1 mark]***

= 251.3... = **250 rad s$^{-1}$ (to 2 s.f.)** ***[1 mark]***

4 a) Angular impulse = $\Delta(I\omega) = I\Delta\omega = 0.2 \times (24 - 2.2)$
= 4.36 = **4.4 Nms (to 2 s.f.)** ***[1 mark]***

b) Angular impulse = $T\Delta t = 4.36$
$T = 4.36 \div 4 = 1.09 = \mathbf{1.1\ Nm}$ **(to 2 s.f.)** ***[1 mark]***

## Page 122 — The First Law of Thermodynamics

1 a) For isothermal processes, $pV$ = constant
Before compression $pV = 1.2 \times 10^4 \times 0.4 = 4800$ Pa m$^3$
So after compression $p = 4800 \div 0.3 = 16\ 000$ ***[1 mark]***
= **1.6 × 10$^4$ Pa (to 2 s.f.)** ***[1 mark]***

b) $pV = nRT$ so $T = pV \div nR$
$T = 4800 \div (0.82 \times 8.31)$ ***[1 mark]***
= 704.4... = **700 K (to 2 s.f.)** ***[1 mark]***

2 $W = Q - \Delta U = 3000 - 300 = 2700$ J ***[1 mark]***
$W = p\Delta V$ so $\Delta V = 2700 \div (1.1 \times 10^{-4})$
= 0.245... m$^3$ ***[1 mark]***
For constant pressure, $\frac{V_1}{T_1} = \frac{V_2}{T_2}$ so

$T_2 = \frac{V_2 T_1}{V_1} = \frac{0.360 \times 300}{0.360 - 0.245...}$ ***[1 mark]***

$T_2 = 942.8... = \mathbf{940\ K}$ **(to 2 s.f.)** ***[1 mark]***

3 The volume is constant, so the work done is zero. This means that $Q = \Delta U$. ***[1 mark]*** As heat energy is being transferred to the system, this makes $Q$ (and $\Delta U$) positive. $\Delta U$ is dependent only on temperature, so the temperature must be increasing. ***[1 mark]***
For isothermal processes, the temperature remains constant.
***[1 mark]***
For adiabatic processes, $Q = 0$ so $W = -\Delta U$. As the gas is being compressed, the work done is negative, meaning that $\Delta U$ is positive ***[1 mark]***. This means that the temperature must be increasing ***[1 mark]***.

## Page 125 — P-V Diagrams

1
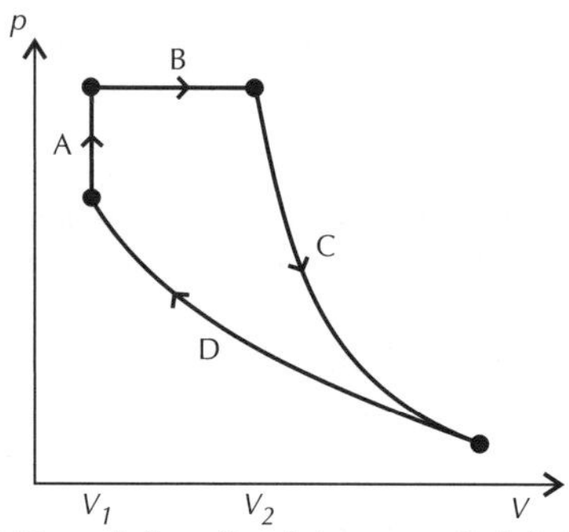


***[1 mark for all points correctly labelled, 1 mark for correct straight lines and arrows representing stages A and B, 1 mark for a curve and arrow pointing downwards representing stage C, 1 mark for a shallower curve representing stage D than stage C.]***

2 a) Change in volume = $0.8 \times 10^{-4}$ m$^3$, $p = 15.0 \times 10^6$ Pa.
$W = p\Delta V = 15.0 \times 10^6 \times 0.8 \times 10^{-4} = \mathbf{1200\ J}$ ***[1 mark]***

b) Horizontally, 10 squares is equal to $2.0 \times 10^{-4}$ m$^3$.
So, one square width equals $(2.0 \times 10^{-4}) \div 10 = 2.0 \times 10^{-5}$ m$^3$.
Vertically, 5 squares is equal to $5.0 \times 10^6$ Pa.
So one square height is equal to $1.0 \times 10^6$ Pa.
***[1 mark for correct calculation of one square's height or width]***
Work done per square = $2.0 \times 10^{-5} \times 1.0 \times 10^6 = 20$ J ***[1 mark]***
The loop encircles around 66 squares, so net work done per cycle is 66 × 20 = **1320 J** ***[1 mark]***.

c) An adiabatic expansion would have a steeper $p$-$V$ curve than an isothermal one ***[1 mark]***. This would make the $p$-$V$ diagram loop area smaller. This area represents the work done per cycle, so the net work would decrease if the system adiabatically expanded ***[1 mark]***.

## Page 127 — Four-Stroke Engines

1 a) During the induction stroke, the piston moves down the cylinder, increasing the volume above it. The air-fuel mixture is sucked in through the inlet valve ***[1 mark]***. The pressure stays roughly constant (just below atmospheric pressure) ***[1 mark]***. In the compression stroke, the inlet valve is closed and the piston is moved up the cylinder, compressing the air-fuel mixture ***[1 mark]***. Just before the end of the stroke, the spark plug creates a spark which ignites the gas inside the cylinder. The temperature and pressure rapidly increase, whilst the volume stays roughly the same ***[1 mark]***.

# Answers

b)

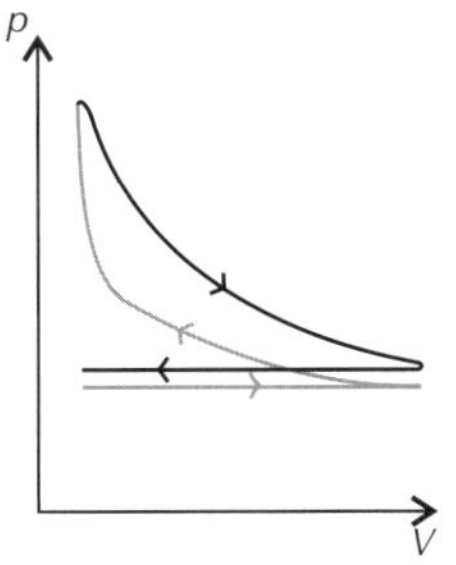


***[1 mark for drawing a curved expansion stroke above the compression stroke curve, 1 mark for drawing a horizontal line for the exhaust stroke]***

c)

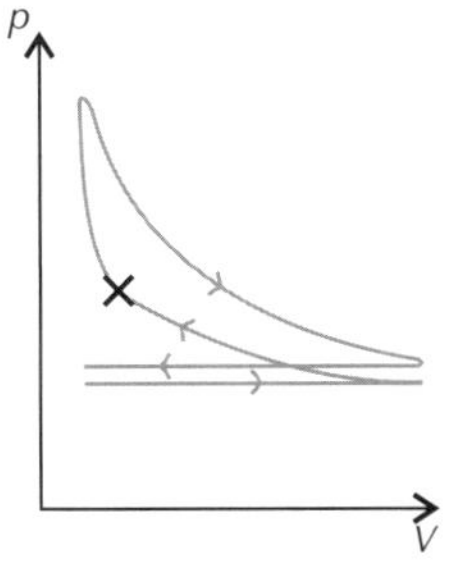


***[1 mark]***

2 Firstly, on the induction stroke, a four-stroke diesel engine takes in only air instead of an air-fuel mixture like a four-stroke petrol engine ***[1 mark]***. There is also no spark plug in a diesel engine, so during the compression stroke, the air inside the cylinder is compressed until it reaches a high enough temperature to ignite diesel ***[1 mark]***. Diesel is sprayed in through a fuel injector just before the end of the compression stroke, where it is then ignited ***[1 mark]***.

## Page 129 — Using Indicator Diagrams

1 a) Indicated power = (area of $p$-$V$ loop) × (number of cycles per second) × (number of cylinders)
= 120 × 29 × 8 = 27 840 = **28 000 W (to 2 s.f.)** ***[1 mark]***

b) Friction power = indicated power – brake power
Brake power = $T\omega$ = 130 × 58π = 7540π W ***[1 mark]***
Friction power = 27 840 – 7540π = 4152.3...
= **4200 W (to 2 s.f.)** ***[1 mark]***

2 Indicated power is related to the area of the indicator diagram loop. As the loop for engine A has a smaller area than for engine B, engine A has a lower indicated power ***[1 mark]***. The frictional power of both engines is the same, so this means that engine A also has a lower output power ***[1 mark]***. Output power, $P = T\omega$. Both engines have the same angular velocity, so the torque of engine A must be less than the torque of engine B ***[1 mark]***.

## Page 131 — Engine Efficiency

1 input power = calorific value × fuel flow rate
= 44.8 × $10^6$ × 2.8 × $10^{-3}$ = 125 440 W ***[1 mark]***

overall efficiency = $\frac{\text{brake power}}{\text{input power}} = \frac{44\,700}{125\,440}$ ***[1 mark]***

= 0.356... = **36% (to 2 s.f.)** ***[1 mark]***

2 a) Theoretical maximum efficiency = $\frac{T_H - T_C}{T_H}$

$= \frac{1200 - 290}{1200}$ ***[1 mark]*** = 0.758... = **76% (to 2 s.f.)** ***[1 mark]***

b) $W = Q_H - Q_C$ = 1000 – 550 = 450 J ***[1 mark]***

Efficiency = $\frac{W}{Q_H} = \frac{450}{1000}$ = 0.45 = **45%** ***[1 mark]***

c) E.g. frictional forces inside the engine, energy is needed to move internal parts***[1 mark for one correct reason]***.

## Page 133 — Reversed Heat Engines

1 a) $W = Q_H - Q_C$ so $Q_H = W + Q_C$
= 2.02 × $10^6$ + 5.66 × $10^6$ = **7.68 × 10⁶ J** ***[1 mark]***

b) $COP_{ref} = \frac{Q_C}{W} = \frac{5.66 \times 10^6}{2.02 \times 10^6}$ = 2.801... = **2.80 (to 3 s.f.)** ***[1 mark]***

2 a) $T_H$ = 25 + 273 = 298 K
$T_C$ = 3 + 273 = 276 K
$COP_{hp} = \frac{T_H}{T_H - T_C} = \frac{298}{22}$ = 13.5... = **14 (to 2 s.f.)** ***[1 mark]***

b) $W = \frac{Q_H}{COP} = \frac{4.10 \times 10^6}{3.5}$ ***[1 mark]***

= 1.17... ×$10^6$ = **1.2 MJ (to 2 s.f.)** ***[1 mark]***

# Section 7: Option D — Turning Points in Physics

## Page 135 — Specific Charge of the Electron

1 a) 1000 eV ***[1 mark]***

b) 1000 eV × 1.60 × $10^{-19}$ J/eV = **1.60 × $10^{-16}$ J (to 3 s.f.)** ***[1 mark]***

c) Kinetic energy = ½$mv^2$ = 1.60 × $10^{-16}$ J ***[1 mark]***
$v^2$ = (2 × 1.60 × $10^{-16}$) ÷ (9.11 × $10^{-31}$) = 3.512... × $10^{14}$
$v = \sqrt{3.512... \times 10^{14}}$ = 1.874... × $10^7$ ms$^{-1}$
= **1.87 × $10^7$ ms$^{-1}$** ***[1 mark]***

$\frac{1.874... \times 10^7}{3.00 \times 10^8} \times 100\%$ = 6.247...

= **6.25% (to 3 s.f.) of the speed of light** ***[1 mark]***

2 Your answer will depend on which experiment you describe, e.g.:
Electrons are accelerated using an electron gun ***[1 mark]***.
A magnetic field ***[1 mark]*** exerts a centripetal force ***[1 mark]*** on the electrons, making them trace a circular path. By measuring the radius of this path and equating the magnetic and centripetal forces ***[1 mark]*** you can calculate $e/m_e$.
***[1 mark for quality of written communication]***.

## Page 137 — Millikan's Oil-Drop Experiment

1 a) The forces acting on the drop are its weight, acting downwards ***[1 mark]*** and the equally sized force due to the electric field, acting upwards ***[1 mark]***.

b) Weight = electric force, so $mg = \frac{QV}{d}$, and $Q = \frac{mgd}{V}$

$Q = \frac{1.63 \times 10^{-14} \times 9.81 \times 3.00 \times 10^{-2}}{4995}$

= 9.603... × $10^{-19}$ C ***[1 mark]***
Divide by e: 9.603... × $10^{-19}$ ÷ 1.60 × $10^{-19}$ = 6.002... ***[1 mark]***
So $Q$ = **6.00e (to 3 s.f.)** ***[1 mark]***

c) The forces on the oil drop as it falls are its weight and the viscous force from the air ***[1 mark]***. As the oil drop accelerates, the viscous force increases until it equals the oil drop's weight ***[1 mark]***. At this point, there is no resultant force on the oil drop, so it stops accelerating, but continues to fall at terminal velocity ***[1 mark]***.

d) At terminal velocity, $F = mg = 6\pi\eta rv$

Rearranging, $v = \frac{mg}{6\pi\eta r}$

Find the radius of the oil drop,
using mass = volume × density: $m = \frac{4}{3}\pi r^3 \rho$.

So $r^3 = \frac{3m}{4\pi\rho} = \frac{3 \times 1.63 \times 10^{-14}}{4 \times \pi \times 885}$ ***[1 mark]***
= 4.396... × $10^{-18}$

$r = \sqrt[3]{4.396... \times 10^{-18}}$ = 1.638... × $10^{-6}$ ***[1 mark]***

So, $v = \frac{1.63 \times 10^{-14} \times 9.81}{6\pi \times 1.84 \times 10^{-5} \times 1.638... \times 10^{-6}}$ = 2.814... × $10^{-4}$

= **2.81 × $10^{-4}$ ms$^{-1}$ (to 3 s.f.)** ***[1 mark]***

# Answers

## Page 140 — Light — Particles vs Waves

1 a) Light consists of particles *[1 mark]*. The theory was based on Newton's laws of motion, with the straight-line motion of light as evidence *[1 mark]*.

b) Newton's corpuscular theory intuitively explained reflection and refraction and fitted with existing laws of physics *[1 mark]*. There was no experimental evidence for Huygens' theory *[1 mark]*, and scientists didn't think it could explain double refraction *[1 mark]*. Newton became a very successful physicist with a strong reputation *[1 mark]*.

2 Young's double-slit experiment proved that light could diffract and interfere like a wave, which particles couldn't do *[1 mark]*. Fizeau measured the speed of light *[1 mark]*, which allowed Maxwell to show that light travelled at the same speed as electromagnetic waves, and so was likely to be an electromagnetic wave *[1 mark]*. Hertz discovered radio waves and showed that their speed was the same as electromagnetic waves, proving Maxwell's prediction of a spectrum of electromagnetic waves including light to be correct *[1 mark]*.

## Page 143 — The Photoelectric Effect and the Photon Model

1 a) Wave theory was unable to explain why, for a given metal, radiation below a certain frequency doesn't cause any photoelectrons to be emitted *[1 mark]*, or why the kinetic energy of photoelectrons doesn't vary with intensity, but has a maximum value for a given frequency of radiation *[1 mark]*. Wave theory predicted that photoelectrons would be emitted due to radiation of any frequency, but that it would take longer for electrons to be emitted by lower frequency waves *[1 mark]*, and that the higher the intensity of the radiation, the higher the kinetic energy of the photoelectrons emitted should be *[1 mark]*.

b) The photon model says each photon has a particular energy given by its frequency *[1 mark]*. When a photon hits a free electron in the metal, this energy is transferred to the electron, and if it is greater than the work function of the metal, the electron can be emitted *[1 mark]*. As each electron can only absorb one photon at a time, only photons with energy greater than the work function can cause photoelectrons to be emitted, hence the threshold frequency *[1 mark]*. Because electrons only absorb one photon at a time, the maximum kinetic energy a photoelectron can have is only dependent on the frequency of the photons, not the intensity of the radiation, which increases the number of photoelectrons emitted, but not their energy *[1 mark]*.

2 The ultraviolet catastrophe was the prediction by wave theory that the peak radiation emitted from a black body would be infinitely high *[1 mark]* towards the ultraviolet region of the spectrum *[1 mark]*. It meant that wave theory must be incorrect as it couldn't correctly explain the behaviour of light *[1 mark]*.

## Page 145 — Wave-Particle Duality

1 a) i) Velocity is given by $\frac{1}{2}mv^2 = eV$ so $v = \sqrt{\frac{2eV}{m}}$ *[1 mark]*

$$v = \sqrt{\frac{2 \times 1.60 \times 10^{-19} \times 515}{9.11 \times 10^{-31}}} = 1.3449... \times 10^7$$

**$= 1.34 \times 10^7$ ms$^{-1}$ (to 3 s.f.)** *[1 mark]*

ii) de Broglie equation $p = \frac{h}{\lambda}$ so wavelength $\lambda = \frac{h}{mv}$ *[1 mark]*

$$\text{so } \lambda = \frac{6.63 \times 10^{-34}}{9.11 \times 10^{-31} \times 1.3449... \times 10^7} = 5.4109... \times 10^{-11}$$

**$= 5.41 \times 10^{-11}$ m (to 3 s.f.)** *[1 mark]*

b) This is in the X-ray region of the EM spectrum *[1 mark]*.

2 a) A stream of electrons is accelerated towards the sample using an electron gun *[1 mark]*. The beam of electrons is focused onto the sample using magnetic and electric fields *[1 mark]*. The parts of the beam that pass through the sample are projected onto a screen to form an image of the sample *[1 mark]*.

b) To resolve detail around the size of an atom, the electron wavelength needs to be around 0.100 nm *[1 mark]*. The relationship between anode voltage and electron wavelength is given by $\lambda = \frac{h}{\sqrt{2meV}}$, which rearranges to give

$V = \frac{h^2}{2me\lambda^2}$ *[1 mark]*.

Substituting $m = 9.11 \times 10^{-31}$ kg, $e = 1.60 \times 10^{-19}$ C, $\lambda = 0.100 \times 10^{-9}$ m gives:

$$V = \frac{(6.63 \times 10^{-34})^2}{2 \times 9.11 \times 10^{-31} \times 1.60 \times 10^{-19} \times (0.100 \times 10^{-9})^2}$$

= 150.78... = **151 V (to 3 s.f.)**, showing that the minimum anode voltage has to be around 150 V *[1 mark]*.

## Page 147 — The Speed of Light and Relativity

1 a) The interference pattern would move/be shifted *[1 mark]*.

b) The speed of light has the same value for all observers *[1 mark]*. It is impossible to detect absolute motion / the ether doesn't exist *[1 mark]*.

2 a) An inertial reference frame is a reference frame in which Newton's 1st law is obeyed *[1 mark]*, e.g. a train carriage moving at constant speed along a straight track (or any other relevant example) *[1 mark]*.

b) The speed of light is unaffected by the motion of the observer *[1 mark]* or the motion of the light source *[1 mark]*.

## Page 149 — Special Relativity

1 time $t = \frac{t_0}{\sqrt{1 - \frac{v^2}{c^2}}}$ and $t_0 = 20.0 \times 10^{-9}$ s *[1 mark]*

$$t = \frac{20.0 \times 10^{-9}}{\sqrt{1 - \frac{(0.995c)^2}{c^2}}}$$ *[1 mark]*

$= 2.0025... \times 10^{-7}$

$= 2.00 \times 10^{-7}$ s **(to 3 s.f.)** *[1 mark]*

You could also give your answer as **200 ns (to 3 s.f.)**.

2 Your description must include:
A diagram or statement showing relative motion *[1 mark]*.
An event of a specified duration in one reference frame *[1 mark]*.
Measurement of the time interval by a moving observer *[1 mark]*.
Time interval for "external" observer greater than time interval for the "stationary" observer or equivalent *[1 mark]*.

3 a) $E = \frac{m_0c^2}{\sqrt{1 - \frac{v^2}{c^2}}}$ and $E = mc^2$ so $m = \frac{E}{c^2} = \frac{m_0}{\sqrt{1 - \frac{v^2}{c^2}}}$ *[1 mark]*

$$m = \frac{1.67 \times 10^{-27}}{\sqrt{1 - \frac{(2.80 \times 10^8)^2}{(3.00 \times 10^8)^2}}} = 4.6516... \times 10^{-27}$$

**$= 4.65 \times 10^{-27}$ kg (to 3 s.f.)** *[1 mark]*

b) $E = mc^2 = 4.6516... \times 10^{-27} \times (3.00 \times 10^8)^2 = 4.1865... \times 10^{-10}$

$= 4.19 \times 10^{-10}$ J **(to 3 s.f.)** *[1 mark]*

# Index

# Index

# Index

# Index